DEFENDING LIFE

Defending Life is arguably the most comprehensive defense of the pro-life position on abortion – morally, legally, and politically — that has ever been published in an academic monograph. It offers a detailed and critical analysis of *Roe v. Wade* and *Casey v. Planned Parenthood* as well as arguments by those who defend a Rawlsian case for abortion choice, such as J. J. Thomson. The author defends the substance view of persons as the view with the most explanatory power. The substance view entails that the unborn is a subject of moral rights from conception. While defending this view, the author responds to the arguments of thinkers such as Boonin, Dworkin, Stretton, Ford, and Brody. He also critiques Thomson's famous violinist argument and its revisions by Boonin and McDonagh. *Defending Life* includes chapters critiquing arguments found in popular politics and the controversy over cloning and stem cell research.

Francis J. Beckwith is associate professor of philosophy and jurisprudence, Baylor University. He teaches in the departments of philosophy and political science as well as the J. M. Dawson Institute of Church-State Studies, where he served as associate director from 2003 until 2007. A 2002–2003 Madison Research Fellow in the politics department at Princeton University, he is a graduate of Fordham University (Ph.D., philosophy) and the Washington University School of Law, St. Louis (M.J.S.), where he won the CALI Award for academic work in the Reproductive Control Seminar. His more than a dozen books include *Is Statecraft Soulcraft? Christianity and Politics* (2008); *To Everyone an Answer: A Case for the Christian Worldview* (2004); *Law, Darwinism, and Public Education: The Establishment and the Challenge of Intelligent Design* (2003); *Do the Right Thing: Readings in Applied Ethics and Social Philosophy*, Second Edition (2002); and *The New Mormon Challenge: Responding to the Latest Defenses of a Fast-Growing Movement* (2002), which was a finalist for the Gold Medallion Award in theology and doctrine. With interests in jurisprudence, politics, philosophy of religion, and public policy, Professor Beckwith has published in a wide variety of academic journals including the *Harvard Journal of Law and Public Policy*, *Journal of Social Philosophy*, *International Philosophical Quarterly*, *Hastings Constitutional Law Quarterly*, *Journal of Medicine and Philosophy*, *American Journal of Jurisprudence*, *Journal of Medical Ethics*, *Public Affairs Quarterly*, *Notre Dame Journal of Law, Ethics and Public Policy*, *Social Theory and Practice*, *Southern Baptist Journal of Theology*, *Christian Bioethics*, *Nevada Law Journal*, *Journal of Law and Religion*, and *Philosophia Christi*. His Web site is http://www.francisbeckwith.com.

To Frankie

DEFENDING LIFE

A Moral and Legal Case against
Abortion Choice

FRANCIS J. BECKWITH

Baylor University

CAMBRIDGE
UNIVERSITY PRESS

CAMBRIDGE UNIVERSITY PRESS
Cambridge, New York, Melbourne, Madrid, Cape Town, Singapore, São Paulo, Delhi

Cambridge University Press
32 Avenue of the Americas, New York, NY 10013-2473, USA

www.cambridge.org
Information on this title: www.cambridge.org/9780521870849

First published 2007

Printed in the United States of America

A catalog record for this publication is available from the British Library.

Library of Congress Cataloging in Publication Data

Beckwith, Francis
Defending life : a moral and legal case against abortion choice / Francis J. Beckwith.
    p.   cm.
Includes bibliographical references and index.
ISBN 978-0-521-87084-9 (hardback) – ISBN 978-0-521-69135-2 (pbk.)
1. Abortion.   2. Abortion – Moral and ethical aspects.   I. Title.
HQ767.B427   2007
363.46–dc22   2006101329

ISBN   978-0-521-87084-9 hardback
ISBN   978-0-521-69135-2 paperback

CONTENTS

ACKNOWLEDGMENTS

I would like to thank the James Madison Program in American Ideals and Institutions (Department of Politics, Princeton University) and its director Robert P. George (McCormick Professor of Jurisprudence, Princeton) for providing me with a research fellowship in an idyllic environment with brilliant colleagues and a proficient staff so that I was able to work on this book free of my ordinary responsibilities as a faculty member. Although the bulk of my work was completed at Princeton (2002–2003), it was at Baylor University, in the 2003–2006 school years, that I finished the book's final chapters and prepared the manuscript and its edited legacies for the publisher. For this reason, I would like to single out for special thanks several of my graduate assistants who were assigned to me by the chair of the Department of Church-State Studies, the academic unit at Baylor University in which I held my faculty appointment during the writing and production of this book. My three 2003–2004 graduate assistants – T. Hunter Baker, Jennifer Clary, and Matthew Tapie – were especially helpful with proofreading an earlier version of the manuscript as well as offering their suggestions and insights. Hunter compiled the book's selected bibliography. After Cambridge University Press accepted the manuscript for publication, another one of my graduate assistants, John Lee (2004–2006), performed the task of reading a later incarnation of the manuscript. Two other graduate assistants, Gerard Figurelli (2005–2007) and Jeremiah Russell (2005–2006), proofread earlier versions of portions of the book that had appeared in a variety of academic journals. In Spring 2007 Gerard took on the tasks of producing an index for the book as well as reviewing the copyedited version of the manuscript. He excelled in both tasks, exceeding even my high expectations of him.

Many colleagues and friends, as well as scholars and writers whom I admire from a distance, have helped sharpen and shape the arguments I present and assess in this book in either my conversations with them or while I was immersing myself in their published works. Among these wise souls are a select few whose insights stand out as particularly illuminating: Robert P. George, Hadley Arkes, Michael Bauman, J. P. Moreland, Scott B. Rae, Gregory P. Koukl, John Conley, Teresa Collett, Peter Kreeft, Patrick Lee, Diane Nutwell Irving, W. Norris Clarke, Keith Pavlischek, Seana Sugrue, Jim Stoner, Frederica Matthews-Green, John Finnis, Alexander Pruss, Joe Koterski, Doris Gordon, Edwin C. Hui (Xu Zhi-Wei), David Reardon, Robert Passantino, Gretchen Passantino, Steve Schwarz, Frank Pavone, Marvin Olasky, Steven D. Thomas, Don Marquis, Tom King, Jorge Garcia, Nigel Cameron, A. A. Howsepian, Norm Geisler, Richard Stith, Scott Klusendorf, J. Budziszewski, Leon Kass, Harold O. J. Brown, Mark Foreman, Ronald Tacelli, and Francis Canavan.

Other scholars and writers – those who oppose the position (or aspects of the position) I defend in this book – have forced me, with their philosophical ingenuity and careful analysis, to hone my arguments and clarify their premises: Dean Stretton, David Boonin, Kenneth Himma, Frances Kamm, Eileen McDonagh, James Sadowsky, Craig Walton, Ronald Wilburn, Mark Michael, Tris Englehardt, Louis P. Pojman, Peter Singer, Michael Tooley, Laurence Tribe, Robert Baird, Susan Appleton, Jeffrey Stout, Ronald Dworkin, Judith Jarvis Thomson, Robert Wennberg, John Rawls, Stuart Rosenbaum, and Paul Simmons. Without these noble adversaries, my task would have been far less challenging and thus far from complete.

Of all the folks mentioned above, three deserve special recognition. First, my dear friend J. P. Moreland, who in 2003 and 2004 fought the same demons as I. But we gained the victory together as brothers in arms. Second, Bob Passantino, who passed away (November 17, 2003) in the midst of my completing this book. So many of us already miss Bob's quick wit and uncommon wisdom in philosophical matters. Well done, good and faithful servant. And third, Louis P. Pojman, a wonderful philosopher and dear friend who departed from this mortal realm on October 15, 2005. Louis and I had debated each other on the issue of abortion (in 1993 at Taylor University in Indiana) and edited a widely used anthology on the subject, *The Abortion Controversy: 25 Years after* Roe v. Wade, Second Edition (Wadsworth, 1998). Louis set a great example for me and so many other philosophers. He showed us how one can be intellectually honest, philosophically rigorous, and politically passionate while at the same time conducting oneself in a way that is gracious, respectful, and generous in spirit. He lived the virtues he taught. He will be missed, but not forgotten.

As always, my lovely wife, Frankie Beckwith, to whom this book is dedicated, continues to support my work and has been especially patient in the writing of this tome. No heart is bigger, and no face has a prettier smile. She's my "precious angel," to borrow a phrase from Bob Dylan. My parents (Harold J. "Pat" and Elizabeth Beckwith), as well as my siblings (James, Patrick, and Elizabeth) and their spouses (Kimberly, Paige, and Patrick) and children (Dean, Dylan, Devin, Riley, Darby, Sophie, John Paul, Camilla Grace, and Michael Aniello), are a constant source of comfort and encouragement. It is through our understanding of the unity of spouses and the generation of their children that we gain a greater appreciation, and a deeper wisdom, of who and what we are as human beings in community and the obligation we have to both honor our predecessors and preserve for our progeny a moral framework that makes the achieving of the good life for them more likely and easier to sustain.

Earlier versions of portions of this book were published elsewhere but have been revised, in some cases significantly, for inclusion in the present volume:

"Defending Abortion Philosophically: A Review of David Boonin's *A Defense of Abortion.*" *Journal of Medicine & Philosophy* 31 (April 2006): 177–203.

"Thomson's 'Equal Reasonableness' Argument for Abortion Rights: A Critique." *American Journal of Jurisprudence* 49 (2004): 118–134.

"The Explanatory Power of the Substance View of Persons." *Christian Bioethics* 10.1 (April 2004): 33–54.

"When You Come to a Fork in the Road, Take It? Abortion, Personhood, and the Jurisprudence of Neutrality." *Journal of Church & State* 44.3 (Summer 2003): 485–487.

"*Roe v. Wade*: Its Logic and Its Legacy." *The Southern Baptist Journal of Theology* 7.2 (Summer 2003): 4–29. A revised and updated version of this article was published under the title "The Supreme Court, *Roe v. Wade*, and Abortion Law." *Liberty University Law Review* 1.1 (2006): 37–72.

(with Steven D. Thomas). "Consent, Abortion, and the Pre-Natal Rapist: A Brief Critique of McDonagh's Suggested Revision of *Roe v. Wade.*" *Journal of Libertarian Studies* 17.2 (Spring 2003): 1–16.

"Cloning and Reproductive Liberty." *Nevada Law Journal* 3.1 (Fall 2002): 61–87.

"Why I Am Not a Relativist." In *Why I Am a Christian: Leading Thinkers Explain Why They Believe*, revised edition. Edited by N. L. Geisler and P. Hoffman. Grand Rapids, MI: Baker Books, 2006, 17–31.

"Law, Religion, and the Metaphysics of Abortion: A Reply to Simmons." *Journal of Church & State* 43.1 (Winter 2001): 19–33.

"Abortion, Bioethics, and Personhood: A Philosophical Reflection." *The Southern Baptist Journal of Theology* 6 (Spring 2000): 14–28.

"Ignorance of Fetal Status as a Justification of Abortion: A Critical Analysis." In *The Silent Subject: Reflections on the Unborn in American Culture*. Edited by Brad Stetson. Westport, CT: Praeger Books, 1996, 33–42.

Politically Correct Death: Answering the Arguments for Abortion Rights. Grand Rapids, MI: Baker Book House, 1993; portions of chapters 4, 5, and 6.

"Utilitarian Arguments, Abortion Rights, and Justice Blackmun's Dissent in *Webster*: Some Philosophical Observations." *Simon Greenleaf Review of Law and Religion: A Scholarly Forum Interrelating Law, Theology and Human Rights* 8 (1988–89): 5–24.

I would like to thank the editors and publishers of these publications for not only allowing my work to first appear in print in these venues but also for permitting me to republish revised versions of those works here as parts of this book.

Special thanks to Stephen D. Schwarz for granting permission to republish in Chapter 4 a reworked, amended, and updated version of a chart that originally appeared in his book, *The Moral Question of Abortion* (Chicago: Loyola University Press), 1990, 22–25.

INTRODUCTION

Who and What Are We and Can We Know It?

The primary purpose of this book is to provide a thorough defense of the pro-life position on abortion and its grounding in a particular view of the human person, a view I will argue is the most rational and coherent one that is at the same time consistent with our deeply held intuitions about human equality. A secondary purpose of this book is to offer an analysis of the abortion question as it touches on law, politics, and public discourse. This book's third purpose is to examine the extent to which our political and legal disagreements on abortion do not adequately capture, and seem almost deliberately framed not to capture, the narrow questions of philosophical anthropology and political theory that are the only ones that really matter if we have any hope of resolving a dispute some believe is intractable. This book is, in a sense, then, not really a book *about* abortion, but rather, a book about human equality, one that makes the argument that the project that began centuries ago – having its metaphysical roots in the biblical notion of the imagio dei (image of God) that provided the intellectual scaffolding for the Declaration of Independence, the abolitionist movement, Abraham Lincoln's second inaugural address, and Martin Luther King Jr.'s speech on the steps of the Lincoln Memorial – can be, and ought to be, extended to include the true wideness of our human community, that is, to include the unborn.

The climate of America and of the world has changed since the U.S. Supreme Court reaffirmed *Roe v. Wade* (1973) in its 1992 decision, *Casey v. Planned Parenthood* (1992). The enthusiasm for moral relativism that seemed to be in ascendancy in those days has been disciplined by the terrorist atrocities of September 11, 2001, and those that followed in Spain (2003), the United Kingdom (2005), and India (2006). With the attendant questions about war and national security that these events raise, moving to the forefront of our public discourse is an acute awareness of the fragility and preciousness of life, the importance of ethical clarity, and the need to require moral justification when the taking of another's life may be required. In addition, the debates over partial-birth abortion, stem-cell research, and human cloning in the mid-to-late 1990s and early 21st century have served to underscore that the question often skirted by jurists, politicians, and professional bioethicists – what is the scope of the human community? – can no longer be ignored. After all, if Christopher Reeve was identical to his embryonic self, then we were no more justified in killing an embryo to acquire its stem cells so that Mr. Reeve might walk again than we would be in stealing Mr. Reeve's eyes so that Stevie Wonder might see again.

The pro-life position I defend in this book can be outlined by the following argument:

1. The unborn entity, from the moment of conception, is a full-fledged member of the human community.
2. It is prima facie morally wrong to kill any member of that community.
3. Every successful abortion kills an unborn entity, a full-fledged member of the human community.
4. Therefore, every successful abortion is prima facie morally wrong.[1]

I intend to show that each one of the premises of this argument is at best true or at least more likely true than not. In Chapter 9 I review this argument-outline and summarize the conclusions I reach in Chapters 4 through 8. These conclusions are the basis on which I support the premises of my argument.

It is important that I define some terms. First, when I say that the unborn entity is a *full-fledged member of the human community* (or *fully human* for short) I mean to say that she is just as much a bearer of rights as any human being whose rights-bearing status is uncontroversial, for example, her mother, you, or me. That is, the unborn entity is entitled to all the rights to which free and equal persons are entitled by virtue of being free and equal persons. So, for example, one cannot deprive the standard unborn entity of her life without the sort of justification we would expect if we were depriving a standard 10-year-old of his rights. To illustrate, if it is wrong to kill a 10-year-old as a result of taking his kidneys and giving them to people the government thinks will benefit society (e.g., scientific geniuses on the verge of curing cancer or AIDS), it is wrong to kill a 20-week-old fetal-clone as a result of taking his kidneys and giving them to his genetic progenitor, a scientific genius, who needs them to survive so that he may continue his work on cures for cancer and AIDS.

Second, when I say that killing a member of the human community is prima facie morally wrong I mean to say that in ordinary circumstances no one is morally justified in killing another human being. However, this does not mean that it is *always* wrong in *every* circumstance to kill someone who is fully human. There could be circumstances in which killing is justified, such as in cases of self-defense or just war. In the case of abortion, the killing of an unborn entity is justified if her presence in her mother's womb poses a significant threat to her mother's life. For if the unborn entity is not surgically removed (which will undoubtedly result in her death if performed early on in the pregnancy), then *both* mother *and* child will die. The specific intention is not to kill the unborn entity but to save the life of the mother. The child's death is an unfortunate, though anticipated, consequence that cannot be avoided unless one is willing to let both mother and child die. Such a decision is the *result of* applying pro-life principles: it is prima facie a higher good that one human being should live rather than two die if one cannot save both.

This book is divided into three parts. Part I, which contains three chapters, concerns moral reasoning, abortion law, and politics. Chapter 1 is a brief defense of the possibility and importance of moral reasoning. I offer a case against moral relativism, arguing that there are objective moral principles that apply to all persons, in all times, and in all places. As part of my case against relativism I make the point that the disagreement over abortion is not a dispute over moral principles per se, but a clash over the question of who counts as a member of the human community (i.e., whether it includes the unborn) and/or how we ought to apply our moral principles. Chapter 2 deals with the current state of abortion law in the United States. I correct the general public's misunderstanding on the nature of that law by presenting, explaining, and critiquing the reasoning of the Supreme Court's majority opinion in *Roe v. Wade* (1973). I also address how court cases since *Roe* have shaped the constitutional right to abortion. In Chapter 3 I address the objection that the pro-life position on abortion – even if it is the morally correct point of view – cannot be reflected in our laws because it is "religious" and hence would violate the First Amendment's prohibition of religious establishment.

Part II is the core of my case. In Chapter 4, I present the scientific facts of prenatal development as well as the different methods physicians use in performing abortions. In Chapters 5 through 7, I critique many arguments that are used to justify abortion at some stage during pregnancy. There are three questions fundamental to the abortion debate that I answer in these chapters. (1) Do the popular arguments for the abortion-choice position really support abortion as a fundamental *right* (Chapter 5)?[2] (2) Is there any decisive moment in the unborn's development at which it becomes "fully human" or a "person" (Chapter 6)? (3) Even if the unborn entity is fully human, is it possible that abortion is *still* morally justified and thus legally permissible (Chapter 7)?

Part III contains two chapters. In Chapter 8, I address the issue of human cloning, whose moral and legal difficulties are similar to those found in the abortion question. Although contemporary bioethical debate is dominated by this and other issues (e.g., embryonic stem-cell research) that are perceived as more pressing than abortion, the answer to the philosophical question lurking behind abortion – who and what are we? – turns out to be the key that unlocks the ethical quandaries posed by these other issues. After all, if human persons ought not to be either subjects of research or killed without justification, and if the unborn from conception is a full-fledged member of the human community, then killing embryos to use their stem cells or to perfect human cloning is prima facie morally wrong. In Chapter 9, my concluding chapter, I sum up my case for the pro-life position by briefly reviewing the conclusions arrived at in Chapters 1 through 8.

I do *not* argue for the pro-life position by appealing to theological reasoning or the authoritative writings of any particular religious tradition. The main thrust of this book is philosophical and jurisprudential. Hence, if my arguments are sound, an atheist, agnostic, or humanist is intellectually obligated to become pro-life. Consequently, those who want to label and dismiss the pro-life position as a *merely* "religious view" (an argument with which I deal in some detail in Chapter 3) will be disappointed by my strategy to ground the pro-life perspective in an array of arguments that can be apprehended by engaging in reasoning unaided by anyone's holy scripture and/or divine revelation. This is not to say, of course, that a citizen may not be fully warranted in holding a pro-life position even if her only basis for doing so is theological. For I am not saying that theological reasons are de facto epistemologically inferior to so-called secular reasons.[3] In fact, I have, on occasion, defended theological arguments for the pro-life position.[4] But because the immediate discounting of religious reasons, or religiously motivated reasons,[5] is not considered bad form among many in our public and academic cultures, I have chosen not to employ theological arguments in this book and thus not to tempt fate.

To make the text more readable, I have dealt with some technical arguments in the endnotes rather than in the text of each chapter. To cite just two instances. In Chapter 2, I relegate to the endnotes an analysis of David Boonin's assessment of using the Supreme Court's viability standard as an argument for denying personhood to pre-viable fetuses. Also in Chapter 2, I critique in the endnotes Justice Blackmun's argument that the severity of punishments found in pre-Roe anti-abortion statutes demonstrates that these statutes did not recognize the unborn as a constitutional person or a full-fledged member of the human community. So, the reader may want to consult the endnotes on occasion.

At the end of the day, the abortion debate is about who and what we are and whether we can know it. The cultural conflict over the permissibility of abortion is really a dispute over whether we are justified in extending our nation's moral progress toward the elimination of unjust discrimination to include those who are the most vulnerable in the human family, the unborn. It is, in the end, whether we like it or not, a testimony to that inescapable truth penned by Aristotle more than two millennia ago, "Statecraft is soulcraft."

PART I

MORAL REASONING, LAW, AND POLITICS

ABORTION AND MORAL ARGUMENT

I have participated in a number of public discussions on the question of abortion.[1] Inevitably, either my opponent or a member of the audience will make the assertion, "Don't like abortion, don't have one," followed by rousing applause by like-minded audience members. This assertion, though common, reveals not only a deep misunderstanding about the nature of the abortion debate but also a confusion about what it means to say that something is morally wrong.

The culprit, I believe, is moral relativism: the view that when it comes to questions of morality, there is no absolute or objective right and wrong; moral rules are merely personal preferences and/or the result of one's cultural, sexual, or ethnic orientation. So choosing an abortion, like choosing an automobile, a vacation spot, or dessert, is merely a matter of preference. Some people like Häagen Dazs™, others abortion. To each his own. Just like it is wrong for one to judge another's taste in ice cream – "You will burn in hell for eating almond roca" – it is wrong for one to judge another's reproductive choices and to ask for the law to reflect that judgment.

Many people see relativism as necessary for promoting tolerance, non-judgmentalism, and inclusiveness, for they think if one believes one's moral position is correct and others' incorrect, one is close-minded and intolerant. I will argue in this chapter that not only do the arguments for relativism fail, but that relativism itself cannot live up to its own reputation, for it is promoted by its proponents as the only correct view on morality. This is why relativists typically do not tolerate nonrelativist views, judge those views as mistaken, and maintain that relativism is exclusively right.

Relativism, admittedly, has lost a lot of its rhetorical edge as of late, largely due to its inadequacy in accounting for the deep wickedness of the reality of terrorist and state-sponsored atrocities of which we continue to grow more aware. For this reason, a rapidly growing number of citizens have no problem with embracing the judgment that there are just some activities that are simply wrong no matter what a particular culture, religion, individual, or public figure may think. Nevertheless, many of these same citizens still resort to embracing relativism when it comes to the issue of abortion, maintaining that reasoning, especially moral reasoning, has no place in this dispute. Thus, in this chapter I critically assess moral relativism. In a section of this critique, I argue that both pro-life and abortion-choice advocates hold a number of moral principles in common, and that the difference between these two contrary points of view does not rest on inconsistent moral principles but on disagreements about the application of these principles and the truth of certain "facts." I will conclude by showing how it is possible to provide reasons for a particular moral point of view, by employing several examples.

MORAL RELATIVISM AND MORAL DISCOURSE

Moral relativism has stunted the ability of many to grasp the nature of moral claims.[2] Some people often confuse *preference-claims* with *moral-claims* or reduce the latter to the former. To understand what I mean by this, consider two statements:[3]

1. I like vanilla ice cream.
2. Killing people without justification is wrong.

The first statement is a preference-claim, as it is a description of a person's subjective taste. It is not a *normative* claim. It is not a claim about what one ought or ought not to do. It is not saying, "Because I like vanilla ice cream, the government ought to coerce you to eat it as well" or "Everyone in the world ought to like vanilla ice cream too." A claim of subjective preference tells us nothing about what one *ought to* think or do. For example, if someone were to say, "I like to torture children for fun," this would tell us nothing about whether it is wrong or right to torture children for fun.

The second claim, however, is quite different. It has little if anything to do with what one likes or dislikes. In fact, one may *prefer* to kill another person without justification and still know that it is morally wrong to do so. This statement is a *moral-claim*. It is not a descriptive claim, for it does not tell us what, why, or how things are, or how a majority of people in fact behave and/or think. Nor is it a preference-claim, for it does not tell us what anyone's subjective preference may be or how one prefers to behave and/or think. Rather, it is a claim about what one *ought to do*, which may be contrary to how one in fact behaves and/or prefers to behave.

Unfortunately, the espousal of moral relativism has made it difficult for many people in our culture to distinguish between preference-claims and moral-claims. Rather than pondering and struggling with arguments for and against a particular moral perspective, people sometimes reduce the disagreement to a question of "personal preference" or "subjective opinion." For example, some who defend the abortion-choice position sometimes tell pro-lifers: "Don't like abortion, then don't have one." This instruction reduces the abortion debate to a preference-claim. That is, the objective moral rightness or wrongness of abortion (i.e., whether it involves the unjustified killing of a being who is fully human) is declared, without argument, to be not relevant. But it is clearly a mistake, for those who oppose abortion do so because they believe that the unborn during most if not all of a woman's pregnancy is a full-fledged member of the human community, and it is prima facie wrong, both objectively and universally, to kill such a being. For this reason, when the pro-lifer hears the abortion-choice advocate tell her that if she doesn't like abortion she doesn't have to have one, it sounds to her as if the abortion-choicer is saying, "Don't like murder, then don't kill any innocent persons." Understandably, the pro-lifer, committed to objective moral norms, finds such rhetoric perplexing as well as unpersuasive. Of course, many sophisticated abortion-choice advocates are opponents of moral relativism as well.[4] But it just seems that in the popular debate abortion-choicers tend to reduce the issue of abortion to a matter of preference and thus seem to have been more affected by moral relativism than have their opponents. (But they are *not completely* affected, for they do appeal to "fundamental rights" which are typically grounded in some objective morality.)[5] It is true that the pro-lifer's arguments may be flawed, but the abortion-choice advocate does not critique those flawed arguments when he mistakenly turns a serious moral disagreement into a debate over preferences.

ARGUMENTS FOR MORAL RELATIVISM

There are two arguments that are often used to defend moral relativism. The first is the argument from cultural and individual differences and the second is the argument from tolerance.

Argument from Cultural and Individual Differences

In this argument, the relativist concludes that there are no objective
moral norms because cultures and individuals disagree on moral issues.
To defend this premise the relativist typically cites a number of examples,
such as cross-cultural and intra-cultural differences over the morality of
sexual practices, abortion, war, and capital punishment. In the words of
Hadley Arkes, an opponent of moral relativism, "In one society, a widow
is burned on the funeral pyre of her husband; in another, she is burned on
the beach in Miami. In one society, people complain to the chef about the
roast beef; in another, they send back the roast beef and eat the chef."[6]
There are at least four problems with this argument.

Relativism does not follow from disagreement

The fact that people disagree about something does not mean that there
is no truth of the matter. For example, if you and I were to disagree
on the question of whether the earth is round, our disagreement would
certainly not be proof that the earth has *no* shape. The fact that a skin-
head (a type of young neo-Nazi) and I may disagree on the question of
whether we should treat people equally and with fairness is certainly not
sufficient reason to conclude that equality and fairness are not objective
moral truths. Even if individuals and cultures hold no values in common,
it does not follow from this that nobody is right or wrong about what
is moral truth. That is, there could be a mistaken individual or culture,
such as Adolf Hitler and Nazi Germany.

If the mere fact of disagreement were sufficient to conclude that objective norms do not exist, then we would have to believe that there is no
objectively correct position on such issues as slavery, genocide, and child
molestation, for the slave owner, genocidal maniac, and pedophile have
an opinion that differs from the one held by those of us who condemn
their actions. In the end, moral disagreement proves nothing.

Disagreement counts against relativism

Suppose, however, that the relativist, despite the logical failure of his
case, sticks to his guns and maintains that disagreement over objective
norms proves the correctness of relativism. But this will not work. For
the relativist has set down a principle – disagreement means there is no
truth – that unravels his own case. After all, some of us believe that relativism is a mistaken view. We, in other words, *disagree* with the relativist
over the nature of morality. We believe that objective moral norms exist

whereas the relativist does not. But, according to the relativist's own principle – disagreement means there is no truth – he ought to abandon his opinion that relativism is the correct position. And to make matters worse for the relativist, his principle is a proposition for which there is no universal agreement, and thus on its own grounds must be rejected. As Arkes points out, "My disagreement establishes that the proposition [i.e., disagreement means there is no truth] does not enjoy a universal assent, and by the very terms of the proposition, that should be quite sufficient to determine *its own invalidity*."[7]

Disagreement is overrated

Although it is true that people and cultures disagree on moral issues, it does not follow from this that they do not share the same principles or that there are not moral norms that are binding on all nations in all times and in all places. Take for example the Salem witch trials. In 1692, in the colony of Massachusetts, nearly three dozen citizens (mostly women) were put to death as punishment for allegedly practicing witchcraft.[8] We do not execute witches today, but not because our moral principles have changed. Rather, the reason why we don't execute witches is because we do not believe, as some of the 17th-century residents of Salem did, that the practice of witchcraft has a fatal effect upon the community. Even if one believes, as I do, that the trials and executions of these alleged witches were travesties of justice, based on flimsy evidence and trumped-up charges fueled by hysteria,[9] the principle to which the trials' apologists appealed seems prima facie correct: communities and their leaders should support and enforce policies that advance the public good. After all, suppose that we had good evidence that the practice of witchcraft did affect people in the same way that secondhand cigarette smoke affects the nonsmoker. We would alter practices to take this into consideration. We might set up non-witch sections in restaurants and ban the casting of spells on interstate airplane flights. The upshot of all this is that advancing the public good is a principle of just government that we share with the 17th-century residents of Salem, but we have good reason to believe that they were factually wrong about the effect of witchcraft upon the achievement of that good and/or that religious liberty better advances the public good than does religious coercion (even if one may have good reason to believe that the practice of witchcraft is in fact not good).[10]

Consider again the issue of abortion. The conventional wisdom is that the moral and legal debate over abortion is a dispute between two factions that hold incommensurable value systems. But the conventional wisdom is mistaken, for these factions hold many moral principles in common.

First, each side believes that all humans possess certain rights regardless of whether their governments protect these rights. That is why both sides appeal to what each believes is a fundamental right. The pro-life advocate appeals to "life" whereas the abortion-choice advocate appeals to "liberty" (or "choice"). Both believe that a constitutional regime, to be just, must uphold fundamental rights.

Second, each side believes that its position best exemplifies its opponent's fundamental value. The abortion-choice advocate does not deny that "life" is a value, but argues that his position's appeal to human liberty is a necessary ingredient by which an individual can pursue the fullest and most complete life possible.

On the other hand, the pro-life advocate does not eschew "liberty." She believes that all human liberty is at least limited by another human person's right to life. For example, one has a right to freely pursue any goal one believes is consistent with one's happiness, such as attending a Los Angeles Lakers basketball game. One has, however, no right to freely pursue this goal at the expense of another's life or liberty, such as running over pedestrians with one's car so that one can get to the game on time. And, of course, the pro-life advocate argues that the unborn are persons with a full right to life. And because the act of abortion typically results in the death of the unborn, abortion, with few exceptions, is not morally justified, and for that reason ought to be made illegal.

The abortion-choice advocate does not deny that human persons have a right to life. He just believes that this right to life is not extended to the unborn because they are not full members of the human community. Others, such as Judith Jarvis Thomson, Eileen McDonagh, and David Boonin,[11] argue that even if the unborn entity is a full-fledged member of the human community, he or she has no right to use the body of another against that person's will, because such a usage of another's body demands of that person great risk and sacrifice that goes beyond any ordinary moral obligation. Hence, because a pregnant woman is not morally obligated to put herself at great risk and to make a significant sacrifice for another, she is morally justified in removing her unborn offspring even if such a removal results in his or her death (see Chapter 7 for a critical assessment of this position). The pro-life advocate does not deny that people have the liberty to make choices that they believe are in their best interests. She just believes that this liberty does not entail the right to choose abortion, for such a choice conflicts with the life, liberty, and interests of another human being (the fetus), who is defenseless, weak, and vulnerable, and has a natural claim upon its parents' care, both pre- and postnatally. Thus, when all is said and done, the debate over abortion is not really about conflicting moral systems. After all, imagine if a pro-life politician were to say the following in a campaign speech: "My party's platform affirms a woman's right to terminate her pregnancy if and only if it does not result in the death of her unborn child." Disagreement over such a plank would not be over the morality of killing human persons; it would be over the metaphysical question of whether the unborn human is included in that category.

Absurd consequences follow from moral relativism

First, if there are no objective moral norms that apply to all persons in all times and in all places, then certain moral judgments, such as the following, cannot be universally true: Mother Teresa was morally better than Adolf Hitler; rape is always wrong; and it is wrong to torture babies for fun. But to deny that these judgments are not universally true seems absurd. For there seem to be some moral judgments that are absolutely correct regardless of what cultures or individuals may think.

Second, if the relativist claims that morality is relative to the individual, what happens when individual moralities conflict? For example, suppose that Jeffrey Dahmer's morality permits him to cannibalize his neighbor, but his neighbor disagrees. What would the relativist suggest be done in this case, as, according to this form of relativism, nobody's morality is in principle superior to any other? In addition, if the moral life is no more than a reflection of people's individual tastes, preferences, and orientations, then we cannot tell young people that it is morally wrong to lie, steal, cheat, smoke, abuse drugs, kill their newborns, and drop out of school, even though these behaviors may be consistent with the students' own personal tastes, preferences, and/or orientations.

Third, even if the relativist were to make the more modest claim that morality is not relative to the individual but to the individual's culture, that one is only obligated to follow the dictates of one's society, other problems follow.

1. The cultural relativist's position is self-refuting. What does it mean for a position to be self-refuting? J. P. Moreland explains:

> When a statement fails to satisfy itself (i.e., to conform to its own criteria of validity or acceptability), it is self-refuting. . . . Consider some examples. "I cannot say a word in English" is self-refuting when uttered in English. "I do not exist" is self-refuting, for one must exist to utter it. The claim

"there are no truths" is self-refuting. If it is false, then it is false. But if it is true, then it is false as well, for in that case there would be no truths, including the statement itself.[12]

How is cultural relativism self-refuting? The supporter of cultural relativism maintains that there are no objective and universal moral norms and for that reason everyone ought follow the moral norms of his or her own culture. But the cultural relativist is making an absolute and universal moral claim, namely, that everyone is morally obligated to follow the moral norms of his or her own culture. So, if this moral norm is absolute and universal, then cultural relativism is false. But if this moral norm is neither absolute nor universal, then cultural relativism is still false, for in that case I would not have a moral obligation to follow the moral norms of my culture.

2. Because each of us belongs to a number of different "societies" or "cultures," which one of them should be followed when they conflict? For example, suppose a woman named "Carla" is a resident of a liberal upscale neighborhood in Hollywood, California, attends a Christian church, and is a partner in a prestigious law firm. In her neighborhood, having an adulterous affair is considered "enlightened" and those who do not pursue such unions are considered repressed prudes. At her church, however, adultery is condemned as sinful, while at her law firm adultery is neither encouraged nor discouraged. Suppose further that Carla chooses to commit adultery in the firm's back office with a fellow churchgoer, Winston, who resides in a conservative neighborhood in which adultery is condemned. The office, it turns out, is adjacent to the church as well as precisely halfway between Carla's neighborhood and Winston's neighborhood. It is not clear which society is morally relevant.[13]

3. There can be no moral progress or moral reformers. If morality is reducible to culture, then there can be no real moral progress. For the only way one can say that a culture is *getting better*, or progressing, is if there are objective moral norms that are not dependent on culture to which a society may draw closer. But if what is morally good is merely what one's culture says is morally good, then we can only say that cultural norms change, not that the society is progressing or getting better. Yet, it seems, for example, that the abolition of slavery and the establishment of civil rights of African Americans in the United States were instances of moral progress. In addition, there can be no true moral reformers if cultural relativism is true. Moreland writes:

If [cultural] relativism is true, then it is impossible in principle to have a true moral reformer who changes a society's code and does not merely bring out what was already implicit in that code. For moral reformers, by definition, *change* a society's code by arguing that it is somehow morally inadequate. But if [cultural] relativism is true, an act is right if and only if it is in society's code; so the reformer is by definition immoral (since he adopts a set of values outside the society's code and attempts to change that code in keeping with these values). It is odd, to say the least, for someone to hold that every moral reformer who ever lived – Moses, Jesus, Gandhi, Martin Luther King – was immoral by definition. Any moral view which implies that is surely false.[14]

Thus, to remain consistent, the cultural relativist must deny that there can be any real moral progress or any real moral reformers. For such judgments presuppose the existence of real, objective, moral norms.

Argument from Tolerance

Many people see relativism as necessary for promoting tolerance, non-judgmentalism, and inclusiveness, for they think if you believe your moral position is correct and others' incorrect you are close-minded and intolerant. They usually base this premise on the well-known differences of opinion on morality between cultures and individuals. So, the moral relativist embraces the view that one should not judge other cultures and individuals, for to do so would be intolerant. There are at least four problems with this argument, all of which maintain that tolerance (rightly understood) and relativism are actually *incompatible* with each other.

Tolerance supports objective morality, not relativism
Ironically, the call to tolerance by relativists presupposes the existence of at least one nonrelative, universal, and objective norm: tolerance. Bioethicist Tom Beauchamp explains:

> If we interpret normative relativism as requiring tolerance of other views, the whole theory is imperiled by inconsistency. The proposition that we ought to tolerate the views of others, or that it is right not to interfere with others, is precluded by the very strictures of the theory. Such a proposition bears all the marks of a non-relative account of moral rightness, one based on, but not reducible to, the cross-cultural findings of anthropologists. . . . But if this moral principle [of tolerance] is recognized as valid, it can of course be employed as an instrument for criticizing such cultural practices as the denial of human rights to minorities and such beliefs as that of racial superiority. A moral commitment to tolerance of other practices and beliefs thus leads inexorably to the abandonment of normative relativism.[15]

Thus, if everyone ought to be tolerant, then tolerance is an objective moral norm. And therefore, moral relativism is false. Also, tolerance presupposes that there is something good about being tolerant, such as being able to learn from others with whom one disagrees or to impart knowledge and wisdom to that person. But that presupposes objective moral values, namely, that knowledge and wisdom are good things. Moreover, tolerance presupposes that someone may be correct about his or her moral perspective. That is to say, it seems that part of the motivation for advocating tolerance is to encourage people to be open to the possibility that one may be able to gain truth and insight (including moral truth and insight) from another who may possess it. If that is the case, then there are objective moral truths that one can learn.

In addition, tolerance presupposes a moral judgment of another's viewpoint. That is to say, I can only be tolerant of those ideas that I think are mistaken. I am not tolerant of that with which I agree; I embrace it. And I am not tolerant of that for which I have no interest (e.g., European professional soccer); I merely have benign neglect for it. (That is, I don't care one way or another.) Consider the following example. Suppose I tell a friend that I believe that homosexuality is immoral. And suppose my friend requests that I be tolerant toward homosexuals in my community. If I accept this advice and choose to be civil, respectful, and gracious to gay men and women with whom I have contact, while at the same time judging their sexual practices as immoral, it seems that I would be truly tolerant. But suppose that someone says that my judging of homosexuality as immoral still makes me "intolerant." At that point, given my understanding of "tolerance," I have no idea what I am supposed to do. For if I change my view of homosexuality, and say either that it is not immoral or that I have no opinion (i.e., I have benign neglect), then I cannot be tolerant, for I can only be tolerant of what I believe is wrong or mistaken. On the other hand, if judging another's position as wrong or mistaken makes one intolerant, then the person who judges my negative assessment of homosexuality is, by that person's own definition, intolerant. But that is absurd. For if "tolerance" means that one ought not to judge a view as morally wrong, then it seems to be consistent with either embracing the view or having benign neglect for it. If that is the case, then "tolerance" has lost its meaning and is simply a cover for trying to shame and coerce others not to publicly (and/or perhaps privately) disagree with one's controversial and disputed position on human sexuality. This, ironically, is an example of intolerance (as traditionally understood). So, it seems to me that the appeal to tolerance, once we have a clear understanding of its meaning, is *inconsistent* with relativism.

Relativism is itself a closed-minded and intolerant position

After all, the relativist dogmatically asserts that there is no moral truth. To illustrate this, consider a dialogue (based loosely on a real-life exchange) between a high school teacher and her student Elizabeth.[16] The teacher instructs her class, "Welcome, students. This is the first day of class, and so I want to lay down some ground rules. First, because no one has the truth about morality, you should be open-minded to the opinions of your fellow students." The teacher recognizes the raised hand of Elizabeth, who asks, "If nobody has the truth, isn't that a good reason for me not to listen to my fellow students? After all, if nobody has the truth, why should I waste my time listening to other people and their opinions? What's the point? Only if somebody has the truth does it make sense to be open-minded. Don't you agree?"

"No, I don't. Are you claiming to know the truth? Isn't that a bit arrogant and dogmatic?"

"Not at all. Rather I think it's dogmatic, as well as arrogant, to assert that no single person on earth knows the truth. After all, have you met every person in the world and quizzed these people exhaustively? If not, how can you make such a claim? Also, I believe it is actually the opposite of arrogance to say that I will alter my opinions to fit the truth whenever and wherever I find it. And if I happen to think that I have good reason to believe I do know the truth and would like to share it with you, why wouldn't you listen to me? Why would you automatically discredit my opinion before it is even uttered? I thought we were supposed to listen to everyone's opinion."

"This should prove to be an interesting semester."

Another student blurts out, "Ain't that the truth," provoking the class to laughter.

Relativism is judgmental, exclusivist, and partisan

This may seem like an odd thing to say as the relativist would like you to think his viewpoint is nonjudgmental, inclusivist, and neutral when it comes to moral beliefs. But consider the following.

First, the relativist says that if you believe in objective moral truth, you are *wrong*. Hence, relativism is judgmental. Second, it follows from this that relativism is *excluding* your beliefs from the realm of legitimate options. Thus, relativism is exclusivist. And third, because relativism

is exclusivist, all nonrelativists are automatically not members of the
"correct thinking" party. So, relativism is partisan.

Tolerance only makes sense within the framework of a moral order,
for it is within such a framework that one can morally justify tolerating
some things while not tolerating others. For tolerance without a moral
framework, or absolute tolerance, leads to a dogmatic relativism, and
thus to an intolerance of any viewpoint that does not embrace relativism.
It is no wonder that in such a climate of "tolerance" any person who
maintains that there is an objective moral order to which society ought
to subscribe is greeted with contempt.

The "tolerance" of moral relativism either condones barbarism or is self-refuting

As I pointed out above, some moral relativists embrace tolerance because
they believe that such a posture is appropriate given the diversity of moral
and cultural traditions in the world today. Humanist author Xiaorong
Li points out the fallacy in this reasoning:

> But the existence of moral diversity does no more to justify that we ought
> to respect different moral values than the existence of disease, hunger,
> torture, slavery do to justify that we ought to value them. Empirical
> claims thus are not suitable as the basis for developing moral principles
> such as "Never judge other cultures" or "We ought to tolerate different
> values." ...
>
> What if the respected or tolerated culture disrespects and advocates
> violence against individuals who dissent? When a girl fights to escape
> female genital circumcision or foot-binding or arranged marriage, when
> a widow does not want to be burned to death to honor her dead husband,
> the relativist is obligated to "respect" the cultural or traditional customs
> from which the individuals are trying to escape. In so doing, the relativist
> is not merely disrespecting the individual but effectively endorsing the
> moral ground for torture, rape, and murder. *On moral issues, ethical
> relativists can not possibly remain neutral – they are committed either to
> the individual or to the dominant force within a culture.*
>
> Relativists have made explicit one central value – equal respect and tol-
> erance of other ways of life, which they insist to be absolute and universal.
> *Ethical relativism is thus repudiated by itself.*[17]

REASONING ABOUT MORAL MATTERS

Morality is clearly more than mere reasoning, just as architecture is more
than mere mathematics. One can immediately grasp as well as appreciate
the moral virtue of Mother Teresa or the monumental elegance of the

Eiffel Tower without having studied Thomas Reid's moral philosophy or mastered geometry and calculus. Nevertheless, just as one cannot build the Eiffel Tower without mastering certain mathematical disciplines, one cannot attribute the label "just" or "right" to one's point of view without offering justification for its rightness.

The logic of moral reasoning has been part and parcel of our discourse for as long as human beings have occupied the Earth. It has stirred souls, shamed sinners, moved nations, energized social movements, and provided for us a potent grammar in numerous areas of private and public life. Consider just three examples, though numerous others could be conscripted for our purposes.

In the book of II Samuel (chapter 11) in the Jewish Tanuch (the Christian Old Testament) one finds the story of King David's encounter with Nathan after the king had taken himself a wife, Bathsheba, a woman whom he had first observed one evening while he strolled on the palace roof. From a distance, he saw Bathsheba bathing. Overwhelmed by her beauty, he sent his messengers to fetch her, and he quickly came to know her (in the biblical sense). That union, however, resulted in a pregnancy. But there was a problem, for Bathsheba, as David knew, was married to Uriah the Hittite. So the King assigned Uriah, a member of the army, to the front lines where the fighting is the most ferocious, and instructed Joab, the leader of the Israelite army, to leave Uriah there unprotected so that he would surely be killed. David married Bathsheba soon after Uriah died on the battlefield.

But David did not live happily ever after, for first among the punishments that followed was Nathan's rebuke, which Nathan introduced with an elegant form of moral reasoning that forced the King to confront the gravity of his offense:

> When [Nathan] came to [David], he said, "There were two men in a certain town, one rich and the other poor. The rich man had a very large number of sheep and cattle, but the poor man had nothing except one little ewe lamb he had bought. He raised it, and it grew up with him and his children. It shared his food, drank from his cup and even slept in his arms. It was like a daughter to him.
>
> "Now a traveler came to the rich man, but the rich man refrained from taking one of his own sheep or cattle to prepare a meal for the traveler who had come to him. Instead, he took the ewe lamb that belonged to the poor man and prepared it for the one who had come to him."
>
> David burned with anger against the man and said to Nathan, "As surely as the LORD lives, the man who did this deserves to die! He must

pay for the lamb four times over, because he did such a thing and had no
pity."

Then Nathan said to David, "You are the man!" (II Sam. 12:1b-7a).

David fully grasped the moral principles by which we judge that the
rich man's behavior was wicked and that it should result in severe punishment against him. But those very same moral principles, and the punishments that follow from violating them, apply to David as well. One
need not accept the divine inspiration and/or historicity of this biblical
account to appreciate the wisdom of Nathan's judgment, the aptness of
his analogy, and the clarity that one acquires when grasping a scintillating
instance of moral reasoning.

In his failed 1858 bid for a U.S. Senate seat from Illinois, Abraham Lincoln engaged in a series of public debates with his Democratic opponent,
Stephen A. Douglas. Among the many topics on which they disputed was
the question of whether U.S. territories should be allowed by the federal government to permit slavery if they so chose. Douglas maintained
that although he believed that slavery was wrong (i.e., he personally
opposed it), he was not willing to require that the federal government
eliminate slavery, for to do so would be to violate the principle of popular sovereignty – that local majorities should be permitted to vote on
such issues free of any and all federal constraints.[18] But, as Lincoln aptly
pointed out, "when Judge Douglas says he 'don't care whether slavery is
voted up or down,'...he cannot thus argue logically if he sees anything
wrong in it;...He cannot say that he would as soon see a wrong voted
up as voted down. When Judge Douglas says that whoever, or whatever
community, wants slaves, they have a right to have them, he is perfectly
logical if there is nothing wrong in the institution; but if you admit that
it is wrong, he cannot logically say that anybody has a right to do a
wrong."[19] Lincoln, a practical man with uncommon wisdom, grasped
an important conceptual truth not often apprehended by those, such as
Douglas, who inadvertently stumble into the arena of moral reasoning
and think they are somewhere else: to claim that something is a wrong
is to claim that it is impermissible, but it would inexorably follow from
that truth that one cannot claim that one has a *right* to perform the
wrong, for that would mean the impermissible is permissible.[20] Or, as
Arkes puts it: "Once we come to the recognition that any act stands in
the class of a wrong...the logic of that recognition forbids us from treating that act any longer as a matter merely of personal taste or private
choice."[21]

In notes he had prepared for himself, Lincoln provided another example of principled moral reasoning in assessing the sorts of arguments that his contemporaries put forth to defend the enslavement of black people by white people:

> You say A. is white and B. is black. It is *color*, then: the lighter having the right to enslave the darker? Take care. By this rule, you are to be a slave to the first man you meet, with a fairer skin than your own.
>
> You do not mean *color* exactly? – You mean the whites are *intellectually* the superiors of the blacks, and therefore, have the right to enslave them? Take care again. By this rule, you are to be a slave to the first man you meet, with an intellect superior to your own.
>
> But, say you, it is a question of interest; and, if you can make it your *interest*, you have the right to enslave another. Very well. And if he can make it his interest, he has the right to enslave you.[22]

Lincoln was making the point that if one were to apply the arguments for slavery to the prospective and current slave owners, whites, then one has put in place premises that may be employed by the government to undermine the rights of all human beings under its authority.[23] For the premises of the pro-slavery arguments contain propositions that appeal to degreed properties that carry no moral weight – color, intellect, and interest – when it comes to the question of human equality. Lincoln's assessment of these arguments is an impressive example of moral reasoning.

CONCLUSION

Moral relativism is a philosophical failure. The two main arguments for moral relativism – the argument from disagreement and the argument from tolerance – are seriously flawed in numerous ways. Given the failure of moral relativism, it seems reasonable to believe in objective morality. Moreover, there is a logic of moral reasoning that has been employed by numerous people throughout the ages for the purpose of providing for their fellow citizens moral clarity and/or moral justification. There is no reason that we cannot do the same in the debate over abortion.

THE SUPREME COURT, *ROE v. WADE,* AND ABORTION LAW

No collection of U.S. Supreme Court opinions has been more misunderstood, and its arguments more misrepresented to the general public, than *Roe v. Wade* (1973) and its jurisprudential progeny.[1]

To fully grasp the reasoning of *Roe*, its paucity as a piece of constitutional jurisprudence, and the current state of abortion law, we will look at three different but interrelated topics: (1) what the Court actually concluded in *Roe*; (2) the Court's reasoning in *Roe;* and (3) how subsequent Court opinions, including *Casey v. Planned Parenthood* (1992), have shaped the jurisprudence of abortion law.

WHAT THE COURT ACTUALLY CONCLUDED IN *ROE*

The case of *Roe v. Wade* (1973) concerned Jane Roe (a.k.a. Norman McCorvey), a resident of Texas, who claimed to have become pregnant as a result of a gang rape (which was found later to be a false charge years after the Court had issued its opinion).[2] According to the Texas law at the time (essentially unchanged since 1856), a woman may procure an abortion only if it is necessary to save her life. Because Roe's pregnancy was not life threatening, she sued the state of Texas. In 1970, the unmarried Roe filed a class action suit in federal district court in Dallas. The federal court ruled that the Texas law was unconstitutionally vague and overbroad and infringed on a woman's right to reproductive freedom. The state of Texas appealed to the U.S. Supreme Court. After the case was argued twice before it, the Court issued *Roe v. Wade* on January 22, 1973, holding that the Texas law was unconstitutional and that not only must all states including Texas permit abortions in cases of rape but in all other cases as well.

The public does not seem to fully understand the scope of what the Court declared as a constitutional right on that fateful day in 1973. The current law in the United States, except in a few states,[3] does not restrict a woman from procuring an abortion for practically any reason she deems fit during the entire nine months of pregnancy. That may come as quite a shock to many readers, but that is in fact the state of the current law.

In *Roe* Justice Harry Blackmun, who authored the Court's opinion, divided pregnancy into trimesters. He ruled that aside from procedural guidelines to ensure maternal health, a state has no right to restrict abortion in the first six months of pregnancy. Writes Blackmun:

> A state criminal abortion statute of the current Texas type, that excepts from criminality only a *life-saving* procedure on behalf of the mother without regard to pregnancy stage and without recognition of the other interests involved, is violative of the Due Process Clause of the Fourteenth Amendment.
>
> (a) For the stage prior to approximately the end of the first trimester, the abortion decision and its effectuation must be left to the medical judgment of the pregnant woman's attending physician.
> (b) For the stage subsequent to approximately the end of the first trimester, the State, in promoting its interest in the health of the mother, may, if it chooses, regulate the abortion procedure in ways that are reasonably related to maternal health.
> (c) For the stage subsequent to viability the State, in promoting its interest in the potentiality of human life, may, if it chooses, regulate, and even proscribe, abortion except where necessary, in appropriate medical judgment, for the preservation of the life or health of the mother.[4]

Thus a woman could have an abortion during the first six months of pregnancy for *any* reason she deems fit. Restrictions in the second trimester should be merely regulatory to protect the pregnant woman's health. In the last trimester (after fetal viability, the time at which the unborn can live outside the womb) the state has a right, although not an obligation, to restrict abortions to only those cases in which the mother's life or health is jeopardized, because after viability, according to Blackmun, the state's interest in prenatal life becomes compelling. *Roe*, therefore, does not prevent a state from having unrestricted abortion for the entire nine months of pregnancy if it so chooses.

Nevertheless, the Court explains that it would be a mistake to think of the right to abortion as absolute.[5] For the Court maintained that it took into consideration the legitimate state interests of both the health of the pregnant woman and the prenatal life she carries. Thus, reproductive liberty, according to this reading of *Roe*, should be seen as a limited freedom established within the nexus of three parties: the pregnant woman, the unborn, and the state. The woman's liberty trumps both the value of the unborn and the interests of the state except when the unborn reaches viability (and an abortion is unnecessary to preserve the life or health of the pregnant woman) and/or when the state has a compelling state interest in regulating abortion before and after viability to make sure that the procedure is performed in accordance with accepted medical standards. Even though this is a fair reading of *Roe*'s reasoning, it seems to me that the premises put in place by Justice Blackmun have not resulted in the sensible balance of interests he claimed his opinion had reached. Rather, it has, in practice, resulted in abortion on demand.

Because Justice Blackmun claimed that a state has a compelling interest in protecting prenatal life only after that life is viable (which in 1973 was between 24 and 28 weeks' gestation), and because the viability line is being pushed back in pregnancy (now it is between 20 and 24 weeks) as a result of the increased technological sophistication of incubators and other devices and techniques, Justice Sandra Day O'Connor made the comment in her dissent in *Akron v. Akron Center for Reproductive Health, Inc.* (1983) that *Roe* is on a "collision course with itself."[6] In other words, if viability is pushed back far enough, the right to abortion will vanish for all practical purposes. That is, in principle, a state's "interest" in a viable fetus can extend back to conception. Furthermore, Blackmun's choice of viability as the point at which the state has a compelling interest in protecting prenatal life is based on a fallacious argument, which I will assess below in my presentation and critique of *Casey v. Planned Parenthood*.

But there is a loophole to which abortion-choice supporters may appeal to avoid O'Connor's "collision course." Consider one state law written within the framework of *Roe*. Nevada restricts abortions after viability by permitting them after the 24th week of pregnancy only if "there is a substantial risk that the continuance of the pregnancy would endanger the life of the patient or would gravely impair the physical or mental health of the patient."[7] But this restriction is a restriction in name only. For the Supreme Court so broadly defined health in *Roe*'s companion decision, *Doe v. Bolton* (1973), that for all intents and purposes *Roe* allows for abortion on demand. In *Bolton* the court ruled that health must be taken in its broadest possible medical context and must be defined "in light of all factors – physical, emotional, psychological, familial, and the woman's age – relevant to the well being of the patient. All these factors relate to health."[8] Because all pregnancies have consequences for a woman's emotional and family situation, the court's health provision has the practical effect of legalizing abortion up until the time of birth if a woman can convince a physician that she needs the abortion to preserve her emotional health. This is why in 1983 the U.S. Senate Judiciary Committee, after much critical evaluation of the current law in light of the Court's opinions, confirmed this interpretation when it concluded that "no significant legal barriers of any kind whatsoever exist today in the United States for a woman to obtain an abortion for any reason during any stage of her pregnancy."[9]

Even former Chief Justice Warren Burger, who originally sided with the majority in *Roe* because he was under the impression that abortion after viability would occur only if the mother's physical life and health were in imminent peril, concluded in his dissent in *Thornburg v. American College of Obstetricians and Gynecologists* (1986) that *Roe* did, contrary to his own earlier interpretation of the decision, support abortion on demand: "We have apparently already passed the point at which abortion is available merely on demand.... The point at which these [State] interests become 'compelling' under *Roe* is at viability of the fetus.... Today, however, the Court abandons that standard and renders the solemnly stated concerns of the 1973 *Roe* opinion for the interests of the States mere shallow rhetoric."[10] Others had come to the same conclusion much earlier than Justice Burger.[11]

Moreover, it is not clear that when the Court refers to viability as the time when the state has a compelling interest in prenatal life that it is referring only to the physical survival of the unborn apart from her mother. Rather, it may be suggesting a largely philosophical notion of "meaningful life,"[12] a determination that is exclusively in the hands of the pregnant woman. Although in *Roe* "meaningful life" seemed to mean a life that is physically independent of its mother (for more on this, see my analysis of *Casey* below), the Court made the point in a later opinion, "There must be a potentiality of 'meaningful life,' . . . not merely momentary survival."[13]

THE COURT'S REASONING IN *ROE*: HOW IT FOUND A RIGHT TO ABORTION

Because the Court had already established a right to contraceptive use by married couples[14] and then by single people[15] based on the right of privacy,[16] it would seem that abortion, because it is a means of birth control, would be protectable under this right of privacy. However, to make this move, there were at least two legal impediments that Justice Blackmun had to eliminate: (1) *Starting in the 19th century anti-abortion laws had been on the books in virtually every U.S. state and territory for the primary reason of protecting the unborn from unjust killing.* If, as Justice Douglas asserts in *Griswold*, the "right of privacy [is] older than the Bill of Rights – older than our political parties, older than our school system,"[17] then the Court must account for the proliferation of anti-abortion laws, whose constitutionality were not seriously challenged until the late 1960s, in a legal regime whose legislators and citizens passed these laws with apparently no inclination to believe that they were inconsistent with a right of privacy "older than the Bill of Rights." (2) *The unborn is constitutionally a person protectable under the Fourteenth Amendment.* After all, unlike contraception, in which all the adult participants in the sexual act consent to its use, a successful abortion entails the killing of a third party, a living organism, the unborn, who has already come into being.[18] So, to justify abortion the Court had to show that the unborn is not a person under the Fourteenth Amendment. If the Court had good reasons to reject these two jurisprudential challenges, then it could establish a right to abortion as a species of the right of privacy.

Justice Blackmun agreed with opponents of abortion rights that anti-abortion laws have been on the books in the United States for quite some time. However, according to Blackmun, the purpose of these laws, almost all of which were passed in the 19th century, was not to protect prenatal life but rather to protect the pregnant woman from a dangerous medical procedure.[19] Blackmun also argues that prior to the passage of these statutes, under the common law, abortion was permissible prior to quickening and was at most a misdemeanor after quickening.[20] (Quickening refers to the "first recognizable movement of the fetus *in utero*, appearing usually from the 16th to the 18th week of pregnancy.")[21] So, because abortion is now a relatively safe procedure, there is no longer a reason for prohibiting it.[22] Consequently, given the right of privacy, and given the abortion liberty at common law, there is a constitutional right to abortion.

The history of abortion figures prominently in the Court's opinion in *Roe*.[23] Justice Blackmun, in 23 pages, takes the reader on a historical excursion through ancient attitudes (including the Greeks and Romans), the Hippocratic Oath, the common law, the English statutory law, the American law, and the positions of the American Medical Association (AMA), the American Public Health Association (APHA), and the

American Bar Association (ABA). The purpose for this history is clear: if abortion's prohibition is only recent, and primarily for the purpose of protecting the pregnant woman from dangerous surgery, then the Court would not be creating a new right out of whole cloth if it affirms a right to abortion. However, only the history of common law is relevant to assessing the constitutionality of this right, because, as Blackmun himself admits, "it was not until after the War Between the States that legislation began generally to *replace* the common law,"[24] even though, as Joseph W. Dellapenna points out, Justice Blackmun's historical chronology is "simply wrong," for 26 of 36 states had already banned abortion by the time the Civil War had ended.[25] Nevertheless, when statutes did not address a criminal wrong, common law was the authoritative resource from which juries, judges, and justices found the principles from which, and by which, they issued judgments.

However, since 1973 the overwhelming consensus of scholarship has shown that the Court's history, especially its interpretation of common law, is almost entirely mistaken. Justice Blackmun's history (excluding his discussion of contemporary professional groups: AMA, APHA, and ABA) is so flawed that it has inspired the production of scores of scholarly works, over the last quarter of the 20th century, that are nearly unanimous in concluding that Justice Blackmun's "history" is untrustworthy and essentially worthless.[26] However, for our modest purposes here, we will assess the two aspects of the Court's history that are the most central, and to which I alluded above: (1) the purpose of 19th-century anti-abortion statutes, and (2) the unborn's status as a Fourteenth Amendment person.

Were Anti-Abortion Laws Meant to Protect the Unborn?

Blackmun was wrong about the primary purpose of the anti-abortion laws. Although protecting the pregnant woman was an important though secondary purpose of these statutes,[27] there is no doubt that their primary purpose was to protect the unborn from harm. In what is perhaps the most definitive scholarly article on this subject,[28] law professor James S. Witherspoon conclusively shows that this was in fact the case. After an extensive analysis of the 19th-century statutes, their legislative histories, and the political climate in which they were passed, Witherspoon concludes:

> That the primary purpose of the nineteenth-century antiabortion statutes was to protect the lives of unborn children is clearly shown by the terms of the statutes themselves. This primary purpose, or legislative recognition

of the personhood of the unborn child, or both, are manifested, in the following elements of these statutes, taken individually and collectively: (1) the provision of an increased range of punishment for abortion if it were proven that the attempt caused the death of the child; (2) the provision of the same range of punishment for attempted abortions killing the unborn child as for attempted abortions killing the mother; (3) the designation of attempted abortion and other acts killing the unborn child as "manslaughter"; (4) the prohibition of all abortions except those necessary to save the life of the mother; (5) the reference to the fetus as a "child"; (6) the use of the term "person" in reference to the unborn child; (7) the categorization of abortion with homicide and related offenses and offenses against born children; (8) the severity of punishments assessed for abortions; (9) the provision that attempted abortion killing the mother is only manslaughter or a felony rather than murder as at common law; (10) the requirement that the woman on whom the abortion is attempted be pregnant; (11) the requirement that abortion be attempted with intent to produce abortion or to "destroy the child"; and (12) the incrimination of the woman's participation in her own abortion. Legislative recognition of the personhood of the unborn child is also shown by the legislative history of these statutes.

In short, the Supreme Court's analysis in *Roe v. Wade* of the development, purposes, and the understandings underlying the nineteenth-century antiabortion statutes, was fundamentally erroneous. That analysis can provide no support whatsoever for the Court's conclusions that the unborn children are not "persons" within the meaning of the fourteenth amendment, and that states do not otherwise have a "compelling interest" in protecting their lives by prohibiting abortion.[29]

The primary reason for Justice Blackmun's historical mistake, according to many scholars, is his almost total reliance on two articles by Professor Cyril Means,[30] who was an attorney for the National Association for the Repeal of Abortion Laws (NARAL). Since 1973, however, Means's work has come under devastating criticism, and for that reason it is no longer considered an authoritative rendering of abortion law,[31] though once in a while it is cited positively by authors.[32]

It is interesting to note that as biological knowledge of both human development and the unborn's nature began to increase, the laws prohibiting abortion became more restrictive. Justice Blackmun was correct when he pointed out that at common law pre-quickening abortion "was not an indictable offense,"[33] for it was thought that prior to quickening the unborn was not animated or infused with a soul.[34] But this is an erroneous belief based on primitive embryology and outdated biology. People indeed believed that prior to quickening there was no life and thus no soul, but they were mistaken, just as they were mistaken about Ptolemaic astronomy, the divine right of kings, and white supremacy, none of which seem to be an acceptable belief today even though each is of more ancient origin than its widely accepted counterparts of heliocentricity, constitutional democracy, and human equality.[35] As biology acquired more facts about human development, quickening began to be dismissed as an arbitrary, and irrelevant, criterion by which to distinguish between protectable and unprotectable human life. "When better knowledge was acquired in the nineteenth century," writes Stephen Krason, "laws began to be enacted prohibiting abortion at every stage of pregnancy."[36] Legal scholar Victor Rosenblum explains:

> Only in the second quarter of the nineteenth century did biological research advance to the extent of understanding the actual mechanism of development. The nineteenth century saw a gradual but profoundly influential revolution in the scientific understanding of the beginning of individual mammalian life. Although sperm had been discovered in 1677, the mammalian egg was not identified until 1827. The cell was first recognized as the structural unit of organisms in 1839, and the egg and sperm were recognized as cells in the next two decades. These developments were brought to the attention of the American state legislatures and public by those professionals most familiar with their unfolding import – physicians. It was the new research finding which persuaded doctors that the old "quickening" distinction embodied in the common and some statutory law was unscientific and indefensible.[37]

Legal scholar and theologian John Warwick Montgomery points out that when the common law and American statutory law employed the quickening criterion "they were just identifying the first evidence of life they could conclusively detect.... They were saying that as soon as you had life, there must be protection. Now we know that life starts at the moment of conception with nothing superadded."[38] Witherspoon writes:

> Clearly, the quickening doctrine was not based on an absurd belief that a living fetus is worthy of protection by virtue of its capacity for movement or its mother's perception of such movement. The occurrence of quickening was deemed significant *only* because it showed that the fetus was alive, and because it was *alive* and *human*, it was protected by the criminal law. This solution was deemed acceptable as long as the belief persisted that the fetus was not alive until it began to move, a belief that would be refuted in the early nineteenth century.[39]

One could say, therefore, that the quickening criterion, prior to the discoveries of modern biology, was employed as an evidential criterion

so that the law may *know* that a human life existed, for one could not
be prosecuted for performing an abortion if the being violently removed
from the womb was not alive to begin with.

Is the Unborn a Person under the Fourteenth Amendment?

The Fourteenth Amendment became part of the U.S. Constitution in
1868. It was passed for the purpose of protecting U.S. citizens, including
recently freed slaves, from having their rights violated by local and state
governments. The portion of the amendment germane to our study reads:

> All persons born or naturalized in the United States, and subject to the
> jurisdiction thereof, are citizens of the United States and of the state
> wherein they reside. No State shall make or enforce any law which shall
> abridge the privileges or immunities of citizens of the United States; nor
> shall any State deprive any person of life, liberty, or property, without
> due process of law; nor deny any person within its jurisdiction the equal
> protection of the laws.

There are two concerns for which Justice Blackmun conscripts the
Fourteenth Amendment to make his argument. First, he argues that the
right of privacy is a fundamental liberty protected by the amendment, and
that the right to abortion is a species of the right of privacy.[40] Second, he
argues that the unborn is not a person under the Fourteenth Amendment.
Because the first depends on the second, and Blackmun admits as much,[41]
my critique will focus exclusively on the latter use of the Fourteenth
Amendment in Blackmun's analysis.

Justice Blackmun offers three reasons in combination for his conclusion that the unborn are not Fourteenth Amendment persons. (1)
He maintains that "the Constitution does not define 'person' in so
many words," and goes on to list all the places in the Constitution in
which the word "person" is mentioned including the Fourteenth Amendment (sections 1, 2, and 3), "the listing of qualifications for Representatives and Senators, . . . the Apportionment Clause, . . . the Migration
and Importation provision, . . . the Emolument Clause, . . . the Electors
provision, . . . the superseded cl. 3, . . . the provision outlining qualifications for President, . . . the Extradition provisions, . . . the superseded
Fugitive Slave Clause 3[,] . . . and . . . the Fifth, Twelfth, and Twenty-
second Amendments."[42] According to Blackmun, "in nearly all these
instances, the use of the word is such that it has application postnatally"
with no "possible prenatal application."[43,44] (2) Texas could not cite one
case in which a court held that an unborn human being is a person under

the Fourteenth Amendment.[45] (3) Throughout most of the 19th century, abortion was practiced with fewer legal restrictions than in 1972. Based on these three reasons the Court was persuaded that "the word 'person,' as used in the Fourteenth Amendment does not include the unborn."[46] Each reason is seriously flawed.

1. In citing the constitutional provisions that apply to postnatal human beings, Justice Blackmun begs the question, for none of the provisions defines the meaning of "person," and thus does not exclude the unborn. Rather, with the exceptions of the Fugitive Slave Clause (Art. IV, Sec. 2, Cl. 3) and the Migration and Importation provision (Art. I, Sec. 9, Cl. 1), both of which were eliminated by the Thirteenth and Fourteenth Amendments, the constitutional provisions Justice Blackmun cites concern matters that apply *to already existing persons*. For example, the Fourteenth Amendment defines *citizens* as "all persons born or naturalized in the United States, and subject to the jurisdiction thereof," but it does not define *persons* (though it seems to be saying that birth is a state that persons undergo rather than an event that makes them persons, and thus the unborn are persons who shift from prenatal to postnatal when they undergo birth). The reference to the qualifications of congressmen (Art. I, Sec. 2, Cl. 2; Art. I, Sec. 3, Cl. 3) tells us that a senator must be at least 30 years old and a representative at least 25, but clearly the Court cannot be saying that because the fetus cannot hold these offices that he or she is not a person (for this would mean that 20-year-olds are not persons either). To cite one more example, the Apportionment Clause (Art. I, Sec. 2, Cl. 3) instructs the government on whom to count in the census to determine every 10 years the reapportionment to states of seats in the House of Representatives. Although the clause excludes the unborn from the census, it also excludes nontaxed Indians and declares black slaves as three-fifths of a person, even though Indians and black slaves are in fact persons. There were, of course, important practical reasons that a government might exclude the unborn from the census: it is extremely difficult and highly inefficient to count unborn persons because we cannot see them and some of them die before birth without the mother ever being aware that she was pregnant. Also, as Krason notes, at the time of the American Founding, "because of the high mortality rate then, it was very uncertain if a child would even be born alive." Moreover, "it was not yet known that the child from conception is a separate, distinct human organism."[47]

2. Although it is true that Texas did not cite a case that held that the unborn is a Fourteenth Amendment person, there was at least one

federal court case that did issue such a holding. That case, *Steinberg v. Brown* (1970),[48] ironically, was cited by the Court in *Roe*,[49] but Justice Blackmun failed to mention that the federal court in Steinberg provided the following analysis:

> Contraception, which is dealt with in *Griswold*, is concerned with preventing the creation of a new and independent life. The right and power of a man or a woman to determine whether or not to participate in this process of creation is clearly a private and personal one with which the law cannot and should not interfere.
>
> It seems clear, however, that the legal conclusion in *Griswold* as to the rights of individuals to determine without governmental interference whether or not to enter into the process of procreation cannot be extended to cover those situations wherein, voluntarily or involuntarily, the preliminaries have ended, and a new life has begun. Once human life has commenced, the constitutional protections found in the Fifth and Fourteenth Amendments impose upon the state the duty of safeguarding it.[50]

What the Court in *Steinberg* is suggesting should be uncontroversial: a legal principle has universal application. So, for example, if a statute that forbids burglary became law at a time when no computers existed, it would not follow that the prohibition against burglary does not apply to computers, that one is free to burgle computers from the homes of one's neighbors because the "original intent" of the statute's framers did not include computers. What matters is whether the entity stolen is *property*, that it is a thing that can be owned, not whether it is a particular thing (in this case, a computer) that the authors of the anti-burglary statute knew or did not know to be property at the time of its passage. To employ another analogy, the religion clauses of the First Amendment apply to religious believers whose faiths came to be after the Constitution was ratified: a Baha'i is protected by the First Amendment even though the Baha'i World Faith did not exist in 1789.[51] Therefore, if the unborn *is* a person, the Fourteenth Amendment is meant to protect him or her even if the authors of the Fourteenth Amendment did not have the unborn in mind.[52] As we shall see below, Texas presented this premise as part of its case for the unborn's humanity. The Court, ironically, accepted this premise, but refused to fairly assess the argument offered by Texas, settling instead for taking "no position" on the status of the unborn.

3. Blackmun's third reason is misleading. For, as we saw in our analysis of the 19th-century anti-abortion laws, state governments grasped the inadequacy of the common law's quickening criterion when they became aware of the knowledge that science had acquired about the nature of

prenatal human life. Consequently, by the end of the 19th century, abortion was prohibited throughout pregnancy. And, as we saw, the primary purpose of these statutes was to protect prenatal human life. Moreover, some scholars have offered compelling reasons to think that at the times of the passage of the Constitution (1789) and the Fourteenth Amendment (1868) common understanding held that the unborn is a person (at least after quickening), and/or at least that a state or the federal government may legislate in such a way so as to place the unborn (even before quickening) under the protections of the law without violating the Constitution.[53]

The state of Texas suggested, as the *Steinberg* court held, that the unborn is protected by the Fourteenth Amendment because it is *in fact* a person. That is, even if Justice Blackmun was correct that the unborn has never been considered a full person under the law, Texas argued that the evidence for the unborn's humanity requires that the Court in the present treat the unborn as a Fourteenth Amendment person. For example, if the Earth were visited by members of an alien race, such as the Vulcans of *Star Trek* lore, it would seem correct to say that these aliens would have Fourteenth Amendment rights, even though they are not homo sapiens. They would have these rights because they would be beings whose natures have properties (e.g., the capacity for moral choice) identically possessed by the sorts of beings the Fourteenth Amendment was intended to protect.[54]

Confronting, though not disputing, Texas's evidence for the unborn's humanity, Justice Blackmun replied: "We need not resolve the difficult question of when life begins. When those trained in the respective disciplines of medicine, philosophy, and theology are unable to arrive at any consensus, the judiciary, at this point in the development of man's knowledge, is not in a position to speculate"[55] Hence, the state should not take one theory of life and force those who do not agree with that theory to subscribe to it, which is the reason Blackmun writes in *Roe*, "In view of all this, we do not agree that, by adopting one theory of life, Texas may override the rights of the pregnant woman that are at stake."[56] Thus for the pro-life advocate to propose that non-pro-life women should be forbidden from having abortions, on the basis that individual humanity begins at conception or at least sometime before birth, is clearly a violation of the right of privacy of non-pro-life women.

But the problem with this reasoning is that it simply cannot deliver on what it promises. For to claim, as Justices Blackmun does, that the Court should not propose one theory of life over another, and that the decision to abort should be left exclusively to the discretion of each pregnant woman, *is* to propose a theory of life that hardly has a clear consensus. For it has all the earmarks of a theory of life that morally segregates the unborn from full-fledged membership in the human community, for it in practice excludes the unborn from constitutional protection. Although verbally the Court denied taking sides on the issue of when life begins, part of the theoretical grounding of its legal opinion, whether it admits to it or not, is that the unborn in this society is not a human person worthy of protection. Thus, the Court actually did take sides on the question of when life begins. It concluded that the unborn is not a human person, because the procedure permitted in *Roe*, abortion, is something that the Court itself admits it would not have ruled a fundamental right if it were conclusively proven that the unborn is a human person: "If the suggestion of personhood [of the unborn] is established, the appellant's case, of course, collapses, for the fetus' right to life is then guaranteed specifically by the [Fourteenth Amendment]."[57]

But if we are to accept the Supreme Court's holding in *Roe* and agree with Justice Blackmun that the right to abortion is contingent upon the status of the unborn, then the allegedly disputed fact about life's beginning means that the right to abortion is disputed as well. For a conclusion's support – in this case, "abortion is a fundamental right" – is only as good as the veracity of its most important premise – in this case, "the unborn is not fully human." So, the Court's admission that abortion choice is based on a widely disputed fact, far from establishing a right to abortion, entails that it not only does not know when life begins, but it does not know when if ever the right to abortion begins. Consequently, the Court's admitted ignorance of not knowing when life begins *undermines* the right to abortion.

Justice Blackmun's argument is flawed in another peculiar way, a way that actually provides a compelling reason to *prohibit* abortion, for, according to the logic of Blackmun's argument, an abortion *may* result in the death of a human entity who has a full right to life. When claiming that experts disagree on when life begins, Justice Blackmun seems to be implying that the different positions on life's beginning all have able defenders, persuasive arguments, and passionate advocates, but none really wins the day. To put it another way, the issue of the unborn's full humanity is up for grabs; all positions are in some sense equal, none is better than any other. But if this is the case, then it is safe to say that the odds of the unborn being fully human are 50/50 (if we wanted to put a number on a reasonable, though disputed, position held by a sizable number of well-informed and educated adults in the world). Given these odds, it would seem that society has a moral obligation to err on the side of life, and therefore to legally prohibit virtually all abortions. After all, if one kills another being without knowing whether that being is a human being with a full right to life, and if one has reasonable, though disputed, grounds (as Blackmun admits) to believe that the being in question is fully human, such an action would constitute a willful and reckless disregard for others, even if one later discovered that the being was not fully human.

Consider this illustration. Imagine the police are able to identify someone as a murderer with only one piece of evidence: his DNA matches the DNA of the genetic material found on the victim. The police subsequently arrest him, and he is convicted and sentenced to death. Suppose, however, that it is discovered several months later that the murderer has an identical twin brother who was also at the scene of the crime and obviously has the same DNA as his brother on death row. This means that there is a 50/50 chance that the man on death row is the murderer. Would the state be justified in executing this man? Surely not, for there is a 50/50 chance of executing an innocent person. Consequently, if it is wrong to kill the man on death row, it is then wrong to kill the unborn when the arguments for its full humanity are just as reasonable as the arguments against it.

AFTER *ROE*

From 1973 to 1989 the Supreme Court struck down every state attempt to restrict an adult woman's access to abortion.[58] The U.S. Congress tried, and failed, to pass a Human Life Bill (1981) to protect the unborn by means of ordinary legislation, and later it failed to pass a Human Life Amendment (1983) to the U.S. Constitution. Although the Court upheld Congress's ban on federal funding of abortion except to save the life of the mother,[59] it never wavered on *Roe*. Given these political and legal realities, pro-lifers put their hopes in the Supreme Court appointees of two pro-life presidents, Ronald Reagan (1981–1989) and George H. W. Bush (1989–1993), to help overturn *Roe*. Reagan and Bush appointed five justices to the Court (Sandra Day O'Connor, Antonin Scalia, Anthony Kennedy, Clarence Thomas, and David Souter) who, pro-lifers mistakenly thought, all shared the judicial philosophies of the presidents who appointed them. Ironically, it would be three of those

justices – O'Connor, Kennedy, and Souter – who would author the
Court's opinion in *Casey v. Planned Parenthood* (1992) and uphold *Roe*.
And two of them – O'Connor and Souter – would go even further, join-
ing three of their brethren in *Stenberg v. Carhart* (2000) in imparting the
blessings of our Constitution on partial-birth abortion.

Nevertheless, three years before *Casey*, the Court seemed to be moving
toward a rejection of *Roe*. Many pro-lifers read *Webster v. Reproductive Health Services* (1989)[60] as a sign that the Court was preparing to
dismantle the regime of *Roe*. In *Webster* the Court reversed a lower-
court decision and upheld several provisions of a Missouri statute that
would not have survived constitutional muster in earlier days. First, the
Court upheld the statute's preamble, which states that "'the life of each
human being begins at conception,' and that '[u]nborn children have
protectable interest in life, health, and well-being.'"[61] Furthermore, it
requires that under Missouri's laws the unborn should be treated as full
persons who possess "all rights, privileges, immunities available to other
persons, citizens, and residents of the state,"[62] contingent upon the U.S.
Constitution and prior Supreme Court opinions. Because these precedents would include *Roe*, the statute poses no threat to the abortion
liberty.

Second, the *Webster* Court upheld the portion of the Missouri statute
that forbade the use of government facilities, funds, and employees in performing and counseling for abortions unless the procedure is necessary
to save the life of the mother.

Third, the Court upheld the statute's provision mandating that "before
a physician performs an abortion on a woman he has reason to believe
is carrying an unborn child of twenty or more weeks gestational age,
the physician shall first determine if the unborn child is viable by using
and exercising that degree of care, skill, and proficiency commonly exercised by the ordinarily skillful, careful, and prudent physician engaged
in similar practice under the same or similar conditions."[63] To properly assess the unborn's viability, the statute requires that the physician
employ procedures as are necessary and enter the findings of these procedures in the mother's medical record.[64] In passing this statute, Missouri's
legislature took seriously *Roe*'s viability marker – that at the time of viability the state has a compelling interest in protecting unborn life. This
is why the Court, in *Webster*, correctly concluded that "the Missouri
testing requirement here is reasonably designed to ensure that abortions
are not performed where the fetus is viable – an end which all concede
is legitimate – and that is sufficient to sustain its constitutionality."[65]

Webster, however, modified *Roe* in at least two significant ways: it rejected both *Roe*'s trimester breakdown as well as its claim that the state's interest in prenatal life becomes compelling only at viability:

> The rigid *Roe* framework is hardly consistent with the notion of a Constitution cast in general terms, as ours is, and usually speaking in general principles, as ours does. The key elements of the *Roe* framework – trimesters and viability – are not found in the text of the Constitution or in any place else one would expect to find a constitutional principle.[66]

According to the Court, "we do not see why the State's interest in protecting potential human life should come into existence only at the point of viability, and that there should therefore be a rigid line allowing state regulation after viability but prohibiting it before viability."[67] Although *Webster* chipped away at *Roe*, it did not overturn it.

In *Casey v. Planned Parenthood* (1992) the Court was asked to consider the constitutionality of five provisions of the Pennsylvania Abortion Control Act of 1982, which the state amended in 1988 and 1989.[68] The Court upheld as constitutional four of the five provisions, rejecting the third one (which required spousal notification for an abortion) based on what it calls the *undue burden* standard, which the Court defined in the following way: "A finding of an undue burden is a shorthand for the conclusion that a state regulation has the purpose or effect of placing a substantial obstacle in the path of a woman seeking an abortion of a nonviable fetus."[69] The undue burden standard is, according to most observers, a departure from *Roe* and its progeny, which required that any state restrictions on abortion be subject to strict scrutiny. That is, to be valid, any restrictions on access to abortion must be essential to meeting a compelling state interest. For example, laws that forbid yelling "fire" in a crowded theater pass strict scrutiny and thus do not violate the First Amendment right to freedom of expression. The *Casey* Court, nevertheless, claimed to be more consistent with the spirit and letter of *Roe* than the interpretations and applications of *Roe*'s principles in subsequent Court opinions.[70] But the *Casey* Court, by subscribing to the undue burden standard, held that a state may restrict abortion by passing laws that may not withstand strict scrutiny but nevertheless do not result in an undue burden for the pregnant woman. For example, the Court upheld as constitutional two provisions in the Pennsylvania statute – a 24-hour waiting-period requirement and an informed-consent requirement (i.e., the woman must be provided the facts of fetal development, risks of abortion and childbirth, and information about abortion alternatives) – that would most likely not have met constitutional muster with the Court's pre-*Webster* composition.[71]

Although the *Casey* Court upheld *Roe* as a precedent, the plurality opinion, authored by three Reagan-Bush appointees – O'Connor, Kennedy, and Souter – rejected two aspects of *Roe*: (1) its requirement that restrictions be subject to strict scrutiny; and (2) its trimester framework (which *Webster* had already discarded). The trimester framework, according to the Court, was too rigid as well as unnecessary to protect a woman's right to abortion.[72] However, the *Casey* Court reaffirmed viability as the time at which the state has a compelling interest in protecting prenatal life, though it seemed to provide a more objective definition than did the *Roe* Court (which, as we saw above, included the nebulous notion of "meaningful life"), despite the fact that it claimed to derive its definition from *Roe*: "Viability, as we noted in *Roe*, is the time at which there is a realistic possibility of maintaining and nourishing a life outside the womb."[73] At this point I want to look critically at the Court's viability criterion and the arguments presented for it in both *Roe* and *Casey*. In *Roe* Justice Blackmun wrote:

> With respect to the State's important and legitimate interest in potential life, the "compelling" point is at viability. This is so because the fetus presumably has the capability of meaningful life outside the mother's womb. State regulation protective of fetal life after viability thus has both logical and biological justification.[74]

Assuming that Justice Blackmun is using "meaningful life" to mean "independent life,"[75] he commits one of two fallacies, depending on how he defines independent life. If he means by independent life a being that does not require the physical resources of another particular being for it to survive – that is, a viable fetus – then Blackmun's argument amounts to a vicious circle, for in that case he is arguing that viability is justified as the time at which the state's interest in prenatal life becomes compelling because at that time the fetus is an independent life, or viable.

Stuart Rosenbaum responds to my charge that Blackmun's argument is circular by denying that Blackmun is presenting an argument: "Since Blackmun does not present an argument, he quite obviously does not present a circular argument. Blackmun *observes* that the state has an interest in protecting fetal life. Period."[76] It is not clear how Blackmun's opinion becomes *better* because he offers no argument, rather than a fallacious one, for his viability standard. Rosenbaum, ironically, critiques my assessment of Blackmun as a "strawman" argument.[77] I suppose I could respond to this charge by claiming that I was not actually offering an argument, but, like Rosenbaum's Justice Blackmun, I was merely stipulating the correctness of my point of view without offering any reasons, good or bad, whatsoever. A better response – and one that I prefer – would be to show that Rosenbaum is simply mistaken, that he has not read Blackmun correctly.

Let me again quote Justice Blackmun's argument, putting in bold the words logicians call inference indicators, words that show that the author is offering a reason or reasons for a conclusion and/or a conclusion inferred from a reason or reasons:

> With respect to the State's important and legitimate interest in potential life, the "compelling" point is at viability. This is so **because** the fetus presumably has the capability of meaningful life outside the mother's womb. State regulation protective of fetal life after viability **thus** has both logical and biological justification.[78]

In the second sentence, "this" is shorthand for the first sentence. So Blackmun is saying that the first sentence is a conclusion for what follows "because," just as one would say "Fred is guilty. This is so **because** the police found the murder weapon in his apartment." In the third and last sentence Blackmun summarizes his argument by concluding that "state regulation protective of fetal life after viability ... has both logical and biological **justification**," that is, the Court is *justified* in its holding because there is logical and biological support for it. Although a fallacious argument, it is an argument: it offers a conclusion and appeals to reasons.

What if, however, Blackmun means by independent life a being that is a separate and distinct being even if it is does require the physical resources of another particular being for it to survive, as in the case of one of two conjoined twins who share vital organs. But in that case, the unborn has independent life from the moment of conception (see Chapter 4) and viability is merely the time at which it need not physically depend on its mother to survive. That is, undergoing an accidental change from dependent to independent does not change the identity of the being undergoing the change. Christopher Reeve did not become less of a being, or cease to be Christopher Reeve, merely because a tragic accident left him dependent on others for his very survival.[79] The "he" who underwent that change remained the same "he." Consequently, changing from nonviable to viable or vice versa does not impart to, or remove from, a being any property or properties that would change that being's identity. In fact, when Blackmun claims that the unborn undergoes change – goes from nonviable to viable – he is implying that the unborn is in fact a being distinct from, though changing its dependence in relation to, its mother. Because viability is a measure of the sophistication and/or accessibility of our neonatal life-support systems (including both technological and parental caregivers), the fetus remains the same while viability changes. For this reason, the viability standard seems to be arbitrary and not applicable to the philosophical question of whether the unborn is a full-fledged member of the human community. Thus, according to the Court, a viable child born at 22-weeks gestation in 2007 is fully human while a nonviable prenatal child at 30-weeks gestation in 1907 is not fully human. But this is absurd, for our technological advances do not change the nature of the dependent being.[80] Blackmun, therefore, seems to be confusing *physical* independence with *ontological* independence; he mistakenly argues from the fact of the pre-viable unborn's lack of independence from its mother that it is not an independent being, a "meaningful life."[81] "Once again," writes Hadley Arkes, "the Court fell into the fallacy of drawing a moral conclusion (the right to take a life) from a fact utterly without moral significance (the weakness or dependence of the child). The Court discovered, in other words, that novel doctrines could be wrought by reinventing old fallacies."[82]

There are two other observations one may make about the viability criterion. First, one could argue that the nonviability of the unborn, and the dependence and vulnerability that goes with that status, should lead one to have more rather than less concern for that being. That is, a human being's dependence and vulnerability is a call for her parents, family, and the wider human community to care and nurture her, rather than a justification to kill her. Second, each of us, including the unborn, is nonviable in relation to his environment. If any one of us were to be placed naked on the moon or the earth's North Pole, we would quickly become aware of our nonviability. Therefore, the unborn prior to the time she can live outside her mother's womb is as nonviable in relation to her environment as we are nonviable in relation to ours.[83]

The *Casey* Court's defense of the viability criterion offers two reasons. First, the Court appeals to *stare decisis*, the judicial practice of giving great deference to precedents. But because the precedent to which the Court appealed, *Roe*, relies on fallacious reasoning to ground the viability criterion and is thus a precedent that is not justified, this first reason has no merit. But that does not stop the Court from offering as a second reason the *reasoning* employed by Justice Blackmun in *Roe* to defend the viability criterion. This is a peculiar strategy of argument, for if precedent, *stare decisis*, is sufficient, why also appeal to the *reasoning* for that precedent? Could the reasoning for the precedent be flawed and the precedent itself still be employed to "justify" a subsequent legal opinion? Or could a precedent be justifiably rejected in an applicable case even though the precedent is grounded in impeccable reasoning? In any event, the Court's second reason is an argument that contains, along with a conclusion, its *definition* of viability (which I have already quoted above) as the argument's premise: "Viability, as we noted in *Roe*, is the time at which there is a realistic possibility of maintaining and nourishing a life outside the womb, so that the independent existence of the second life can in reason and fairness be the object of state protection that now overrides the rights of the woman."[84] This argument is as fallacious in *Casey* as it was in *Roe*. The Court first defines viability and then from that premise of biological fact draws the normative conclusion that it is only fair and reasonable that after viability the State has a right to protect the unborn. The premise – the biological fact of fetal nonviability through roughly the first six months' pregnancy – cannot possibly provide sufficient warrant for the conclusion that the Court is trying to draw: it is fair and just, and required by our Constitution, for the government to permit, with virtually no restrictions, the unborn's mother to kill it before it is viable. For the Court to make its argument valid, it would have to add to its factual premise the normative premise: whenever a human being cannot live on its own because it uniquely depends on another human being for its physical existence, it is permissible for the second human being to kill the first to rid the second of this burden. But if it were to add that premise, the argument, though now valid, would contain a premise even more controversial than the abortion right it is attempting to justify, and for that reason would require a premise or premises to justify *it*.

The *Casey* Court also ignored the scholarly criticisms of *Roe*'s justification of the abortion right. To review some of what we covered above: (1) The key premises of Justice Blackmun's case – that abortion was a common law liberty, and the primary purpose of 19th-century abortion law was to protect women from dangerous operations – have been soundly refuted in the scholarly literature. (2) His case against the unborn's status as a Fourteenth Amendment person is questionable. (3) His argument from expert disagreement over the unborn's full humanity – that the unborn is not a Fourteenth Amendment person because experts disagree on its status – undermines the right to abortion as well as provides a reason to prohibit abortion.

Instead of restating these bad arguments, the *Casey* Court invented new ones. It upheld *Roe* on the basis of *stare decisis* for which the Court provided two reasons: (1) the reliance interest,[85] and (2) the Court's legitimacy and the public's respect for it. Concerning the first, the Court argued that because the nation's citizens had planned and arranged their lives with the abortion right in mind, that is, because they have relied on this right, it would be wrong for the Court to jettison it.[86] And second, if the Court were to overturn *Roe*, it would suffer a loss of respect in the public's eye and perhaps chip away at its own legitimacy, even if rejecting *Roe* would in fact correct an error in constitutional jurisprudence.[87] The Court, nevertheless, in its opening comments in *Casey* speaks of abortion as a liberty grounded in the due process clause of the Fourteenth Amendment, an extension of the right of privacy cases we covered earlier.[88] Yet, even the *Roe* Court understood that abortion had been banned nearly everywhere in the United States for quite some time, and thus it could not easily be construed as a fundamental liberty found in our nation's traditions and history unless the reason for banning abortion was now obsolete and the fetus was not protected under the Fourteenth Amendment. The *Roe* Court, as we saw, made that argument, one that we now know was largely based on a distortion of history that virtually all scholars concede was false and misleading. So nothing of any substance was left for the *Casey* Court to hang its hat on except for an appeal to *stare decisis* based on the reliance interest and the public's perception of the Court's legitimacy.[89] After all, if the *Casey* Court really believed that *Roe*'s reasoning was sound, that abortion was really a fundamental liberty found in our nation's traditions and history, it would have made *that* argument rather than relying on these other reasons. But the implications of this deal with the devil are daunting. By putting in place the premises of jurisprudence that it did, the Court gave cover to future courts to "justify" about any perversity it wants to uphold or "discover." For example, given the premises of *Casey*, the Court could knowingly, and "justifiably," deprive a citizen of his or her fundamental rights if the Court believes that a vast majority of other citizens have relied on that deprivation, and to declare it unjust would make the Court look bad in the eyes of the beneficiaries of this injustice. Here's the lesson: if a bad decision cannot be overturned because it is bad, then we cannot rely on the Court to protect a good opinion when it is good, if what is doing all the work is *narcissus stare decisis*.

It seems to me that Chief Justice Rehnquist, the author of the Court's *Webster* opinion, got it right when he made the comment in his dissenting opinion in *Casey*: "*Roe v. Wade* stands as a sort of judicial Potemkin Village, which may be pointed to passers-by as a monument to the importance of adhering to precedent. But behind the facade, an entirely new method of analysis, without any roots in constitutional law, is imported to decide the constitutionality of state laws regulating abortion. Neither *stare decisis* nor 'legitimacy' are truly served by such an effort."[90]

Beginning in 1996, then-President Bill Clinton vetoed several bills passed by the U.S. Congress to prohibit what pro-life activists call "partial-birth abortion."[91] Also known as D & X (for dilation and extraction) abortion, this procedure is performed in some late-term abortions. Using ultrasound, the doctor grips the fetus's legs with forceps. The fetus is then pulled out through the birth canal and delivered with the exception of its head. While the head is in the womb the doctor penetrates the live fetus's skull with scissors, opens the scissors to enlarge the hole, and then inserts a catheter. The fetus's brain is vacuumed out, resulting in the skull's collapse. The doctor then completes the womb's evacuation by removing a dead fetus.

Although none of the congressional bills became law, 30 states, including Nebraska, passed similar laws that prohibited D & X abortions. However, in *Stenberg v. Carhart* (2000),[92] the Supreme Court, in a 5–4 decision, struck down Nebraska's ban on partial-birth abortions, on two grounds. (1) The law lacked an exception for the preservation of the mother's health, which *Casey* required of any restrictions on abortion. (2) Nebraska's ban imposed an undue burden on a woman's fundamental right to have an abortion.

Although Nebraska's statute had a "life of the mother" exception, the Court pointed out that *Casey* requires an exception for *both* the life and *health* of the mother if a state wants to prohibit post-viability abortions.[93] But Nebraska did not limit its ban to only D & X abortions performed after viability. Its ban applied throughout pregnancy. So, according to the Court, unless Nebraska can show that its ban does not increase a woman's health risk, it is unconstitutional: "The State fails to demonstrate that banning D & X without a health exception may not create significant health risks for women, because the record shows that significant medical authority supports the proposition that in some circumstances D & X would be the safest procedure."[94] But, as Justice Kennedy points out in his dissent, "The most to be said for the D & X is it may present an unquantified lower risk of complication for a particular patient but that other proven safe procedures remain available even for this patient."[95] But the relative risk between procedures,

if in fact D & X is in some cases relatively safer,[96] cannot justify overturning the law if the increased risk is statistically negligible and if the
State, as the Court asserted in *Casey*[97] and *Webster*,[98] has an interest in
prenatal life throughout pregnancy which becomes compelling enough
after viability to prohibit abortion except in cases when the life or the
health of the mother are in danger. After all, if "the relative physical
safety of these procedures, with the slight possible difference"[99] requires
that the Court invalidate Nebraska's ban on partial-birth abortion, then
the Court proves too much. For with such premises in hand one may conclude that a ban on infanticide is unconstitutional as well, for a parent
who kills her handicapped newborn eliminates the possibility that this
child from infancy to adulthood will drain her resources, tax her emo-
tions, and require physical activity not demanded by nonhandicapped
children. Consequently, to conscript Justice Stephen Breyer's language,
the state that bans infanticide fails to demonstrate that this prohibition
without a health exception may not create significant health risks for
women, because the record shows that significant medical authority supports the proposition that in some circumstances, infanticide would best
advance the mother's health.

The Court's second reason for rejecting Nebraska's law is that the
ban on D & X imposed an undue burden on a woman's fundamental
right to have an abortion. For the type of abortion performed in 95%
of the cases between the 12th and 20th weeks of pregnancy, D & E
abortion (dilation and evacuation),[100] is similar to D & X abortion. So,
the Court reasoned, if a ban on D & X abortions is legally permissible,
then so is a ban on D & E abortions. But that would imperil the right
to abortion. Hence Nebraska's ban imposes an undue burden on the
pregnant woman, and thus violates the standard laid down in *Casey*. But
as both Justice Thomas and Justice Kennedy point out in their separate
dissents,[101] by reading Nebraska's law in this way, the Court abandoned
its long-standing doctrine of statutory construction, that statutes should
be read in a way that is consistent with the Constitution if such a reading is
plausible. What the Court did in *Stenberg* was to read Nebraska's statute
in the least charitable way one could read it. Moreover, Justice Thomas,
in a blistering dissent, shows, in meticulous and graphic detail,[102] that
D & X and D & E procedures are dissimilar enough that it is "highly
doubtful that" Nebraska's D & X ban "could be applied to ordinary D
& E."[103]

In 2003, President George W. Bush signed into law a federal partial-
birth abortion ban,[104] which contains both a more circumspect definition

of D & X abortion as well as a life of the mother exception.[105] It was immediately challenged in federal court by abortion-choice groups.[106] Nevertheless, on April 18, 2007, in *Gonzales v. Carhart* (2007), the Supreme Court upheld the federal statute.[107]

In 2002, the U.S. Congress, with the signature of President Bush, passed the "Born-Alive Infants Protection Act," the brainchild of the inestimable Hadley Arkes.[108] The Act requires that any child who survives an abortion be immediately accorded all the protections of the law that are accorded all other postnatal human beings. Although it is, in the words of Arkes, a "modest first step,"[109] it is a first step, but not an insignificant one. For it affirms that an abortion entails the expulsion of a being who, if she survives, should receive all the protections of our laws. But this, of course, raises an awkward question for abortion-choice supporters: What is it, then, about that vaginal passageway that changes the child's nature in such a significant fashion that it may be killed without justification before exit but only with justification post-exit? The Act put in place a premise that elicits questions that lead one back to the most important question in this debate: Who and what are we?

3

ABORTION, LIBERALISM,
AND STATE NEUTRALITY

"Statecraft," Aristotle wisely instructed his pupils, "is soulcraft," by which he meant that the moral premises embedded in the social and legal fabric of a political regime provide direction and sustenance for the character and beliefs of its citizens. That is, what is tacitly accepted by a people and its institutions, in its practices and principles, will tell us more about what it embraces as good, true, and beautiful than all of its verbal declarations to the contrary. Nevertheless, on the issue of abortion, a number of thinkers have argued that the current regime in American law – the *Roe v. Wade* framework – is proof that Aristotle was mistaken, that the state may, and ought to, remain impartial on abortion without commiting itself to any particular view of humanity. We have already seen in our assessment of *Roe* (Chapter 2) that the Court did not succeed. Several thinkers, however, have presented arguments they believe can rescue this opinion and provide explicit philosophical justification for abortion rights while the state remains impartial on the question of whether the unborn has protected moral status. In this essay we will assess the cases made by Paul D. Simmons and Judith Jarvis Thomson.

Although the late John Rawls's political liberalism is often associated with the point of view I critique in this chapter, his last published words on the matter seem to be consistent with the sort of case I am making in this book, that the pro-life position can be defended with publicly accessible reasons that may be incorporated into our laws without violating any fundamental rights, or what Rawls called "constitutional essentials."[1] But because in an earlier publication he recommended Thomson's essay as an example of the sort of case that could be made for the abortion-choice position that is also consistent with his theory of political liberalism,[2] I have chosen to engage Thomson's argument[3] as well as the case made by Simmons.

SIMMONS AND THE RELIGIOUS LIBERTY ARGUMENT

In his essay, "Religious Liberty and Abortion Policy: *Casey* as 'Catch-22'," [4] Paul D. Simmons argues that the U.S. Supreme Court's decisions on abortion have resulted in a dilemma for the pregnant woman. On the one hand, the Court seems to be saying in *Roe v. Wade* [5] (and in portions of *Casey v. Planned Parenthood*) [6] that the right to abortion is a fundamental liberty, and that the decision to abort is one that is best considered by the woman in light of her own deeply held personal and religious convictions. On the other hand, the Court seems to be saying that states, though they may not ban abortion completely, may create some obstacles for abortion, such as 24-hour waiting periods and providing patients with the facts of prenatal development, [7] as well as permiting pro-life protesters to verbally dissuade women who are entering abortion clinics for the purpose of procuring an abortion. [8] According to Simmons, this "amounts to a 'Catch-22' for women whose decision to undertake an abortion, based on their own personal understanding of morality, may be compromised by the activities of others who oppose abortion for moral or religious reasons." [9]

Simmons suggests that the Court, so as to remove the "Catch-22," should "examine abortion as an issue of religious liberty and First Amendment guarantees." [10] For, according to Simmons, the position of the pro-lifers, that the unborn is a full-fledged person from conception, is the result of "speculative metaphysics," indeed "religious reasoning," and for that reason, ought not to be part of public policy, because if it were it would amount to one religious position being foisted upon those who do not agree with it. This would violate the Establishment Clause, the portion of the U.S. Constitution's First Amendment that asserts that government may not establish a religion. [11] It would also violate the Free Exercise Clause of the First Amendment, for to allow such a public policy would be inconsistent with the Court's obligation "to protect the free exercise of the woman's conscientious (i.e., religious) judgment." [12]

I have great sympathy for Simmons's concern that one group's metaphysical position may become, as a result of political power and not reason and/or democratic deliberation, the one exclusively reflected in our legal framework. [13] I will argue in this reply, however, that the nature of the abortion debate is such that *all positions* on abortion presuppose some metaphysical point of view, and for this reason, the abortion-choice position Simmons defends is not entitled to a privileged philosophical standing in our legal framework. I am not denying there may be other reasons that the law might permit abortion. I am merely arguing in this chapter that the reason Simmons suggests – that the pro-life view is "religious" while the abortion-choice position is not – cannot be one of those reasons.

Metaphysics is an area of philosophy that deals with questions having to do with the ultimate grounding and nature of things in the world. It is concerned with such diverse topics as the mind/body problem, identity, God, the existence and nature of universals, the existence and nature of the soul, and so on. Thus, the morality of abortion, if it is to be construed as contingent upon the nature of the unborn, is an issue whose resolution depends on which metaphysical view of the human being is correct.[14] Given this, let us take a look at Simmons's argument.

Although he makes many provocative and interesting claims that deserve a reply, I will focus on a small portion of his essay that I believe is the core of his case. According to Simmons, "the first principle of religious liberty is that laws will not be based upon abstract metaphysical speculation, but will be fashioned through the democratic processes in which every perspective is subject to critical analysis. Any proposal must be open either to revision or rejection."[15] He then cites, as an example of what is not speculative metaphysics, the viability standard proposed by the Court in *Roe*.[16]

I will first critique Simmons's use and defense of the viability standard, move on to a general critique of Simmons's view of "abstract metaphysical speculation," and then respond to a subsequent defense of Simmons offered by Stuart Rosenbaum.

Abortion and Viability

In *Roe*, as I pointed out in Chapter 2, the Supreme Court ruled that at fetal viability a state has a compelling interest in protecting prenatal (or "potential") life, and thus may restrict abortion during that time as long as the restrictions allow for abortion to preserve the health and/or life of the pregnant woman. Simmons's argument for the viability standard is nearly identical to the one presented by Blackmun:

> Part of the genius in *Roe v. Wade* (now affirmed in *Casey*) was putting forward the standard of viability: that stage of development at which the fetus has sufficient neurological and physical maturation to survive outside the womb. Prior to that, the fetus simply is not sufficiently developed as an independent being deserving and requiring the full protection of the law, i.e., a person. The notion of viability correlates biological

maturation with personal identity in a way that can be recognized and accepted by reasonable people.[17]

It is interesting to note that Simmons praises the Court's legal use of the standard and then employs the standard as a decisive moment at which he believes it is reasonable to say that the unborn acquires full humanity (or becomes a "person"), even though that is *not the way* the Court employed viability. In *Roe*, as we saw in Chapter 2, the Court divided pregnancy into trimesters. It ruled that aside from normal procedural guidelines to ensure protection for the pregnant woman, a state has no right to restrict abortion in the first six months of pregnancy. In the last trimester (when the unborn is viable) the state has a right, although *no obligation*, to restrict abortions to only those cases in which the mother's life or health is in danger, because the state, at that point in the unborn's development, has a compelling interest in protecting potential human life. If, however, the Court held that viability was the time at which the unborn becomes a person (as Simmons apparently believes), then the states would have an obligation, not merely a right, under the Fourteenth Amendment to protect the life of the unborn from unjust harm. Remember that Blackmun, in *Roe*, writes of the unborn's *potential* human life and not its *actual* constitutional personhood. This follows from his comment in *Roe* that "the word 'person,' as used in the Fourteenth Amendment, does not include the unborn."[18] So, it is at the moment of birth, not viability, that the Court maintains that the unborn becomes a person. Viability is merely the time at which a state may increase its restrictions on abortion because of its interest in prenatal life.

Nevertheless, Simmons's use of viability, like Blackmun's use of it (which we assessed in Chapter 2), is unsuccessful. First, Simmons's argument, like Blackmun's, is circular. Simmons writes that prior to viability, "the fetus simply is not sufficiently developed as an independent being deserving and requiring the full protection of the law, i.e., a person."[19] And this standard is reasonable, according to Simmons, because "the notion of viability correlates biological maturation with personal identity in a way that can be recognized and accepted by reasonable people."[20] For Simmons, a nonviable fetus should not have legal standing because it is not an independent organism (that is, nonviable). Thus, the circularity of Simmons's argument is easy to discern: a nonviable fetus should not have legal standing because it is nonviable.

Second, although Simmons writes that the viability standard "correlates biological maturation with personal identity in a way that can be recognized and accepted by reasonable people,"[21] many reasonable people reject it on the grounds that the standard is, in fact, unreasonable (as I argue in Chapter 2). In light of those criticisms, if one is to take seriously one aspect of the standard by which, Simmons suggests, pro-lifers should evaluate their position on the unborn's humanity – "*the question is whether the definition is reasonable*"[22] – then it would seem correct to reject Simmons's viability standard on the grounds that it is logically flawed and thus unreasonable. Therefore, given his claim that "any proposal [on the unborn's humanity] must be open either to revision or rejection,"[23] it would seem that Simmons should either revise or reject his use of the viability standard.

In a response to my charge that Simmons argues in a circle, Stuart Rosenbaum maintains, as he did in his response to the same charge I leveled against Justice Blackmun's similar argument, that Simmons, who employs Justice Blackmun's argument,[24] does not argue in a circle because Simmons, like Blackmun, is not offering an argument.[25] Rosenbaum, however, is mistaken.

First, as I noted in Chapter 2 in reference to Blackmun's argument, it is not clear how Simmons's view becomes *better* because he offers for his viability standard no argument rather than a fallacious one.

Second, although not employing inference indicators, Simmons clearly presents an argument for his point of view. He defines viability as "that stage of development at which the fetus has sufficient neurological and physical maturation to survive outside the womb."[26] And then from that definition he draws a *normative* conclusion: "Prior to that, the fetus simply is not sufficiently developed as an independent being deserving and requiring the full protection of the law, i.e., a person."[27] If it does not seem clear that this is an argument, imagine if Simmons had said exactly the same thing but inserted "therefore" between these two propositions: viability is "that stage of development at which the fetus has sufficient neurological and physical maturation to survive outside the womb." Therefore, "prior to that, the fetus simply is not sufficiently developed as an independent being deserving and requiring the full protection of the law, i.e., a person." There is a reason and a conclusion, and thus an argument. But imagine if we changed the topic and removed "therefore": the age of 18 is the stage of development at which a human being has sufficient neurological and physical maturation to control a heavy piece of equipment. Prior to that, the human being is not sufficiently developed to receive the full privileges of the department of motor vehicles, that is, a driver's license. One instantly recognizes this as an *argument* for 18 as the minimum age at which a person may receive a driver's license, for it offers a reason and a conclusion. Thus, Simmons offers an argument as well, one just as fallacious as Blackmun's.[28]

Abortion and Metaphysics

Not only is the viability standard flawed, but a careful analysis of Simmons's use of it reveals that it is, like the pro-life position, based on a particular metaphysics of the human person. Simmons's defense of the viability standard as a legal criterion by which to distinguish persons from non-persons is an example of employing a particular view of human persons to support a particular public policy (i.e., abortion choice). He defends this philosophical anthropology by arguing that certain prenatal entities – pre-viable fetuses – are not entitled to protection by the state since they lack a property which, if present, would make them persons. This is an example of the accidental-essential division employed by some metaphysicians when they discuss, defend, or critique a particular philosophical anthropology. J. P. Moreland illustrates: "If something (say Socrates) has an accidental property (e.g., being white), then that thing can lose the property and still exist. For example, Socrates could turn brown and still exist and be Socrates. Essential properties constitute the nature or essence of a thing; and by referring to essential properties, one answers in the most basic way this question: What kind of thing is x?"[29] So, for Simmons, viability is an essential property of human persons, and thus when the unborn lacks it, it is not a human person. Simmons is, therefore, doing the work of a metaphysician. He is attempting, through philosophical reflection and argument, to defend a disputed view of the human person. Thus, if Simmons is correct that laws should "not be based upon abstract metaphysical speculation,"[30] then either his viability standard has no place in public policy or laws can (or perhaps can't) be based on metaphysics.

Other thinkers offer other metaphysical views on the nature of human beings, which we will critically assess in Chapter 6. Some argue that personhood does not arrive until brain waves are detected (40 to 43 days after conception).[31] Others, such as Mary Anne Warren,[32] define a person as a being who can do certain things, such as have consciousness, solve complex problems, have a self-concept, and engage in sophisticated communication, which would put the arrival of personhood *after birth*. Presenting views similar to Warren's, Michael Tooley[33] and Peter Singer[34] argue that not only is abortion permissible, but so is infanticide, for they maintain that the newborn (for some months after birth, I might add) is not a person and thus is not entitled to the protections we accord beings who have such a status. David Boonin takes a more conservative abortion-choice position, maintaining that the unborn does not become a subject of moral rights until the arising of organized cortical brain activity (25 to 32 weeks after conception).[35] Still others, such as L. W. Sumner,[36] take a moderate position and argue that human personhood does not arrive until the fetus is sentient, the ability to feel and sense as a conscious being. This, according to Sumner, occurs possibly as early as the middle weeks of the second trimester of pregnancy and definitely by the end of that trimester.

There are also theologically argued variations on these positions. They are, in my judgment, as much based on metaphysical considerations as the secular theories. However, they either rely on or add premises that appeal to Scripture, religious tradition, or theological reasoning. For instance, theologian Beverley Harrison, whose work is cited by Simmons in his article,[37] denies the personhood of both the infant as well as the post-viable fetus:

> An infant is a biologically discrete entity, an individual human being – though not a full person. In the first half of pregnancy, a fetus could not be considered this.... There is no analogue between a conceptus and a human being except certain protoplasm – the former is human tissue but not human life.... In regard to infanticide, one has to weigh the moral concerns carefully. It is wise for the community to discourage infanticide and would be unwise to make abortion illegal.... Infanticide is not a great wrong. I do not want to be construed as condemning women who, under certain circumstances, quietly put their infants to death.[38]

Theologian and ethicist Joseph Fletcher, who maintains that his ethical views are within the Christian tradition,[39] presents criteria of personhood that exclude infants.[40] The Religious Coalition for Reproductive Choice (RCRC), a group from whose website one may download an article authored by Simmons,[41] affirms that "the common belief is that life begins at birth, when the baby begins to breathe on his/her own and is not dependent on oxygen from the mother. Therefore, Jewish and biblical tradition defined a human being with the word 'nephesh' – the breathing one.... Biblically, a human being is one who breathes."[42] Christian ethicist John Swomley agrees, arguing that "the Bible's clear answer is that human life begins at birth, with the first breath. In Gen. 2:7, God 'breathed into his nostrils the breath of life and man became a living being' (in some translations, 'a living soul')."[43]

Given the philosophical and religious diversity on the question of personhood, it is not clear how Simmons can say that "to provide protections for a viable fetus" does not violate any "group's religious teachings or any premise of logic."[44] For it would seem that Simmons's view, that personhood begins at viability, is inconsistent with the views of those who believe that fetal protection should be extended to include pre-viable fetuses (e.g., Brody, Sumner) as well as those whose views would exclude from protection post-viable fetuses and/or postnatal babies (e.g., Harrison, Tooley, Fletcher, RCRC, Swomley).

As one might guess, those who believe that full humanity begins at conception have developed and defended highly sophisticated arguments for their position.[45] These arguments, like those of their adversaries including Simmons, are put forth to defend a particular metaphysical view of human persons. The following is a brief example of the sort of philosophical anthropology defended by some of these pro-lifers. (In Chapter 6 I offer a defense of this viewpoint.)

As I write in Chapter 6, according to *the substance view*, each kind of living organism or *substance*, including the human being, maintains identity through change and possesses a nature or essence that makes certain activities and functions possible. "A substance's *inner nature*," writes J. P. Moreland "is its ordered structural unity of ultimate capacities. A substance cannot change in its ultimate capacities; that is, it cannot lose its ultimate nature and continue to exist."[46] Consider the following illustration.

A domestic feline, because it has a particular nature, has the ultimate capacity to develop the ability to purr. It may die as a kitten and never develop that ability. Regardless, it is *still* a feline as long as it exists, because it possesses a particular nature, even if it never acquires certain functions that by nature it has the capacity to develop. In contrast, a frog is not said to lack something if it cannot purr, for it is by nature not the sort of being that can have the ability to purr. A feline that lacks the ability to purr *is still a feline* because of its nature. A human being who lacks the ability to think rationally (either because she is too young or she suffers from a disability) *is still a human person* because of her nature. Consequently, a human being's lack makes sense *if and only if* she is an actual human person.

Second, the feline remains the same particular feline over time from the moment it comes into existence. Suppose you buy this feline as a kitten and name him "Cartman." When you first bring him home you notice that he is tiny in comparison to his parents and lacks their mental and physical abilities. But over time Cartman develops these abilities, learns a number of things his parents never learned, sheds his hair, has his claws removed, becomes 10 times larger than he was as a kitten, and undergoes significant development of his cellular structure, brain, and cerebral cortex. Yet, this grown-up Cartman is identical to the kitten Cartman, even though he has gone through significant physical changes. Why? The reason is because living organisms, substances, maintain identity through change.

Another way to put it is to say that organisms, including human beings, are ontologically prior to their parts,[47] which means that the organism as a whole maintains absolute identity through time while it grows, develops, and undergoes numerous changes, largely as a result of the organism's nature that directs and informs these changes and their limits. The organs and parts of the organism, and their role in actualizing the intrinsic, basic capacities of the whole, acquire their purpose and function *because* of their roles in maintaining, sustaining, and perfecting the *being as a whole*. This is in contrast to a thing that is not ontologically prior to its parts, like an automobile, cruise ship, or computer. Just as a sporting event (e.g., a basketball game, a tennis match) does not subsist through time as a unified whole, an automobile, ship, or computer does not as well.[48] It is, rather, in the words of Moreland, "a sum of each temporal (and spatial) part." Called *mereological essentialism* (from the Greek "meros" for "part"), it "means that the parts of a thing are essential to it as a whole; if the object gains or loses parts, it is a different object."[49] Organisms, however, are different, for they may lose and gain parts, and yet remain the same thing over time.

Thus, if you are an intrinsically valuable human person now, then you were an intrinsically valuable human person at *every moment in your past* including when you were in your mother's womb, for you are identical to yourself throughout the changes you undergo from the moment you come into existence. But if this were not the case, that it is only one's present ability to exercise certain human functions, such as rationality, awareness of one's interests, and consciousness, that makes one a person, then it is not the organism that is intrinsically valuable, but merely one's states or functions. "It would follow" from this, writes Patrick Lee, "that the basic moral rule would be simply to maximize valuable states or functions." For example, "it would not be morally wrong to kill a child, no matter what age, if doing so enabled one to have two children in the future, and thus to bring it about that there were two vehicles of intrinsic value rather than one. On the contrary, we are aware that persons themselves, which are things enduring through time, are intrinsically valuable."[50]

Among the ways that some thinkers reply to this argument is to advance a case that there is no substantial self that remains the same through all the accidental changes the human being undergoes, that is, there is no absolute identity between any stages in the existence of a human being. Proponents of this view maintain that personal identity consists in a series of experiences that do not require an underlying substance that has the experiences. My "personhood" is merely a string of psychological experiences connected by memory, beliefs, and/or character as well as causal, bodily, and temporal continuity. And because this continuity does not extend to the fetal stages of existence, and perhaps not even to infancy, the unborn and perhaps the newborn are not persons.[51] Some call this the *no-subject* view.[52] In a 1990 essay, Simmons seems to be embracing this metaphysical perspective: "No one can deny that there is a continuum from fertilization to birth, maturity, and adulthood, but not every stage on the continuum has the same value or constitutes the same entity."[53] An implication of this view is that even when a human being becomes a "person" she is literally not the same entity she was 10 years ago or even one second ago. That is, she does not maintain absolute identity through change. This view has been subject to trenchant, and I believe convincing, philosophical criticism.[54]

A motivation for maintaining the no-subject view, on the part of many thinkers, is a commitment to materialism. The dominant metaphysical view of intellectuals in the West, materialism maintains that all that exists is the physical world, that nonphysical things like God, angels, natures, substances, and souls do not actually exist and/or cannot be the object of knowledge. Materialist Paul Churchland writes: "The important point about the standard evolutionary story is that the human species and all of its features are the wholly physical outcome of a purely physical process.... If this is the correct account of our origins, then there seems neither need, nor room, to fit any nonphysical substances or properties into our theoretical account of ourselves. We are creatures of matter. And we should learn to live with that fact."[55]

Another sort of response (one to which I respond in Chapter 6) is to agree with the pro-lifer that one's adult self is identical to one's prenatal self, that it is in fact the same substance that remains identical to itself through time, but that intrinsic value is an *accidental*, rather than an *essential*, *property* had by human beings as long as they exist.[56] This view is the most dominant one in the literature.

The point here is not to marshal a defense, or to reply to criticisms, of any one view of the human person, for I do that in Chapter 6. Rather, the point is to show that one's philosophical anthropology is grounded in some metaphysical perspective, or as Simmons pejoratively calls it, speculative metaphysics. So, for example, if one is a materialist like Churchland, one will likely develop a philosophical anthropology that excludes nonphysical properties and substances. Or if one ties the achievement of personhood to the acquisition and development of certain physical properties – as Simmons apparently does[57] – one would seem to be accepting the view that the human person is merely a physical system, denying that a human being is a substance ontologically prior to its parts.[58] Or if one argues, like many pro-lifers do, that the human being is a substance that maintains absolute identity through change as long as it exists, then an ordinary adult human being is the same substance that was in her mother's womb from conception, and thus, that unborn entity, who later became the adult, was a person as well. Thus, Simmons is simply mistaken when he affirms that "abstract metaphysical speculation has its rightful place in theology[,] but must finally be rejected as inappropriate to the logic necessary for democratic rule,"[59] for no position on abortion, including his, is without metaphysical presuppositions whether or not those presuppositions are consciously recognized or affirmed by its advocates.

It is apparent that Simmons is not correct when he asserts that the anti-abortionist view of fetal personhood is *merely* a claim of "Catholic dogma"[60] and/or "special knowledge"[61] that is neither "subject to critical analysis"[62] nor rooted in "reason."[63] For many of the pro-life thinkers cited in this chapter – Moreland, Rae, Irving, Schwarz, Joyce, George, and Lee, in particular – have presented their views and made their arguments in numerous books, essays, lectures, paper presentations, and peer-reviewed publications. They have, in other words, made public arguments in public settings and subjected their views to critical analysis by peers. Whether their arguments work or not is another question that is outside the scope of this chapter. Simmons, however, does not further his call for "civility that is necessary to maintain tolerance among and for all religious groups in a free and open society"[64] as well as ending "intolerance toward people with different opinions"[65] when he depicts the arguments and philosophical sophistication of his adversaries in a way that may be perceived by some as uncharitable caricature.[66]

In a critique of a previously published analysis of Simmons's view,[67] Stuart Rosenbaum claims that "Beckwith simply cannot by reference to anything Simmons has written about abortion legitimate his claim that Simmons is engaging metaphysics or ontology or philosophical anthropology."[68] Rosenbaum is mistaken. For example, in both footnote 56 and in the text of this chapter, I quote Simmons as saying that prior to viability "the fetus simply is not sufficiently developed to speak meaningfully of it as an independent being deserving and requiring the full protection of the law, that is, a person. The notion of viability correlates biological maturation with personal identity in a way that can be recognized and accepted by reasonable people."[69] Here Simmons is telling us that the fetus is not a person ("an independent being deserving and requiring the full protection of the law") and then tells us why ("the fetus simply is not sufficiently developed"). He is suggesting a philosophical anthropology. Part of that philosophical anthropology involves the notion of what it means to be, in the words of Simmons, "an independent being," a claim of ontology and metaphysics. I also cite in the same footnote a statement by Simmons from a 1990 piece: "Viability, by definition, deals with that stage of gestation at which the fetus has a developed neo-cortex and physiological maturation sufficient to survive outside the womb. Biological maturation is correlated with personal identity that can be recognized and accepted by reasonable people."[70] To claim that "biological maturation is correlated with personal identity" is to make a claim about the relationship between biology, a science, and personal identity, a philosophical concept, in addition to making a disputed claim about what it means to be a person; that is, Simmons's claim is a piece of philosophical anthropology, a branch of metaphysics. Or consider one more comment from Simmons, which is quoted above in this chapter: "No one can deny that there is a continuum from fertilization to birth, maturity, and adulthood, but not every stage on the continuum has the same value or constitutes the same entity."[71] Simmons is claiming that the human being does not remain identical to itself, nor possess the same value, throughout its existence, and that you are mistaken if you hold that the early embryo is identical to the adult she will become and possesses the same value throughout her existence from conception to adulthood until natural death. This is a metaphysics, a philosophical anthropology, and a value theory all wrapped into one sentence.[72] But, as we have seen, Simmons's position is in fact rejected by reasonable people offering sophisticated and reasonable arguments in respected venues. Because all three of these passages from Simmons are quoted in the very article of mine to which Rosenbaum is responding,[73] it is a mystery to me why Rosenbaum thinks he's rebutting my argument when he states that "reading the quotes" Beckwith "cites, as well as reading more widely in Simmons's work, is enough to persuade serious readers that Simmons in fact believes that he is avoiding metaphysical views about persons and that he intends to avoid such views."[74] This claim is a mystery because I do not dispute that Simmons *believes* that he is avoiding metaphysical views about persons; what I am arguing is that Simmons, as well as others who hold similar views, *cannot* avoid metaphysical views about persons even if they believe they are doing so. After all, Simmons offered to his readers *reasons*, that is, grounds, that he believes establish his view that the law *ought to* mark off one set of human beings (pre-viable ones) as objects that may be killed without justification and mark off another set of human beings as subjects that may do the killing without justification. Because these grounds appeal to properties certain human beings may or may not possess, they are metaphysical grounds, whether or not Simmons or Rosenbaum believes that they are.

Consequently, Rosenbaum offers no actual arguments in rebuttal, but merely repeats what Simmons thinks about his own views and then *says* that I have Simmons all wrong.[75] Rosenbaum also assigns to me and my views unkind, inaccurate, and pejorative descriptions and labels.[76] Yet despite these philosophical shortcomings, his essay is not without philosophical value. For he has provided the discerning reader another excellent example of the same mistake made by Simmons. But Rosenbaum's mistake is more subtle than Simmons's. To see this mistake, we have to remove, very carefully, the layers of philosophical jargon that conceal it. To accomplish this task, I will employ the very "unmasking" strategy he suggests has undermined the Western tradition of rational argument and natural law reasoning that he finds in my work and considers to be "most egregious and most offensive."[77] Writes Rosenbaum:

> Beginning in the nineteenth century, the Achilles' heel of Western rationalist fundamentalism became apparent through the work of Ralph Waldo Emerson and Friedrich Nietzsche. The work of these two thinkers, one American and one German, gave rise to different traditions on different continents, traditions dedicated to unmasking the pretensions of reason to adjudicate properly among positions on complex intellectual, moral, and "metaphysical" issues.[78]

In the cause of unmasking reasons' pretentiousness, Rosenbaum offers his readers *reasons* for why one should embrace his cause, and he expects others to provide adequate reasons for their viewpoints as well.[79] He believes that the reasons for his position are sufficient in establishing the veracity of it. If not, why does Rosenbaum maintain that those who disagree with his analysis are *wrong*,[80] and that he is *right*? (Those who disagree are not only corrected but labeled and their honesty called into question).[81] In fact, "for the sake of intellectual integrity,"[82] Rosenbaum instructs us that one must open oneself to this "unmasking" tradition. That is, one should be teachable (i.e., open) so that one may increase the likelihood that one will discover and embrace the right point of view (Rosenbaum's), a view (in its American pragmatist version) that "is constructive, optimistic, and forward-looking,"[83] apparently because these are good reasons to consider a philosophical perspective. Certain virtues may follow from embracing this view, including not only intellectual integrity but *wisdom*, the ability to understand diverse practices of diverse cultures,[84] and to be tolerant of those practices and cultures.[85] In sum, one has an obligation to be open to the correct point of view, to embrace what is right when one discovers it, and to seek wisdom and understanding to be more tolerant of differences.

Moreover, Rosenbaum claims that I incorrectly interpreted *Roe v. Wade* and the works of Simmons,[86] and for that reason he issues a strong condemnation for my apparent lapse in judgment.[87] Evidently, Rosenbaum believes my scholarship failed to reach a standard for which I should be aware and to which I am obligated to abide: texts should be interpreted accurately. This, of course, is grounded in more primitive moral notions: to accurately interpret a text one should do so fairly and honestly, and one should pursue the truth while interpreting texts. Both these moral commands are logically prior to, and thus not derived from, the texts themselves or the historical circumstances in which one finds oneself, for to extract truths from texts and facts from history, obedience to these moral commands is a necessary condition, one that Rosenbaum admits is the case.[88]

Apparently, Rosenbaum believes that these norms and virtues, delineated in the previous two paragraphs, are goods that one ought not to lack, and that they are not culturally bound or contingent upon any historical circumstances or texts, for he offers these norms and virtues as conditions and consequences for agents bound by their finitude and their place in history: "Beckwith's incipient metaphysical imperialism and paternalism is inconsistent with the *wisdom* of Blackmun and Simmons, a *wisdom* appropriate for historical people living in historical communities and having historical traditions and historical documents."[89] Evidently, there are not only norms and virtues that are universally commendable, such as wisdom, intellectual integrity, optimism, forward-lookingness, and tolerance, but there are vices that are universally condemnable, such as "metaphysical imperialism" and "paternalism," not to mention "philosophical fundamentalism,"[90] pretentiousness,[91] and distorting another's views.[92]

Rosenbaum, however, is now in a peculiar position, for he asks us to join him in the unmasking of the pretentiousness of reason (and its attendant moral notion, natural law)[93] by offering us a cluster of *reasons* that include moral judgments, not contingent on time or historical circumstance, whose purpose is to make us wise and virtuous, assuming that we are the sorts of beings who ought to be wise and virtuous. He, therefore, offers to us what he claims the unmaskers have shown cannot be offered: reason, natural law, and a philosophical anthropology. In the same way that Simmons must employ the metaphysics he says he will not use, Rosenbaum must use reason and natural law in his project to unmask the pretentiousness of reason and natural law. He does what comes naturally without knowing it. The unmasking is complete.

JUDITH JARVIS THOMSON'S ARGUMENT FOR LEGALIZED ABORTION FROM THE EQUAL REASONABLENESS OF THE PRO-LIFE AND ABORTION-CHOICE POSITIONS

Thomson is best known for a defense of abortion that concedes the unborn's personhood but nevertheless maintains that there is a right to abortion (with which I deal in Chapter 7).[94] She is also the author of a widely read piece that appeared in the *Boston Review* in 1995.[95] In this essay she seems to set aside her earlier argument by granting to opponents of abortion that if abortion is prima facie unjustified homicide, then there are sufficient grounds for restricting a woman's liberty to abort.[96] She also concedes that the pro-life position on the moral status of the unborn is reasonable, but denies that reason requires that abortion-choice advocates embrace it, for the abortion-choice view, that the unborn is not a full-fledged member of the human community (at least during the earliest stages of pregnancy), is just as reasonable as the pro-life point of view. Consequently, no side of the issue really wins the day.

THOMSON'S ARGUMENT

Given this state of affairs,[97] Thomson defends the continued legalization of abortion in the United States, based on three ideas she summarizes at the end of her essay:

> First, restrictive regulation severely constrains women's liberty. Second, severe constraints on liberty may not be imposed in the name of considerations that the constrained are not unreasonable in rejecting. And third, the many women who reject the claim that the fetus has a right to life from the moment of conception are not unreasonable in doing so.[98]

Recall the pro-life position I offered in the introduction:

1. The unborn entity, from the moment of conception, is a full-fledged member of the human community.
2. It is prima facie morally wrong to kill any member of that community.
3. Every successful abortion kills an unborn entity, a full-fledged member of the human community.
4. Therefore, every successful abortion is prima facie morally wrong.[99]

Thomson is not saying that any of the premises in the above argument are false or that the conclusion does not follow from the premises. Rather, she is arguing that the soundness of the pro-life argument is *not relevant* to resolving the political question of abortion. What is relevant, however, is whether those who reject the pro-life argument – abortion-choice proponents and women seeking abortions – are not unreasonable in rejecting it.

Critique of Thomson's Argument

There are at least three problems with Thomson's argument: (1) It does not adequately present the most sophisticated arguments against abortion, (2) anti-abortionists are not unreasonable in rejecting the most important premise in Thomson's argument, and (3) she stipulates, without argument, that "liberty" is the value at stake in the abortion debate.

Thomson does not adequately present the pro-life case
One may reasonably question whether Thomson has adequately assessed the point of view she claims an abortion-choice proponent is not unreasonable in rejecting. Here's her presentation of the pro-life case:

A familiar argument starts from the premise that a human being's life begins at conception. (We are invited to accept that premise on the ground that the conceptus – a fertilized human egg – contains a biological code that will govern its entire future physical development, and therefore is already a human being.). Moreover, human beings have a right to life. A human being can forfeit that right by, for example, unjustly aggressing against another. But, the argument continues, the fetus, at all stages is innocent of any aggression.... And so the argument concludes: abortion at any stage, from conception on, is a violation of the right to life, and thus is murder.[100]

As we saw in our analysis of Simmons's argument, this is not what sophisticated pro-lifers argue. Granted, in popular presentations at pro-life rallies and in other settings, pro-lifers typically appeal to the embryo's possession of a human genetic code as evidence of its humanity. But in the philosophical literature with which Thomson should be conversant, pro-life thinkers present a careful, and metaphysically rich, defense of the unborn's full humanity from conception. (I offer this type of case in Chapters 4 and 6 of this present volume.) But it should be evident to the reader, even from the modest presentation of the pro-life case in this chapter, that the arguments for that point of view are far more sophisticated than Thomson lets on. This is not to say that these arguments have not been countered with rebuttals.[101] However, for Thomson's audience to properly assess her claim that neither the pro-life position nor the abortion-choice position is unreasonable, she should have not only provided the analytic tools for such an assessment but also the best materials partisans on either side have to offer.

It is not unreasonable to reject Thomson's position
In support of her position, she offers three ideas, the most important of which is the principle that "severe constraints on liberty may not be imposed in the name of considerations that the constrained are not unreasonable in rejecting." For this principle to be acceptable, according to the standard of rational acceptance Thomson's position requires, it must be a principle that is unreasonable to reject when applied to the debate over abortion. But that does not seem to be correct, for at least two reasons.

First, Thomson presents no argument for why pro-lifers would be unreasonable in rejecting this principle. In fact, she merely stipulates the principle's truth and thus provides no argument for it. Consequently, given the absence of a reason to support it, and given the fact that its truth is not self-evident, it seems prima facie not unreasonable to reject it.

Second, Thomson wants to procure the law to severely constrain the liberty of those who oppose abortion, for she is offering an argument that makes it almost always unjustified for pro-life citizens to employ the resources of their government to protect beings that they are not unreasonable in believing are full-fledged members of the human community deserving of our protection. But these citizens are being constrained from influencing and shaping the laws and practices of their communities on grounds – the pregnant woman has a right to abort – that Thomson *concedes* that pro-lifers are not unreasonable in rejecting, for their position *entails* the denial of those grounds. That is to say, the reasonableness of the pro-life position on the protected moral status of the fetus – which, Thomson concedes, entails a constraint on the right to abort – is reason enough, according to the standard of rational acceptance Thomson's position requires, to reject her call to constrain the liberty of pro-life citizens.

Thomson claims that opponents of abortion "ought not say that reason requires us to accept" the pro-life position, "for that assertion is false."[102] However, she does not hesitate to imply that reason requires that the central principle of her case be employed by the state as a justification for it to constrain the political activities of pro-life citizens, even though, as we have seen, it is not unreasonable for these citizens to reject this principle.

Thomson does not seem to appreciate the true scope and implications of conceding the reasonableness of the pro-life position. Consider, for example, her claim that some pro-life activists engage in fraud:

> There is already far too much falsehood in the prolife movement. A recent newspaper photograph showed an prolife protester holding a placard that said 'Abortion kills'; that much is true. But under those words was a photograph of a baby. The baby looked to me a year and a half old – counting in the ordinary way, from birth, not conception. The message communicated by that placard was that abortion kills fully developed babies, and that is false, indeed, fraudalent. Exaggeration for a political purpose is one thing, fraud quite another.[103]

This is a strong accusation to make, and one that opponents of abortion should not take lightly. However, it seems to me that Thomson unwittingly reveals in this rhetorical flourish a misunderstanding of the pro-life position. The protester holds to the view – that Thomson herself maintains is not unreasonable – that the baby in the placard is no different in nature or in moral status than her prenatal self from the moment of conception. For the protester, he or she is offering the baby's picture as a guide to help extend and inspire the imagination of those who need images and props to start on the path of moral reasoning. It seems that this tactic of protest is not unlike the instances of abortion-choice activists holding up placards with coat-hangers to symbolize the dangers of illegal abortions performed by black market nonphysicians prior to *Roe v. Wade*, even though "coat-hanger" abortions constituted a tiny percentage of those procured in the pre-*Roe* years.[104]

Thomson stipulates, without argument, that "liberty"
is the value at stake in the abortion debate

Even if Thomson is correct about the equal reasonableness of the pro-life
and abortion-choice positions, it does not follow that the abortion-choice
position *must be* the one that is reflected in our laws. Thomson, however,
maintains that because the arguments for the contrary positions on the
moral standing of the unborn are equally reasonable, and because the
liberty of certain citizens (i.e., pregnant women) hangs in the balance,
we should err on the side of liberty and grant the right to abortion. She
writes:

> One side says that the fetus has a right to life from the moment of
> conception, the other side denies this. Neither side is able to prove its
> case.... [W]hy should the deniers win?... The answer is that the situa-
> tion is not symmetrical. What is in question here is not which of two values
> we should promote, the deniers' or the supporters'. What the supporters
> want is a license to impose force; what the deniers want is a license to be
> free of it. It is the former that needs justification.[105]

But this clearly begs the question, for Thomson has to show, rather
than merely stipulate, that in the debate over abortion's permissibility
reason requires us to conclude that liberty is the good that is at stake. Or
to conscript Thomson's language for our purposes, it is not unreasonable
to reject the notion that we should err on the side of liberty when all sides
in the abortion debate hold equally reasonable arguments. Consider the
following argument (which is nearly identical to the one employed in
Chapter 2 in reply to Justice Blackmun's "experts disagree" argument).

If it is true that no one position on the unborn's moral status wins
the day, this is an excellent reason *not* to permit abortion, because an
abortion *may* result in the death of a human entity who has a full right
to life. If one kills another being without knowing whether that being is
a person with a full right to life, and if one has reasonable grounds (as
Thomson admits) to believe that the being in question is a person, such
an action would constitute a willful and reckless disregard for others,
even if one later discovered that the being was not a person.

Thomson, like Justice Blackmun, seems to be saying that the different
positions on the unborn's moral status all have able defenders, persuasive
arguments, and passionate advocates, but none really wins the day. To put
it another way, the issue of fetal personhood is up for grabs; all positions
are in some sense equal, none is better than any other. Thomson writes
that "while I know of no conclusive reason for denying that fertilized

eggs have a right to life, I also know of no conclusive reason for asserting that they do have a right to life."[106] But if this is the case, then it is safe to say that the odds of the unborn being a human person are 50/50. Given these odds, it would seem that society has a moral obligation to err on the side of life, and therefore, to legally prohibit virtually all abortions.

Consider again the illustration I used in Chapter 2. Imagine the police are able to identify someone as a murderer with only one piece of evidence: his DNA matches the DNA of the genetic material found on the victim. The police subsequently arrest him, and he is convicted and sentenced to death. Suppose, however, that it is discovered several months later that the murderer has an identical twin brother who was also at the scene of the crime and obviously has the same DNA as his brother on death row. This means that there is a 50/50 chance that the man on death row is the murderer. Would the state be justified in executing this man? Surely not, for there is a 50/50 chance of executing an innocent person. Consequently, if it is wrong to kill the man on death row, it is then wrong to kill the unborn when the arguments for its full humanity are just as reasonable as the arguments against it.

One may also employ Thomson's own principle – "severe constraints on liberty may not be imposed in the name of considerations that the constrained are not unreasonable in rejecting" – to show that liberty is not the value at stake in the abortion debate. Consider the following example. Suppose that there is a shooting range in Central Texas, located only 1,000 feet from the playground of a local elementary school. The county commission, at the request of concerned parents and teachers, prohibits the shooting range to operate when the students at the school are on the playground, because there is a 1 in 100 chance that a bullet will ricochet off one of the targets and hit a child. Imagine that the marksmen who practice at the range, with the support of the range's ownership, employ Thomson's principle to rebut the commission's policy: "severe constraints on liberty may not be imposed in the name of considerations that the constrained are not unreasonable in rejecting." The response on the part of the commission would likely be: "Yes, your principle may be correct, *but* you are in fact *unreasonable* in rejecting the policy's constraint on your liberty, for reason requires that you accept a public policy to protect the innocent from unjust harm even if there is only a 1 in 100 chance of it occurring." To apply the commission's response to Thomson's argument: yes, your principle may be correct, *but* you are in fact *unreasonable* in rejecting the pro-life constraint on the pregnant woman's abortion liberty, for reason requires that you accept a public policy to protect the innocent from unjust harm if it is reasonable to believe that abortion is prima facie unjustified homicide. After all, the burden that abortion is employed to terminate (pregnancy) is less of a harm than the wrong that Thomson concedes is not unreasonable to believe occurs in the termination of that burden (unjustifed homicide of a human person).[107]

CONCLUSION

It seems, then, that the abortion debate can not be politically and legally resolved by merely appealing to a "first principle of religious liberty,"[108] as Simmons calls it, or the supposed equal rationality of the abortion-choice and pro-life positions on the unborn's moral status while stipulating that liberty is the default position, as Thomson suggests. For there does not seem to be any neutral ground. After all, to say that a woman should have the right to choose to terminate her pregnancy without public justification is tantamount to denying the pro-life position that the unborn are human persons who by nature are worthy of protection by the state. And to affirm that the unborn are human persons with a natural right to life that ought to be protected by the state is tantamount to denying the abortion-choice position that a woman has a fundamental right to terminate her pregnancy, because such a termination would result, in most cases, in an unjustified homicide. Consequently, when abortion-choice advocates, in the name of tolerance and religious liberty, call for pro-life citizens to completely cease employing the legitimate avenues of our constitutional democracy for the purpose of protecting the unborn from harm, these abortion-choice supporters are in fact instructing their fellow citizens to silently, politely, and without resistance acquiesce to the metaphysical status quo, namely, that the unborn are not full-fledged members of the human community and therefore are not entitled to protection by the state. To the opponent of abortion, this request hardly seems tolerant or liberating.

PART II

ASSESSING THE CASE FOR ABORTION CHOICE AND AGAINST HUMAN INCLUSIVENESS

4

SCIENCE, THE UNBORN, AND ABORTION METHODS

What does it mean to say that a particular being is *human*, that he or she is a member of the species *Homo sapiens*? How, for example, may one distinguish a human being from, let's say, a dog, a cat, a grapefruit, or a human being's part such as a finger or a blood cell? And if the being in the womb is a *human* being, what are the methods by which the abortionist accomplishes his goal of extinguishing that being's life? In this chapter we will answer these questions. We will do so by presenting the facts of prenatal development as well as the methods used by physicians to terminate an unwanted pregnancy. Given the gravity of a woman's choice to abort – as all parties in this dispute concede – we have an obligation to become conversant with these matters, troubling though they are.

It surprises many people when they are told that most sophisticated defenders of abortion choice concede that the unborn, long before birth,[1] is a human being, though they argue that it lacks a property essential to acquiring the status of a moral *person*. And thus, a pregnant woman may kill that entity prior to its acquisition of that property. Although an important subject – one that is addressed in great detail in Chapter 6 – in this chapter we take up the more modest task of simply showing that the unborn is a human being from conception as well as presenting the methods by which it may be killed in an abortion.

A HUMAN BEING BEGINS AT CONCEPTION[2]

We will first look at the scientific facts that establish the claim that a human being begins her existence at conception. We will then critically assess several arguments that are employed to reject this claim.

The Facts of Fetal Development[3]

Pregnancy begins at *conception*, the *successful* result of the process of fertilization at which the male sperm and the female ovum unite.[4] That is, fertilization is a process, taking from 24 to 36 hours, that culminates in conception. And what results is an entity called a *zygote*. It is a misnomer to refer to this entity as a "fertilized ovum." For both ovum and sperm, which are genetically parts of their owners (mother and father, respectively), cease to exist at least at the moment of conception and perhaps earlier in the fertilization process. For that reason, it may not even be correct to refer to the sperm and egg as "uniting," for, as philosopher Robert Joyce points out, "that suggests that they remain and form a larger whole." But that is not accurate, for they are not like machine parts cobbled together to form something larger though remaining identifiable parts. Rather, "the nuclei of the sperm and ovum *dynamically interact*," and "in so doing, they both cease to be. One might say they die together."[5]

There is a dispute among human embryologists concerning the point in the fertilization process at which a new human being comes to be. Many maintain that this occurs *before* syngamy, the time at which the maternal and paternal chromosomes cross over and form a diploid set. Some, for example, argue that a human being comes to be when the sperm penetrates the ovum, whereas others argue that this occurs when the pronuclei of the maternal and paternal chromosomes blend in the oocyte. It seems to me that the penetration criterion is flawed because the sperm and ovum still seem to be two distinct entities and thus no new individual human being exists. The pre-syngamy pronuclei standard is less problematic as at that time sperm and ovum have ceased to exist as distinct entities and the oocyte, though not possessing the diploid set of chromosomes of the zygote and embryo, seems to behave like an individual living organism with an intrinsically directed nature. Nevertheless, even though a new human being *may have* come to be prior to syngamy (and there is good reason to hold this view), it seems indisputable that at syngamy a new human being, an individual human being, exists and is in the process of development and is not identical to either the sperm or the ovum from whose uniting it arose.[6]

David Boonin argues that the dispute about the precise moment at which a new human organism comes into existence counts against the claim that a human being begins at conception.[7] Although he brings up many of the same points I have briefly summarized above, Boonin's raising of this important epistemological question (When do we know X is an individual organism and its germ cell progenitors cease to be?) does not detract from the claim that a complete and living zygote is a whole human organism. It *may be* that one cannot, with confidence, pick out the precise point at which a new being comes into existence between the time at which the sperm initially penetrates the ovum and a complete and living zygote is present. But how does it follow from that acknowledgment of agnosticism that one cannot say that zygote X is a human being? It seems to me that Boonin commits the fallacy of the beard: just because I cannot tell you when stubble ends and a beard begins does not mean that I cannot distinguish bearded faces from clean-shaven ones. After all, abortion-choice supporters typically pick out what they consider value-making properties – for example, rationality, having a self-concept, sentience, or organized cortical brain activity (as in the case of Boonin) – that they justify concluding that a being lacking one or all of them does not have a right to life. (These arguments will be critically assessed in Chapter 6). But it is nearly impossible to pick out at what precise point in a being's existence it acquires the correct trait, for example, when it becomes rational enough or has a sufficient amount of organized cortical brain activity to warrant a right to life. But it's doubtful whether the abortion-choice advocate would abandon her position on those grounds.

Resulting from the dynamic interaction, and organic merger, of the female ovum (which contains 23 chromosomes) and the male sperm (which contains 23 chromosomes), the conceptus is a new, although tiny, individual with a human genetic code with its own genomic sequence (with 46 chromosomes),[8] which is neither her mother's nor her father's.[9] From this point until death *no new genetic information is needed* to make the unborn entity an individual human being. Her genetic makeup is established at conception, determining to a great extent her own individual physical characteristics – gender, eye color, bone structure, hair color, skin color, susceptibility to certain diseases, and so on. That is to say, at conception, the "genotype" – the inherited characteristics of an individual human being – is in place and it plays the same role in the human organism as it does in all living organisms: it is highly complex information that instructs the unfolding of the organism's intrinsic potential. The conceptus, from the very beginning, is a whole organism, with certain capacities, powers, and properties, whose parts work in concert to bring the whole to maturity.

The organism's genotype will remain with it as long as it exists. The only thing necessary for its growth and development, as with the rest of us, is oxygen, food, water, and healthy interaction with its natural environment, because this organism, like the newborn, the infant, and the adolescent, needs only to develop in accordance with her given nature that is present at conception. This is why French geneticist Jerome L. LeJeune, while testifying before a Senate Subcommittee, asserted: "To accept the fact that after fertilization has taken place a new human has come into being is no longer a matter of taste or opinion. The human nature of the human being from conception to old age is not a metaphysical contention, it is plain experimental evidence."[10]

LeJeune's conclusion is substantiated by a host of other authorities, some of which were cited in a U.S. Senate subcommittee report to the U.S. Senate Judiciary Committee (1981). The following is a limited sample:

Dr. Hymie Gordon, professor of medical genetics and physician at the Mayo Clinic:

I think we can now also say that the question of the beginning of life – when life begins – is no longer a question for theological or philosophical dispute. It is an established scientific fact. Theologians and philosophers may go on to debate the meaning of life or purpose of life, but it is an established fact that all life, including human life, begins at the moment of conception. ...

I have never ever seen in my own scientific reading, long before I became concerned with issues of life of this nature, that anyone has ever argued that life did not begin at the moment of conception and that it was a human conception if it resulted from the fertilization of the human egg by a human sperm. As far as I know, these have never been argued against.[11]

Dr. M. Krieger, *The Human Reproductive System*, 88 (1969):

All organisms, however large and complex they may be when fullgrown, begin life as but a single cell.

This is true of the human being, for instance, who begins life as a fertilized ovum.[12]

Dr. B. Patten, *Human Embryology*, 43 (3rd ed. 1968):

The formation, maturation and meeting of a male and female sex cell are all preliminary to their actual union into a combined cell, or *zygote*, which definitely marks the beginning of a new individual.[13]

Dr. Micheline Matthews-Roth, a principal research associate in the department of medicine, Harvard Medical School:

So, therefore, it is scientifically correct to say that an individual human life begins at conception, when egg and sperm join to form the zygote, and this developing human always is a member of our species in all stages of its life.[14]

Dr. Ronan O' Rahilly and Dr. Fabiola Muller, *Human Embryology and Teratology*, 2nd ed. (1996):

> It needs to be emphasized that life is continuous, as is also human life, so that the question "When does (human) life begin?" is meaningless in terms of ontogeny. Although life is a continuous process, fertilization is a critical landmark because, under ordinary circumstances, a new, genetically distinct human organism is thereby formed.[15]

The U.S. Senate Subcommittee, which cited four of the above authorities in its report, made the observation that "no witness [who testified before the subcommittee] raised any evidence to refute the biological fact that from the moment of conception there exists a distinct individual being who is alive and is of the human species. No witness challenged the scientific consensus that unborn children are 'human beings,' insofar as the term is used to mean living beings of the human species." On the other hand, "those witnesses who testified that science cannot say whether unborn children are human beings were speaking in every instance to the value question rather than the scientific question.... [T]hese witnesses invoked their value preferences to redefine the term 'human being.'" The committee report explains that these witnesses "took the view that each person may define as 'human' only those beings whose lives that a person wants to value. Because they did not wish to accord intrinsic worth to the lives of unborn children, they refused to call them 'human beings,' regardless of the scientific evidence."[16] I will critique these "value" arguments in Chapter 6.

So from a strictly scientific point of view, it seems reasonable to believe that the development of an individual human life begins at conception. Consequently, each human being begins her physical existence as a zygote and that organism does not acquire its humanness at some later stage in its development. The human organism remains a human *being* throughout her life, from zygote to embryo to fetus to newborn to adolescent and throughout adulthood until natural death at which the existence of the living organism ends. None of these stages imparts to the human being her humanity.

Because the conceptus can be brought into existence in a petri dish, as evidenced in the case of the so-called test-tube baby, and since this entity, if it has white parents, can be transferred to the womb of a black woman and be born white, we know conclusively that the conceptus is *not* part of the woman's body. Of course, the conceptus attaches to the woman's body and draws sustenance from her, and in that sense it is physically engaged with the mother's body. But it is still a separate *being* that is *not* her mother.

Although the zygote is a one-celled organism it is simply not *just a cell* like the rest of the cells of either the mother's or father's body. It is an individual human organism whose cells all have the same genomic sequence – just like those in her mother's body as well as in our own – except the zygote is a human being at a stage in her development at which her body just happens to have only one cell. But the fact that the zygote is a one-celled entity should not take away from the intricate complex information found in her genomic sequence. Bart T. Hefferman, M.D., tells us:

> The new combination of chromosomes [i.e., the zygote's genetic structure] sets in motion the individual's life, controlled by his own individual code (genes) with its fantastic library of information projected from the past on the helix of . . . DNA. A single thread of DNA from a human cell contains information equivalent to six hundred thousand printed pages with five hundred words on a page, or a library of one thousand volumes. The stored knowledge at conception in the new individual's library of instruction is fifty times more than that contained in the *Encyclopedia Britannica*. These unique and individual instructions are operative over the whole of the individual's life and form a continuum of human existence even into succeeding generations.[17]

As Dr. Gordon writes, "Even at that early stage, the complexity of the living cell is so great that it is beyond our comprehension. It is a privilege to be allowed to protect and nurture it."[18]

Cell division occurs after the zygote stage. The early human being increases to over 100 cells within the first week after conception. *Implantation* occurs around six days after conception. This is the time at which the conceptus "nests" or implants in her mother's uterus. During this time, and possibly up to 14 days after conception,[19] a splitting of the conceptus may occur and resulting in monozygotic (or identical) twins. In some instances the two concepti may recombine and become one conceptus. (I will respond below to the argument that the possibility of the conceptus twinning and the subsequent conceptus recombining refutes the claim that a human being begins her existence at conception.) The primitive streak – precursor to the nervous system – appears between days 12 and 17. At about three weeks a primitive heart muscle begins to pulsate. Other organs begin to develop during the first month, such as a liver, umbilical cord, kidneys, and a digestive tract (albeit in their incipient forms). This organism has a head with a developing face with nascent ears, mouth, and eyes, even though it is no larger than "the size of half a pea."[20] Toward the end of the first month (between 26 and 28 days) the arms and legs begin to appear as tiny buds. The first month ends with a fully formed human embryo.[21]

From the 18th day after conception, Stephen Krason points out, development of the central nervous system and brain is considerable.[22] One group of obstetricians and gynecologists explains:

> Such early development is necessary because the nervous system integrates the action of all the other systems. By the end of the 20th day the foundation of the child's brain, spinal cord and entire nervous system will have been established. By the 6th week after conception this system will have developed so well that it is controlling movements of the baby's muscles, even though the woman may not be aware that she is pregnant. By the 33rd day the cerebral cortex, that part of the central nervous system that governs motor activity as well as intellect may be seen.[23]

Although tiny, the unborn by the beginning of the second month *looks* "distinctly human" (though it *is* human from conception), and yet it is highly likely that the mother does not even know she is pregnant.[24] During the second month, the eyes, ears, nose, toes, and fingers make their appearance. Her skeleton develops, her heart beats, and her blood, with its own type, flows. The unborn at this time has reflexes and her lips become sensitive to touch. Brain waves can be detected at about 40 to 43 days after conception, although they could very well be *occurring* weeks earlier. "*By the end of the seventh week we see a well-proportioned small scale baby*. [emphasis mine.] In its seventh week, it bears the familiar external features and all the internal organs of the adult, even though it is less than an inch long and weighs only 1/30th of an ounce."[25] By the eighth week her own unique fingerprints as well as the lines in her hands begin to take shape. The heart beats strongly as the unborn's stomach, liver, and kidneys perform the tasks for which they were designed. "After the eighth week no further primordia will form; *everything* is already present that will be found in the full term baby.... From this point until adulthood, when full growth is achieved somewhere between 25 and 27 years, the changes in the body will be mainly in dimension and in gradual refinement of the working parts."[26] That is, at eight weeks post-conception all bodily systems are present in at least their rudimentary form.

Movement is what distinguishes the third month of pregnancy from its predecessors. Although just an ounce in weight and no more than a goose egg in size, the unborn begins to display movement including swallowing, squinting, swimming, sucking her thumb, and grasping with her hands. Her organs continue to develop, including rudimentary sperm and egg cells (depending on whether it is male or female). It is possible to observe parental features in the unborn's facial expressions. "The vocal cords are completed. In the absence of air they cannot produce sound; the child cannot cry aloud until birth although he is capable of crying long before."[27]

Growth is characteristic of the fourth month. The weight of the unborn expands sixfold by the end of the month, a time at which she is about eight to ten inches in height or 50% of what her height will be at birth. In the fifth month of pregnancy the unborn becomes *viable*. That is, she now has the ability, under our current technological knowledge, to live outside her mother's womb. Some babies have survived as early as 20 weeks after conception. The fifth month is also the time at which the mother begins to feel the unborn's movements, although mothers have been known to feel stirrings earlier. During the fifth month, the unborn's hair, skin, nipples, and nails develop. Because rapid eye movement (REM) sleep can be observed in the unborn, she is likely dreaming. She can also hear her mother's voice.

In the remaining four months of pregnancy the unborn continues to develop. The child's chances of survival outside the womb increase as she draws closer to her expected birthday. During this time she responds to sounds, her mother's voice, pain, and the taste of substances placed in the amniotic fluid. Some studies have shown that the child can actually learn before it is born.[28] The child is born approximately 38 weeks after conception.

Given the facts of embryology and fetal development, at conception, a *whole human being*, with its own genome, comes into existence, needing only food, water, shelter, and oxygen, and a congenial environment in which to interact, to grow and develop itself to maturity in accordance with her own intrinsically ordered nature. Like the infant, the child, and the adolescent, the conceptus is a being who is in the process of unfolding its potential, that is, the potential to grow and develop itself but not to change what it is. This being, because of its nature, is actively disposed to develop into a mature version of herself, though never ceasing to be herself. Thus, the same human being that begins as a zygote continues to exist to its birth and through its adulthood unless disease or violence stops it from doing so. For there is no decisive break in this physical organism's continuous development from conception until death from which one can reasonably infer that the being undergoes a substantial change and literally ceases to exist and a new being comes into existence (like the substantial change that the sperm and ovum undergo when they cease to exist and a new being comes into existence). This is why it makes perfect sense for any one of us to say, "When *I* was conceived ..."

Objections

Although it is widely acknowledged in the scientific literature that the individual human being begins at conception, there are some who have challenged this notion. Unlike the thinkers who maintain that the unborn is a human being from conception but does not become a person until sometime later (we will assess their arguments in Chapter 6), those whose arguments we evaluate in this section do not address the personhood question but rather offer reasons for *denying* that conception is the time at which an individual human being comes into existence. They believe that the human being comes into existence very early in pregnancy, but not at conception. We will look at five of those arguments.

Objection 1: The unborn is not a human being until implantation because it is at that time that it establishes its presence by transmitting hormonal signals to its mother.

Bernard Nathanson argues that at the moment of implantation the unborn "establishes its presence to the rest of us by transmitting its own signals – by producing hormones – approximately one week after fertilization and as soon as it burrows into the alien uterine wall." For Nathanson implantation is significant because prior to this time the unborn "has the genetic structure but is incomplete, lacking the essential element that produces life: an interface with the human community and communication of the fact that it is there."[29] So for Nathanson the unborn's hormonal communication to her mother is essential for a human being to begin its existence.

This argument is flawed for at least two reasons. First, it seems wrong to say that whether one is a human being by nature is dependent on whether others are aware of one's existence. It seems correct to say that it is not *essential* to your existence as a human being whether anyone *knows* you exist, for you *are* who you *are* regardless of whether others are aware of your existence. One interacts with a human being, one does not make a being human by interacting with it. In philosophical terms,

Nathanson confuses *epistemology* (the study of how we know things) with *ontology* (the study of being or existence).

A second objection is, ironically, mentioned by Nathanson himself. He writes, "If implantation is biologically the decisive point for alpha's [the unborn's] existence, what do we do about the 'test-tube' conceptions? The zygote in these cases is seen in its culture dish and could be said to announce its existence even before it is implanted?" Nathanson responds to these questions by asserting, "It seems to me that when it is in the dish the zygote is already implanted, philosophically and biochemically, and has established the nexus with the human community, before it is 're'-implanted into the mother's womb."[30] This response, however, does not support Nathanson's position, for he is admitting that there is no *real* essential difference between the implanted and the non-implanted conceptus, just an accidental difference (the former's existence is known while the latter's is not). Hence, just as there is no *essential* difference between a Bill Clinton who, in a possible world, pumps gas in Little Rock and a Bill Clinton who, in another possible world that is the actual world, is a former president of the United States (there are only accidental differences between the two Clintons), there is no essential difference between an unknown conceptus and a known conceptus. In sum, it seems counterintuitive to assert that one's nature is dependent on another's knowledge of one's existence.[31]

Objection 2: Some products of conception are not human beings and some human beings may not result from conception.

There is a second argument for implantation, and not conception, as the beginning of a human being's existence: "Some entities that stem from the union of sperm and egg are not 'human beings' and never will develop into them" and there may be some human beings who come into being without the union of sperm and egg.[32] Concerning the former, Nathanson offers three examples of nonhuman entities that result from the sperm-egg union: the hydatidiform mole ("an entity which is usually just a degenerated placenta and typically has a random number of chromosomes"), the choriocarcinoma ("a 'conception-cancer' resulting from the sperm-egg union is one of gynecology's most malignant tumors"), and the "blighted ovum" ("a conception with the forty-six chromosomes but which is only a placenta, lacks an embryonic plate, and is always aborted naturally after implantation"). A human clone, on the other hand, is an example of a human entity that may come into being without the benefit of a sperm-egg union.[33]

The problem with Nathanson's argument is that it confuses necessary and sufficient conditions. One who holds that a human being begins to exist as a single organism at conception is not arguing that everything that results from the sperm-egg union is necessarily a conception. That is, every conception of a human being is the result of a sperm-egg union, but not every sperm-egg union results in such a conception. Hence, the sperm-egg union is a *necessary* condition for conception, but not a *sufficient* condition.

Furthermore, Nathanson is correct in asserting that a human clone would be a human being who has come into existence without benefit of conception. (The issue of cloning is dealt with in great detail in Chapter 9.)[34] But this would only mean that conception is not a *necessary* condition for a human being to come into existence, just as the sperm-egg union is not a *sufficient* condition for a conception. In sum, all human beings that are the result of conception come to be at conception, but not all human beings are the result of conception (e.g., clones) and not everything that results from a sperm-egg union is a conception (e.g., "blighted ovum").

Objection 3: Because so many pregnancies result in miscarriages or spontaneous abortions, it is difficult to believe the unborn are complete human beings during their entire gestation.

Not every conception results in the birth of a child. In fact, some have estimated that between 20% and 50% of all concepti die before birth. And some have claimed that up to 30% die before *implantation*.[35] Thomas Shannon and Allan Wolter maintain that only 45% of sperm-egg unions result in live births, with the remaining ending in miscarriage,[36] which leads them to hold that the individual human being does not come to be at conception.[37] That is, because of the apparently vast number of unborn entities that perish prior to birth (and usually very early in pregnancy), some people find it difficult to believe that the newly conceived unborn entity is fully human. But this is clearly an invalid argument, for it does not logically follow from the *number* of unborn entities who die that these entities are by *nature* not human beings who have begun their existence. To cite an example, it does not follow from the fact that underdeveloped countries have a high infant mortality rate that their babies are not as human as those born in countries with low infant mortality rates.[38] After all, what if it were discovered that the numbers cited above are mistaken, that in fact 90% of all conceptions come to term? Would it now be the case that the early embryo *is* an individual human being that began her existence at conception? Again, why would the number of entities who perish make a difference as to whether these entities were human beings who had begun their existence at conception? After all, *all* human beings who are conceived *die*, whether they die as a result of a miscarriage at three months gestation or as an adult in Memphis, Tennessee, at the age of 42. Are we to infer from this 100% mortality rate that none of these beings are human beings who have begun their existence?

It should be noted, as Patrick Lee points out, that "the percentages mentioned by proponents" of the spontaneous abortion "argument are disputable. For one thing... [as we saw earlier], in many cases the fertilization process is in effect incomplete, so that what is growing is not a complete human being. Many of the products of fertilization which fail to implant are no doubt the results of incomplete fertilizations and so are not human persons [or human beings]."[39]

But suppose someone were to respond to this analysis by arguing that if we really believe that every conception is a human being, are we not obligated to prevent all spontaneous abortions even though it may lead to overpopulation and an appropriation of medical and other resources that may have catastrophic results?

First, this response does not show that the newly conceived entity is *not* a human being who began her existence at conception; rather, it is an attack upon the intellectual consistency of those who offer arguments to support their belief that the newly conceived entity is a human being whose existence began at conception. It is those arguments, and not the people who offer them, that are the proper object of analysis.

Second, in this chapter I am not arguing that all human beings are full-fledged members of the moral community (i.e., persons). Rather, I am making the argument that a human being begins her existence at conception. Whether that human being while in her mother's womb should be a subject of moral concern from conception on par with typical adult human beings is another question and the focus of Chapter 6. So, in reply to the response, I could simply say that a human being dies as a result of a spontaneous abortion, but whether that human being is a subject of moral concern on par with a typical adult human being is another question altogether.

Third, assuming that the unborn from conception is a subject of moral concern (i.e., a person), this response is flawed in another way: it confuses our obvious prima facie moral obligation not to commit homicide (that is, to intentionally kill an innocent human person) with the questionable moral obligation to interfere with natural death of a human person in every instance. Clearly the former does not entail the latter. "Protecting life is a moral obligation, but resisting natural death is not necessarily a moral duty.... There is no inconsistency between preserving natural life, opposing artificial abortion and allowing natural death by spontaneous abortion."[40] Consider an illustration outside of the context of abortion: a healthy 82-year-old man is clearly a human person as would be his twin. Imagine that the twin is in the last stages of cancer and no known remedy can save him. Suppose, however, he could prolong his life for a little bit more but only if he undergoes painful chemotherapy that will result in several months of misery. Our prima facie duty not to kill the healthy twin does not entail that we have a duty to require that the dying twin undergo the chemotherapy, even though both are human persons. Consequently, just as difficult questions about withholding and withdrawing treatment from dying patients do not count against our prohibition against killing innocent healthy adults, the question of how we should ethically respond to spontaneous abortions does not count against the pro-life position that it is morally wrong to *directly* and *intentionally* kill the healthy and normally developing unborn.

Objection 4: Because the early embryo has the potential to twin and recombine and possesses cellular totipotency, it is not an individual human being.

Some argue that because twinning (the division of a single conceptus into two), and perhaps recombination (the reuniting of two concepti into one conceptus), may occur roughly within the first two weeks of pregnancy, an individual human being is not present until twinning and recombination are no longer possible. Moreover, because the very early embryo consists of totipotent cells, any one of which could be detached from the cluster and become an individual human being in its own right, some thinkers argue that until the cells are differentiated and lose their totipotency,[41] the embryo, though genetically human, is not an *individual* human *being*. According to Shannon and Wolter:

> Because of the possibility of twinning, recombination, and the potency of any cell up to gastrulation to become a complete entity, the particular zygote cannot necessarily be said to be the beginning of a specific, genetically unique individual human being. While the zygote is the beginning of a genetically distinct life, it is neither an ontological individual nor necessarily the immediate precursor of one.[42]

Norman Ford suggests that "the early embryo is really a cluster of distinct individual cells, each one of which is a centrally organized living individual or ontological entity in simple contact with the others enclosed in the protective zona pellucida. It would be difficult to justify attributing the natural unity property to a single ontological individual to the cluster of cells as a whole."[43] Thus, according to Ford, the embryo is not a single *being*, but rather, a cluster of *beings* held together by the zona pellucida, "a natural surface 'coat' that covers the embryo."[44]

The objection assessed in this section may be put this way:

1. The early embryo is merely a cluster of totipotent cells that may divide into separate entities that may later recombine.
2. Any "entity" that may divide into separate "entities" that may later recombine is not an individual *being*.
3. Therefore, the early embryo is not an individual being.

This is a valid argument, for if both premises are true, the conclusion follows. However, there are good reasons to reject both premises, which means that the argument is unsound. Concerning the second premise – any "entity" that may divide into separate "entities" that may later recombine is not an individual *being* – it is clearly not true. Patrick Lee offers as an illustration, the flatworm, a being that has the potential to result in two flatworms if it is cut in two. Lee explains:

> The reason the division does not simply result in death seems to be that the parts of the flatworm have the capacity to de-differentiate. This fact surely does not imply that prior to the division the flatworm is merely an aggregate of cells or tissues. It simply means that the parts of the flatworm have the potential to become a whole flatworm when isolated from the present whole of which they are parts. Likewise, at the early stages of development of the human embryo the cells seem to be as yet relatively unspecialized and therefore can become whole organisms if they are divided and have an appropriate environment after the division. But that fact does not in the least indicate that prior to such an extrinsic division the embryo is an aggregate rather a single, multicellular organism.[45]

Simply because two concepti result from a split conceptus or one conceptus results from two concepti that recombine, it does not logically follow that any of the concepti prior to twinning or recombining were not individual human beings.[46]

Recall the first premise: the early embryo is merely a cluster of totipotent cells that may divide into separate entities that may later recombine. But, as we shall see, there is good reason to reject the notion that the early embryo is merely a "cluster" of cells rather than an individual organism. I suspect that the reason it is tempting to think of the early embryo in this way is that its cells are totipotent and thus each has the capacity, if detached from the others, to develop into an individual human being. But it does not follow from the totipotency of the early embryo's cells that he or she is merely a cluster of cells with no organizing principle, or substantial unity, that unifies these cells as the parts of an individual biological entity. "As the flatworm example shows," writes Lee, "a totipotency of a part does not show that *prior to the division* the part is not functioning as a part."[47] What evidence is there for the early embryo's unity as a being?

First, totipotent cells do not detach from the embryo willy-nilly; they detach for a reason, either by a force external to the embryo (e.g., a scientist who intentionally splits an embryo or detaches one of its totipotent cells) or perhaps something intrinsic to the entity itself. If the former, then the divided embryo is like the split flatworm, a being whose totipotent cells were detached by an outside force. But this clearly does not mean that either the embryo(s) or the flatworm(s) is (are) not unified being(s) before or after the artificial detachments. After all, suppose that science one day is able to take one of my skin cells and make it totipotent and provide an artificial womb for the cell so that it grows, develops, and after nine months becomes an adopted baby. Would such a scenario – an artificial detachment and manipulation of my cell so that it becomes totipotent – prove that I am not a unified being? If not, why would the artificial detachment (minus the manipulation because it is unnecessary) of an early embryo's cell prove that it is not a unified being simply because all its cells are totipotent?

Concerning the latter – that there may be something intrinsic to the entity itself that results in the detachment of one of its totipotent cell – physician and theologian Edwin Hui points out that there is no intrinsically directed potential for monozygotic twinning in every conceptus. (Twinning, of course, may occur as a result of an early embryo being manipulated artificially, as noted earlier.) That is, twinning is not "always present in the normal conditions of embryogenesis."[48] It is, after all, quite rare, "occurring in only three or four out of a thousand births." Nevertheless, writes Hui, even though "scientists are still uncertain as to why it actually takes place," they "do know that some unknown agents seem to be needed to break down the intercellular bonds that normally hold the cells together as an individual organism."[49] Because there is strong evidence that monozygotic twinning has a genetic cause (hence, it runs in certain families), it seems that some zygotes have a basic duality prior to their splitting – an intrinsically directed potential – that is not present in virtually all other zygotes. Thus, according to Hui, "the two beings that emerge as twins are in actuality two from conception, although in a 'latent' form."[50]

But even if every early embryo were to possess an intrinsically directed potential for twinning – that may be triggered by some external stimulus – it would not follow that the early embryo is not a unified organism. It would only mean that the human being, early in her existence, possesses a current capacity that becomes latent after a certain level of development, just as some latent capacities become current later in the human being's existence (e.g., the ability to philosophize).

Second, the early embryo, though consisting of totipotent cells, behaves like a single organism with an intrinsic goal-directedness for which its cellular parts interact and communicate with one another *unless* one of the cells is separated from the whole. There are at least four reasons to believe this is the case.

1. If the early embryo were not a unified organism, Benedict Ashley and Albert Moraczewski point out, the totipotent cells of the embryonic cluster "should each develop into a mature organism." But because "they do so only if they are *separated* from the others," it follows "that at least some interaction is taking place between them within the zona pellucida which restrains them from individually developing as *whole* organisms and normally directs them collectively to remain *parts* of a single organism continuous with the zygote."[51]

2. The zona pellucida (which Ford and Shannon and Wolter admit holds the embryonic cell-cluster together) as well as other embryonic tissues, Anthony Fisher writes, are "formed by the embryo, usually with its genetic constitution, and for its sole benefit and use, and are indeed its organs; they are clearly not the mother's organs, nor a tumor, nor some alien third organism living symbiotically with mother and embryo."[52] Lee aptly points out that "such activities – formation of organs for the benefit of the whole – constitute the defining trait of organisms."[53]

3. Although the embryo consists entirely of totipotent cells after its initial cell divisions, "genetic restriction of the cells [i.e., cell differentiation] begins after day five, at the blastocyst stage."[54] However, what is significant in terms of the present discussion is that "the evidence also shows that the time" when this cell differentiation "begins is determined from within by a 'clock mechanism' intrinsic to the developing embryo."[55] Ann McLaren explains:

There appears to be an inbuilt "clock" in the time of blastocyst differentiation. When cleavage is delayed or arrested, or when the number of cells in an embryo is reduced artificially, the secretion of blastocoelic fluid occurs at approximately the same time as intact blastocysts. The "clock" is not necessarily related to chronological age, and it could be provided by the number of nuclear cytoplasmic divisions in the embryo. The "clock" appears to be set and, if development is delayed, the embryo makes up for the delay later.[56]

This seems to show that the early embryo is a substantial unity whose parts, triggered by an intrinsically directed "clock mechanism," work in concert with one another for the growth, development, and continued existence of the whole.[57]

4. Other evidence for the early embryo's substantial unity includes the fact that its cells function "in distinct ways even from the two-cell stage," such as when compaction occurs on day three,[58] and the fact that "even before compaction, the positional differences between the cells is important, the top from the bottom, the right from the left, even though this differentiation is reversible."[59] Moreover, according to developmental biologist, Michael Buratovich, "the blastosmeres [the totipotent cells of the early embryo] are held together by tight junctions and gap junctions, which allow cells to communicate with each other. . . . By the eight-cell stage the cells are very tightly bound to each other. These cells are talking to each other in complex and wonderful ways. They are totipotent because they need to be – how else are they going to make everything from skin to sperm?"[60]

The significance of these activities should not be missed: they show that the cells of the early embryo, though totipotent, are functioning in ways consistent with their being constituent parts of a unified organism. That is, the cells function in concert to unfold what the early embryo's intrinsically directed nature has apparently instructed it to do. The unfolding is orderly and goal-directed with the end being the continuing development and subsistence of the embryo itself as a whole.

Objection 5: The zygote relies on maternal molecules to initially direct its development.

Some thinkers have argued that the zygote is not an individual human being at conception because in the initial stages of cell division it does not rely on the informational content of its own genes to direct its development. Rather, the mother's messenger ribonucleic acid (mRNA), inherited from the ovum responsible for the zygote's existence, directs its development until the four- to eight-cell stage. After that time, the zygote's own genes are activated and it begins to develop in accordance with the information encoded in those genes.[61] Consequently, "the zygote does not possess sufficient genetic information within its chromosomes to develop into an embryo that will be the precursor of an individual member of the human species."[62] There are several reasons this argument is unconvincing.

First, it rests on the faulty assumption that an entity is not an individual being unless it relies exclusively on its own chromosomes entirely throughout its existence. But why should we believe that's true? For chromosomes, like hearts, fingers, and lungs, are parts of the organism. Granted, chromosomes are important parts, parts that help direct the growth and development of the organism and whose information content helps shape some of the unique features and characteristics that make up a mature human being. But if these parts are present but not active, it does not follow that the organism is not a unified being if their working is not necessary at that point in its development. If, for example, hearts, fingers, and lungs cease working and are replaced by artificial versions of them, the organism remains the same though undergoing change. However, it's not as if the zygote or the early embryo does not have, or has lost, its chromosomes; it always had them from the moment it came to be. They just have not been activated yet, for they are not required to be activated for the organism's development at that time in its existence, just as the zygote or early embryo does not need a central nervous system at that time, though it certainly needs it several years later when it is a toddler. Consequently, a more fruitful way to look at the zygote or early embryo is to see it as a unified being with its own genetic structure whose nature requires that in its initial stages it use the maternal mRNA to direct its development. That is, the zygote or early embryo is a *living organism* with certain powers and properties, including the capacity to be acted upon by maternal molecules to facilitate its intrinsically directed purpose for continued development and subsistence of itself as a *whole*.

Second, the central argument for this objection is unsound. The argument goes like this: because a biologically perfect zygote could just as well develop into a hydatidform mole or teratoma as it could a blastocyst, the zygote is not intrinsically directed to develop into a mature human being.[63] This is so because a zygote's continued development "depends at each moment on several factors: the progressive actualization of its own genetically coded information, the actualization of pieces of information that originate *de novo* during the embryonic process, and exogenous information independent of the control of the zygote."[64] But this argument is based on a false premise. As Antoine Suarez points out, complete hydatidform moles and teratomas do not result from normal, biologically complete, conceptions but arise from entities that are in fact flawed or deficient "fertilizations" and thus have no intrinsically directed capacity to develop into a normal human being.[65]

Nevertheless, Lee has argued that "even if it were true that some information is received from maternal molecules, this would not show that the preimplantation embryo was not a complete human individual."[66] He goes on to illustrate this point by showing that the human organism, like every other organism, operates in such a way throughout its existence that it interacts with, and is affected by, other entities without ceasing to be itself:

> There is no reason to expect that *all* of the future features of the developing organism should be already determined by its internal genetic make-up. Environmental conditions, which could include maternal molecules within the uterus, can determine many of the future characteristics of the developing organism. Indeed, throughout his or her life, many of this organism's important characteristics will arise from interaction between his or her own internal power and the environment. If informational factors are received from maternal molecules, still, how this information fits within the overall development of this organism is determined from within the organism's own directed growth. Thus, if any information is received from maternal molecules, it does not determine the primary organization and direction of the multitude of cell differentiations and acquisitions and uses of nutrition occurring in this organic system. That primary organization comes from within the embryo itself.[67]

Consider an illustration. When one contracts pneumonia, one does not have within one's chromosomes the necessary components to fight off the disease. That is why one takes antibiotics to kill the microorganisms that infect the lungs. Thus, without the antibiotics, one may die. But if one is no less a whole human organism simply because one relies on the antibiotics for one's survival and continued development, the zygote or early embryo is no less a whole human organism simply because it relies on maternal molecules.[68]

Abortion Methods

We will now move on to present the different methods of abortion that are employed by physicians and other medical personnel to terminate a pregnancy and, consequently, end the life of the unborn human being. Although there are some forms of birth control, such as the IUD, that result in the killing of the early embryo, we will focus on abortions that are performed by medical personnel at abortion clinics and hospitals.

Most Frequently Used Methods

Abortion surveillance statistics of any given year are published several years later. So the most recent statistics available for this book are from 2002. According to a late-2005 report published by the Centers for Disease Control (CDC), there were 854,122 legal abortions performed in the United States in 2002, a 0.1% increase from the 2001 number of 853,485.[69] The number of legal abortions per year in the United States went from 615,831 in 1973 to 1,429,247 in 1990.[70] However, after 1990, the number of legal abortions began to steadily decline, dropping below the 1 million mark in 1998 (884,273) for the first time since 1976 (988,267).[71]

Of the legal abortions procured in 2002, 92.4% were performed by methods under the general category "curettage," which means that some scraping of the uterus is employed as part of the abortion procedure.[72] According to the CDC, this category includes "suction curettage," "sharp curettage" (or D & C, dilation and curettage), and D & E (dilation and evacuation).[73] The first two are performed in the first trimester,[74] though D & C has become increasingly rare.[75] The third method, according to Planned Parenthood Federation of America (PPFA),[76] is performed after the first trimester. The following brief descriptions of each procedure rely mostly, though not entirely, on abortion choice and official government publications.

Suction curettage

The state of Michigan's Department of Community Health offers the following description of suction curettage, by far the most frequently used method of abortion:

> After dilation, a plastic tube about the diameter of a pencil is then inserted into the uterus through the enlarged cervix. The tube is attached to a pump which then suctions out the fetus, the placenta and other uterine contents. After the suctioning, the physician may find it necessary to use a curette (a sharp, spoon-like instrument) to gently scrape the walls of the uterus to make sure all the fragments of the fetus and placenta have been removed from the uterus.[77]

Another type of suction abortion, though performed early in pregnancy, is manual vacuum aspiration (MVA). It is a form of surgical abortion (according to PPFA), involves "suction," and is performed early in pregnancy and usually up to the 10th week of pregnancy. The Planned Parenthood website explains: "MVA can be done from the time when a woman suspects pregnancy up to about 10 weeks from her last period. The cervix is dilated, and the uterus is emptied with a handheld syringe. If a definitive gestational sac is not identified within the removed tissue, the woman is tested for possible ectopic pregnancy. MVA takes about 10 minutes."[78]

Abortion provider and physician, Warren Hern, M.D., notes that during a suction abortion "the physician will usually first notice a quantity of amniotic fluid, followed by placenta and fetal parts, which are more or less identifiable."[79]

Dilation and curettage (D & C)   rare

Former U.S. Surgeon General C. Everett Koop, an opponent of abortion choice, explains this type of abortion in graphic detail:

> In this procedure, usually before the twelfth or thirteenth week of pregnancy, the uterus is approached through the vagina. The cervix is stretched to permit the insertion of a curette, a tiny hoelike instrument. The surgeon then scrapes the wall of the uterus, cutting the baby's body to pieces and scraping the placenta from its attachments on the uterine wall. Bleeding is considerable.[80]

As I noted above, this procedure has become increasingly rare, largely because a suction abortion is much more efficient in evacuating the unborn human being from the womb. In fact, according to the 2002 CDC report, only 2.4% of all abortions performed that year were "sharp curettage,"[81] which includes both D & C and D & E,[82] the method we will look at next.

Dilation and evacuation (D & E)

According to abortion-choice advocate K. Kaufmann, "at some clinics, D & Es are only done up to the 16th and 18th week of pregnancy; at others, the limit is 20 or 22 weeks. Only a handful of providers go up to 24 or 25 weeks."[83] On its official website, Planned Parenthood describes this method of abortion in the following way:

Dilation and evacuation (D & E) is performed in two steps.

The first step of a D & E involves cervical preparation (softening and dilation).

- The vagina is washed with an antiseptic.
- Absorbent dilators may be put into the cervix, where they remain for several hours, sometimes overnight. Misoprostol may also be used to facilitate dilation of the cervix.

During the second step of a D & E

- The woman may be given medication to ease pain and/or prevent infection.
- A local anesthetic is injected into or near the cervix. General anesthesia can also be used.
- The dilators are removed from the cervix.

The fetus and other products of conception are removed from the uterus with surgical instruments and suction curettage. This procedure takes about 10–20 minutes.[84]

Dr. Hern is much more illustrative in his description of this procedure: "We have reached a point in this particular technology [D & E abortion] where there is no possibility of denial of an act of destruction by the operator. It is before one's eyes. The sensations of dismemberment flow through the forceps like an electric current."[85] Hern writes in his text, *Abortion Practice*, on the difficulties that may arise in performing this method in the latter portion of the second trimester: "The procedure changes significantly at 21 weeks because the fetal tissues become much more cohesive and difficult to dismember. . . . A long curved Mayo scissors may be necessary to decapitate and dismember the fetus."[86]

Lesser Used Methods

The following methods of abortion are used less often for a variety of reasons, though mostly because they are employed early in pregnancy (long before a vast majority of potential abortion clients seek out an abortion provider), late in pregnancy (when there are far fewer abortions), or are not as efficient as alternative methods.

Medical (or "chemical") abortions

These are nonsurgical methods of abortion offered by some, though not all, abortion clinics in the United States. According to Planned Parenthood's website, either one of two combinations of drugs may be used to induce a medical abortion: Methotrexate-Misoprostol, and Mifepristone (RU-486)-Misoprostol. Concerning the former, "studies have shown this method to be effective up to 49 days after the first day of the last menstrual period."[87] It is administered in the following way:

A woman receives an injection of methotrexate from her clinician. About five days later she inserts misoprostol tablets into her vagina. The pregnancy usually ends at home within a day or two, although 15–20 percent of women undergoing this procedure require up to four weeks to terminate their pregnancies successfully.... The pre-embryo or embryo and other products of conception that develop during pregnancy are passed out through the vagina. Complete abortion will occur in 92–96% of women receiving this regimen.[88]

The latter drug combination, Mifepristone-Misoprostol, has been shown by studies "to be effective up to 63 days after the first day of the last menstrual period."[89] Planned Parenthood's website describes how it works:

A woman swallows a dose of mifepristone under the guidance of her clinician. In a few days she uses the second medication, misoprostol. The pregnancy usually ends within four hours after taking the misoprostol. The pre-embryo or embryo and other products of conception that develop during pregnancy are passed out through the vagina. Complete abortion will occur in 96–97 percent of women receiving this regimen.[90]

According to the 2002 CDC report, medical abortions (which it calls "intrauterine instillation") make up 0.8% of all the abortions. However, the report includes in this number saline or prostaglandin abortions, which it states "was used rarely (0.3% of all abortions), primarily at" less than "8 weeks' or" more than "16 weeks' gestation" (see Induction).[91]

Induction

Although induction is a method not often employed in abortions in the second or third trimester, it may be accomplished in one of two ways. "The doctor may insert a medication called prostaglandin into the vagina or give the medication in the form of an injection to start contractions that will expel the fetus." Or he may inject saline solution "into the uterus to start contractions and cause a stillbirth." According to Planned Parenthood, "the discomfort from the contractions, which usually last from six to 24 hours, may be relieved with oral medication." The procedure "is usually done in a hospital and usually requires staying overnight or longer."[92] According to the CDC, as I noted above, saline and prostaglandin made up only 0.3% of all legal abortions in 2002,[93] which is about 2,562 abortions.

Dr. Koop points out that because the saline abortion requires that the physician inject concentrated salt solution into amniotic fluid in which the unborn lives, this solution "is absorbed" by the unborn "both through the lungs and the gastrointestinal tract, producing changes in the osmotic pressure." In addition, "the outer layer of skin is burned off by the high concentration of salt. It takes about an hour to kill the baby by this slow method. The mother usually goes into labor about a day later and delivers a dead, shriveled baby [if it is a post 16-week saline abortion]."[94]

Dilation and extraction (D & X) or "partial-birth abortion"

As I noted in Chapter 2, D & X abortion is sometimes the procedure of choice for physicians performing abortions in the late second and third trimesters.[95] Using ultrasound, the doctor grips the fetus's legs with forceps. The unborn is then pulled out through the birth canal and delivered with the exception of its head. While the head is in the womb the doctor penetrates the live fetus's skull with scissors, opens the scissors to enlarge the hole, and then inserts a catheter. The fetus's brain is vacuumed out, resulting in the skull's collapse. The doctor then completes the womb's evacuation by removing a dead fetus.

Martin Haskell, M.D., the creator of the procedure, offers a more clinical description of the procedure:

> At this point [i.e., when the child has been delivered except for the head], the right-handed surgeon slides the fingers of the left hand along the back of the fetus and "hooks" the shoulders of the fetus with the index and ring fingers (palm down). Next he slides the tip of the middle finger along the spine towards the skull while applying traction to the shoulders and lower extremities. The middle finger lifts and pushes the anterior cervical lip out of the way. While maintaining this tension, lifting the cervix and applying traction to the shoulders with the fingers of the left hand, the surgeon takes a pair of blunt curved Metzenbaum scissors in the right hand. He carefully advances the tip, curved down, along the spine and under his middle finger until he feels it contact the base of the skull under the tip of his middle finger. Reassessing proper placement of the closed scissors tip and safe elevation of the cervix, the surgeon then forces the scissors into the base of the skull or into the foramen magnum. Having safely entered the skull, he spreads the scissors to enlarge the opening. The surgeon removes the scissors and introduces a suction catheter into this hole and evacuates the skull contents. With the catheter still in place, he applies traction to the fetus, removing it completely from the patient.[96]

It is not clear how many such abortions are performed yearly in the United States as the CDC does not have a category for D & X, although it does have a category it labels "other" which may include D & X. Nevertheless, it is likely the numbers are in the thousands. Dr. Haskell admitted, in 1992, that he had already applied his then-new surgical invention on 700 patients and that he "routinely performs this procedure on all patients 20 through 24 weeks...with certain exceptions... [and] on selected patients 25 through 26 weeks."[97] A 1997 article in *The New Republic*, a magazine whose editorial position is generally supportive of abortion choice, cites the work of Ruth Padawer, a staff writer for the local Bergen County, New Jersey, newspaper, *The Record*: "She called local clinics, asked how many [partial-birth abortions] they performed, did some math and wrote up her conclusions: 'Interviews with physicians who use the method reveal that in New Jersey alone, at least 1,500 partial-birth abortions are performed each year, three times the supposed national rate. Moreover, doctors say only a minuscule amount are for medical reasons.'"[98] Dr. Haskell's practice and Ms. Padawer's story were confirmed by a stunning confession by Ron Fitzsimmons, then–executive director of the National Coalition of Abortion Providers. Since 1995, when the political debate over partial-birth abortion began, Fitzsimmons and his abortion-choice colleagues had claimed that partial-birth abortion was extremely rare (about 450 per year) and performed only in late-term pregnancy for serious reasons such as severe fetal deformity and to save the life of the mother. In 1997, Fitzsimmons, on an episode of ABC News' *Nightline* admitted, in answer to Ted Koppel's question, "What were you lying through your teeth about?" "When I said that the procedures were performed only in about 450 cases and only in those severe circumstances. That was not accurate. But we have no apologies for this procedure."[99] According to *The New Republic*'s account, "Fitzsimmons tried, several times, to tell Koppel that, in fact, 3,000 to 5,000 partial-birth abortions were performed every year on fetuses twenty weeks or older; and, of course, only 500 to 750 were performed for reasons of maternal health in the third trimester."[100] Fitzsimmons told the *New York Times* that "in the vast majority of cases, the procedure is performed on a healthy mother with a healthy fetus that is 20 weeks or more along" and is "performed far more often than his colleagues have acknowledged."[101]

Hysterotomy

Performed in some late-term abortions, this technique's use has dropped significantly since the first decade of legalized abortion in the United States. Dr. Koop explains the procedure:

A hysterotomy is exactly the same as a Cesarean section with one difference – in a Cesarean section the operation is usually performed to save

Number of Weeks	Status of Development	Type of Abortion	% of total abortions

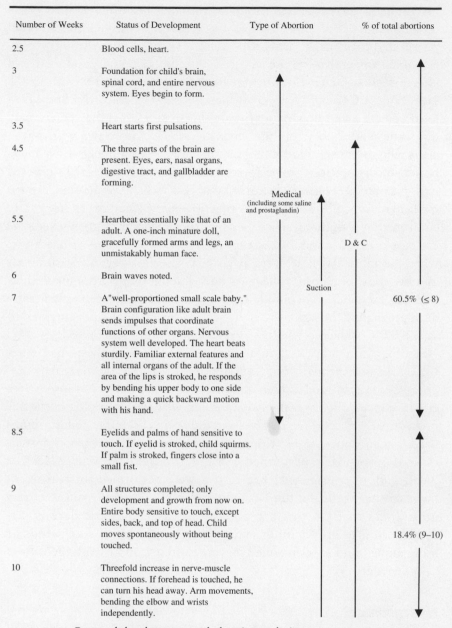

2.5	Blood cells, heart.		
3	Foundation for child's brain, spinal cord, and entire nervous system. Eyes begin to form.		
3.5	Heart starts first pulsations.		
4.5	The three parts of the brain are present. Eyes, ears, nasal organs, digestive tract, and gallbladder are forming.		
		Medical (including some saline and prostaglandin)	
5.5	Heartbeat essentially like that of an adult. A one-inch miniature doll, gracefully formed arms and legs, an unmistakably human face.	D & C	
6	Brain waves noted.		
		Suction	
7	A "well-proportioned small scale baby." Brain configuration like adult brain sends impulses that coordinate functions of other organs. Nervous system well developed. The heart beats sturdily. Familiar external features and all internal organs of the adult. If the area of the lips is stroked, he responds by bending his upper body to one side and making a quick backward motion with his hand.		60.5% (≤ 8)
8.5	Eyelids and palms of hand sensitive to touch. If eyelid is stroked, child squirms. If palm is stroked, fingers close into a small fist.		
9	All structures completed; only development and growth from now on. Entire body sensitive to touch, except sides, back, and top of head. Child moves spontaneously without being touched.		18.4% (9–10)
10	Threefold increase in nerve-muscle connections. If forehead is touched, he can turn his head away. Arm movements, bending the elbow and wrists independently.		

FIGURE 4.1. Prenatal development and abortion techniques.

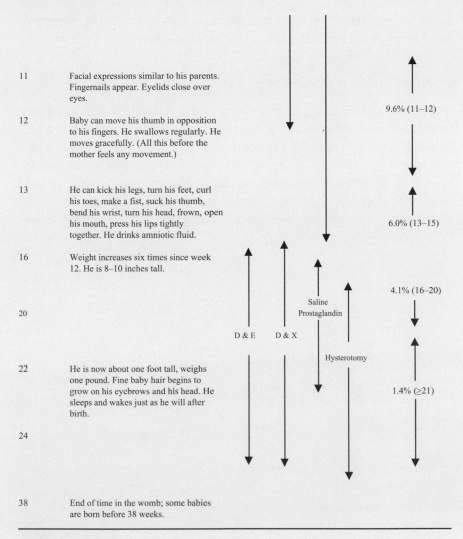

FIGURE 4.1. (cont.)

the life of the baby, whereas a hysterotomy is performed to kill the baby. These babies look very much like other babies except that they are small and weigh, for example, about two pounds at the end of a twenty-four week pregnancy. They are truly alive, but they are allowed to die through neglect or sometimes killed by a direct act.[102]

Although hysterotomies do occur, their numbers are so small that the CDC since 1997 has included them under the category "other."[103] In fact, in the last year the CDC reported them in a separate category (1996), it listed them with hysterectomies with a total number of 36.[104]

CONCLUSION: TYING IT ALL TOGETHER

To better grasp the connection between prenatal development and when certain abortion techniques are most often performed in pregnancy, see Figure 4.1, which originally appeared as a table in Schwarz's 1990 book, *The Moral Question of Abortion*.[105] I have amended and updated it in light of contemporary changes in the use of certain abortion procedures. I have also added a column that lists the percentage of the total abortions performed during the weeks in question (as of the latest CDC report).

5

POPULAR ARGUMENTS

Pity, Tolerance, and Ad Hominem

Arguments for abortion choice are put forth in popular culture – in newsprint, online, and in the broadcast media – with much verve and vigor. But as we shall see, these arguments are offered with little relation to the rules of rational argument, rules that defenders of abortion choice, in their more candid moments and with other issues, would never abandon. The purpose of this chapter is to present and assess those arguments. Of course, not every defender of abortion choice holds to all or any of these arguments. Some of the more sophisticated apologists eschew much of the popular rhetoric and defend their position on other grounds. (These grounds and the arguments for them are the focus of Chapters 3, 6, and 7). But because most people will come into contact with the popular arguments, and because some of them are found in some Supreme Court opinions, it is necessary that we carefully assess them.

In this chapter we will cover three general categories of popular abortion-choice arguments: (1) arguments from pity; (2) arguments from tolerance; and (3) arguments ad hominem.

ARGUMENTS FROM PITY

An argument from pity is an attempt to show the plausibility of one's point of view by trying to move others emotionally, although the reasonableness of the position really stands or falls on the basis of other important factors. Philosopher James B. Freeman writes that one appeals to pity when "one pulls on the 'heartstrings,' presents a most pathetic, tear-jerking story to obtain agreement – not because any good reason has been given but because the hearer feels sorry."[1] Freeman cites a letter to the editor as an example:

> Dear Sir:
>   As a mother of nine children I would like to speak out on the draft everyone is talking about.
>   I am one that is very much against it. I lost a husband in Korea and if they draft from age 18 to 26 I stand to lose fours sons and one daughter.
>   As a mother in poor health I don't think I could take that.
>   Why can't [the president] leave well enough alone and try and find our boys missing or being held some place? – Mrs. L. T.[2]

The problem with Mrs. L. T.'s argument is not that it does not accurately convey to us her true feelings, but that it fails to present any relevant reasons to support her position that draft registration is not the correct public policy. After all, one could readily admit that Mrs. L. T. may be correct when she claims that she would not be emotionally capable of handling a situation in which all her children were war fatalities. But this fact alone is insufficient in establishing that draft registration as a public policy is an unjust idea. For another mother could argue in the same manner that it is unjust to send her money-embezzling children to prison on the basis that she will not be able to handle it emotionally. But whether they morally and legally *deserve* prison is independent of their mother's emotional ability to handle their prison term. Hence, in a moral argument, an appeal to pity is inappropriate when one argues for a position primarily on that basis and ignores relevant facts or philosophical insights that would make such an appeal irrelevant, as in the case of Mrs. L. T.'s letter to the editor. The following arguments for abortion choice are examples of such fallacious appeals to pity. I will conclude with an analysis of the use of such arguments by the U.S. Supreme Court.

Argument from the Dangers of Illegal Abortions

Anyone who has witnessed an abortion-choice demonstration has likely seen on placards and buttons a drawing of a coathanger. This symbol, according to the demonstrators, represents the many women who were either harmed or killed because they either performed illegal abortions on themselves (i.e., the surgery was performed with a "coathanger") or went to unscrupulous physicians (or "backalley butchers"). Hence, as the argument goes, if abortion is made illegal, then women will once again be harmed. Needless to say, this argument serves a powerful rhetorical purpose. However, it is flawed in a significant way: it begs the question.

This fallacy, as we shall see, lurks behind a good percentage of the popular arguments for abortion choice. One begs the question when one assumes what one is trying to prove. For example, if one *concludes* that the Baylor Bears are the best team in the Big 12 conference *because* no team is better, then one is not giving any reasons for this belief other than the conclusion one is trying to prove, since to claim that a team is the *best team* is exactly the same as saying that *no team is better*. Sometimes this fallacy is committed in a more subtle way. For instance, an unsophisticated Christian may argue that he believes in God because the Bible says that God exists and the Bible is God's Word. The Christian is assuming that there is a God who inspired the Bible, but this is the Being whose existence is in question ("Does God exist?"). Hence, by implicitly assuming his conclusion to be true in his appeal to the Bible's authority, the Christian commits the logical fallacy of begging the question.

The question-begging nature of the coathanger argument is easy to discern: only by assuming that the unborn are not fully human does the argument work. For if the unborn are *not* fully human, then the abortion-rights advocate has a legitimate concern, as one would have in overturning a law forbidding appendectomies if countless people were needlessly dying of both appendicitis and illegal operations. But if the unborn *are* fully human, this abortion-choice argument is tantamount to saying that because people die or are harmed while killing other people (i.e., unborn people), the state should make it safe for them to do so. This argument would be advocating a state of affairs in which the government permits its citizens to kill innocent human beings without providing any justification whatsoever. Hence, only by assuming that the unborn are not fully human does this abortion-choice argument work. Therefore, it begs the question.

Even some abortion-choice proponents, who argue for their position in other ways, admit that the coathanger/backalley argument is fallacious. Mary Anne Warren, for example, writes that "the fact that restricting access to abortion has tragic side effects does not, in itself, show that the restrictions are unjustified, since murder is wrong regardless of the consequences of prohibiting it."[3] In other words, one must *first* show that the unborn is not a subject of rights.

Argument from Economic Inequity

Abortion-choice advocates often argue that prior to abortion being legalized, pregnant women who did not go to unscrupulous physicians or "backalley butchers" traveled to foreign nations where abortions were legal. This was an option open only to rich women who could afford such an expense. Hence, *Roe v. Wade* has made the current situation fairer for poor women. Therefore, if abortion is prohibited it will not prevent rich women from having safe and legal abortions elsewhere.[4]

This argument is fallacious. For it *assumes* that legal abortion is a *moral good* that poor women will be denied if abortion is made illegal. But because the morality of abortion is the point under question, the abortion-choice proponent assumes what he is trying to prove and therefore begs the question. One can think of a number of examples to better understand this point. To cite one, we would consider it bizarre if someone argued that the hiring of hit men to kill one's enemies should be legalized, because, after all, the poor do not have easy economic access to such professionals.

In the abortion debate the question of whether abortion entails the death of a being who is fully human must be answered before the question of fairness is even asked. Because equal opportunity to eliminate an innocent human person is not a moral good, the question of whether it is fair that certain rich people will have privileged access to abortion if it becomes illegal must be answered *after* we answer the question of whether abortion in fact is *not* the killing of an innocent human person. For it is not true that the vices of the wealthy are virtues simply because the poor are denied them.

Furthermore, the pro-life advocate could turn this argument on its ear by admitting to the abortion-choice advocate that indeed something economically unjust will occur if abortion on demand is made illegal, namely, that rich unborn humans will be less safe from unjust homicide than are poor unborn humans. But this is more preferable than what is currently occurring, namely, that rich and poor unborn humans are not safe. Of course, the pro-life advocate is assuming that the unborn entity is fully human and the abortion-choice advocate is assuming that it is not. Therefore, the real issue is *not* one of economic inequity but whether the unborn are fully human and hence deserving the protections of our law enjoyed by those of us who are already born.

Argument from Population, Poverty, and Financial Burden

Some abortion-choice advocates make much of both the use of abortion as a means of population control and the financial and emotional burden a child may put on a family. It is argued that in such situations abortion is justified. A number of abortion-choice advocates argue that if abortion is forbidden, then the poor will keep producing more children to draw more welfare. Hence, there is an economic incentive in permitting abortion. There is a major problem with this argument: it is based on bad moral reasoning.

First, this argument does not really support the pro-*choice* position that abortion is a fundamental right that pregnant woman can exercise for any reason she deems fit during the entire nine months of pregnancy (see Chapter 2). For if this argument is successful it only establishes the right to an abortion in the cases of overpopulation, poverty, and financial burden, *not* "for any reason the pregnant woman deems fit." Futhermore, suppose that the world were overpopulated but that pregnant women in such a world *refused* to have abortions. Would the abortion-choice advocate *force* these women to have abortions? If yes, then appealing to overpopulation is not a pro-*choice* argument, for it entails *compulsory abortions*. If the answer is no, then abortion for population control is not relevant to establishing the pro-*choice* position, for it is obvious that women can always choose to not have abortions in the face of an overpopulation problem.

Second, this argument, like the other arguments we have gone over, begs the question. That is, only if the abortion-choicer *assumes* that the unborn poor are not fully human does his argument carry any weight. For if the unborn poor are fully human, the abortion-choicer's plan to eliminate overpopulation and poverty by permitting the extermination of the unborn poor is inconsistent with his own ethic of personal rights. Thus, the question of aborting the unborn poor hinges on the status of the unborn. Furthermore, if the unborn are fully human, then this is also a good argument for infanticide and the killing of all humans we find to be financially burdensome or emotionally taxing. Therefore, only by assuming that the unborn are not fully human does the abortion-choice advocate avoid such horrendous consequences. Thus for this argument to work, the abortion-choicer must beg the question.

Third, underlying this type of abortion-choice argument is a fundamental confusion between the concept of "finding a solution" and the concept of "eliminating a problem." For example, one can eliminate the problem of poverty by executing all poor people, but this would not *really* solve the problem, as it would directly conflict with our basic moral intuition that human persons should not be gratuitously exterminated for the sake of easing economic tension. This "solution" would undermine the very moral principles that ground our compassion for poor people – namely, that they are humans of great worth and should be treated with dignity regardless of their predicament. Similarly, one can eliminate the problem of having a headache by cutting off one's head just as a society can eliminate wife-beating by legalizing wife-killing, but these are certainly not real solutions. Therefore, the argument of the abortion-choice advocate is superfluous unless he can first show that the unborn are not fully human and hence do not deserve to be treated as moral subjects. Philosopher and bioethicist Baruch Brody comments:

> In an age where we doubt the justice of capital punishment even for very dangerous criminals, killing a fetus who has not done any harm, to avoid a future problem it may pose, seems totally unjust. There are indeed many social problems that could be erased simply by destroying those persons who constitute or cause them, but that is a solution repugnant to the values of society itself. In short, then, if the fetus is a human being, the appeal to its being unwanted justifies no abortions.[5]

This is not to minimize the fact that there are tragic circumstances, such as the poor woman with four small children who has become pregnant by her alcoholic husband. But once again we must ask whether the unborn entity is fully human, for *hardship does not justify homicide*. For example, if I knew that killing you would relieve me of future hardship, that in itself would not be sufficient justification for me to kill you. If an abortion-choice supporter knew that his death would help heal a dysfunctional family, would he be morally obligated to agree that the members of this family have a *right* to kill him to achieve this goal? But if the abortion-choice supporter is not obligated to die for others who perceive his death as a benefit for them, why is the unborn obligated to do so?

In rare cases in which a child may bring extra hardship, those in the religious and charitable communities should help lend financial and emotional support to the family, as they well do in many cases. And it may be wise, if it is a case of extreme hardship, for the woman to put her baby up for adoption, so that she may give to others the gift of parenthood. But if the unborn is fully human, killing her is never a morally viable option, just as killing born children, who are fully human (as nearly everyone agrees), is never a morally viable option for parents who seek relief from the burdens of parenthood.

Argument from the Unwanted Child and Child Abuse

Many people in the abortion-choice movement argue that legal abortion will help eliminate unwanted children. They believe that unwantedness is indirectly responsible for a great number of family problems, such as child abuse. Hence, if a family can have the "correct" amount of children at the "proper" times, then these family problems will be greatly reduced if not eliminated.[6] There are several serious problems with this argument.

First, it begs the question, because only by assuming that the unborn are not fully human does this argument work. For if the unborn are fully human, like the abused born children whom we readily admit are fully human, then to kill the unborn is itself a form of child abuse. Would the killing of three-year-olds be morally acceptable if it would eliminate the abuse of five-year-olds? Of course not. But what morally distinguishes the unborn from the born infant, the three-year-old, or the five-year-old? That is the *real* question – "Are the unborn fully human?" – not, "Does abortion help curb child abuse?"

Second, it is very difficult to demonstrate that the moral and metaphysical value of a human being is dependent on whether someone wants or cares for that human being. For example, no one disputes that the homeless are intrinsically valuable even though they are, for the most part, unwanted. But suppose the abortion-choice supporter responds to this by saying, "But you are treating the unborn as if they were as human as the homeless." And this is exactly my point. The question is not whether the unborn are wanted; the question is whether the unborn are fully human.

Third, the unwantedness of children in general tells us a great deal about our moral character as a people but very little about the intrinsic value of the children involved. For it is a self-centered, hedonistic people who do not consider it a self-evident obligation to care for the most vulnerable and defenseless members of the human race. A lack of caring is a flaw in the one who ought to care, not in the person who ought to be cared for. Hence, whether abortion is morally justified depends on whether the unborn are fully human, not on their wantedness.

Fourth, the appeal to wantedness for determining value applies only to *things* that have economic value based on their demand. For example, tickets to the Super Bowl are valuable because they are desired by people. If nobody cared about the Super Bowl, ticket prices would be lowered to attract more people to the game. Hence, their value would decrease as demand decreased. The musical talents of Bob Dylan are another example of such a "thing." Sony Records is willing to pay Mr. Dylan millions of dollars to record an album simply because his talents help Sony earn profits for its investors. Now Mr. Dylan's value as a *human person* is the same regardless of whether his skills as a musician and composer are wanted. For to say that his human value is equal to the economic value of his skills would be to undermine the very system of rights and obligations that serve as the foundation for our claim that civil and human rights are universal in scope and no respector of persons. Hence, only if the unborn entity is a *thing*, and *not* fully human, does its wantedness have a bearing on its value. Therefore, the question is not whether the unborn entity is wanted but whether it is fully human, for if it is fully human its wantedness is irrelevant to its intrinsic value.

Psychologist Dr. Sidney Callahan has made the observation that the problem with the abortion-choice argument from "unwantedness" is that it sets a terrible social precedent, for it is clearly implying that "the powerful" (in this case, parents) can determine at will the worth of "the powerless" (in this case, their unborn children). She writes:

> The powerful (including parents) cannot be allowed to want and unwant people at will....
>
> It's destructive of family life for parents even to think in these categories of wanted and unwanted children. By using the words you set up parents with too much power, including psychological power, over their children. Somehow the child is being measured by the parent's attitudes and being defined by the parent's feelings. We usually want only objects, and wanting them or not implies that we are superior, or at least engage in a one-way relationship, to them.
>
> In the same way, men have "wanted" women through the ages. Often a woman's position was precarious and rested on being wanted by some man. The unwanted woman could be cast off when she was no longer a desirable object. She did not have an intrinsic dignity beyond wanting.[7]

It seems, then, that abortion-choice feminists have espoused the least virtuous and most repulsive aspect of "machoism."

Argument from the Deformed and Handicapped Child

Because it is now possible to detect through amniocentesis and other tests whether the unborn entity will turn out to be physically or mentally handicapped,[8] some abortion-choicers argue that abortion should remain a choice for women who do not want to take care of such a child. Another reason cited for advocating the aborting of the defective preborn is that it is better for such children to never be born than to live a life with a serious mental or physical handicap. There are several problems with this argument.

First, this argument, like many of the appeals to "hard cases," does not *really* support the abortion-choice position, the position that abortion is a fundamental right the pregnant woman can exercise for any reason she deems fit during the entire nine months of pregnancy (see Chapter 2). In other words, if this argument is successful in showing that abortion is justified in the case of a woman pregnant with a deformed or handicapped fetus, it only establishes the right to an abortion in such cases, *not* "for *any* reason the pregnant woman deems fit" including when her unborn child is perfectly healthy (which is the case in almost every abortion performed in America).

Second, like many of the abortion-choice arguments, this argument begs the question by assuming that the unborn entity is not fully human. For if the unborn are fully human, then to promote the aborting of the handicapped unborn is tantamount to promoting the execution of hand-icapped people who are already born. But such a practice is morally reprehensible. Are not adults with the same deformities human? Then so too are smaller people. In fact, abortion-choicers Peter Singer and Helga Kuhse, who argue for their position in other ways, admit that "pro-life groups are right about one thing: the location of the baby inside or outside the womb cannot make such a crucial moral difference.... The solution, however, is not to accept the pro-life view that the fetus is a human being with the same moral status as yours or mine. The solution is the very opposite: to abandon the idea that all human life is of equal worth."[9] Although I do not agree with this conclusion, and will argue against it in Chapter 6, Singer and Kuhse make an important observation: the question is not whether a particular unborn entity is physically or mentally handicapped, but whether it is fully human and deserving of all the rights of such a status.

Third, it is not clear that we can make sense of the notion that certain human beings are better off not existing. For one thing, how can one compare nonexistence with existence when they do not have any-thing in common? How can one be better off not existing if one is not there to appreciate the joy of such a "state" (whatever that means)? Former Surgeon General C. Everett Koop, who worked for years with severely deformed infants as a pediatric surgeon at Philadelphia's Chil-dren's Hospital, observed that "it has been my constant experience that disability and unhappiness do not necessarily go together."[10] He states:

> Some of the most unhappy children whom I have known have all of their physical and mental faculties, and on the other hand some of the happi-est youngsters have borne burdens which I myself would find very diffi-cult to bear. Our obligation in such circumstances is to find alternatives

for the problems our patients face. I don't consider death an acceptable alternative. With our technology and creativity, we are merely at the beginning of what we can do educationally and in the field of leisure activities for such youngsters. And who knows what happiness is for another person?[11]

This is not to say that there are not tragedies in life and that having a handicapped child is not a difficult burden to carry. But it is important to realize that if the unborn entity is fully human, homicide cannot be justified simply because it relieves one of a terrible burden. Though it may be rather harsh to accept, it seems fundamental to correct moral reasoning that *it is better to suffer evil rather than to inflict it*.[12] For if this moral precept were not true, all so-called moral dilemmas would be easily soluble by simply appealing to one's own relief from suffering. But in such a world the antidote would be worse than the poison, for people would then have a right to harm another if it relieved them of a burden. None of us has a right to expect someone else, whether it is an unborn child or a full-grown adult, to forfeit his or her life so that we may be relieved of a burden. I, and I'm sure a great number of other people, would find such a world morally intolerable.

Moreover, it should not be forgotten that a handicapped child can give both society and the family into which it has been born an opportunity to exercise true compassion, love, charity, and kindness. It is an assault upon our common humanity to deny our capacity to attain virtue in the presence of suffering and/or disability.

A society whose ethic asserts that certain preborn human beings forfeit their right to life simply because they have a certain physical deformity or mental handicap is a society that has put in its social fabric premises that will make it more likely for its citizens to judge those born human beings with the same flaws as having lives "not worth living." For passing through the birth canal, as passing through the Panama Canal, does nothing to change who one is. The logic of this conclusion was played out in a real-life situation in 1982.[13] That year, an Indiana newborn, Infant Doe, who was born with Down's syndrome and a congenital defect that prevented food from reaching her stomach, was permitted to die at the request of her parents who asked the attending physician to withold food and water from the infant. This parental decision was upheld by an Indiana court. Since her stomach problem was correctable by surgery, if Infant Doe had not been "retarded," there is no doubt that the parents would have requested the necessary surgery. So it was not her inability to eat that killed Infant Doe, but parents who neglected her simply because she had Down's syndrome. While commenting on this case, columnist George Will, writes about his own son, Jonathan, who is a Down's syndrome citizen:

> When a commentator has a direct personal interest in an issue, it behooves him to say so. Some of my best friends are Down's syndrome citizens. (Citizens are what Down's syndrome children are if they avoid being homicide victims in hospitals.)
>
> Jonathan Will, 10, fourth-grader and Orioles fan (and the best Wiffle-ball hitter in southern Maryland), has Down's syndrome. He does not "suffer from" (as newspapers are wont to say) Down's syndrome. He suffers from nothing, except anxiety about the Orioles' lousy start. He is doing nicely, thank you. But he is bound to have quite enough problems dealing with society – receiving rights, let alone empathy. He can do without people like Infant Doe's parents, and courts like Indiana's asserting by their actions the principle that people like him are less than fully human. On the evidence, Down's syndrome citizens have little to learn about being human from people responsible for the death of Infant Doe.[14]

Someone may respond to all of the above by asking the question, "But how can you force someone to bring a handicapped child into the world?" This question, of course, *assumes* that the unborn human is not fully a person. Thus, like the arguments we have already gone over, it begs the question. But suppose the unborn is fully human, then the child in the womb is *already in the world*. Hence, the question would be misguided, since nobody would be forcing anyone to bring a handicapped child into the world; the child is already in the world. Pro-lifers just want the handicapped children who are already in the world, born and unborn, to be protected from unjust homicide.

What about the case of severe handicap, such as anencephaly? According to the *American Medical Association Encyclopedia of Medicine*, anencephaly is the "absence at birth of the brain, cranial vault (top of the skull), and spinal cord. Most affected infants are stillborn or survive only a few hours." Anencephaly occurs "due to a failure in development of the neural tube, the nerve tissue in the embryo that eventually develops into the spinal cord and brain." A woman can know early in pregnancy that she is carrying an anencephalic baby "by measurement of *alphafetoprotein*, by *ultrasound scanning*, and by *amnio-centesis*."[15]

Although severely damaged, the anencephalic child is still a self-integrated human organism. Krason offers a helpful analogy found in the work of Germain Grisez: the anencephalic is much like a human being who remains alive for a short period of time after his head is blown off by a gunshot. "Such a person," writes Krason "is human and remains such until he dies." Because "the anencephalic originated as a human and developed normally up to the point when the neural tube failed to close," the child "thus can be viewed as a human being, albeit a damaged one, whose abnormality will cause his death shortly after birth, like the gunshot wounded person will die a short while after his wound."[16] A damaged human is not a nonhuman. Thus, the anencephalic child, or any preborn human being who is severely handicapped, raises the same questions that arise whenever we deal with postnatal human beings who are damaged. However, their humanness is not diminished as a result of their unfortunate state. Some philosophers, nevertheless, argue that the unborn – anencephalic or not – are not moral persons. These arguments will be assessed in Chapter 6. Consequently, if the unborn is a moral person, that is, fully human, the case of the severely deformed preborn should be assessed in the same way we assess the case of the person who is alive but has had his head blown off. So, again, the real question is whether the unborn is a full-fledged member of the moral community of persons. Therefore, the appeal to the unborn's handicap or deformity to justify abortion begs the question.

Argument from Interference in Career

This argument has been used by many abortion-choicers in popular debate. It has been put forth in a scholarly forum by Virginia Ramey Mollenkott.[17] She begins her article by pointing out the perils of being a woman in today's society. She cites the fact that even if a sexually active woman uses the most effective contraceptives available, failure could occur and she could still get pregnant. She then asks, "How is a married woman able to plan schooling or commit herself to a career or vocation as long as her life is continually open to the disruption of unplanned pregnancies?" Mollenkott then concludes, "Unless, of course, she can fall back on an abortion when all else fails."[18]

The fundamental problem with this argument, like all the others we have covered thus far, is that it begs the question by assuming that the unborn are not fully human. For what would we think of a parent who killed his two-year-old because the child interfered with the parent's ability to advance in his occupation? We would find such an act morally reprehensible. Therefore, the abortion-choice position hinges on whether the unborn human being is a full-fledged member of the human community, not on appeals to careers or occupations.

Argument from Rape and Incest

A woman who becomes pregnant due to an act of either rape or incest is a victim of a horribly violent and morally reprehensible crime. Although pregnancy as a result of either rape or incest is extremely rare,[19] pregnancy does occur in some instances. Bioethicist Andrew Varga, an opponent of abortion, summarizes the argument from rape and incest:

> It is argued that in these tragic cases the great value of the mental health of a woman who becomes pregnant as a result of rape or incest can best be safe-guarded by abortion. It is also said that a pregnancy caused by rape or incest is the result of a grave injustice and that the victim should not be obliged to carry the fetus to viability. This would keep reminding her for nine months of the violence committed against her and would just increase her mental anguish. It is reasoned that the value of the woman's mental health is greater than the value of the fetus. In addition, it is maintained that the fetus is an aggressor against the woman's integrity and personal life; it is only just and morally defensible to repel an aggressor even by killing him if that is the only way to defend personal and human values. It is concluded, then, that abortion is justified in these cases.[20]

There are several problems with this argument. First, this argument is not relevant to the case for abortion on demand, the position defended by the popular abortion-choice movement. This position states that a woman has a *right* to have an abortion for virtully *any* reason during the entire nine months of pregnancy (see Chapter 2). To argue for abortion on demand from the hard cases of rape and incest is like trying to argue for the elimination of traffic laws from the fact that one might have to violate some of them in rare circumstances, such as when one's spouse or child needs to be rushed to the hospital. It is important to remember that the abortion-choice position, and the current regime in American law, is that abortion is a fundamental right that may be exercised solely at the discretion of the pregnant women in consultation with a physician prepared to perform the procedure. Consequently, if there were not cases of rape or incest, there would still be a right to abortion, according to this jurisprudential understanding. Thus, the appeals to rape and incest are *literally irrelevant* to establishing a right to abortion. (For more on the question of abortion *rights* and popular appeals to pity, see the section, Social Necessity of Abortion for Women's Equality).

Second, the unborn entity is *not* an aggressor when its presence does not endanger its mother's life (as in the case of a tubal pregnancy). It is the rapist who is the aggressor. The unborn entity is just as much an innocent victim as its mother. Hence, abortion cannot be justified on the basis that the unborn is an aggressor.

Third, this argument begs the question by assuming that the unborn is not fully human. For if the unborn is fully human, then we must ask whether the relieving of the woman's mental suffering justifies the killing of an innocent human being. *But homicide of another is never justified to relieve one of emotional distress.* Although such a judgment is indeed anguishing, we must not forget that the same innocent unborn entity that the career-oriented woman will abort to avoid interference with a job promotion is biologically and morally indistinguishable from the unborn entity that results from an act of rape or incest. Hence, the argument from rape and incest is successful only if the unborn is not fully human.

Fourth, if the unborn is fully human (which is the *real* question), to request that its life be forfeited for the alleged benefit of another is to violate a basic intuition of ethical judgment: "we may never kill innocent person B to save person A." For example, "we cannot kill John by removing a vital organ in order to save Mary, who needs it. This is not a lack of compassion for Mary; it is the refusal to commit murder, even for a good cause. John has a right not to be killed to benefit Mary, even to save her life. Mary has the same right. We could not kill the woman to benefit the child. Equally, we cannot kill the child to benefit the woman." In abortion, "the child is being sacrificed for the benefit of another. He has no duty to do this; it is not right to force him. Would those who favor abortion for rape volunteer their lives so that another may be benefited in a similar way? If not, is it right to force this on another person? If yes, at least they have the opportunity to make a choice; the child does not."[21] Simply because some people believe that an unborn child's death may result in the happiness of another does not mean that the child has a duty to die.

Some abortion-rights advocates claim that the pro-lifer lacks compassion, since the pro-lifer's position on rape and incest forces a woman to carry her baby against her will. Nothing could be further from the truth. It is the rapist who has already *forced* this woman to carry her child, not the pro-lifer. The pro-life advocate merely wants to prevent another innocent human being (the unborn entity) from being a victim of another violent and morally reprehensible act, abortion, for two wrongs do not make a right. What makes abortion evil is the same thing that makes rape evil: an innocent human person is brutally violated and dehumanized. Unwillingness to endorse unjustified homicide is no lack of compassion.

As Schwarz points out with the following example, sometimes the moral thing to do is not the most pleasant:

> A person in a concentration camp may have the opportunity to become an informer, which means a better life for him. But it also means betraying his friends and causing them additional suffering. Morally, he is forced to remain in his present, pitiable state, rather than do a moral evil, namely, betraying his friends, perhaps causing their deaths. If a woman is forced to continue a pregnancy, the case is similar in this respect, that she too is forced to remain in a pitiable state because the alternative is a moral evil, the killing of an innocent child.[22]

Fifth, Michael Bauman has observed: "A child does not lose its right to life simply because its father or its mother was a sexual criminal or a deviate."[23] Bauman also points out that in using the rape/incest argument the abortion-choicer is making the problematic assumption that the *rape victim* is the one best suited to administer justice and should be permitted to kill the criminal's offspring. But if the unborn entity is fully human (which is the *real* question), this type of "justice" does not resemble what reasonable people have thought of as justice, for "a civilized nation does not permit the victim of a crime to pass a death sentence on the criminal's offspring. *To empower the victim of a sex offense to kill the offender's child is an even more deplorable act than the rape that conceived it.* The child conceived by rape or incest is a victim, too. In America, we do not execute victims."[24] Bauman concludes:

> Because ours is a government of laws and not of men, we must not consign justice and morality to the pain-beguiled whims of victims. They, of all people, might be the least able to render a just verdict or to identify the path of highest virtue. I am convinced that the more monstrously one is mistreated, the more likely it is that revenge and personal expedience will look to that person like goodness. While rape victims most certainly know best the horror and indignity of the crime in question, being its victims does not confer upon them either ethical or jurisprudential expertise. Nor does it enable them to balance the scales of justice or satisfy the demands of the moral imperative with care, knowledge, finesse, or precision. If one was an uninformed or inept ethicist or penologist before the crime, as most of us undoubtedly are, being a victim does not alter that fact at all. Justice is traditionally portrayed as blind, not because she was victimized and had her eyes criminally removed, but because she is impartial. Rape victims, like all other crime victims, rarely can be trusted to be sufficiently impartial or dependably ethical, especially seeing that they so often decide that the best alternative open to them is to kill the criminal's child.[25]

No moral person denies the tragedy and degradation of rape and incest. These are horrible crimes that result in emotional, psychological, physical, and spiritual damage to their victims. However, to countenance abortion in such cases is to turn on its head a principle of ethics that seems to be as well-grounded a moral intuition as one can find: "That one has been wronged does not make permissible imposing on one who did not do the wrong (and was not otherwise to blame for it) burdens it would otherwise be impermissible to impose on him."[26] Although, as I argue in Chapter 7, a mother may have less responsibility for a child conceived in rape than a child who came to be as a result of voluntary intercourse, it is does not follow that she, or anyone else, has the moral right to kill the rape-produced child.

Argument from Pity for the Women Prosecuted, Convicted, and/or Sentenced for Murder if Abortion Is Made Illegal

According to abortion-choice supporters, if abortion is made illegal, many women will be prosecuted, convicted, and/or sentenced for murder (a capital offense in some states) because the changed law will entail that abortion in almost every circumstance is the unjustified and premeditated killing of an innocent human person (the unborn). Abortion-choice activists argue that such a situation will unnecessarily cause emotional and familial harm to women who are already in a difficult situation. Such laws, if they are instituted, will lack compassion. But according to the abortion-choice supporter, if the pro-lifer is to remain consistent with her position that the unborn are human persons, then she *must* institute such compassion-lacking laws. On the other hand, if the pro-lifer does not institute such laws, then it is highly doubtful that she *really* believes that the unborn are human persons. In any event, the pro-life position appears to be inconsistent.

There are several problems with this argument. First, if this argument is correct about the pro-lifer's inconsistency, it does not prove that the unborn are not human persons or that abortion is not a great moral evil. It simply reveals that pro-lifers are unwilling to "bite the bullet" and consistently apply their position. The fact that pro-lifers may possess this character flaw does not mean that their arguments for the unborn's full humanity are flawed.

Second, this argument ignores the pre-legalization laws and penalties for illegal abortion and possible reasons they were instituted. Although it is clear that these laws considered the unborn human persons,[27] in most states women were granted immunity from prosecution and in other states the penalties were very light. As I noted in Chapter 2, the Supreme Court in *Roe v. Wade* employed these latter two facts and did not properly assess the former, to conclude that state anti-abortion statutes were not intended to protect the unborn's life but only to protect maternal health, and that this was not consistent with the view offered by the state of Texas that the unborn is a human person under the Fourteenth Amendment of the U.S. Constitution.[28] The problem with the Court's conclusion is that it did not take into account the possible *reasons* the statutes granted women immunity and light sentences, especially considering that in other places the law saw the unborn as persons. Legal scholar James Witherspoon suggests three reasons:

> First, they [the legislatures] might have considered that the woman who would attempt such an act would only do so out of desperation, and that it would be inhumane to inflict criminal penalties on her after having suffered through such an experience. That legislators were moved by such considerations is indicated by the fact that legislatures which did incriminate the woman's participation generally imposed less severe penalties on the woman for this participation than on the person who actually attempted to induce the abortion.
>
> Second, it is also possible that this immunization of women from criminal liability for participation in their own abortions was a result of the paternalism of the era, which limited criminal responsibility of women at the same time that it limited their civil rights. Despite her consent to the act, the woman was considered a victim rather than a perpetrator of the act.
>
> Third, the immunity might have been motivated in part by practical considerations. Often the only testimony which could be secured against the criminal abortionist was that of the woman on whom the abortion was performed; perhaps the woman was granted complete immunity so that she would not be deterred from revealing the crime or from testifying against the abortionist by any risk of incurring criminal liability herself. That the non-incrimination of the woman's participation was motivated by this practical consideration is indicated by the fact that those states which *did* incriminate the woman's participation often enacted statutes granting a woman immunity from prosecution in exchange for her testimony, or providing that this evidence would not be admissible in any criminal prosecution against her.[29]

Thus, it seems likely that by prudently balancing the unborn's personhood, the evil of abortion, the desperation of the woman, and the need for evidence to insure a conviction, jurists and legislators in the past believed that the best way to prevent abortions from occurring and at the same time uphold the sanctity of human life was to criminalize abortion, prosecute the abortionist,[30] grant immunity or a light penalty to the woman, and show her compassion by recognizing that she is the second victim of abortion.

Consequently, if abortion is made illegal because the law comes to recognize the unborn as intrinsically valuable human persons, legislatures, while crafting laws and penalties, and courts, while making judgments as to sentencing, will have to take into consideration the following facts. (1) Unborn human beings are full-fledged members of the human community and to kill them with no justification is unjustified homicide. (2) Because of a general lack of understanding of the true nature of the unborn child – likely due to decades of cultural saturation by abortion-choice rhetoric and little serious philosophical reflection on the pro-life position by the general public – most citizens who procure abortions do so out of well-meaning ignorance. (3) The woman who will seek and obtain an illegal abortion is really a second victim. Women who seek illegal abortions will probably do so out of desperation. Not realizing at the time of the abortion that the procedure kills a real human being, some of these women suffer from depression and guilt feelings after finding out the true nature of the unborn.[31] And because both those who may encourage these women to seek an illegal abortion (family and friends), as well as the abortionist who will be paid for performing this deed, have no intention of discouraging her, it is likely that the pregnant woman will not be fully informed of the unborn's nature (e.g., "You're not carrying a baby, it's a 'product of conception,' 'blob of tissue,' 'a bunch of cells,' etc."). (4) Even if his intention may be to help the woman, the illegal abortionist will not be ignorant of the demands and purpose of the law and the nature of the being that the abortion kills. However, because juries may be reluctant to sentence such a physician to decades in prison let alone the death penalty, a lighter penalty may be easier to secure.[32] (5) The government has an interest in preventing unjustified and premeditated killing of human beings, whether born or unborn, who live within its jurisdiction. Legislators and jurists who intend to pass and enforce laws and penalties prohibiting almost all abortions, if they are to be just, fair, and compassionate, must take into consideration these five points, as the legislators and jurists of the past did prior to the legalization of abortion. There is no doubt, therefore, that the law will reflect these sentiments if abortion is made illegal again.

Third, given my second response to this argument, those who defend it seem to embrace a simplistic view of the purpose of criminal law and the penalties for violating it. For sometimes the purpose of a penalty is to provide an incentive to a polity for the realization of the best possible circumstances for elimination of the prohibited act and protection for its victim, *precisely because* the act in question and the violation of its victim so morally transgresses what is good. For example, in some states it is a capital offense to kill a police officer in the line of duty but not an ordinary citizen on the job, but this does not mean that the ordinary citizen has less value as a person than the police officer. Consequently, precisely because prohibiting the act of abortion advances the public good – because abortion entails in most cases the unjustified killing of an unborn human being – a prudent legislature will take into consideration all the variables and types of individuals ordinarily involved in the act to protect as many unborn human beings as possible.

The Social Necessity of Abortion for Women's Equality

In his famous dissent in *Webster v. Reproductive Health Services* (1990), Justice Harry A. Blackmun claims that without freedom to choose abortion there will be no "full participation of women in the economic and political walks of American life."[33] Blackmun is echoing the call of popular abortion-choice rhetoric that asserts that women cannot achieve social and political equality without control of their reproductive lives. In addition to Blackmun's comments, consider the following put forth by other abortion-choice supporters:

Laurence Tribe, Tyler Professor of Constitutional Law, Harvard Law School:

> Laws restricting abortion so dramatically shape the lives of women, and only of women, that their denial of equality hardly needs detailed elaboration. While men retain the right to sexual and reproductive autonomy, restrictions on abortion deny that autonomy to women. *Laws restricting access to abortion thereby place a real and substantial burden on women's ability to participate in society as equals.*[34] (emphasis mine)

Kate Michelman, President of the National Abortion Rights Action League (NARAL):

> We have to remind people that abortion is the guarantor of a woman's . . . right to participate fully in the social and political life of society.[35]

Nancy S. Erickson, abortion-rights attorney:

This right [to abortion], of necessity *must* be absolute, for if it is not, women will never truly have the ability to plan and to control their own lives.[36]

But the assumption behind this rhetoric – that equality can only be achieved through special surgery (abortion) – implies that women are *naturally* inferior to men, that they need abortion (a form of corrective surgery) to become equal with men. This is hardly consistent with any feminism that claims that men are *not* naturally superior to women. As one feminist publication has pointed out: "How can women ever lose second-class status as long as they are seen as requiring surgery to avoid it? . . . [This] is the premise of male domination throughout the millennia – that it was nature which made men superior and women inferior. Medical technology is offered as a solution to achieve equality; but the premise is wrong. Nature doesn't provide for inequality, and it's an insult to women to say women must change biology in order to fit into society."[37]

It seems to me that this argument is rhetorically powerful in some circles because it taps into an unconscious sexism that assumes that male sexuality is the paradigm of *human* sexuality. Consequently, the inequality does not lie in the nature of women but in the disordered way in which our society places value on that nature. The key to ending this inequality is not to socialize women into the male paradigm, but to celebrate and honor the indispensable role that mothers play in caring for the most vulnerable and defenseless members of our population, the unborn.

There is another reason to reject this argument: it begs the question as to the unborn's full humanity. After all, if the unborn is fully human, then a 30-year-old pregnant woman is identical to her prenatal self 30 years and 5 months ago. And if that is the case, then to have allowed that pregnant woman's mother to abort her 30 years and 5 months ago without justification is to deny the 30-year-old pregnant woman's equal protection under the law as well as the equal protection of the unborn child she is carrying who may herself become a mother in 30 years.

In the July 9, 2000, edition of the *Los Angeles Times* (Orange County edition), Eileen Padberg, a Republican consultant in Irvine, California, offers an argument that serves as a nice foil by which to better grasp the inadequacies, and the ironies, of the social inequality argument. She writes that an implication of the pro-life position is that "the fetus has more rights than" our "wives, sisters, and daughters."[38] But that is not what follows from the pro-life position. Rather, what follows is that all human persons, including wives, sisters (born and unborn), and daughters (born and unborn), retain their dignity and rights as long as they exist, from the moment they come into being. Ironically, by excluding the unborn from the human community, Ms. Padberg diminishes, and puts in peril, the very rights she jealously, and correctly, guards. For once she asserts that it is legally obligatory for our government to exclude certain small, vulnerable, defenseless, and dependent human beings from protection for no other reason than because someone considers their destruction vital to that person's well-being, then it is difficult to know on what moral grounds Ms. Padberg could oppose a totalitarian state or government policy that allows for the exploitation and destruction of wives, sisters, and daughters by powerful people who believe they will live better lives by engaging in such atrocities against these women.

In one place Ms. Padberg seems on the verge of understanding this logic: "We must protect the right for women to make choices about their bodies, for all women, no matter where they live, how old they are or how much money they have."[39] If Ms. Padberg had only taken the principles that undergird this sentiment and extended them, by her imagination, a bit further, she would have discovered a silent group of females, no different in nature from her, who are also entitled to the protection of these principles. For they are being denied the shelter of our Constitution merely because of where they live (they live in wombs), how old they are (they are quite young), and how much money they have (they are naked and penniless), reasons Ms. Padberg correctly judges as irrelevant.

Of course, if there are good philosophical reasons to reject the unborn's full humanity, then *those reasons*, and not the postnatal parental burdens that result from not killing one's unborn offspring, are the proper reasons by which to advance one's case.

Abortion Rights, Arguments from Pity, and the Supreme Court

In his dissenting opinion in *Webster v. Reproductive Health Services* (1989), Justice Harry Blackmun, the author of *Roe*, employs some of the arguments from pity we have already critiqued in this chapter. I will quote him at length:

> Thus, "not with a bang, but a whimper," the plurality discards a landmark case of the last generation [i.e., *Roe v. Wade*], and casts into darkness the hopes and visions of every woman in this country who had come to believe that the Constitution guaranteed her the right to exercise some control over her unique ability to bear children. The plurality does so

either oblivious or insensitive to the fact that millions of women, and their families, have ordered their lives around the right to reproductive choice, and this right has become vital to the full participation of women in the economic and political walks of American life. The plurality would clear the way once again for government to force upon women the physical labor and specific and direct medical and psychological harms that may accompany carrying a fetus to term. The plurality would clear the way again for the State to conscript a woman's body and to force upon her a "distressful life and future." *Roe*, 410 U.S., at 153

The result, as we know from experience, . . . would be that every year hundreds of thousands of women, in desperation, would defy the law, and place their health and safety in the unclean and unsympathetic hands of back-alley abortionists, or they would attempt to perform abortions upon themselves, with disastrous results. Every year, many women, especially poor and minority women, would die or suffer debilitating physical trauma, all in the name of enforced morality or religious dictates or lack of compassion, as it may be.[40]

Blackmun is arguing that because the Supreme Court in the *Webster* decision has given the states greater leverage in restricting abortion rights, all types of horrible consequences will eventually result. But suppose that none or few of the consequences which Blackmun predicts will in fact occur. Suppose that for the most part people obey the new abortion restrictions, and these restrictions do not hinder the "full participation of women in the economic and political walks of American life." Suppose that due to the full reversal of *Roe v. Wade* the pro-life movement gains enormous momentum and convinces a vast majority of Americans of the full humanity of the unborn and our special responsibility in caring for them. If the above occurs, would Blackmun (if he were alive) recant and say that he was wrong in dissenting in *Webster* or would he continue to defend a woman's right to abortion because this right is in his view found in the Fourteenth and Ninth Amendments to the Constitution as he argued in *Roe*? If he opts for the latter and chooses to defend the right to abortion regardless of whether the consequences he warned us about would occur, then these consequences are not relevant to the question of abortion rights. If, however, Blackmun opts for the former and claims that his views are contingent upon these consequences, then abortion is not a right grounded in the right to privacy (as we saw in Chapter 2). It seems then that popular arguments for abortion rights, although a source of powerful rhetoric for a Supreme Court justice, have little to do with the real question of whether there really is a constitutional right to abortion.

Moreover, because it is an emotional appeal that ignores the evidence for the unborn's full humanness, Justice Blackmun's case is a question-begging rhetorical flourish and not a serious argument. We would easily recognize the question-begging nature of this reasoning if Justice Blackmun had applied it in response to the U.S. Congress passing the Fourteenth Amendment to include black Americans as full-fledged citizens:

> Thus, "not with a bang, but a whimper," the Congress in passing the 14th amendment discards a landmark case of the last generation (*Dred Scott*), and casts into darkness the hopes and visions of every property owner in the South who had come to believe that the Constitution guaranteed him the right to exercise some control over his God-given right to own property. The Congress does so either oblivious or insensitive to the fact that millions of property owners, and their families, have ordered their lives around the right to ownership of property, and that this right has become vital to the full participation of Southern gentlemen in the economic and political walks of American life.

ARGUMENTS FROM TOLERANCE

Many people in the abortion-choice movement argue that their position is more tolerant than the pro-life position. After all, they reason, the abortion-choice movement is not forcing pro-life women to have abortions, but the pro-life movement *is* trying to deny all women the option to make a choice. There are at least six arguments offered to defend this abortion-choice position. Because the philosophical basis for these arguments was critically assessed in Chapter 3, my analysis of the following arguments should be read in light of that chapter.

Argument from Religious Pluralism

According to this argument, the question of when protectable human life begins is a personal religious question that one must answer for oneself. As abortion-choicer Mollenkott argues:

> Women who believe that abortion is murder may *never* justly be required to have an abortion. Anti-abortion laws would not affect such women for obvious reasons. But for women whose religious beliefs do permit them to consider abortion (and under certain circumstances require them to do so), anti-abortion legislation would forbid their following these religious convictions.[41]

This argument is flawed in numerous ways. First, it begs the question. For it assumes that in an aborton the only subject of rights is the pregnant woman. Granted, if the unborn is not fully human, then Mollenkott is likely correct that abortion is a matter of preference that the state should not forbid. But, of course, Mollenkott's burden is to show that this accounting of abortion is correct and that the unborn is not a subject of rights.

Second, Mollenkott seems to be saying that because abortion is a "religious" question, the state has no right (or obligation) to restrict or prohibit its practice. But that cannot be right. After all, what if a religious group arose that believed that human personhood did not begin until the age of two and prior to that time parents could sacrifice their children to the Devil? And what if society were to enforce its homicide laws and start prosecuting and convicting group members who engage in this practice? It is hard to believe that anyone would say that Mollenkott would have warrant in applying her principle to this case. Consider what it would sound like:

> Women who believe that child-killing is murder may *never* justly be required to sacrifice their child to the Devil. Anti-child-killing laws would not affect such women for obvious reasons. But for women whose religious beliefs do permit them to consider child-killing (and under certain circumstances require them to do so), anti-child-killing legislation would forbid their following these religious convictions.

Third, the fact that a view on abortion is *consistent* with a religious view does not mean that it is exclusively religious or that it is in violation of the Establishment Clause of the Constitution. For example, many pro-life advocates argue for their position by offering nontheological support for their position (as I do in this book),[42] while many abortion-choice advocates,[43] such as Mollenkott, argue that their position is theologically grounded in the Bible. Hence, it seems right to say that just because a political or moral position may also be found in religious literature, such as the Bible, does not make such a view exclusively "religious." For if it did, then our society, on establishment grounds, would have to dispense with laws forbidding such crimes as murder and robbery simply because such actions are prohibited in the Hebrew-Christian Scriptures. Furthermore, some public policies, such as civil rights and environmental legislation, that are supported by many citizens on religious grounds, would have to be abolished on establishment grounds as well. It is well known, for instance, that those who sought to abolish slavery in 19th-century America – the abolitionists – were unashamed to admit that their moral convictions flowed from their Christian beliefs. Even abortion-choice advocate and Harvard Law Professor, Laurence Tribe, agrees that simply because one's morality has its origin in a religious tradition does not mean that one cannot help shape public policy:

> But as a matter of constitutional law, a question such as this [abortion], having an irreducibly moral dimension, cannot properly be kept out of the political realm merely because many religions and organized religious groups inevitably take strong positions on it. . . . The participation of religious groups in political dialogue *has never been constitutional anathema in the United States*. Quite the contrary. The values reflected in the constitutional guarantees of freedom of religion and political expression argue strongly for the inclusion of church and religious groups, and of religious beliefs and arguments, in public life.[44] (emphasis mine)

Hence, the pro-life position is a legitimate public policy option and does not violate the Establishment Clause of the Constitution.

Fourth, Mollenkott's argument is requesting that pro-lifers act as if their fundamental view of human life is incorrect in addition to requiring that they accept the abortion-choice view of what constitutes both a just society and the moral community of persons. But such a posture is hardly "tolerant" or "accommodating," as philosopher George Mavrodes eloquently points out with the following illustration:

> Let us imagine a person who believes that Jews are human persons, and that the extermination of Jews is murder. Many of us will find that exercise fairly easy, because we are people of that sort ourselves. So we may as well take ourselves to be the people in question. And let us now go on to imagine that we live in a society in which the "termination" of Jews is an everyday routine procedure, a society in which public facilities are provided in every community for this operation, and one in which any citizen is free to identify and denounce Jews and to arrange for their arrest and termination. In that imaginary society, many of us will know people who have themselves participated in these procedures, many of us will drive past the termination centers daily on our way to work, we can often see the smoke rising gently in the late afternoon sky, and so on. And now imagine that someone tells us that if we happen to believe that Jews are human beings then that's O.K., we needn't fear any coercion, nobody requires us to participate in the termination procedure ourselves. We need not work in the gas chamber, we don't have to denounce a Jew, and so on. We can simply mind our own business, walk quietly past the well-trimmed lawns, and (of course) pay our taxes.
>
> Can we get some feel for what it would be like to live in that context? . . . And maybe we can then have some understanding of why they [the right-to-lifers] are unlikely to be satisfied by being told that they don't have to get abortions themselves.[45]

Because the abortion-choice advocate is asking the pro-lifer to act as if her fundamental view of human life is false, the pro-lifer may view her adversary's position as a subtle and patronizing form of intolerance. When the abortion-choice advocate offers the pro-lifer suggestions on how to practice her moral convictions – for example, "Don't like abortion, don't have one" – the pro-lifer does not hear tolerance and openness, but rather something that sounds downright counterintuitive, such as "Don't like murder, don't commit one" or "Don't like slavery, don't own a slave."

Argument from Imposing Morality

There is a variation of the above argument. Some abortion-choice advocates argue that it is simply wrong for anyone to "force" his or her own view of what is morally right on someone else. Consequently, they argue that pro-lifers, by attempting to forbid women from having abortions, are trying to force their morality on others.

But this argument cannot be right, for it is not *always* wrong for the community to institute laws that require that people behave in accordance with certain moral principles.[46] For instance, laws against drunk driving, murdering, smoking crack, robbery, and child molestation are all intended to impose a particular moral perspective on the free moral agency of others. Such laws are instituted because the acts they are intended to limit often obstruct the public good and/or the free agency of other persons, for example, a person killed by a drunk driver is prevented from exercising his free agency. These laws seek to maintain a just and orderly society by limiting some free moral agency (e.g., drunk driving, murdering) so that society sustains a moral ecology hospitable to advancing the public good and in the long run increases free moral agency for a greater number (e.g., fewer people will be killed by drunk drivers and murderers, and hence there will be a greater number who will be able to act as free moral agents). Therefore, a law prohibiting abortion would *unjustly* impose one's morality upon another *only if* the act of abortion is good, morally benign, or does not *unjustly* limit the free agency of another. That is to say, if the unborn entity is fully human, forbidding abortions would be perfectly just, because nearly every abortion would be an unjust act that unjustly limits, or more accurately, does not permit to be actualized, the free agency of another. Consequently, the issue is not whether the pro-life position is a moral perspective that may be forced on others who do not agree with it, but rather, the issue is who and what counts as "an other," a person, a full-fledged member of the human community.

Argument against a Public Policy When There Is Deep Disagreement

There is another, though secular, variation on the first argument from religious pluralism. Some people argue that it is unjust to make a public policy decision in one direction when there is wide diversity of opinion within society. This argument can be outlined in the following way:

1. There can never be a just law requiring uniformity of behavior on any issue on which there is widespread disagreement.
2. There is widespread disagreement on the issue of forbidding abortion.
3. Therefore, any law that forbids people to have abortions is unjust.

Because I critique Judith Jarvis Thomson's sophisticated version of this argument in Chapter 3, I will offer here a response only to this more generic version of the argument.

Premise (1) is clearly false, a judgment for which I offer five reasons. First, if (1) is true, then the abortion-choice advocate must admit that the United States Supreme Court decision, *Roe v. Wade*, is an unjust decision, because the Court ruled that the states that make up the United States, whose statutes prior to the ruling disagreed on the abortion issue, must behave uniformly in accordance with the Court's decision. If, however, the abortion-choice advocate denies that *Roe* was an unjust decision, then he is conceding that it is false that "there can never be a just law requiring uniformity of behavior on any issue on which there is widespread disagreement." Second, if (1) is true, then the abolition of slavery was unjust because there was widespread disagreement of opinion among Americans in the 19th century. Yet nobody would say that slavery should have remained as an institution. Third, if (1) is true, then much of civil rights legislation, about which there was much disagreement, would have been unjust. Fourth, if (1) is true, then a favorite abortion-choice public policy proposal is also unjust. Some abortion-choice advocates believe that the federal and/or state government should use the tax dollars of the American people to fund the abortions of poor women. There are large numbers of Americans, however, some of whom support abortion choice, who do not want their tax dollars used in this way. And fifth, if (1) is true, then laws forbidding pro-life advocates from preventing their unborn neighbors from being aborted would be unjust. One cannot say that there is not widespread disagreement concerning this issue. But these are the very laws the abortion-choice advocate supports. Hence, this argument is self-refuting, since by legislating the abortion-choice perspective the government is "requiring uniformity of behavior on an issue on which there is widespread disagreement." That is to say, the abortion-choice advocate is forcing the pro-lifer to act *as if* her view of prenatal life is false. By making "no law," the government is implicitly affirming the view that the unborn are *not* fully human, which is hardly a neutral position.

Argument from the Impossibility of Legally Stopping Abortion

Maybe the defender of the above argument is making the more subtle point that because there is widespread disagreement on the abortion issue, enforcement of any laws prohibiting abortion would be difficult. In other words, abortions are going to happen anyway, so we ought to make them safe and legal. There are several problems with this argument.

First, it begs the question, because it assumes that the unborn is not fully human. For if the unborn is fully human, this argument is tantamount to saying that because people will unjustly kill other people anyway, we ought to make it safe and legal for them to do so. But unjust killing *is never justified*, even if there is a social penalty in forbidding it.

Second, the evidence strongly suggests that the legalization of abortion has resulted in a dramatic increase in the number of abortions, and that the number of women who died as a result of illegal abortion has been greatly exaggerated.

One sophisticated study concluded that "a reasonable estimate for the actual number of criminal abortions per year in the prelegalization era [prior to 1967] would be from a low of 39,000 (1950) to a high of 210,000 (1961) and a mean of 98,000 per year."[47] On the other hand, Christopher Tietze, an abortion-choice advocate of some standing, "had estimated that there were about 600,000 illegal abortions every year" and that those numbers would remain roughly the same after the procedure was legalized.[48] But as Hadley Arkes points out, "the argument was quickly embarrassed ... by the news – reported by Tietze – that by 1974 [the year after *Roe*] the number of abortions had risen to 900,000 per year, 53 percent about their level in 1972."[49] The number rose to 1.2 million in 1977 and over 1.5 million in 1982.[50]

Bernard Nathanson, M.D., one of the original leaders of the American abortion-choice movement and co-founder of N.A.R.A.L. (the National

Association for the Repeal of Abortion Laws) who has since become pro-life, admits that he and others in the abortion-choice movement intentionally fabricated the number of women who died as a result of illegal abortions. Nathanson writes:

> How many deaths were we talking about when abortion was illegal? In N.A.R.A.L. we generally emphasized the drama of the individual case, not the mass statistics, but when we spoke of the latter it was always "5,000 to 10,000 deaths a year." I confess that I knew the figures were totally false, and I suppose the others did too if they stopped to think of it. But in the "morality" of the revolution, it was a *useful* figure, widely accepted, so why go out of our way to correct it with honest statistics. The overriding concern was to get the laws eliminated, and anything within reason that had to be done was permissible.[51]

Laurence Lader, one of the leaders in the early days of the contemporary abortion-choice movement, once tried to support the figure cited by Nathanson when he claimed that "one study at the University of California's School of Public Health estimated 5,000 to 10,000 abortion deaths annually. Dr. Tietze places the figure nearer 1,000."[52] In response, James T. Burtchaell writes that "it is enlightening to consult the sources to which Lader refers the reader. No University of California study is cited. Instead, Lader refers to a source that depends on a deputy medical examiner of Los Angeles, who simply passes on a conjecture of 5,000 to 10,000 deaths annually. As for Tietze, the article to which Lader refers contains no estimate of or comment upon national abortion mortality."[53] Ironically, Dr. Tietze, in a *New York Times* article, described the numbers offered by advocates like Lader and the early-Nathanson as "unmitigated nonsense."[54] According to moderate abortion-choice bioethicist, Daniel Callahan, Tietze claimed that there were about 500 such deaths per year.[55]

As one would suspect, pro-lifers cite even lower mortality numbers. Physician John Willke and his wife, Barbara Willke, write that according to the U.S. Bureau of Vital Statistics, only 39 women died from illegal abortions in 1972, the year before *Roe*.[56] Andre Hellegers, M.D., the late professor of obstetrics and gynecology at Georgetown University Hospital, testified before a U.S. Senate Judiciary Committee that there had been a steady decrease of abortion-related deaths since 1942. That year there were 1,231 deaths. Because of improved medical care and the use of penicillin, this number fell to 133 by 1968.[57]

Even though all serious people in this debate, whether pro-life or abortion choice, concede that the early abortion-mortality numbers were greatly exaggerated for political purposes, one should not minimize that such deaths were significant losses to the families and loved ones of those who had died. On the other hand, one cannot ignore the more sobering fact that if the unborn is a full-fledged member of the human community, these abortion-related maternal deaths, though tragic, pale in comparison to the nearly 40 million preborn human beings who have been killed by abortion in the United States since 1973.

Third, if virtually all abortions are instances of unjust killing, perhaps a change in the law to forbid virtually all abortions would have a teaching role in helping people to understand the seriousness of abortion and the obligations we have to the most vulnerable and defenseless members of the human family. After all, the function of law is not always to reflect the attitudes and behavior of society but to serve as "a mechanism by which people are encouraged to do what they know is right, even when it is difficult to do so."[58] David C. Reardon points out that "studies in the psychology of morality reveal that the law is truly the teacher. One of the most significant conclusions of these studies shows that existing laws and customs are *the most* important criteria for deciding what is right or wrong for most adults in a given culture."[59] Citing legal philosopher John Finnis, Nathanson writes that "sometimes the law is ahead of public morality. Laws against dueling and racial bias preceded popular support for these attitudes."[60]

If the abortion-choice advocate, in reply to this analysis, were to claim that the law cannot stop *all* abortions, he makes a trivial claim, for this is true of all laws that forbid illegal acts. For example, since hiring paid assassins and purchasing child pornography are forbidden by the law, some people have no choice but to acquire them illegally. But there is no doubt that their illegality does hinder a number of citizens from obtaining them. Should we then legalize child pornography and the hitman profession because we can't stop *all* people from obtaining such "goods" and services? Such reasoning is absurd.

Argument from "Compulsory" Pregnancy

Some abortion-choice advocates, in wanting to get a rhetorical edge in public debate, refer to pro-life legislation as "tantamount to advocating *compulsory pregnancy*."[61] This is not really an argument in a technical sense, since it has only a conclusion and contains no premises to support the conclusion. It is merely an assertion. But as an assertion it is entirely question-begging, for it assumes the non-personhood of the unborn. To cite an example, an angry father would be begging the question as to the personhood of his victims if he referred to laws that forbid murder as tantamount to advocating *compulsory marriage* and *compulsory fatherhood*, for such laws indeed forbid him from murdering his wife and his children. Can you imagine a father, or a mother for that matter, arguing that he (or she) is not obligated to obey the child support laws because they are "tantamount to advocating *compulsory parenthood*?" A rapist, I suppose, could argue on the same grounds and conclude that laws against rape are "tantamount to advocating *compulsory chastity*." And the slave owner, the "pro-choicer" of the mid-19th-century political scene, could easily conclude that the Thirteenth Amendment to the Constitution, since it robbed him of slave ownership, was "tantamount to advocating *compulsory government relinquishing of private property*."

In sum, a law that forbids the brutal victimizing of another person is inherently a just law, whether the victim is an unborn human being, an adult woman, a youngster, or an African American. Hence, the *real* question is whether the unborn is fully human, *not* whether pro-life legislation advocates "compulsory pregnancy."

More sophisticated versions of this argument are defended by Judith Jarvis Thomson, Eileen McDonagh, and David Boonin. I critique them in Chapter 7.

Argument from Tolerance for the Woman's Privacy

Much of abortion-choice literature argues that the pro-life position should not be reflected in our laws because the abortion decision is a very private and intimate one that should be kept between a woman, her physician, and her family, as they know what is best for the pregnant woman. There are, however, several problems with this argument.

First, it is not legally accurate. As I pointed out in Chapter 2, an adult woman in the United States is free to procure an abortion performed by a physician she met five minutes ago; and there is no law that requires that it be performed by *her* physician. And legally she is not obligated to either inform or receive consent from any family members, including her husband if she is married; the U.S. Supreme Court has consistently struck down statutes that require spousal notification.

Second, as with the other arguments in this chapter, this one begs the question. The fact that a decision is intimate and private has no bearing on the question of whether the unborn entity who is killed by abortion is fully human and deserving of legal protection. If the unborn is fully human, then killing her, even in the most intimate and private of settings, is still morally wrong. If the unborn is *not* fully human, then its death is of little moral significance, whether it is performed in the most intimate and private of settings. Consequently, the privacy and the intimacy of the decision is completely irrelevant to the morality of abortion.

Third, if the unborn is fully human, then it seems to be reasonable to seriously consider the strong possibility that abortion undermines, rather than sustains, privacy and intimacy. Stephen Schwarz, for example, maintains that because the unborn developing in the pregnant woman's womb is her own offspring, this human being is "entrusted to her, residing in her, nourished in her, protected by her." Thus, writes Schwartz, "it is abortion, not the prohibition of it, that violates the intimate realm of a woman who is pregnant. It is abortion that intrudes into this beautiful sanctuary, where a small, innocent, defenseless child is nestled and protected." The fact that it is the woman who requests the abortion does not invalidate Schwarz's point. Because the abortion "is objectively a violent sundering of this natural, intimate relationship," by requesting the abortion, the mother "becomes a part of this terrible evil, and often suffers from it as the second victim."[62] Schwarz continues: "Yes, there is something private and intimate that we should protect: the child. Abortion is a violation of the child's privacy, an intrusion into what is intimate for him, his own person. The methods of abortion and the pain they cause are violations of intimacy and privacy."[63]

It seems, then, that the appeal to intimacy and privacy may drive one away from abortion choice rather than toward it. After all, "the child's right to live, not to be killed, especially by the painful methods of abortion, that right surely outweighs anyone's claim to a right to privacy. And the state must protect that right, just as it protects other civil rights."[64] Men cannot beat their wives in the name of "privacy" and neither can parents molest or physically abuse their children because the family circle is "a private and intimate sanctuary." Therefore, it is the full humanity of the unborn that ought to be doing the moral work, not appeals to privacy or intimacy.

AD HOMINEM ARGUMENTS

"*Ad hominem*" literally means to "attack the man (or person)...[T]o attack *ad hominem* is to attack the man who presents an argument rather than the argument itself."[65] This is a bad form of reasoning because the person offering the argument has no bearing on the quality of the *argument*, unless the person is appealing to his or her own authority as a premise in the argument (e.g., "I'm an expert on X, and thus you should believe me"). Aside from that exception, attacking a person is a disreputable form of argument.

Why Don't Pro-Lifers Adopt the Babies They Don't Want Aborted?

In a *Dear Abby* column, a letter writer offers the following assessment of the character of pro-lifers (with which Abby acknowledges her agreement in her response):

> Dear Abby: This is a message to those men and women who try to prevent women from entering abortion clinics and carry big signs that say, "They Kill Babies Here!"
>
> Have you signed up to adopt a child? If not, why not? Is it because you don't want one, can't afford one or don't have the time, patience or desire to raise a child?
>
> What if a woman who was about to enter a family planning clinic saw your sign, then decided not to have an abortion but chose to give her baby to you? Would you accept it? What if the mother belonged to a minority group – or was addicted to drugs, or tested positive for AIDS? . . .
>
> So, to those carrying those signs and trying to prevent women from entering family planning clinics, heed my message: If you must be against abortion, don't be a hypocrite – make your time and energy count.[66]

This argument can be summarized in the following way: unless the pro-life advocate is willing to help bring up the children she does not want aborted, she has no right to prevent a woman from having an abortion. As a principle of moral action, this seems to be a bizarre assertion. For one reason, it begs the question by assuming that the unborn is not fully human. For would we not consider the killing of a couple's children unjustified even if we were approached by the parents with the following offer, "Unless you adopt my three children by noon tomorrow, I will put them to death"? The fact that I may refuse to adopt these children does not mean that their parents are justified in killing them. Hence, it all depends on whether the unborn is fully human.

Second, think of all the unusual precepts that would result from the moral principle put forth by the letter writer: unless I am willing to marry my neighbor's wife, I cannot prevent her husband from beating her; unless I am willing to adopt my neighbor's daughter, I cannot prevent her mother from abusing her; unless I am willing to hire ex-slaves for my business, I cannot say that the slave-owner should not own slaves. Although pro-life

groups are active in helping women in crisis pregnancies, the point I
am making is that it does not logically follow that abortion ipso facto
becomes a moral good simply because individual pro-life advocates are
not currently involved in such works of mercy.

And finally, this argument cuts both ways. The pro-lifer can ask the
abortion-choice advocate why *he* does not help with the upbringing of
poor children whose mothers have chosen *not* to kill them, since the
postnatal existence of these children is a result of the abortion-choice
advocate's public policy of *choice*. It is odd, to say the least, that the
groups that speak the most passionately about "choice" – Planned Parenthood, the National Abortion Rights Action League, or the National
Organization for Women – are not the ones who create and manage crisis pregnancy centers and other institutions that meet the physical and
spiritual needs of women who *choose* not to have an abortion and help
counsel women who suffer from post-abortion depression.[67] Pro-lifers
are the ones who fund and dedicate their time to such institutions.[68]

Aren't Pro-Lifers Inconsistent if They Support Capital Punishment?

Some abortion-choice (and even pro-life) advocates argue that the pro-
lifers who support capital punishment are inconsistent because, on the
one hand, they oppose killing in abortion but, on the other hand, support killing in capital punishment. There are several problems with this
reasoning.

First, how does this help the abortion-choice position or hurt the pro-
life position on abortion? Wouldn't this argument make people who are
against capital punishment and for abortion choice equally inconsistent?

Second, inconsistent people can draw good conclusions. For example, a person may inconsistently believe that it is permissible to unjustly
discriminate against black people but not white people. But this inconsistency in his thinking would not make his correct conclusion about the
wrongness of discriminating against white people ipso facto incorrect.
Hence, this argument is a red herring and does not deal with the ethical
legitimacy of either abortion or the pro-life position.

Third, there are a number of pro-life advocates who do not believe
that capital punishment is morally justified.[69] The abortion-choice advocate can't say that *these pro-lifers* are inconsistent. Why does he not then
give up his abortion-choice position and embrace *this* pro-life position,
as it should seem to him even more consistent than the anti–capital punishment abortion-choice position?

Fourth, one can plausibly argue that the pro-life position on abortion *is* consistent with capital punishment. Pro-life advocates, for the most part, do *not* argue that killing is *never* justified, for there are instances in which killing is justified, such as in the cases of self-defense and capital punishment, both of which do *not* entail the killing of an *innocent* human life. But the typical abortion does entail such killing. Hence, the pro-life advocate who believes in capital punishment is saying, "It is wrong to take the life of an innocent human person, but the capital offender is not innocent. Therefore, capital punishment is morally justified."

Moreover, a murder suspect before he is found guilty and/or sentenced to death can be justly convicted only if he is provided with the constitutional right of due process, which places the burden of proof on the state to prove his guilt in accordance with the rules of evidence. On the other hand, the unborn, who has murdered no one, is killed without any due process. Thus, one may be logically consistent in affirming both that capital punishment is morally justified and that the pro-life position on abortion is correct.

In sum, this argument commits the ad hominem fallacy, for it is a direct attack on the character of the pro-life advocate. Instead of dealing with the pro-lifer's arguments against abortion, the abortion-choicer attacks the pro-lifer's intellectual consistency.

Men Don't Get Pregnant

This argument is so silly I fear that by acknowledging it I may be giving it undeserved credibility. But because I hear it so frequently, it ought to be dealt with. I was confronted with this argument for the first time in a debate at the University of Nevada, Las Vegas (December 4, 1989). One of the debate participants, Esther Langston (professor of social work, UNLV), told the audience that she thought that it was rather strange that a man would offer arguments against abortion. After all, she claimed, men don't get pregnant; abortion is therefore a woman's issue.

There are several problems with this argument. First, I responded to Professor Langston by pointing out that *arguments don't have penises*, people do.[70] Because many pro-life *women* use the same arguments as I did in the debate, it was incumbent upon my opponent to answer my arguments, which stand or fall apart from my genitalia. I pointed out that because she could not offer the same "rebuttal" if a woman were putting forth the same arguments, therefore, my gender is absolutely irrelevant to whether the pro-life position is correct. In a subtle and clever way she dodged my arguments and attacked *me*, a clear case of the ad hominem fallacy.

Second, on the same rationale, Professor Langston would have to reject the *Roe v. Wade* decision, since it was arrived at by nine *men* (7–2).

Third, if Professor Langston's reasoning is correct, then mothers could never rightfully consent to have their newborn baby boy's foreskin circumcised, because, after all, how can any mother know how it feels to have a portion of her penis cut off?[71]

Fourth, abortion is a *human* issue, not just a women's issue, for it has consequences for everybody in society. It is from men's salaries that tax dollars may be taken to fund abortions; it is men who must help in child-rearing or pay child support if the mother *chooses not to abort*; and it is the man's seed that is one of the material causes (along with the female's ovum) of the unborn's being.

Fifth, the appeal to the pregnant woman's *personal involvement* is a two-edged sword. Could not someone argue that precisely because men don't get pregnant, and are thus less tainted by personal involvement, their opinion concerning the morality of abortion is more *objective*?

CONCLUSION

The arguments assessed in this chapter – though emotionally compelling to some – are logically fallacious and thus cannot bear the weight of the case for which they are offered. Realizing this, some sophisticated abortion-choice advocates agree with pro-lifers that the nature of the unborn is the only important question. However, they argue that the unborn, though a human being, is not a full-fledged member of the human community, that is, a person. They admit that the unborn entity is *genetically* human but they argue that it does not possess the full attributes of personhood until some time prior to or after birth.[72] Hence, to kill an unborn entity via abortion at a particular point in its gestation prior to its achievement of personhood is not to violate anyone's rights, for there is no one whose rights are being violated. We critically assess the arguments for this position in Chapter 6.

Others, however, take a different approach.[73] They argue that even if the unborn is fully human (or a person), it is not wrong for a woman to procure an abortion. For the unborn entity, to survive, must use another's body. If the state were to force the woman to continue the pregnancy, it would be no different from the state forcing a person to donate his kidney to save another's life. That is, one does not have an obligation to act heroically for another's sake. By conceding the full humanity of the unborn and arguing that abortion is justified on other grounds, the defender of this sort of argument seemingly avoids the question-begging nature of virtually all the arguments we covered in this chapter. We critically examine this type of argument in Chapter 7.

Nevertheless, in terms of our legal tradition and the jurisprudential parameters set down in *Roe*, the popular arguments we covered in this chapter are woefully inadequate to establish a right to abortion. As Justice Blackmun admits in *Roe*: "If this suggestion of personhood [of the unborn] is established, the appellant's case, of course, collapses, for the fetus' right to life is then guaranteed specifically by the [Fourteenth] Amendment."[74]

Consequently, the most important question in the legal debate over abortion is: "Are the unborn full-fledged members of the human community?" As we have seen, the leading popular arguments for abortion choice beg this fundamental question. For if the unborn is a human person, then these arguments collapse into jurisprudential irrelevancy. As Gregory P. Koukl puts it: "If the unborn is not a human person, no justification for abortion is necessary. However, if the unborn is a human person, no justification is adequate."[75]

6

THE NATURE OF HUMANNESS AND WHETHER THE UNBORN IS A MORAL SUBJECT

Most supporters of abortion choice agree with pro-life advocates that the question of abortion's permissibility rests on the moral status of the unborn: abortion is prima facie unjustified homicide if and only if the unborn entity is a full-fledged member of the human community (i.e., a person or a subject of moral rights). Most abortion-choice advocates also agree with pro-life supporters that the unborn entity is a human being insofar as it belongs to the species Homo sapiens. Where they disagree is over the question of the moral status of the unborn. These abortion advocates argue that the unborn entity is not a *person* and hence not a subject of moral rights until some decisive moment in fetal or postnatal development.

Consequently, these abortion-choice supporters argue that not all human beings are equally intrinsically valuable (IV) because some do not have the present capacity to exhibit certain properties or functions that would make them IV. I call the defender of this point of view the anti-equality advocate (AEA). Although these thinkers disagree among themselves as to what these properties or functions are – some offer sentience, others suggest "ability to reason" and/or self-awareness or some combination of these – these criteria all have one thing in common: a human being is IV if and only if she presently possesses certain properties and/or is able to exercise certain functions.

In Chapter 3, I defend the notion that the human being, as an organism, begins its existence at conception, that it is a unified organism with its own intrinsic purpose and basic capacities, whose parts work in concert for the perfection and perpetuation of its existence as a whole. Moreover, although some dispute whether the human being, as a unified organism, begins at conception by offering an alternative moment some time soon after conception (e.g., implantation at 72 hours, presence of the primitive

streak at 14 days, etc.), virtually no one disputes – including leading
defenders of abortion-choice[1] – that every mature human being was once
an adolescent, a child, an infant, a baby, a newborn, a fetus, and an
embryo. David Boonin, for example, writes:

> On the desk in my office where most of this book was written and revised,
> there are several pictures of my son, Eli. In one, he is gleefully dancing
> on the sand along the Gulf of Mexico, the cool ocean breeze wreak-
> ing havoc with his wispy hair. . . . In the top drawer of my desk, I keep
> another picture of Eli. The picture was taken September 7, 1993, 24 weeks
> before he was born. The sonogram image is murky, but it reveals clearly
> enough a small head tilted back slightly, and an arm raised up and bent,
> with the hand pointing back toward the face and the thumb extended
> toward the mouth. There is no doubt in my mind that this picture, too,
> shows the same little boy at a very early stage in his physical develop-
> ment. And there is no question that the position I defend in this book
> entails that it would have been morally permissible to end his life at this
> point.[2]

This chapter will focus almost exclusively on the arguments of the
AEAs who maintain that intrinsic value is an accidental property, like
height, weight, or skin pigmentation, all of which could change while
the being undergoing the change remains the same being. As already
noted, proponents of this view do not deny that one's adult self and
one's fetal self are one and the same being. Rather, they argue that your
fetal self was not intrinsically valuable because it had not yet acquired
the property or properties that make it an intrinsically valuable human
being (or IVHB). That is, the human being does not become something
else when in its early life it acquires these value-making properties (this
could occur sometime late in pregnancy or after its birth, depending
on what property or properties count), but rather, it remains the same
being while undergoing the change from not-intrinsically valuable to
intrinsically valuable. In other words, intrinsic value is an accidental, but
not an essential, property of the human being.

I will first offer a brief overview of the view of the human person that I
believe is the correct one: the substance view. And following my critique
of the AEA position, I will critique five popular arguments – the agnostic
approach, the appearance of humanness, birth, human sentiment, and
the beginning of brain activity – followed by a brief presentation of what
is called the SLED test (Size, Level of Development, Environment, and
degree of Dependency). And finally, I conclude by addressing several
common questions about the pro-life position.

THE SUBSTANCE VIEW OF PERSONS

I believe that this view – the substance view – is the correct view of the human person. As will become evident, this view is consistent with our commonsense experience of encountering human beings in the world. For this reason, those who deny this view must offer reasons that, though making abortion morally permissible, result in apparently counterintuitive consequences.

According to the substance view, a human being is intrinsically valuable because of the sort of thing it is and the human being remains that sort of thing as long as it exists. What sort of thing is it? The human being is a particular type of substance – a rational moral agent – that remains identical to itself as long as it exists, even if it is not presently exhibiting the functions, behaving in ways, or currently able to immediately exercise these activities that we typically attribute to active and mature rational moral agents.

A substance is an individual being of a certain sort. So, for example, the substance George W. Bush is a *human* substance, a being with a particular nature that we call "human." The substance Lassie too is an individual being, but she is a *canine* substance, a being with a particular nature that we call "canine." W. Norris Clarke offers a four-part definition of what constitutes a *human* substance:

> (1) it has the aptitude to exist *in itself* and not as a part of any other being; (2) it is the unifying center of all the various attributes and properties that belong to it at any one moment; (3) if the being persists as the same individual throughout a process of change, it is the substance which is the abiding, unifying center of the being across time; (4) it has an intrinsic dynamic orientation toward self-expressive action, toward self-communication with others, as the crown of its perfection, as its very *raison d'etre*.[3]

Each kind of living organism or *substance*, including the human being, maintains identity through change as well as possessing a nature or essence that makes certain activities and functions possible. "A substance's *inner nature*," writes J. P. Moreland, "is its ordered structural unity of ultimate capacities. A substance cannot change in its ultimate capacities; that is, it cannot lose its ultimate nature and continue to exist."[4] Consider the following illustration (which I also offer in Chapter 3).

A domestic feline, because it has a particular nature, has the ultimate capacity to develop the ability to purr. It may die as a kitten and never develop that ability. Regardless, it is *still* a feline as long as it exists, because it possesses a particular nature, even if it never acquires certain functions that by nature it has the capacity to develop. In contrast, a frog is not said to lack something if it cannot purr, for it is by nature not the sort of being that can have the ability to purr. A feline that lacks the ability to purr *is still a feline* because of its nature. A human being who lacks the ability to think rationally (either because she is too young or she suffers from a disability) *is still a human person* because of her nature. Consequently, a human being's lack makes sense *if and only if* she is an actual human person.

Second, the feline remains the same particular feline over time from the moment it comes into existence. Suppose you buy this feline as a kitten and name him "Cartman." When you first bring him home you notice that he is tiny in comparison to his parents and lacks their mental and physical abilities. But over time Cartman develops these abilities, learns a number of things his parents never learned, sheds his hair, has his claws removed, becomes 10 times larger than he was as a kitten, and undergoes significant development of his cellular structure, brain, and cerebral cortex. Yet, this grown-up Cartman is identical to the kitten Cartman, even though he has gone through significant physical changes. Why? The reason is because living organisms, substances, maintain identity through change.

Another way to put it is to say that organisms, including human beings, are ontologically prior to their parts,[5] which means that the organism as a whole maintains absolute identity through time while it grows, develops, and undergoes numerous changes, largely as a result of the organism's nature that directs and informs these changes and their limits. The organs and parts of the organism, and their role in actualizing the intrinsic, basic capacities of the whole, acquire their purpose and function *because* of their roles in maintaining, sustaining, and perfecting the *being as a whole*. This is in contrast to a thing that is not ontologically prior to its parts, like an automobile, cruise ship, or computer. Just as a sporting event (e.g., a basketball game, a golf match) does not subsist through time as a unified whole, an automobile, ship, or computer does not as well.[6] It is, rather, in the words of Moreland, "a sum of each temporal (and spatial) part." Called *mereological essentialism* (from the Greek "meros" for "part"), it "means that the parts of a thing are essential to it as a whole; if the object gains or loses parts, it is a different object."[7] Organisms, however, are different, for they may lose and gain parts, and yet remain the same thing over time.

Robert Joyce has made the observation that a "major flaw" in thinking of human beings as becoming intrinsically valuable when they aquire certain "parts" (i.e., properties) "is its subtle or not so subtle projection of a mechanistic model of development onto an organically developing reality." That is to say, the proponent of this position "fails to distinguish between natural process and artifactual process. Only artifacts, such as clocks and spaceships, come into existence part by part. Living beings come into existence all at once and then gradually unfold to themselves and to the world what they already, but only incipiently, *are*."[8] Because one can only develop certain functions by nature (i.e., a result of basic, intrinsic capacities) because of the sort of being one *is*, a human being, at every stage of her development is *never* a potential person; she is *always* a person with potential even if that potential is never actualized due to premature death or the result of the absence or deformity of a physical state necessary to actualize that potential. For example, a human being without vocal cords in a society in which there are no artificial or transplant vocal cords never loses the potential to speak, but she will in fact never speak because she lacks a physical state necessary to actualize that potential.

In the remaining sections of this chapter, I show that the substance view has more explanatory power in accounting for why we believe that human persons are intrinsically valuable even when they are not exercising certain powers that we attribute to an IVHB (e.g., when one is temporarily comatose), why human persons remain identical to themselves over time, and why it follows from these points that the unborn is a human person.

A CRITIQUE OF THE ANTI-EQUALITY CASE

The AEA argues that your fetal self was not intrinsically valuable because it had not yet acquired the property or properties that make you presently an intrinsically valuable human being (IVHB). I argue that this view is inadequate for several reasons, under two general categories: (1) the AEA cannot account for some apparently clear cases of IVHBs, and (2) the advocate of the substance view can adequately respond to the leading critiques of it, and in the process, offer more reasons for one to accept it.

AEA Cannot Account for Some Apparently Clear Cases of IVHB

When one is asleep, unconscious, or temporarily comatose, one does not have the present ability to reason or exhibit self-awareness, and yet it seems unreasonable to say that one is not IV in such states. The AEA, in response, may want to argue that the analogy between sleeping/

unconscious/comatose human beings and the preborn breaks down because the former *at one time* in their existence functioned as IVHBs and will probably do so in the future, while the latter, the preborn, did not. Consequently, you are identical to your preborn substance, but you now possess a property that made you an IVHB and that you lacked when you were preborn. But this will not work. Consider the following example.

Suppose your Uncle Jed is in a terrible car accident that results in his being in a coma from which he may or may not wake. Imagine that he remains in this state for roughly two years and then awakens. He seems to be the same Uncle Jed that you knew before he went into the coma, even though he's lost some weight, hair, and memories. Was he an IVHB during the coma? Could the physicians have killed Uncle Jed – the living organism we refer to as "Uncle Jed" – during that time because he did not exihibit certain functions or have certain present capacities? If one holds that IV depends on capacities that are immediately exercisable, it is difficult to see why it would be wrong to kill Uncle Jed while he was in the coma. Yet it would be wrong, precisely because Uncle Jed is identical to himself through all the changes he undergoes and that self, by nature, has certain basic capacities.

Consequently, the AEA cannot reply by arguing that Uncle Jed's life was intrinsically valuable during the coma because *in the past* he functioned as an IVHB and probably will do so in the future. For we can change the story a bit and say that when Uncle Jed awakens from the coma he loses virtually all his memories and knowledge including his ability to speak a language, engage in rational thought, and have self-awareness. He then would be in precisely the same position as the standard fetus. He would still literally be the same human being he was before the coma but he would be more like he was before he had a "past." He would have the basic capacities to speak a language, engage in rational thought, and have self-awareness, but he would have to develop and learn them all over again for these basic capacities to result, as they did before, in present capacities and actual abilities.

The AEA does not want to exclude Uncle Jed and others like him. So the AEA must offer an account that includes these people but excludes the human beings he does not think are intrinsically valuable (e.g., the preborn). So, he cannot claim that it is the substance's present capacity that makes him intrinsically valuable, for that would exclude Uncle Jed and his friends. And, as we have seen, having a *past* does not do the trick either. But suppose the AEA says in reply, "Okay, what makes Uncle Jed and his friends intrinsically valuable is that there is a psychological connection between this comatose clan and their post-comatose selves."[9] But that can't be right. For imagine that while in the coma Uncle Jed's physician *tells you* that your uncle will come out of the coma, but when he comes out he will *not* have any of the memories, beliefs, or knowledge that he once possessed, though he will be able to regain his prior abilities and accumulate new memories and experiences over the years following his recovery through the normal process of learning and development. In essence, Uncle Jed would be, while in the coma, in precisely the same position as the standard fetus, but unlike in the previous Uncle Jed story you would *know that fact* prior to his coming out of the coma. But according to the AEA it would be permissible to kill Uncle Jed while he is in the coma, for, given the physician's diagnosis and prognosis, Uncle Jed would not be psychologically connected to an IVHB. Yet, given the fact that the AEA *concedes* that the substance "Uncle Jed" is the same human being who remains identical to himself while undergoing the accidental changes through pre-coma, coma, and post-coma, it is Uncle Jed's basic capacities as a human substance, and not his currently exercisable capacities (as a mature, undamaged substance), that best accounts for Uncle Jed as an intrinsically valuable human being during this entire ordeal. Of course, the typical human being possesses these basic capacities from the moment it comes into being as a zygote. Thus, if the preborn is not an intrinsically valuable human being, neither is Uncle Jed.

Critique of Responses

In this section I will critique three counterarguments to the substance view offered by philosophers David Boonin, Dean Stretton, Judith Jarvis Thomson, and Ronald Dworkin. My critique of these responses will allow me to advance additional reasons to support the substance view, including (1) the substance view's superior explanatory power in accounting for human equality in comparison to the AEA's view, (2) the anti-equality view's incapacity, and the substance view's elegance, in accounting for the wrongness of purposely creating damaged human beings, and (3) why the substance view better accounts for rights than the interest-model offered by AEAs.

Boonin's Argument

In his analysis of Don Marquis's "future-like-ours" account of the prima facie moral wrongness of abortion,[10] David Boonin bites the bullet when he dismisses a counterexample similar to my Uncle Jed story:

Of course, the critic might instead appeal to an imaginary case in which a temporarily comatose adult has had the entire contents in his brain destroyed so that there is no more information contained in his brain than is contained in that of the preconscious fetus. In this case, it seems right that my position does not imply that such an individual has the same right to life as you or I. But, as in the case of the adult who has never had conscious experiences, a critic of abortion cannot appeal to such a case as a means of rejecting my position because we cannot assume ahead of time that killing such individuals is seriously immoral.[11]

Although this reply may adequately rebut Marquis's account, it does not succeed in the case I offer in this chapter. I will explore only one line of reasoning on this matter. Recall that in my example, Uncle Jed once had conscious experiences, memories, particular skills, and abilities but lost any mental record of them, and thus will have to relearn all of his abilities and knowledge as he did before he had any conscious experiences. But they would not be the same experiences and desires he had before. That is, he would be in precisely the same position as the standard fetus, with all the basic capacities he had at the beginning of his existence. So this is Boonin's dilemma: either it's prima facie wrong to kill Uncle Jed or it isn't. Suppose he opts for the first horn of the dilemma, arguing that killing Uncle Jed is seriously wrong because he once exercised abilities that resulted from his basic capacities (which would be the only justification available given Boonin's understanding of personhood). But what precisely is doing the moral work in this judgment? Is it Uncle Jed's past? That does not seem right, for remember that that past will never be regained; so killing Uncle Jed is not preventing the eventual return of a cluster of experiences and desires uniquely associated with Uncle Jed. After all, if Uncle Jed were in precisely the same situation except that he was so damaged that he would stay in a comatose state for the rest of his life (Uncle Jed2), a legitimate, though disputed, question to raise by his attending physicians would be whether continued medical treatment of Uncle Jed2 is warranted. The question would be legitimate because Uncle Jed2's prognosis would be essentially hopeless. However, if there is a very good chance that he will regain his abilities and acquire new knowledge, experiences, and memories over time, his prognosis would not be hopeless. Thus, it seems that if Boonin were to correctly conclude that it would be wrong to kill Uncle Jed before he came out of the coma, what would be doing the moral work would not be Uncle Jed's past but that he is a being of a certain sort with certain basic capacities that make certain functions and abilities possible. That is, Boonin would have to employ the resources of the substance view. But this would mean that abortion is prima facie morally wrong as well, for the standard fetus is a being of the same sort with certain basic capacities that make certain functions and abilities possible.

To tease this illustration out further, imagine that you have another uncle, Herb. Herb is in precisely the same position as Uncle Jed, except that Herb will regain all his memories, prior abilities, and other faculties and it will take Uncle Herb exactly the same amount of time to reacquire what he has lost as it will for Uncle Jed to acquire new memories and relearn old abilities and skills. If I understand correctly Boonin's view of personhood, it would be permissible to kill Uncle Jed but not Uncle Herb, even though the only difference between them would be that the latter will regain what he has lost while the former will gain memories he never had and many abilities he once mastered. Boonin clearly would not want to assert that it is prima facie permissible to kill a reversibly comatose person. Yet, given his position, it is prima facie permissible to kill a similarly situated reversibly comatose human being merely on the grounds that he will not be able to reacquire past traits and memories and he will have to relearn skills and abilities he possessed prior to his coma. It seems to me that the difference between Uncle Jed and Uncle Herb carries no moral weight whatsoever.

Of course, Boonin bites the bullet and asserts a point of view that would seem to require that he opt for the second horn of the dilemma: it is not prima facie wrong to kill Uncle Jed because the entirety of Uncle Jed's past abilities, experiences, and knowledge would be gone forever (which would be consistent with Boonin's understanding of personhood). But the premise on which this argument is based is as controversial as the conclusion for which it is employed to support: having a human nature with intact basic capacities is *not sufficient* for one to have a right to life if one has not engaged in certain value-giving functions or mental activities that result from these basic capacities but will likely do so in the future. Granted, such a premise will support the belief that most abortions are not serious moral wrongs, a conclusion many people, including Boonin, find desirable. But that is precisely the conclusion that Boonin attempts to establish with the help of this controversial premise.

Opting for the second horn of the dilemma fails on two other counts. First, as Patrick Lee aptly points out, the AEA account of intrinsic value, of which Boonin's position is an example, undermines the moral equality of those human beings the AEA considers intrinsically valuable.[12] That is, the AEA cannot explain why fundamental human rights ought not to be distributed on the basis of native intellectual abilities and other value-giving properties, such as rationality and self-awareness. This is because capacities are stages along a continuum, with some basic capacities being exercisable only as a result of other capacities first being actualized (e.g., the proximate capacity to learn a language requires a certain level of brain development) and those capacities presently differ in their degrees of exercisability (e.g., people have a wide range of language skills). Some adult human beings are more or less rational and more or less self-aware in comparison to others, and some human beings, because they are damaged or immature, are in the process of developing, and have not yet achieved, certain second-order capacities (e.g., the requisite brain structure to develop the capacity to learn algebra) that make certain first-order capacities possible (e.g., the present capacity to do algebraic problems if you know algebra).[13] But if that is the case, then some "intrinsically valuable" human beings are more or less "intrinsically valuable" than others. But intrinsic value is not a degreed property; you either have it or you don't, and thus IV cannot be conditioned upon the possession of a degreed property, for if you have more of it then you should have more value. It would follow from this that the notion of the moral equality of human beings is not only illusory when applied to the preborn (which the AEA already believes) but to all human beings as well. But the AEA does not want to deny human equality among IVHBs. Yet, the AEA can reject this undesirable consequence only if he embraces the notion that human beings are intrinsically valuable because they are rational moral agents *by nature* from the moment they come into existence.

Second, not only can the AEA not account for human equality, he cannot account for the wrongness of intentionally creating unequal human beings who are not intrinsically valuable (according to the AEA's perspective). For example, what would be wrong if a developmental biologist manipulated the development of an early embryo-clone in such a way that the result is an infant without higher brain functions but whose healthy organs can be used for ordinary transplant purposes or for spare parts for the person from whom the embryo was cloned?[14] Given the dominant accounts of moral personhood – views that claim that a being's possession of intrinsic value is contingent upon some presently held property or immediately exercisable mental capacity to function in a certain way – it is not clear how intentionally creating such deformed beings for a morally good purpose is morally wrong. I suppose one could argue that it is morally wrong because the unborn is entitled to her higher brain functions. But as abortion-choice proponent Dan W. Brock argues, "this body clone" could not arguably be harmed because of its "lack of capacity for consciousness."[15] Yet he concedes that "most people would likely find" the practice of purposely creating permanently nonsentient human beings "appalling and immoral, in part because here the cloned later twin's capacity for conscious life is destroyed *solely as a means* to benefit another."[16] This, however, makes sense only if the cloned twin is entitled to his higher brain functions. But according to the view embraced by most AEAs, one cannot have rights (including entitlements) unless one has interests (and interests presuppose desires), and the pre-sentient fetus has no interests (because she has no desires).[17] So the entitlement account does not do the trick for the AEA. It seems to me that the substance view is the account of human personhood that best explains the moral repugnance one feels when one first appreciates the prospect of these activities becoming commonplace in our society under the rubric of reproductive rights: it is prima facie wrong to destroy the physical structure necessary for the realization of a human being's basic, natural capacity for the exercisability of a function that is a perfection of its nature. Although this provides moral warrant for the legal prohibition of intentionally producing deformed human beings for an apparently good purpose, it also grounds significant legal restrictions on abortion, a procedure that destroys the physical structure necessary for the realization of a human being's basic, natural capacity for the exercisability of a function that is a perfection of its nature.

Stretton's Argument

Dean Stretton offers a thought-experiment to show that personhood need not be an essential property of a living organism,[18] which Stretton claims is contrary to the substance view of human beings whose advocates claim that the substance, the human being, is a person *by nature* and does not *become a person* by achievement.

Stretton asks us to imagine an organism, such as a dog (that we will call "Phydeaux"),[19] which is not an intrinsically valuable entity. However, suppose we have the technological sophistication to add to Phydeaux's brain the cerebrum of a fully mature human brain and we in fact do it. According to Stretton, because Phydeaux now possesses the properties of an intrinsically valuable being – that is, he has the immediate exercisable capacity for rational thought, moral agency, and other functions – this is an example of an organism remaining identical to itself but changing from nonintrinsically valuable (a non-person) to intrinsically valuable (a person). In the same way, the fetus changes from nonintrinsicially valuable to IV when it acquires certain properties – immediately exercisable capacities – that philosophers such as Stretton consider decisive in correctly attributing personhood to any entity.

But there are reasons to doubt that this thought-experiment properly accounts for our intuitions on this matter. As Lee points out, the thought-experiment "works" for Stretton because he presupposes in his interpretation of it that his view of persons is correct, that is, he reasons in a circle.[20] But one need not interpret the story in this way. Lee offers two options: (1) the person whose cerebrum was transplanted to Phydeaux continues existence while Phydeaux does not. "One could say this," writes Lee, "if one believed that the human being is an organism but that his cerebrum is his only indispensable organ."[21] (2) According to this option (which Lee prefers, and I do too), if the human being "continues to live" minus his cerebrum, "she remains a (damaged) human person; and *if* combining a cerebrum with" Phydeaux's "bodily parts produces a rational animal, a substantial change occurs and so" Phydeaux goes out of existence "and a new rational animal, a new person, comes to be."[22] To employ an analogy, Phydeaux's body and the human's cerebrum are like a sperm and egg, playing the roles of two living parts of other organisms that, when combined, "*dynamically interact*,"[23] and become a brand new organism. According to Lee, the second option makes perfect sense under a substance account, which holds "that a rational animal is a type of substance, and that being rational (having the natural capacity for conceptual and free thought) is a specific difference, a feature expressing (in part) what the substance is instead of an accidental characteristic."[24] To put it another way, a human person is a rational moral agent by nature from the moment it comes into being; it is a substantial unity identical to itself that subsists through time. No being *becomes* such a substance, for substantial change is a change that eliminates the being rather than something that the being undergoes. Phydeaux does not *become* an intrinsically valuable person when his living bodily parts dynamically interact with the human cerebrum; rather, Phydeaux ceases to exist and his living bodily parts contribute to the bringing into being of a substance that never was.

But suppose we grant to Stretton that a being may remain identical to itself and yet change from nonintrinsically valuable to intrinsically valuable. Assuming that intrinsic value is not an essential property – that is, one can lose it and regain it and still not undergo substantial change – Stretton's analogy does not establish his point that the fetus does not have intrinsic value but acquires it later in life while remaining identical to itself through these changes. For in the case of pre-IV Phydeaux, prior to the attachment of the human cerebrum, he had no basic capacity by nature to grow one. The fetus and Uncle Jed – and the IV-Phydeaux if he lapses into an Uncle-Jed-like coma – all possess the basic capacities of a rational moral agent. Consequently, all that Stretton proves – if he is successful – is that IV is not an essential property for Phydeaux. He does not show that IV is not an essential property of human beings from the moment that they come into existence or that the fetus does not have intrinsic value prior to having the present capacity to exercise functions we typically associate with rational moral agents who are mature.

In his rebuttal to Lee's response to his initial argument, Stretton seems to miss the point:

> Putting aside the right to life (which is the very case in dispute), our background knowledge does not include any cases where a being's natural capacities entitle it to any substantial (significant) type or level of respect. Suppose, for example, I have a natural capacity to become a great athlete, or a brilliant intellectual. This natural capacity (or indeed any other essential property) would hardly entitle me to any respect if, say, too much TV has in fact turned me into a fat, lazy dullard. Substantial respect *would* of course be owed to those who *are* great athletes or brilliant intellectuals – perhaps in virtue of their developed capacity for these things, or perhaps in virtue of other accidental properties, such as their achievements in these areas. Generalising, it appears we do not owe to beings, in virtue of their natural capacities (or any other essential property), any substantial type or level of respect. The right to life, however, is surely itself about respect: the fact that a being has a right to life is just the fact that, in virtue of some property it has, we owe that being a certain (very substantial) type and level of respect. But now *because* we do not owe to beings, in virtue of their natural capacities (or any other essential property), any substantial type or level of respect, *it follows that* we do not owe to beings, in virtue of their natural capacities (or any other essential property), the substantial type and level of respect involved in the right to life. And this is just to say that beings do not have a right to life in virtue of their natural capacities (or any other essential property), but in virtue of their *accidental* properties.[25]

Ironically, Stretton's rebuttal makes the very point he is denying. Surely he is correct that one ought not to respect people who, when given the opportunity to hone and nurture certain gifts – such as intellectual skill and athleticism – waste these potentials in a life of sloth and depravity. But the "respect" not owed here is not the respect about which Lee and

I write when it comes to beings who are rational moral agents by nature because of their basic capacities. The respect about which Stretton writes is a second-order respect that is *earned* by persons who properly employ and nurture those natural talents that are not equitably distributed among human beings (and thus come in degrees and thus cannot be the basis of intrinsic value). But the withholding or lavishing of that respect on a particular being makes sense only in light of the *sort of being* it is by nature, that is, a being who has certain intrinsic capacities and purposes that if prematurely disrupted by either its own agency or another agent, results in an injustice. So the human being who wastes his talents is one who does not respect his natural gifts or the basic capacities whose maturation and proper employment make possible the flourishing of talent and skill. That is, the notion of "proper function,"[26] coupled with the observation that certain perfections grounded in basic capacities have been impermissibly obstructed from maturing, is assumed in the very judgment one makes about human beings and the way by which they should treat themselves (as in the case of the lazy person with natural gifts offered by Stretton) or be treated by others (as in the case of the unborn in abortion).

The Desire-Interest Arguments

It is fairly typical for contemporary philosophers, especially those in the analytic tradition, to ground rights in interests that one can have only if one has desires, such as a desire to be treated fairly or not to be killed unjustly and so on. So, prior to the acquisition of desires, a human being has no interests and thus no rights including a right to life. The implication of this to the abortion issue is obvious. In this section we will assess two arguments that offer support for this position, one by Ronald Dworkin as presented by Judith Jarvis Thomson and the second by David Boonin.

Thomson-Dworkin Argument

Thomson relies on the work of Ronald Dworkin, who argues that it is "'very hard to make sense of the idea' that a fetus has rights from the moment of conception. Having rights seems to presuppose having interests, which in turn seems to presuppose having wants, hopes, fears, likes and dislikes. But an early fetus lacks the physical constitution required for such psychological states."[27] Instead of presenting one of the many philosophically sophisticated pro-life responses to this sort of argument, Thomson employs her own, an argument that is intended to show that it is possible to deny Dworkin's thesis insofar as Dworkin is arguing that having rights (and hence interests) is a necessary condition for having protected moral status. (That is, the fetus may not have rights, but that does not mean it may not have protected moral status.) It is, however, an argument that no pro-life philosopher, to my knowledge, has ever, or would ever, employ.

Thomson argues that paintings do not have interests and therefore do not have rights. That is, one cannot wrong a painting, though one can wrong its owner by destroying, stealing, or damaging it. In contrast, writes Thomson, "wronging a creature is impeding its interests unfairly." But because "paintings have no interests, there is no such thing as impeding their interests unfairly, and therefore no such thing as wronging them."[28] Even though she thinks that this account of rights seems very plausible, she does not think that it would "be flatly unreasonable to deny that idea." That is to say, "we may grant that if a thing lacks interests, then it is not possible to impede its interests unfairly, and therefore that it is not possible to wrong it," but if "having rights is a kind of protected moral status," we need to explain "why it should be thought that a thing has that special status only if it is possible to wrong it."[29] To put it another way, there is nothing unreasonable in maintaining that you cannot wrong a painting, but it does not follow that the painting does not have protected moral status, that is, you may have no right to destroy it even though it cannot be wronged. For Thomson, "it seems entirely reasonable" to claim that a painting cannot be wronged, "but how do you get from there to the conclusion that paintings lack the protected moral status?" Although it seems reasonable to embrace this conclusion, "we lack a compelling rationale for doing so."[30] Applying this reasoning to the question of whether an unborn human being has protected moral status, Thomson admits that she knows "of no other reason for denying that fertilized eggs have a right to life than the one that rests on the idea that having rights presupposes having interests," which means that she knows "of no conclusive reason for denying that fertilized eggs have a right to life."[31]

Although Thomson's analysis of Dworkin's notion of protected moral status and its relationship to rights provides another apparently intractable philosophical puzzle on which philosophers may publish for decades to come, it is not the sort of metaphysically robust analysis that one finds in pro-life literature, including some of the works cited in this chapter. How then should a pro-lifer respond to the Dworkin-Thomson argument?

First, as a general point, it seems counterintuitive to claim that having a conscious desire for a particular good or an awareness of an entitlement is a necessary condition to having been wronged if one is deprived of that good or entitlement unjustly. Robert Wennberg provides a helpful example:

> If I were cheated out of a just inheritance that I didn't know I had, I would be harmed regardless of whether I knew about the chicanery. Deprivation of a good (be it an inheritance or self-conscious existence) constitutes harm even if one is ignorant of that deprivation.[32]

Second, on the specific question at issue, the pro-lifer may argue that having interests that presuppose conscious desires cannot adequately account for the wrongness of killing human beings. (1) If the substance view of persons is correct, as I argue in this chapter, then your prenatal self has intrinsic value even if one has no conscious desire for a right to life. (2) As Lee has argued,[33] a person, such as a slave, may be indoctrinated to believe that he has no interests, but he still has a prima facie right not to be killed, even if he has no conscious longing for, or interest in, a right to life. Even if the slave is never killed unjustly, we would still think that he has been harmed precisely because his desires and interests have been obstructed from coming to fruition. Thus, "it seems more reasonable," writes Lee, "to hold that the violation of someone's rights is more closely connected with what truly *harms* the individual rather than with what he or she desires."[34] But if that is the case, the proper question is what sort of a thing is a human being and what types of "conditions or activities truly perfect a human being," and "whether a person is harmed or deprived of a real benefit . . . or not."[35] Thus, the prima facie wrongness of killing the unborn does not rest on its desires that Dworkin argues are the basis of interests and consequently its rights. Rather, the wrongness of killing the unborn, indeed, the wrongness of killing any one of us, is grounded in a nature of a particular sort of being who is deprived of real goods when it is killed, and these goods are ones for which its nature is intrinsically directed to achieve for its own perfection.

Boonin's Organized Cortical Brain Activity Argument

Boonin offers his own desires account of the right to life. He argues that the human being does not achieve this moral status until it acquires organized cortical brain activity, which may occur as early as 25 weeks' gestation or as late as 32 weeks.[36] Here is a summary of his argument:

1. Organized cortical brain activity must be present for a being to be capable of having conscious experience,
2. Prior to having a conscious experience, a being has no desires,
3. Desires (as understood in Boonin's taxonomy, shown later) are necessary for a being to have a right to life,
4. The fetus acquires organized cortical brain activity between 25 and 32 weeks' gestation.
5. Therefore, the fetus has no right to life prior to organized cortical brain activity.

To defend his view of the relationship between desire and a right to life, Boonin reintroduces the reader to distinctions he made earlier in the book in his critique of Don Marquis's future-like-ours argument against abortion.[37] Boonin makes a distinction between *dispositional* and *occurrent* desires, and between *ideal* and *actual* desires. According to Boonin, "a desire of yours is occurrent if it is one you are conspicuously entertaining," such as your desire to read the rest of this sentence. On the other hand, "a desire of yours is dispositional if it is a desire that you do have right now even if you are not thinking about it at just this moment," such as your desire to live a good long life.[38] The temporarily comatose adult, according to Boonin, has dispositional desires rather than occurrent desires.

So, according to Boonin, it is dispositional desires that ground one's right to life, for one has a right to life even if one is not presently aware of desiring it. But, of course, there are people who, because of depression, false beliefs, incomplete information, or other conditions do not have an occurrent desire for a right to life. For this problem, he introduces a distinction between ideal and actual desires. To employ one of Boonin's own examples: although you may have an actual occurrent desire to drink a glass of water that you do not know is laced with poison, "we may confidently consider your ideal desire to avoid drinking from the glass, given that your actual (though likely dispositional rather than occurrent) desire not to be killed strongly outweighs your actual (even if occurrent) desire to quench your thirst."[39]

What these distinctions show, according to Boonin, is that Marquis is right that it is wrong to kill a being who has a future-like-ours, but, contra Marquis who maintains that this occurs very early in pregnancy and perhaps at conception,[40] the fetus does not become such a being until it has acquired organized cortical brain activity. Abortion opponents typically respond to traditional personhood-criteria that exclude fetuses (e.g., rationality, self-consciousness) by citing counterexamples of beings that we know it is prima facie wrong to kill, even though they lack the present ability to exercise these personhood-criteria (e.g., newborns, toddlers, the temporarily comatose); therefore, Boonin's distinctions are ingenious.

Based on these distinctions, Boonin maintains that newborns, toddlers, and the temporarily comatose have a right to life even if they are not occurrently desiring a right to life. They have an ideal dispositional desire because they possess a particular sort of brain that has had a conscious experience and thus has the potential to desire a right to life. Writes Boonin,

> Once an individual does develop such desires, the potential that his brain has for developing further becomes morally relevant: It is because a human infant's brain has a potential that a mature cow or pig does not have that the human infant uncontroversially has a future-like-ours, whereas the cow or pig does not. And it is because of this that the conscious desire that an infant has provides a solid foundation for attributing to it an ideal dispositional desire that its future-like-ours be preserved, whereas this cannot be said of the conscious desires of the cow or the pig.[41]

Although the distinctions between desires offered by Boonin may be uniquely suited for his conscription of Marquis's future-like-ours account, they do not seem to be useful in either overcoming the comatose–Uncle Jed counterexample I suggested earlier (whose prior experiences are forever erased) or establishing organized cortical brain activity as the condition that imparts to the human being a right to life. Thus, I believe that premise (3) in Boonin's argument – "desires are necessary in order for a being to have a right to life" – is false. Concerning the organized cortical brain activity criterion, I offer two criticisms: the problem of the indoctrinated slave, and the problem of creating brainless human beings.

THE PROBLEM OF THE INDOCTRINATED SLAVE. As Lee has argued and as I noted in my critique of the Thomson-Dworkin argument, a person, such as a slave, may be indoctrinated to believe he has no interests, but he still has a prima facie right not to be killed, even if he has no conscious desire for, or interest in, a right to life. Even if the slave is never killed, we would still think that he has been harmed precisely because his desires and interests have been obstructed from coming to fruition.[42] Boonin may respond that the slave's *ideal* desire is to have a right to life. But that judgment seems to assume that the slave is a being of a certain sort that ought to desire a right to life even when he does not actually desire a right to life. Then, it is not *desire* that grounds the right to life, but the nature of the sort of being that would have this correct desire if it had not been indoctrinated, or will have this correct desire when it reaches a certain level of maturity and it is functioning properly.

To better understand this problem, imagine that you own one of these indoctrinated slaves and she is pregnant with a fetus that has not reached the point of organized cortical brain activity. Because you have become convinced that Boonin's view of desires is correct, and thus you are starting to have doubts about the morality of indoctrinating people with already organized cortical brain activity to become slaves, you hire a scientist who is able to alter the fetus's brain development in such a way that its organized cortical brain activity prevents the fetus from ever having desires for liberty or a right to life. That is, the organized cortical brain activity arises in this being in such a way that its basic capacities to desire liberty and a right to life, that it possessed from the moment it came into being, can never come to maturity. Yet it seems that the rights of this fetus have been violated *precisely because* its acquisition of certain presently exercisable abilities to which it is entitled was intentionally disrupted by an external agent prior to the arising of organized cortical brain activity. But if rights presuppose desires and desires presuppose organized cortical brain activity, then Boonin's criterion cannot account for the wrong done to the fetus when a scientist changes the developmental trajectory of the fetus's organized cortical brain activity before it arises.

THE PROBLEM OF CREATING BRAINLESS HUMAN BEINGS. Another problem with Boonin's desire account is that it falls prey to the same problem I brought up earlier in my critique of another of Boonin's arguments: the desire account of rights cannot account for the wrongness of purposely creating brainless human beings for an apparent public good. Because the reader can go back and read my entire argument, I will restate only a portion of it here and apply it to the desire account.

Given Boonin's desire account of rights, it is not clear what would be wrong in cloning brainless human beings for the purpose of harvesting their organs, even though to do so seems wrong. As I noted above, some may be tempted to locate the wrong in the moral intuition that the pre-brain embryo is deprived of something to which he is entitled. But if that is the case, then desire (whether occurrent, dispositional, actual, or ideal) is a condition that is not necessary for a human being to possess both rights and a present capacity to be harmed.

Thus, given these two problems, as well as the comatose–Uncle Jed counterexample, the prima facie wrongness of violating another's rights cannot rest on a human being's desires. Rather, its wrongness seems to be grounded in the notion that a human being is a being of a particular sort who is deprived of real goods when it is killed or maimed, and these are goods its nature is intrinsically directed to achieve for its own perfection. Consequently, organized cortical brain activity fails as a condition that imparts to a human being a right to life.

OTHER CRITERIA

In addition to the criteria already covered, other standards are offered to justify abortion choice. In this section, I will cover five of the most popular ones: (1) the agnostic approach, (2) appearance of humanness, (3) human sentiment, (4) birth, and (5) brain waves. Three others I will *not* cover in this chapter are quickening, viability, and sentience, for each has been covered in another portion of the book. Quickening and viability were assessed in Chapter 2 in analyzing *Roe v. Wade* (and viability was critiqued a second time in Chapter 3). Because sentience is employed by some moderate abortion-choice advocates as one of those properties that the unborn must possess to be considered a "person,"[43] the critique in part II of this chapter may be applied to the sentience criterion as well. I will conclude this section with what has been called the SLED test.

Agnostic Approach to Justify Abortion Choice

Abortion-choice advocates often claim that "no one knows when life begins," but this is a misnomer. No one who knows anything about prenatal development seriously doubts that individual biological human life is present from conception or at least within the first two weeks after conception (see Chapter 4). What the abortion-choice advocate probably means is that there is disagreement as to when the human being in the womb becomes a subject of rights, and thus no one really knows when human life becomes intrinsically valuable.

This argument is typically employed as a justification for legally permitting abortion. As I noted in Chapter 2, a version of this argument was offered by Justice Blackmun in *Roe*. And as we saw, its premise is incapable of establishing a right to abortion, for if one is not sure that one is killing a moral subject, then one should not kill it. That is, the unborn should be given "the benefit of the doubt." Robert Wennberg, however, disagrees with this inference and offers the following illustration to counter it:

> A thirty-six-year-old woman with four children, worn down and exhausted by poverty and terrible living conditions, married to an alcoholic husband finds herself pregnant. Although not the sole source of income for her family, the woman does work and her income is desperately needed. After wrestling with her predicament, the woman decides that an abortion would be in the interests of herself and her family.... Concerned about whether abortion might be the killing of a being with a right to life, she consults two moralists, both of whom appeal to the Benefit of the Doubt Argument. One is a "conservative" who warns her to avoid the possibility of a great moral evil – terminating the life of what *might* be a holder of a right to life. The other is a "liberal" who encourages her to secure what she *knows* to be good – avoiding considerable suffering for herself and her family. It seems to me that both pieces of advice are reasonable and that neither is clearly superior to the other.[44]

The point of this story is that the Benefit of the Doubt Argument can be used by either the conservative or the liberal. For the liberal, the benefit of the doubt should be given to eliminating the woman's predicament, as we know that she is a real person in a real predicament, whereas we are unsure of the fetus's right to life and/or full humanness. On the other hand, for the conservative, the benefit of the doubt should be given to the unborn, because the magnitude of the evil one may be committing (i.e., killing an innocent person for the sake of relieving one's own suffering) is so great that it should be avoided at all costs.

Wennberg's response, however, does not completely capture the prolifer's use of the Benefit of the Doubt Argument. It seems to downplay the moral magnitude of killing an innocent human person when one admits that the arguments on all sides of the moral status of the being in question are so equally compelling that one is forced to an agnostic position on the matter.[45] Consider the following revised version of the above story:

> A thirty-six-year-old woman with four children, worn down and exhausted by poverty and terrible living conditions, married to an alcoholic husband finds herself pregnant. Although not the sole source of income for her family, the woman does work and her income is desperately needed. After wrestling with her predicament, the woman is approached by a wealthy benefactor who presents to her the following proposition that would get her out of her predicament: "If you detonate the building

across the street, which I own, I will pay you $50,000 a year for the next 20 years, adjusting the sum every year in accordance with inflation and the cost of living, and provide you a housekeeper free of charge (This will, of course, more than make up for the burden another child places on the family). However, there is one catch: there is a 1 in 10 chance that in the basement of this building there is a perfectly healthy and innocent 8-year-old child. Thus you run the risk of killing another human being. Is your personal well-being worth the risk?"

If the woman decides to blow up the building, I believe that few if any would judge her actions as morally justified. Even if the odds were 1 in 100, it would seem incredible that anyone would even consider the risk of murdering another human being so insignificant that she would take the chance.

To better understand the flaw in Wennberg's story, let us revise the story even further and suppose that the thirty-six-year-old woman is independently wealthy, childless, lives in a beautiful home, and has a wonderful caring husband. Would Wennberg argue that the risk of murder would be justified in *this* case? If no, then his position is tantamount to saying that risking unjustified homicide is morally justified for poor people but not for the wealthy, which means that relief of personal economic and familial burdens is a sufficient justification for risking unjustified homicide. This seems to be morally counterintuitive. If his answer is yes – that the risk *is* justified in the case of the well-off thirty-six-year-old – then the relieving of personal economic and familial burdens is not relevant in the justification for risking unjustified homicide, and Wennberg's support of a liberal use of the Benefit of the Doubt Argument collapses.

We can revise Wennberg's argument in a different way and suppose that a family wanting to adopt a child will pay the thirty-six-year-old woman $50,000 in addition to hospital expenses so that she can bring the baby to term. Now that her burden has been for the most part lifted, is risk of murder still justified? If yes, then the relieving of her economic and familial burdens is not relevant to Wennberg's case. If no, then, as in the other revised story, Wennberg's argument is essentially saying that risking unjustified homicide is morally justified for people with certain hardships. But, as with the previous story, this seems to be counterintuitive.

Even if the pro-lifer grants Wennberg his point, it has limited applications, as a great number of abortions do not occur because of desperate circumstances such as those described in Wennberg's original story. It follows then that even Wennberg must admit that a great number of abortions are immoral and should be banned, as they risk unjustified homicide and do not relieve the parents of a burden whose elimination is worth the risk of unjustified homicide.

Human Appearance

Some argue that the unborn becomes a "human being," or a subject of rights, at the time it begins to take on the appearance of a child.[46] Ernest Van Den Haag is sympathetic to this criterion. He writes that when the unborn acquires a functioning brain and neural system soon after the first trimester it "starts to resemble an embryonic human being." And after this point "abortion seems justifiable only by the gravest of reasons, such as the danger to the mother; for what is being aborted undeniably resembles a human being to an uncomfortable degree."[47] Van Den Haag does combine the human appearance criterion with one of the criteria embraced by some AEAs: a functioning brain and neural system. However, because we have already critically assessed the AEA's position, and because the "brain wave" criterion will be critiqued below, only the human appearance criterion will be assessed here.

There are several problems with Van Den Haag's case. First, although appearance can be helpful in determining what is or is not a human being, it is certainly not a sufficient or a necessary condition for doing so. After all, manikins in department stores resemble human beings and they are not even remotely such. On the other hand, some oddities, such as the bearded lady or the elephant man, who more closely resemble nonhuman primates, are nonetheless human beings.

Second, as John Jefferson Davis points out, "this objection assumes that personhood presupposes a postnatal form. A little reflection, however, will show that the concept of a 'human form' is a dynamic and not a static one. Each of us, during normal growth and development, exhibits a long succession of different outward forms." That is to say, an early embryo, although not looking like a newborn, does look exactly like a human ought to look at this stage of her development. Thus, "the appearance of an 80-year-old adult differs greatly from that of a newborn child, and yet we speak without hesitation of both as persons. In both cases, we have learned to recognize the physical appearances associated with those developmental stages as normal expressions of human personhood."[48] In other words, the unborn at any stage of her development looks perfectly human because that is what humans look like at that time.

It may be true that it is psychologically easier to kill something that does not resemble the human beings we see in everyday life, but it does not follow from this that the being in question is any less human or that the executioner is any more humane. Once we recognize that the development of a human being is a process that a particular being undergoes and that does not cease at the time of birth, "to insist that the unborn at six weeks look like the newborn infant is no more reasonable than to expect the newborn to look like a teenager. If we acknowledge as 'human' a succession of outward forms after birth, there is no reason not to extend that courtesy to the unborn, since human life is a continuum from conception to natural death."[49] Hence, Van Den Haag confuses appearance with reality.

Human Sentiment

Some abortion-choice proponents argue that since many parents do not grieve at the death of an embryo or fetus as they would at the death of an infant or a small child, the unborn is not a subject of moral rights (i.e., a person).

But this is an inadequate basis for moral judgment. As Judge John T. Noonan has observed, "Feeling is notoriously an unsure guide to the humanity of others. Many groups of humans have had difficulty in feeling that persons of another tongue, color, religion, sex, are as human as they."[50] One usually feels a greater sense of loss at the sudden death of a healthy parent than one feels for the hundreds who die daily of starvation in underdeveloped countries. Does this mean that the latter are less human than one's parent? Certainly not. Noonan points out that "apart from reactions to alien groups, we mourn the loss of a ten-year-old boy more than the loss of his one-day-old brother or his 90-year-old grandfather." The reason for this is that "the difference felt and the grief expressed vary with the potentialities extinguished, or the experience wiped out; they do not seem to point to any substantial difference in the humanity of baby, boy, or grandfather."[51]

Furthermore, if this abortion-choice argument is correct, it leads to an absurdity: by grieving the death of their unborn child, one set of parents can *make* their child a person, whereas another set of parents who do not grieve the death of their child can *make* their child a non-person. And what about the parents of a deceased two-year old who don't grieve their child's death? Is this two-year-old all of a sudden not a person?

Birth

Some abortion-choice proponents argue that birth is the time at which a human entity becomes a subject of moral rights. They usually hold this position for at least two reasons: (1) our culture calculates the beginning of one's entry into society from one's date of birth; and (2) it is only after birth that a child is named, baptized, and accepted into a family. There are several problems with this argument.

First, it is simply a social convention that we count one's beginning from one's birthday and that people name and baptize children after their births. After all, one's nature is not changed if, after birth, one is abandoned, unnamed, and not baptized. Some cultures, such as the Chinese, count one's beginning from the moment of conception. Does that mean that the American unborn are not fully human while the Chinese unborn are?

Second, location is not relevant to one's nature. As Wennberg writes, "surely personhood and the right to life is not a matter of location. It should be *what* you are, not *where* you are that determines whether you have a right to life."[52] In fact, abortion-choice philosophers Peter Singer and Helga Kuhse write, "The pro-life groups are right about one thing: the location of the baby inside or outside the womb cannot make such a crucial moral difference. We cannot coherently hold that it is all right to kill a fetus a week before birth, but as soon as the baby is born everything must be done to keep it alive."[53]

Third, birth, like high school graduation or bar mitzvah, is an event that a particular being *undergoes*; it is not something that imparts to that being a property that changes its essential nature. Just as you remain you as you pass through the Lincoln Tunnel into Manhattan in the backseat of your father's Chevy, you remain you as you pass through the birth canal into the doctor's hands and from there to your mother's breast.

Fourth, as Wennberg points out, a newborn chimpanzee can be treated like a human newborn (i.e., named, baptized, accepted into a family), but this certainly does not mean that it is a subject of moral rights.[54]

Brain Waves

Some bioethicists, such as Baruch Brody, maintain the unborn becomes a subject of rights when its brain starts functioning, which can first be detected by the electroencephalogram (EEG) at about the end of the sixth week of pregnancy.[55] This view differs from Boonin's organized cortical brain activity criterion I critiqued earlier. For Boonin, what is important is that the unborn acquire conscious desires to ground rights; but these desires can take place only when the brain has organized cortical activity, which occurs between 25 and 32 weeks' gestation. Thus, according to

Boonin, the unborn has a right to life no earlier than 25 weeks. In contrast, Brody is arguing that the unborn has a right to life when its primitive brain begins functioning, which occurs early in pregnancy (40–42 *days* after conception), long before the unborn has the present exercisable capacity to have conscious experiences.

Brody argues that to judge whether a being is a human being and thus a subject of moral rights "we must first see ... what properties are such that their loss would mean the going out of existence (the death) of a human being."[56] He reasons that because at brain-death a human being goes out of existence (at least in this mortal realm), the presence of a functioning human brain is the property that makes one fully human. Consequently, Brody argues that "one of the characteristics essential to a human being is the capacity for conscious experience, at least at a primitive level. Before the sixth week, as far as we know, the fetus does not have this capacity. Thereafter, as the electroencephalographic evidence indicates, it does. Consequently, that is the time at which the fetus becomes a human being."[57]

There are several problems with this argument. First, it seems to depend on a Cartesian understanding of the self that locates the person exclusively in mental activity or consciousness.[58] This argument differs little from the AEA arguments critiqued in section I, which put a premium on a being's present capacity for certain value-making activities, such as consciousness, rationality, and/or desire. However, as I noted in that section, the unborn, by nature, has basic capacities for these functions from the moment it comes into being. In addition, the analogies of Uncles Jed and Herb show that presently exercisable capacity and/or the reacquisition of memories and skills are inadequate to ground intrinsic value. Consequently, Brody's notion of "capacity for conscious experience" is in fact had by the pre-brain embryo if we think of a basic capacity as a real capacity (which seems right) or it is not had by either the pre-brain embryo or Uncle Jed if we think of it as a presently exercisable capacity rather than a basic one.

Brody is arguing that the absence of mental function or the cerebral architecture (however primitive) that makes mental functions possible signals the absence of an essential human being. Brody assumes that what is valuable about a human being is consciousness, a psychological self, which he argues correlates with an intact (albeit premature) brain that has the capacity to allow the self to manifest certain functions, such as self-consciousness, self-awareness, and thought. This account seems to beg an important question: Why should the psychological self – the mental activities of a human being – be judged as the locus of intrinsic value rather than the whole being who, from the moment it comes into existence and whose parts work in concert for the maturing and perfecting of its basic capacities, maintains absolute identity through change while losing and gaining parts over time? I suspect that Brody would reply that he is not begging the question as he is relying on people's considered intuitions on this matter, and ethical discussion has to start somewhere. That, of course, is an appropriate way to conduct a philosophical inquiry, and I've done a bit of that myself over the years. Nevertheless, there are counterexamples and metaphysical concerns – many of which we have already covered in this chapter – that result in contrary intuitions that are consistent with the account of human personhood that I am defending. For example, Lee points out that those, like Brody, who maintain that the person is absent if the essential organ by which personal acts are manifested is not present (in this case, the primitive brain),[59] "view the soul [or substance] only in its synchronic function (its effect at a definite time) and ignore its diachronic function (its effect on a sequence spread out in time)."[60] That is, Brody offers a particular notion of substance – a Cartesian one – that does not take into account other phenomena for which the concept of substance defended in this chapter has been traditionally offered, for example, the intrinsic purpose of organisms, absolute identity over time, and substantial unity of the entity,[61] aspects of a being that are central to its existence, continuity, and identity even when that being is not self-aware or self-conscious.

Other difficulties with this argument have been offered by a variety of thinkers.[62] One writer, for instance, has argued that Brody has overstated the symmetry between the beginning and end of life, for there is a distinction between the pre-brain embryo and the brain-dead corpse: "Brain death indicates the end of human life as we know it, the dead brain having no capacity to revive itself. But the developing embryo has the natural capacity to bring on the functioning of the brain."[63] That is to say, an entity's *irreversible* absence of brain waves *after* the brain waves have come into existence indicates that the entity is no longer a fully integrated whole with basic capacities. On the other hand, the unborn who has yet to reach the stage in her development at which she exhibits brain waves, unlike the brain-dead corpse, is a whole fully integrated human organism with basic capacities including the capacity to develop brain waves. Therefore, "the two stages of human life are, then, entirely different from the point of view of brain functioning. The embryo contains the natural [or basic] capacity to develop all the human activities:

perceiving, reasoning, willing, and relating to others. Death means the end of natural growth, the cessation of these abilities."[64] An embryo, in its earliest stages, does not need a brain to be a whole living organism, whereas human beings at later stages do. As Stephen Schwarz points out: "There is clearly a world of difference between no brain activity in the sense of 'no more' and in the sense of 'not yet.' If a human being with irreversible 'no more' is dead, it does not follow that a human being whose lack of brain activity has the character of 'not yet' is dead, or otherwise not a human being."[65]

In reply to this criticism, Brody offers the following fictional scenario:

Imagine that medical technology has reached the stage at which, when brain death occurs, the brain is removed, "liquified," and "recast" into a new functioning brain. The new brain bears no relation to the old one (it has none of its memory traces, and so on). If the new brain were put into the old body, would the same human being exist or a new human being who made use of the body of the old one? I am inclined to suppose the latter. But consider the entity whose brain has died. Is he not like the fetus? Both have the potential for developing into an entity with a functioning brain (we shall call this a weak potential) but it seems to me, that an entity can go out of existence even if it retains a weak potential for having a functioning brain, and that, analogously, the fetus is not a human being just because it has this weak potential. What is essential for being human is the possession of the potential for human activities that comes with having the structures required for a functioning brain. It is this potential that the fetus acquires at (or perhaps slightly before) the time that its brain starts functioning, and it is this potential that the newly conceived fetus does not have.[66]

Once a few conceptual distinctions are made, it is easy to see why this response does not succeed.[67] The unborn's potential is intrinsic to its nature, something for which its parts act in concert to actualize. The unborn that acquires consciousness is the same substance that once did not have consciousness. On the other hand, the corpse and its brain are not parts of a fully integrated organism. Rather they are dis-integrated parts that may be employed as material causes – for example, the pre-recast brain – that may contribute to the existence of a new organism as in Brody's fictional scenario. Consequently, the use of the term "weak potential" is misleading. The unborn does not have a *"weak* potential" for consciousness; it has a basic capacity for consciousness by nature that it is intrinsically directed to acquire and will come to fruition given adequate health, nutrition, and shelter. In contrast, the "weak potential" of the dead brain is not an active, intrinsically directed potential it has by nature but is the sort of passive potential that all things have: a passive potential to be acted upon, shaped, and altered by extrinsic causes including agents. For example, the apple tree in my neighbor's yard has the basic capacity (or active potential) by nature to spawn apples; it has the weak potential (or passive potential) to become my desk, though *it* really can *not* become my desk. Rather, its material parts may be employed by a carpenter to build my desk. It is the carpenter's agency, plan, and tools acting in concert upon the dead wood of the tree that results in my desk. The tree ceases to exist as an organism when it is killed. The "recasting" of the resulting lumber is not, strictly speaking, a potential the tree has by nature. It is merely one of the many ways it may be acted upon by extrinsic agents that may destroy it and use its material parts for any number of projects from desks to tooth picks.

Another problem with the brain-wave criterion is its inability to account for the wrongness of purposely creating brainless human beings for an apparent public good. Although I have already brought this up twice in my critique of the AEA's case, it is worth mentioning again here. Dan W. Brock cites Carol Kahn's proposal, in which she argues that "after cell differentiation, some of the brain cells of the embryo or fetus would be removed so that it could then be grown as a brain-dead body for spare parts for its earlier twin."[68] According to Brock, "this body clone would be like an anencephalic newborn or pre-sentient fetus, neither of whom arguably can be harmed, because of their lack of capacity for consciousness."[69] Yet, Brock maintains, "most people would likely find" the practice of purposely creating nonsentient human beings "appalling and immoral, in part because here the cloned later twin's capacity for conscious life is destroyed solely as a means to benefit another."[70] It is not precisely clear, given the brain-wave account of moral personhood, what would be wrong with cloning brainless human beings for the purpose of harvesting their organs. That is, if there is no injustice done to another and someone receives a benefit, it is difficult to know where exactly the wrong is to be located in the act. I suspect that some would locate it in the moral intuition that the pre-brain embryo is deprived of something to which he is entitled. But if that is the case, then current possession of a brain activity is a condition that is sufficient, but not necessary,[71] for a human being to possess both rights and a present capacity to be harmed. Yet what follows is that the intentional creation of brainless children (or embryos) for the purpose of harvesting their organs is a serious wrong whose prohibition should be reflected in our laws, for their pre-brain selves are rights-bearers entitled to some protection by the wider community. But if we were to extract from this insight the principle that seems to ground this wrong – it is prima facie wrong to destroy the physical structure necessary for the realization of a human being's present capacity for the exercisability of a function that is a perfection of its nature – then the pre-brain embryo is a subject of moral concern.

The SLED Test

Stephen Schwarz has provided a useful acronym (SLED) to describe the four differences between the unborn and the born – *S*ize, *L*evel of development, *E*nvironment, and degree of *D*ependency – all of which are morally irrelevant in deciding whether anyone, born or unborn, has a fundamental right to life.[72] The theories of personhood covered in this chapter either implicitly or explicitly accept one or more of these differences as morally relevant. Because we have already discussed and critiqued these theories, what follows is merely a shorthand way to summarize the problems that these theories have in common.

Size
The unborn is smaller than the newborn. But a 7′7″ basketball player, such as Yao Ming, is much bigger than my wife, Frankie Beckwith, who is 4′11 3/4″. It would be absurd to say that Frankie has less moral value than Yao (although he does have greater economic value than she does since signing a multimillion-dollar contract with the NBA's Houston Rockets).

Level of Development
An adolescent is more physically developed than an infant, but that does not mean that the latter has less of a right to life. As I have already argued in this chapter, human development consists of stages along a continuum, none of which endow the human being with characteristics that change it from nonintrinsically valuable to intrinsically valuable. Writes Schwarz, "he is equally a person; he is the same person at his earlier stage of development as at the later stages, or else it would not be *his* development" (emphasis mine).[73] Therefore, the fact that the unborn is less developed than the newborn has no moral relevancy.

Environment

Where one is is irrelevant to *who* one is. The fact that a child may be in her mother's womb is a geographical fact not a moral judgment. As Schwarz notes, a newborn in an incubator is not worth less than one in her mother's arms or one who is a week younger and still in her mother's womb.[74] It is easy to see that environment is not at all morally relevant.

Degree of Dependency

As I noted in Chapter 2 in my critique of Justice Blackman's viability standard in *Roe v. Wade*, dependency is a notoriously unreliable notion in assessing a being's intrinsic value. After all, a person in a nursing home is more dependent on another's care than a healthy 25-year-old Olympic athlete. Yet it seems obvious that the greater dependency of the patient in the nursing home does not disqualify her as an intrinsically valuable being. As Schwarz points out:

> I remain myself through the various changes, phases of growth and development, phases of relative dependency or independence, that pertain to my body. I am not any less *me* because my body may be in a state of greater dependency than at another time. Thus we see that dependency through connection to another person has nothing to do with being a person. It only has to do with how the body is sustained.[75]

That is, undergoing an accidental change from dependent to independent does not change the identity of the being undergoing the change. Christopher Reeve did not become less of a being, or cease to be Christopher Reeve, merely because a tragic accident left him dependent on others for his very survival. The "he" that underwent that change remained the same "he." Consequently, changing from nondependent to dependent or vice versa does not impart to, or remove from, a being any property or properties that would change that being's identity. Thus, the fact that the unborn through most of its development is physically dependent on her mother has no moral bearing as to her nature or whether she is a person with intrinsic value.

OTHER OBJECTIONS TO THE VIEW THAT A HUMAN PERSON IS A SUBSTANCE THAT COMES TO BE AT CONCEPTION

The following are thirteen common questions raised against the view of the human person I am defending in this monograph. Some of the objections concern philosophical issues whereas others concern questions of public policy and jurisprudence.

If Sperm and Ova Are Genetically Human, Does Not That Make Them "Protectable Life"?

Sperm and ova do not have a right to life because they are not individual human *beings*, but are parts of individual human beings. They are only genetically human insofar as they share the genome of their owners, but this is also true of their owners' other parts (e.g., hands, feet, kidneys). Sperm and ova cease to exist at conception when the zygote, an individual human substance, comes into existence.

Peter K. McInerny, however, argues that "a living human cell that might be stimulated into a clone of a person does not now have a personal future. A fetus similarly has only the potentiality to develop a personal future. For this reason, killing a fetus is morally very different from killing a normal adult human."[76] But this argument is no better than the one we just criticized, for the unstimulated cell (which is genetically *part* of a human being) as well as the thing used to stimulate it are merely causes of the resulting unborn human clone. Likewise, the sperm and ovum (which are genetically each a *part* of an individual human being) are causes of the resulting unborn human non-clone. But none of the causes for either the unborn human clone or the unborn human non-clone is an intrinsically directed, whole organism with basic capacities for personal acts by nature, but in fact ceases to exist when conception results.[77] Hence, there is no similarity between an unstimulated living human cell and a typical unborn human being.

Does Not the Pro-Life View Entail 'Speciesism'?

The pro-life position does not lead to what certain animal rights proponents call "speciesism,"[78] the belief that all human life is sacred and/or special simply because it belongs to the species Homo sapiens. Just as racism is arbitrary because color and ethnicity are irrelevant to assessing a human being's intrinsic worth, those who charge pro-lifers with speciesism argue that preference for the species Homo sapiens is just as arbitrary. But this charge is a red herring. For the pro-life position is based on the *personal nature* of human beings and the presence of that nature from the moment a human being comes into existence regardless of whether it has the present exercisable capacity for, or is currently engaging in, personal acts. Consequently if another species exists, whether in this world or in another (such as Klingons and Vulcans of *Star Trek* lore), which possesses a personal nature from the moment any of its individual members come into being,[79] then pro-lifers would seek to have these creatures protected from unjustified homicide as well.[80]

Wouldn't Your Position Mean That Some Forms of Artificial Birth Control Result in Homicide?[81]

Yes. For there are forms of birth control whose primary, or secondary, purpose is to cause the death of an unborn human being. These birth control methods include the IUD, the "morning-after" pill, and RU-486. They are called *abortifacients*. However, not every form of birth control is designed to cause the death of an unborn human being. Some of these include the condom, diaphragm, and sterilization, all of which merely prevent conception.

This is why the pro-life advocate makes a distinction between *contraception* and *birth control*. Contraception literally means "to prevent conception." Therefore, all contraception is a form of birth control, because it prevents birth. But not all forms of birth control are contraceptive, as some forms, such as the ones cited, may prevent birth by killing the conceptus *after conception*. Hence, the pro-life advocate does not equate *contraception* with abortion, and some pro-lifers have no qualms with contraception as a morally legitimate form of family planning within the context of marriage.

Wouldn't Your Position Mean That Certain Abortifacients, Used *Exclusively* for Birth Control, Would Have to Be Made Illegal?

Yes, it would.[82] This question is sometimes raised because it is presumed that by answering the question "Yes" the pro-lifer is making a totally outrageous claim. But it is only presumed outrageous because those who present the question either explicitly or implicitly deny that the unborn is a moral person. Therefore, the outrageousness of banning abortifacients is contingent upon the moral status of the unborn. If the unborn is not a moral subject, at least in its earliest stages of development, my answer *is* outrageous. But if the unborn is a moral subject, then to call for its protection is certainly not outrageous at all, but something that all just governments are obligated to do. Hence, if the arguments for the unborn's moral personhood in this chapter and Chapter 4 are correct, or more likely correct than not, then those who support the right for citizens to use abortifacients, whose primary or secondary purpose is to kill unborn human beings, are the ones who are supporting something totally outrageous.

However, those drugs that can be beneficial to persons in other contexts, which may also function as abortifacients, obviously cannot be forbidden by law. Just as one cannot ban a butcher knife simply because it *may* be used to kill another person, one cannot ban an otherwise helpful drug because it *may* be used to kill another person.

If the Unborn Is a Moral Subject, Would It Not Follow That the State Must Ban Medical Treatments That Have an Abortifacient Side Effect?

Assuming that the unborn child is a human person, it would depend on the condition from which the woman is suffering.[83] For example, if the unborn is not viable, and if the woman's condition is life threatening, and if the treatment in question is necessary to save the mother's life, then it is justified, because if the woman's life is not saved then both mother and child would die. All things being equal, it is better that one person should live rather than two die; therefore, use of a treatment with an abortifacient side effect in this situation would be morally justified, for the intent would be to save a life (the mother's) even though the death of the unborn is a forseeable though not intended consequence.

On the other hand, if the treatment in question is not intended to preserve the mother's life and the woman's condition is not life threatening, then to risk the death of the unborn child is not morally justified. If the unborn is fully human, it is morally required that we forbid non-life-preserving medical treatment with an abortifacient side effect. As Schwarz points out, "Medical treatments should be proscribed if they include the killing of the child, just as any treatment, or any action, should be proscribed if it includes the killing of an innocent person."[84]

Isn't an Unborn Human, at Least in Its Earliest Stages of Development, Like an Acorn That Is Only a Potential Oak Tree?

This analogy has been used on many occasions by abortion-choice advocates. For example, Frank R. Zindler, in an article that originially appeared in *American Atheist*, argues: "As for potential persons, *an acorn is not an oak tree!*"[85] Aside from the problem of claiming that the unborn are "potential persons," which we have already addressed in this chapter as well as Chapter 4, there is a strong reason to believe this analogy is flawed.

Because a human being is a mammal and an oak tree is a plant, it is unclear why one should even entertain it as a source of insight. A better analogy would be to compare a human being to another mammal, such as a dog, cow, or horse. But because the unborn progeny of these mammals are developing, growing, and living members of the same species as their parents, just as are unborn humans of their parents, this hurts rather than helps the abortion-choice position.

But even if we accept Zinder's analogy, it still fails. After all, if the acorn is numerically identical to the oak tree, then the acorn is the oak tree in the sense that it is the same being, just as the infant is numerically identical to its adult self and thus is in fact the same being. Of course, we value oak trees more than we value acorns. But that is because oak trees provide to us certain aesthetic and practical goods that acorns do not provide. Human beings, however, are not valuable because they are instrumentally useful to others, as the oak tree is to many people. Human beings are valuable because of what they are and not because of what they do. As Robert P. George and Patrick Lee write: "Oak trees and acorns are not equally valuable, because the basis for their value is not *what* they are but precisely those accidental characteristics by which oak trees differ from acorns. We value the ugly, decaying oak tree less than the magnificent, still flourishing one; and we value the mature, magnificent oak more than the small, still growing one. But we would never say the same about human beings."[86]

Isn't the Unborn, at Least in Its Earliest Stages of Development, Just a Blueprint, or "Information Code," of a Human Being?

In response to the pro-life argument that full humanness begins at conception, a booklet published by the Religious Coalition for Abortion Rights, *Words of Choice*, claims that "just as a blueprint for a house is not a house, a genetic blueprint for a human body [i.e., the entity at conception] is not a person."[87] This is a caricature of the pro-life position, which is that the human being from the moment it comes into existence is a whole living being of particular nature who *possesses* a human genome. She is *not* a model, or blueprint, of a human being. Daniel Callahan, an advocate of abortion choice, agrees:

> It is...unscientific to call an embryo or fetus a mere "blueprint." Blueprints of buildings are not ordinarily mixed into the mortar; they

remain in the hands of the architects. Moreover, once a building has been constructed, the blueprint can be thrown away, and the building will continue to stand. The genetic blueprint operates in an entirely different way: it exerts a directly causal action in morphological development; as an intrinsic part of the physiological structure, it can at no point be thrown away or taken out.[88]

Doesn't a "Life of the Mother" Exception Involve a Contradiction?

Some argue that if pro-lifers really believe that life is sacred, why do they say that the killing of the unborn child is justified to save the life of the mother? Although I believe that I have sufficiently addressed this elsewhere in the book I will say a few more words here.

First, when pregnancy endangers a mother's life, medical personnel should try to save the lives of both mother and child. Second, if that is not possible, the physician must choose the course of action that best upholds the sanctity of human life. Because it is the mother's body that serves as the environment in which the unborn is nurtured, it is impossible to save the unborn child before viability (20 to 24 weeks after conception). In fact, almost all abortions performed to save the mother's life occur long before viability, for they are usually for an ectopic (or tubal) pregnancy. Consequently, in such cases, the physician must save the mother's life even if it results in the death of the unborn. The physician's intention is not to kill the child but to save the mother. But because salvaging both is impossible, and it is, all things being equal, better that one should live rather than two die, "abortion" to save the mother's life, in this case, is justified.

Third, after viability, when abortion itself is far riskier for the mother than is childbirth, there are very few if any instances in which an "abortion" will save the mother's life. But when such cases do occur, the same principles apply here as prior to viability. Former Surgeon General C. Everett Koop explains:

> When the woman is pregnant, her obstetrician takes on the care of two patients – the mother-to-be and the unborn baby. If, toward the end of the pregnancy, complications arise that threaten the mother's health, he will take the child by inducing labor or performing a Caesarean section.
>
> His intention is still to save the life of both the mother and the baby. The baby will be premature and perhaps immature depending on the length of gestation. Because it has suddenly been taken out of the protective womb, it may encounter threats to its survival. The baby is never willfully destroyed because the mother's life is in danger.[89]

Is a Zygote Equal to a Mature Adult Woman?

Writes Zindler: "If the single-celled zygote is *equal* to a full-grown woman, it follows that a full-grown woman can't be worth *more* than a single cell! Anyone who values women so little is a menace to society and shouldn't be allowed to run loose without a leash."[90] Aside from being emotionally charged rhetoric, this argument has several problems.

First, it equivocates on the meaning of the word "cell." The pro-lifer is *not* saying that a mature adult woman is equal to *any* single cell, which would imply the absurd conclusion that the single cells that make up a woman's body would each be individually equal to the total number of them together (i.e., the woman's entire body). Rather, the pro-lifer is arguing that when it comes to intrinsic value, all human beings are on an equal footing regardless of their stage of development, whether at the beginning (a single-celled zygote) or at the end (an elderly person). It just happens that an intrinsically valuable human being is a single cell at the beginning, but it does not follow, as Zindler mistakenly assumes, that adult human beings are equal to *any* individual human cell. Zindler attacks a straw man, something nobody believes.

Second, Zindler's argument is a non sequitur, that is, its conclusion does not logically follow from its premise. Recall Zindler's argument: "If the single-celled zygote is *equal* to a full-grown woman, it follows that a full-grown woman can't be worth *more* than a single cell!" But treating intrinsically valuable human beings with dignity at whatever stage of their development does not *logically* make the more developed ones worth less than they would have been worth if we had not come to know about the less developed ones and their intrinsic value. Knowing that the membership of the community of moral persons is larger than we had supposed, that it includes the less developed ones, does not decrease the intrinsic value of the more developed ones whom we have always known to be members. Consequently, the fact that pro-lifers claim that human beings at whatever stage of development are intrinsically valuable no more undermines the intrinsic value of a pregnant woman than does claiming that newborn infants are intrinsically valuable undermines our respect for more developed human beings such as their parents. Ironically, the pro-life position shows a great deal more respect for the pregnant woman's place in society than does Zindler's position. After all, according to the pro-life understanding of human beings, the pregnant woman has the enormous responsibility and privilege of protecting and nurturing a developing human being who is intrinsically valuable. In contrast, according to Zindler's position, the pregnant woman is merely an incubator who serves as a temporary shelter for a blob of cells. Moreover, if I understand Zindler correctly, the pregnant woman is not identical to her prenatal self, which entails that *unborn* females have no intrinsic value. So, one could argue that the pro-life position shows greater respect for women than Zindler's point of view.

Third, Zindler's argument equivocates on the world "equal." When pro-lifers say that all human beings are equal in their intrinsic value, they are not arguing that all human beings are equal as to their present functions or exercisable abilities. When confronted with a similar question posed to me in a debate several years ago, I responded: "It all depends; of course, a zygote cannot ride a bicycle as well as an adult. But insofar as possessing the nature of human personhood the zygote is equal to all other human beings with whom this nature is shared." Granted, zygotes cannot function like older human persons (as newborns cannot function like teenagers), but, as we have seen in this chapter, this certainly does not mean they are not intrinsically valuable.

Fourth, assuming that Zindler is correct, his argument proves too little if it is an argument for abortion choice throughout the entirety of pregnancy. For he emphasizes the one-celled zygote rather than the older fetus which, as we saw in Chapter 4, is a small-scale baby at seven weeks. That is, even if Zindler's argument supports the permissibility of killing zygotes and early embryos, it does not support the permissibility of killing the unborn entity when it is much more developed, when it is not merely one cell and tiny. As Schwarz points out, "When examined carefully, the absurdity of this argument as an attempt to justify abortion confronts us. 'It's alright to destroy a tiny [zygote], because it is so tiny. Therefore it's all right to take a well-developed child at twelve weeks or more, burn her skin and poison her by saline, or cut her to pieces by D & E.'"[91]

Fifth, following from the previous criticism, Zindler's argument, ironically, could be construed as a moderate *anti*-abortion argument. As Schwarz explains:

Suppose [this argument] convinces a person that a [zygote] counts for virtually nothing in comparison to a mature person. The reason would be its tiny size and undeveloped status, implying that with development and a more normal size, the being in question would be valued. But that is precisely what is true of a seven-week-old baby in the womb, or that same child in later phases. Thus, if the zygote may be destroyed because it is so tiny, then precisely for this reason the child who is a victim of standard abortion techniques may not be destroyed, because he is not tiny. Therefore, abortion is wrong.[92]

Sixth, Zindler's case is more of a rhetorical flourish than a sober argument. Consider again his comments: "If the single-celled zygote is *equal* to a full-grown woman, it follows that a full-grown woman can't be worth *more* than a single cell! Anyone who values women so little is a menace to society and shouldn't be allowed to run loose without a leash." But two can play that game. The pro-lifer can take the same data and make Zindler's position look foolish and philosophically naïve: "If the worth of human beings is dependent on such morally irrelevant factors as size, level of development, environment, and dependency, then Zindler is claiming that big, developed, and independent people can wantonly kill tiny, less developed, dependent people. Anyone who sees the value of human life as being subject to such irrelevant factors is a menace to society and shouldn't be allowed to run loose without a leash." This, of course, is an unfair caricature of the more sophisticated cases offered by abortion-choice advocates. But just as it would be wrong for me, or any other pro-life advocate, to offer up such straw men as examples of our opponents' arguments, it would be wrong for an abortion-choice advocate, such as Zindler, to do likewise with our case.

Seventh, if the arguments in this chapter and Chapter 4 are successful, or more likely successful than not, then Zindler's rhetorical flourish is of no effect. That is, Zindler must first show where and why the pro-life arguments are logically flawed rather than merely offering an emotional appeal.

If the Unborn Were Considered Legal Persons, Would Not This Result in Chaos in Our Legal and Social Structure, Such as Census Counting, Tax Laws, Legislature Reapportionment, Population-Based Funding and Services?

No.[93] Treating the unborn as human persons and protecting them from being killed unjustly does not mean that we must overturn our current legal and social structure. Take, for example, the census. We can continue to count only born human beings, and base legislative reapportionment on that sum,[94] for it is extremely difficult and highly inefficient to count unborn human beings because we cannot see them and many of them die before birth, sometimes without the mother ever being aware that she was pregnant. Consequently, there is nothing inconsistent with thinking of the census as a count of *only* born human beings and at the same time acknowledging that the unborn are human beings who ought to be protected. This same rationale can be applied as well to the tax laws, population-based allocating of funding and services, and other matters.[95]

Second, prior to the mid-1960s, when the laws in every state in the United States considered the unborn moral subjects,[96] our legal and social structure was relatively the same as it is today. Because in the past protecting the unborn was consistent with what we know today as the current legal and social structure, there is no reason it cannot be the same today if the law is changed to acknowledge the unborn as full-fledged members of the moral community.

Third, whether our legal and social structure would have to be overhauled as a result of recognizing the unborn's moral status has no bearing on whether the unborn are intrinsically valuable by nature. Certainly the unborn can be intrinsically valuable by nature regardless of how the legal and social structure may be set up. Consider the example of slavery. Suppose a defender of slavery argued that abolishing slavery would not be justified because it would undermine society's legal and social structure – for example, plantations would not have free labor, free blacks would need jobs, unemployment would increase, the census would have to be changed, the tax code would need to be altered. Would this objection have any bearing on the question of whether black slaves are intrinsically valuable human beings by nature?

The Fire in the IVF Clinic Scenario

An anonymous reviewer raises an important counterexample to my case: "Suppose that in an IVF clinic, an earthquake causes (1) a couple of glass dishes to break resulting in ten eggs being accidentally fertilized and (2) a fire in a room in which five patients are trapped. I can either save the fertilized eggs (they will then be implanted in another clinic) or the patients. Most of us believe that I should save the patients but it is not clear that the sort of substance dualism espoused by the author is compatible with this claim."

These types of stories can, of course, always be adjusted to make an entirely different point. For example, suppose the five patients are aging Nazi war criminals and the 10 embryos are one's own offspring. It's pretty clear which group one would save. However, the sort of fictional scenario offered by this referee has been responded to by a number of others. I will offer one reply put forth by Scott B. Rae, who argues that this sort of story confuses epistemology with ontology, that is, it confuses what things appear to us with what things actually are. As Rae writes,

> The surface appearance of an embryo seems too distant and impersonal. But surface appearances and the emotions they engender are, by themselves, inadequate guides for moral reflection. To a lesser degree, this same sort of "argument" could be used to justify racism, an unjustified preference for individuals who share many of one's own surface features. Since the presence or absence of surface features may be the real basis for the intuitions in this argument, we do not consider it has the force its advocates claim it has.[97]

If the Unborn Is Considered a Moral Subject under the Law, Would It Not Follow That Pregnant Women Would Be Prohibited from Smoking, Drinking Alcohol, or Engaging in Other Activities That May Harm the Unborn?

The fact that smoking and drinking alcohol during pregnancy can harm the unborn is well documented in the medical and scientific literature.[98] Consequently, because such activity is harmful to the unborn, and the unborn are moral subjects, a mother has a *moral* responsibility to make sure her unborn child is not harmed, just as she does *after* the child's birth. However, whether the intrusive policing of such harmful activity should be a fixed point of our criminal law is another question.

My view is the one proposed by Schwarz, who draws an analogy with the "born child [who] has a right to good health care, proper diet, protection from harmful effects." He points out, however, that although "to some extent this right can be enshrined in law, to a large extent it cannot. We cannot have police at the family dinner table ensuring that the child gets all the nourishing food and vitamins he needs. Nor can he be protected from all harmful effects in the home, parallel to the harmful effects for the preborn child from his mother's smoking [or drinking]." Yet, Schwarz concludes, "surely the born child's right to live must be enshrined in the law, and given the same legal protection the rest of us enjoy. Exactly the same applies to that child before he is born."[99]

It should be noted, as Schwarz points out, that the question assessed in this section really does not help the abortion-choice position, because the same question can be asked to the abortion-choice supporter who argues that the being in the womb is not an actual person but only a potential person.[100] After all, if the child is brought to term, the pregnant woman's behavior, though immediately impacting the development of the fetus while she is carrying it, will result in harm and suffering to the fetus *after* it is born.[101] Therefore, "the wrongness of smoking [or drinking] while pregnant is no way removed, or even mitigated, by adopting the view that no person is present in the womb. Correspondingly, if smoking [or drinking] is already wrong on the assumption the 'fetus' is merely a potential person, nothing significant is changed or added when we come to realize that he is already a person, an actual person."[102] Consequently, the objection raised in the question assessed in this section applies to the "potential person" view as well.

Furthermore, if abortion is made illegal because the law recognizes the unborn as moral subjects, then the unborn will be treated as born children. And just as the law *presumes* that the parents of born children have the best interests of their children in mind, the law will presume the same about the parents of unborn children. Therefore, unless the state has a *very good* reason to suspect that the activities of the parents are causing harm to their unborn child (as it would have to for parents of born children), the state has to presume that the parents are acting in a way that has the best interests of their child in mind.

If the Unborn Is Considered a Person under the Law, Would Not All Miscarriages Be Suspect and Would Not Women Have to Prove That Their Miscarriages Were Not Elective Abortions?

No.[103] First, this question is a crass appeal to fear. People die all the time, but we do not ask those closest to the deceased to prove that they did not commit a murder. After all, in our criminal law one is *presumed* innocent until *proven* guilty. If the unborn are considered moral subjects under the law, this would be true of women who have had miscarriages as well.

Second, all miscarriages would not be suspect, but only those for which there are reasonable grounds to suspect that deliberate killing was involved.[104] This is how we treat the deaths of children whose demise was the result of an apparent accident. If there is evidence to suspect that the born child was abused and her death was the result of someone's negligence or premeditated act, then an investigation ought to be conducted. If there is no evidence, then the parents ought to be left alone to mourn their loss.[105] The same principle would apply to miscarriages.

7

DOES IT REALLY MATTER WHETHER THE UNBORN IS A MORAL SUBJECT? THE CASE FROM BODILY RIGHTS

Some abortion-choice advocates do not see the status of the unborn as the decisive factor in whether abortion is morally justified. They argue that a pregnant woman's removal of the unborn from her body, even though it is foreseeable that it will result in the unborn's death, is no more immoral than an ordinary person's refusal to donate his kidney to another in need of one, even though this refusal will probably result in the death of the prospective recipient.

In 1971, philosopher Judith Jarvis Thomson published what would become the most famous and influential argument of this sort.[1] Others, including David Boonin[2] and Eileen McDonagh,[3] have defended revised versions of it. The focus of this chapter will be on Thomson's argument as well as refinements of it found in these other works.

THOMSON'S ARGUMENT

Thomson writes that it is "of great interest to ask what happens if, for the sake of argument, we allow the premise [that the unborn is intrinsically valuable (IV)]. How, precisely, are we supposed to get from there to the conclusion that abortion is morally impermissible?"[4] Thomson's argument, therefore, poses a special difficulty for the pro-life advocate. She grants, for the sake of argument, the pro-lifer's most important premise – the unborn is a subject of moral rights – but nevertheless concludes that abortion is morally permissible. In a sense, her query, at the level of principle, is uncontroversial, for she is simply asking whether it follows from the fact that a living being is intrinsically valuable that it is *never* permissible to kill that being or to act in a way that results in its death. After all, many pro-lifers would answer "no." Many of them argue that one can consistently maintain that all human beings are IV, and thus have a prima facie right to life, while at the same time holding there may be some cases in which killing human beings is justified, such as in the cases of just war or self-defense.

Thomson argues that even if the unborn is intrinsically valuable with a right to life, it does not follow that a pregnant woman is morally required to use her bodily organs to sustain the unborn's life. To make her case, Thomson offers a story that accentuates what she believes are the relevant principles that support her argument:

> You wake up in the morning and find yourself back to back in bed with an unconscious violinist. A famous unconscious violinist. He has been found to have a fatal kidney ailment, and the Society of Music Lovers has canvassed all the available medical records and found that you alone have the right blood type to help. They have therefore kidnapped you, and last night the violinist's circulatory system was plugged into yours, so that your kidneys can be used to extract poisons from his blood as well as your own. The director of the hospital now tells you, "Look we're sorry the Society of Music Lovers did this to you – we would never have permitted it if we had known. But still, they did it, and the violinist now is plugged into you. To unplug you would be to kill him. But never mind, it's only for nine months. By then he will have recovered from his ailment, and can safely be unplugged from you." Is it morally incumbent on you to accede to this situation? No doubt it would be very nice of you if you did, a great kindness. But do you *have* to accede to it? What if it were not nine months, but nine years? Or still longer? What if the director of the hospital says, "Tough luck, I agree, but you've now got to stay in bed, with the violinist plugged into you, for the rest of your life. Because remember this. All persons have a right to life, and violinists are persons. Granted you have a right to decide what happens in and to your body, but a person's right to life outweighs your right to decide what happens in and to your body. So you cannot ever be unplugged from him." I imagine that you would regard this as outrageous.[5]

Thomson concludes she is "only arguing that having a right to life does not guarantee having either a right to be given the use of or a right to be allowed continued use of another person's body – even if one needs it for life itself."[6] That is, the unborn does not have a right to life so strong that it outweighs the pregnant woman's right to personal bodily autonomy.[7] Thomson anticipates several objections to her argument, and in the process of responding to them further clarifies her case. It is not important, however, that we go over these clarifications, for some are not germane to the pro-life position I am defending in this book.[8]

According to Thomson, the pregnant woman consented to sex but not to the pregnancy that followed if she did not intend to have children. Just as opening my window for the pleasure of fresh air does not entitle a burglar to my belongings even though while opening the window it was foreseeable that a burglar might crawl through the window wanting to steal from me, engaging in sex for pleasure does not entitle the fetus to the pregnant woman's body even though while engaging in sex it was foreseeable that an unborn human being might result needing the pregnant woman's body for its survival.[9]

It should be noted, however, that Thomson's illustration gives the impression that the typical abortion procedure is merely a matter of *unplugging* the unborn from its mother, perhaps involving nothing more onerous or controversial than flipping a switch or turning a knob. But this is misleading. Stephen Schwarz and Ronald K. Tacelli graphically point out, as I document in Chapter 4, that "a woman who has an abortion is indeed 'withholding support' from her unborn child ... [but] abortion is far more than that. It is the active killing of a human person – by burning him, by crushing him, by dismembering him."[10] Federal judge and legal scholar, Richard A. Posner, whose dissenting opinion in *Hope Clinic v. Ryan* 195 F.3d 857 (1999) held that statutes intended to ban the partial-birth abortion procedure are unconstitutional,[11] offers his own, more detailed, description:

[A] doctor performing an abortion does not merely "pull the plug" on the fetus. In a first-trimester abortion he uses either surgical instruments or a suction pump to remove the fetus from the uterus ("curettage"). In a second-trimester abortion he either uses surgical instruments to the same end or he injects a chemical that either kills the fetus and by doing so induces premature labor or just induces premature labor. Whatever the method, he is employing force for the purpose and with the effect of killing the fetus, and though the killing is a by-product rather than the sole end, the same is true when a child kills his parents in order to inherit their money. The surgical procedure used in second-trimester abortion routinely involves crushing the fetus's cranium, and even in first-trimester abortion the fetus is sometimes removed piecemeal, for we are told that "if a fetus beyond 10 weeks of age is recognized, the fragments should be reassembled to see if the fetus is essentially complete" (because any fetal tissue remaining in the uterus could cause infection). In the rare third-trimester abortion, the doctor kills the fetus either by injecting a chemical into its heart or drilling a hole in its cranium and removing its spinal fluid through the hole.[12]

A CRITIQUE OF THOMSON'S ARGUMENT

There are at least four problems with Thomson's argument. These problems can be put into two categories: (1) metaphysical and (2) ethical. In the course of my critique I will consider and assess arguments by other thinkers who have offered support for Thomson's case or ones similar to it.

A. Metaphysical Problems

As I noted in Chapter 3, *metaphysics* is an area of philosophy that deals with questions having to do with the ultimate grounding and nature of things in the world.[13] It is concerned with such diverse topics as the mind/body problem, identity, God, the existence and nature of universals, the existence and nature of the soul, and so on. Thus, the morality of abortion, if it is to be construed as contingent upon the nature of the unborn, is an issue whose resolution depends on which metaphysical view of the human being is correct.

Thomson is suggesting that the abortion-choice position is still correct even if we table the metaphysical question of the fetus's moral status by conceding that the unborn is a person. Nevertheless, I believe it is a mistake to infer from this that Thomson and her allies are in fact conceding for the sake of argument what pro-lifers believe about the fetus, even though they are claiming that they are doing just that.[14] What Thomson is granting is *not* the pro-life view of personhood, but a view of personhood consistent with the pro-life position *only insofar* as it is aligned with her own liberal and minimalist understanding of autonomy and choice. The success of her case, and the case of those who offer support for her argument, depends on assuming a view of the person that isolates the individual from other persons except as those relationships arise from the individual's explicit choice. It is, in the words of Michael Sandel, the "image of the self as free and independent, unencumbered by aims and attachments it did not choose for itself."[15] But if this is Thomson's understanding of personhood, as it seems to be, then it is *that* understanding she is stipulating when she grants to the abortion opponent, for the sake of argument, that the fetus is a *person*. But that is *not* the pro-life view of personhood. The pro-life view is that human beings are persons-in-community and have certain natural obligations as members of their community that arise from their roles as mother, father, citizen, child, and so on. Therefore, the success of Thomson's case and those of her allies depends on begging questions of philosophical anthropology that are derived from an understanding of personhood that is necessary to arrive at the conclusion that abortion is a fundamental right even if the fetus is *that sort of person*.

Thus, I believe that Thomson and her allies smuggle in a philosophical anthropology – a metaphysical view of the human person – in their defense of abortion choice that is no less controversial than the unborn's personhood they are *apparently* conceding for the sake of argument. I argue that there are two claims they make – one implied and the other explicit – in which this philosophical anthropology is smuggled: (1) pregnancy is not a prima facie good, and (2) consent-to-sex is not consent-to-pregnancy.

Is Pregnancy a Prima Facie Good?

Implied in the works of Thomson[16] and Boonin,[17] and explicit in the work of McDonagh (who compares pregnancy to rape),[18] is the notion that pregnancy is not a prima facie good. Why is this observation important? If pregnancy is a prima facie good, then the analogies employed by Thomson, Boonin, and McDonagh – which are all cases of prima facie wrongs – fail to capture the essence of pregnancy. Consider the following illustration.

A young woman is involved in a car accident and is rendered unconscious by her injuries. She is brought to a hospital where – still comatose – she is examined by a doctor. While performing some tests, the doctor determines that the woman has been pregnant for several weeks. Furthermore, suppose that evidence comes to light to suggest that the woman is unaware of her pregnancy – perhaps her close friends know nothing of the pregnancy, a diary shows no knowledge of being pregnant, and so on.

Adopting either McDonagh's understanding of pregnancy as morally equivalent to rape or assault, or Boonin's[19] and Thomson's notion that pregnancy is a prima facie violation of the woman's bodily integrity, what is the doctor's obligation to his unconscious patient? It would seem that, under these conditions, the doctor is morally required to perform an abortion to rid his patient of the "massive intrusion" being imposed upon her by the unborn. After regaining consciousness, the woman would have to be told that she's undergone an abortion for a pregnancy of which she was not aware, for there was no evidence that consent had been given and that she was under assault or that her bodily integrity was being violated.

I submit that this conclusion, logically drawn, is grossly incompatible with our moral intuitions concerning pregnancy. It is hard to imagine that any doctor, in good conscience, would perform an abortion on this woman merely because he had no evidence that she had consented to the pregnancy. It is likely that those who had undergone such an abortion would experience a tragic sense of loss; a sense of having been robbed of something precious in the pregnancy – something which, at the very least, deserved thoughtful consideration despite the difficulties of bearing a child. It is hard to imagine that a woman in such circumstances would not herself feel significantly violated. In other words, contra McDonagh, the abortion, not the pregnancy, would be more analogous to rape.

An anonymous referee suggests that ongoing or "perhaps most recent" consent may be effective as a reply against my arguments. He writes, "In the accident victim case what matters is not whether the now-unconscious woman consented to pregnancy at the time of the conception, but whether she would consent to pregnancy now. If she would, then the doctor is not justified in proceeding with the abortion." But such speculations about what an unconscious person's desires about her pregnancy's continuance *would be* makes sense if pregnancy is a prima facie good, as I believe that it is. But for that reason, the reply seems to miss the parallel between rape and pregnancy that McDonagh is trying to draw, and the claim of Boonin and Thomson that pregnancy is a prima facie violation of bodily integrity.

To understand what I mean, consider another situation, one that takes the Thomson-McDonagh-Boonin (TMB) thesis at its word, and presses the parallels. Suppose that you come across a man having sex with that same unconscious patient and you correctly intervene to stop the ugly violation. In this light, it is hard to see how someone could dismiss the accident counterexample with the claim that what matters is whether the pregnant woman would consent to pregnancy now. To press the parallel, one could say, "What matters is whether she would consent to sex now." Would anyone really allow a man to have sex with an unconscious woman? If not, and if one would allow the pregnancy to continue in the accident case, then this shows that the TMB parallels are ill-formed and that pregnancy is in fact a prima facie good, which is precisely my point.

Someone who maintains that pregnancy is a prima facie good, and is sympathetic to the difficulties of this case, might respond to my accident-victim story by saying that the doctor should wait until his patient regains consciousness. McDonagh, to the contrary, reinforces the unfortunate conclusion I have drawn from the logic of her position:

> Some might suggest that the solution to coercive pregnancy is simply for the woman to wait until the fetus is born, at which point its coercive imposition of pregnancy will cease. This type of reasoning is akin to suggesting that a woman being raped should wait until the rape is over rather than stopping the rapist. Nonconsensual pregnancy, like nonconsensual sexual intercourse, is a condition that must be stopped immediately because both processes severely violate one's bodily integrity and liberty.[20]

Boonin offers a similar analysis when he states:

> My claim has simply been that the fact that [the woman's] engaging in intercourse was voluntary provides no good reason to suppose that she has in fact [tacitly agreed to give up the right to the exclusive control of her body]. . . . But the assumption that the right to control one's body is inalienable is open to doubt. Suppose, after all, that a woman made the following explicit agreement: Give me some money today, and tomorrow you can use my body in any way that you want even if by that time I have changed my mind and no longer want you to. Most of us would think this sort of contract to be simply invalid. As at least one writer sympathetic to the good samaritan argument [i.e., Thomson's argument] has urged, "one cannot legitimately enslave oneself by waiving in advance one's right to control one's body." . . . And if this is so, then even if we thought that by her actions the woman could legitimately be understood as *attempting* to consent to waive this right, we would still have to conclude that she had not in fact done so.[21]

Consequently, under the TMB thesis, the doctor in the midst of the situation – aware of the pregnancy in the absence of consent – must see it as the rape-in-progress (McDonagh), or at least a prima facie violation of the patient's bodily integrity of his unconscious patient (Thomson/Boonin). How could he do anything else but end the assault?

Someone may object to my use of the quotes from McDonagh and Boonin by which I attempt to show that they would agree that a physician should perform an abortion on the unconscious pregnant woman. The objector may argue that my implicit comparison between waiting until the unconscious woman wakes up and waiting until the pregnancy of a conscious woman comes to term seems forced. This objector might say that the point of waiting until the woman wakes up is to see whether the pregnancy is voluntary, a reason that does not exist in the case of the conscious pregnant woman. But clearly in my second analogy, in which one woman is unconscious during pregnancy and the other during sex, this reason for waiting – the absence of consent – is present. Therefore, this objection fails, for it relies on the intuition that pregnancy is a prima facie good, but my point is that that intuition is not supported by TMB.

Is Consent-to-Sex Consent-to-Pregnancy?

Thomson and her allies make a distinction between consent-to-pregnancy and consent-to-sex. That is, consent-to-sex is a distinct act from consent-to-pregnancy. For when one engages in an act of sexual intercourse without the intent to procreate a child, there is no tacit or explicit consent to caring for, or at least not to kill, the unborn child.

To make their case, proponents offer a number of analogies. McDonagh, for example, makes the point that we do not consent to an injury even if we know that our actions negligently increase our risk of injury and others may benefit from our negligence.[22] She argues that consenting to smoking cigarettes, living in an area known for hurricanes, or wandering into a forest occupied by grizzly bears does not mean that one is consenting to lung cancer, destruction of one's property, or becoming a meal.[23] Boonin provides his own illustrations. He asks to imagine a case in which a man named Ted accidentally leaves his money on the table of a restaurant in which he and his friend Bill had just dined. Although Ted is at fault for this mistake, "still, it is surely unreasonable," writes Boonin, "to insist that by putting the money on the table when he sat down Ted tacitly agreed to let the waiter keep all of it if, as a foreseeable consequence of this act, the money was still on the table when he left."[24] Just as consenting to smoking cigarettes is not consenting to lung cancer and consenting to wandering into a forest is not consenting to being a grizzly bear's meal, analogously, consenting to sex does not mean that one is consenting to pregnancy.

It seems to me that these analogies "work" only because they presuppose a controversial philosophical anthropology that many reasonable people would find prima facie mistaken. That is, if one can show that this philosophical anthropology is at least not prima facie correct, the moral intuitions that are grounded in it and to which abortion-choice proponents appeal to make their case are not prima facie correct either. Let me explain.

Although TMB separate sex and pregnancy in their analysis, it is not clear to everyone that they are detachable, though causally related events, like wandering into a forest and being attacked by a grizzly bear, acquiring lung cancer as a result of smoking cigarettes, accidentally leaving your money at the restaurant and the waiter taking it as his tip, or being hooked up involuntarily to an unconscious violinist. For it seems reasonable to many people that sex is really part of pregnancy; it is the act engaged in by agents from which pregnancy is the designed (though maybe not the desired) result. But not in the same way as lung cancer results from cigarette smoking. For if one thinks of the human organism as a unified substance with certain natural purposes, basic capacities, powers, and properties, as I argue in Chapter 6, then it seems correct to say that the *telos* (or purpose) of reproductive organs *is* reproduction (i.e., pregnancy), for sperm and ova seem intrinsically ordered toward that very purpose. On the other hand, a cigarette is an artificial construct whose purpose is externally imposed upon it by an outside agent, its manufacturer. A cigarette is not a living organism, a unified substance, whose parts work together for a certain purpose because of its internal nature or essence. J. P. Moreland clarifies this notion when he writes that "it is because an entity has an essence and falls within a natural kind that it can possess a unity of dispositions, capacities, parts and properties at a given time and can maintain identity through change." Moreover, "it is the natural kind that determines what kinds of activities are appropriate and natural for that entity."[25]

Thus, to understand one's self and one's nature is to understand that one's sexual organs are ordered toward procreation. And once one understands and appreciates that, it seems that consent to sexual intercourse does entail consent to pregnancy whether or not one intends or desires such a state. It is not that pregnancy is merely "foreseeable," as Boonin writes.[26] Rather, *pregnancy* is *the* intelligible point of the participants' parts acting in concert: the sperm are expelled from the male into the female so that one of them may commingle with an ovum, resulting in a new human life. Sex, of course, has other purposes: to facilitate intimacy, to unify spouses, and so on. But, clearly, there is nothing outrageous in claiming that pregnancy is part of sex; it is what sometimes results when all the participants' parts are functioning properly, for that is to what these parts are naturally ordered.

Given this philosophical anthropology, and given TMB's concession that the fetus is a human person (though implicitly denying the broader teleological considerations that go with that pro-life understanding), one may look at their case in another, less morally compelling, way: they maintain that it is permissible to engage in a pleasurable act whose design is to bring into existence a vulnerable, defenseless, and dependent human person, and if such a person comes into existence, one of the persons responsible for its existence and who is in a unique position to care and nurture it can then destroy it without any justification except an act of will.

To put it another way, the mother, in virtue of the sexual act's reproductive purpose, consents to a process in which she plays a vital procreative, protective, and life-supportive role in relation to her unborn child – one only she can fulfill, and one for which many people think she is prima facie designed to fulfill as the maternal partner of the conjugal act. She has agreed to this course of action knowing that doing so may put her child (a rights-bearing individual) in a state out of which the child cannot opt and in which the government permits its mother to kill it without any public justification.

Of course, TMB may want to reject the philosophical anthropology I am suggesting and maintain that the human being is merely a collection of parts, a property-thing, like a car, computer, or cigarette, with no nature, essence, or natural purposes, and that there are literally no such things as "reproductive organs" as such. But it is not clear how they can do so given their reliance on notions such as "rights," which they seem to believe are essential moral properties that human beings (especially pregnant women) have prior to government (that is, by nature). Yet this seems to imply that when human beings are denied their rights by government they are not being treated in a way that is in accordance with their natural purpose (i.e., human beings are beings such that they have rights that ought to be respected by the state). They may respond by saying that human beings do have a natural purpose but only when it comes to rights and not when it comes to sex and pregnancy. They may *say* that, but it is unclear how they can have it both ways philosophically once they grant teleology as an appropriate category by which to reflect on the nature of human persons. For it seems that once teleology is allowed in, it is difficult to deny that sex as part of pregnancy seems prima facie correct, that sex is ordered toward reproduction. And even if one were to deny the metaphysical foundation that some believe grounds sex as part of pregnancy, one would have to admit that the belief that sex is part of pregnancy is *at least* as well grounded a moral intuition as one may extract from Thomson's violinist illustration, McDonagh's analogies of lung cancer, a hurricane, and a hungry grizzly bear, and Boonin's story of Ted forgetting his money at the restaurant.[27]

Ethical Problems

There are at least two ethical problems with Thomson's argument: (1) it assumes moral volunteerism, and (2) it cannot account for intuitions that result in a pro-life understanding of pregnancy and the unborn. I will conclude with an analysis of (3) the rape exception.

It Assumes Moral Volunteerism

By using the violinist story as an illustration of how the principles about which all human relationships should be ethically applied, Thomson seems to be saying that moral obligations must be voluntarily accepted to have moral, and thus legal, force. But that does not seem correct in some cases. For instance, we do not consider explicit consent to be a necessary condition when we justly ascribe blame and attribute responsibility to a person whose actions resulted in consequences that he did not explicitly intend to bring about. Take, for example, the following tale. Imagine a man and a woman engage in consensual intercourse that results in pregnancy. The couple did not intend this result, for they were careful in their carnal indulgence, employing several of the most efficient and safest forms of birth control short of surgical abortion. And yet, conception occurred. Rather than exercising her legal right to abort, the woman, who had never fancied herself as a mother, chooses to bring the child to term, for she has not been able to suppress the maternal instincts that welled up inside her from the moment her physician informed her that she was pregnant. The father, however, does not share the mother's excitement. In fact, he loathes the idea of being anyone's father. He wants neither the title nor the responsibility. Soon after the child's birth, the mother seeks from the father financial support for the child that he sired. He rejects her request. She hires an attorney and begins legal action against the father, asking the court to garnish the father's wages until his child is 18 years old. There is no doubt that the father was careful and precautionary in his sexual activity with his child's mother, and he had indicated by both his contraceptive actions and his words that he did not want to become a father. Yet, the child support laws virtually everywhere offer a different moral understanding of this man's responsibility,[28] one that does not put a premium on autonomy, choice, or explicit intention. Under these laws, the child's father is obligated to provide financial support for his child *precisely because* of his paternal relationship to this child, a reason that Thomson would consider not morally relevant. These laws are grounded in deep moral intuitions, that seem prima facie correct, that ground our notion that parents have a natural, pre-political, obligation to care for their child even if the child's existence was not the result of a conscious plan to bring the child into being. Our intuitions about parental obligation to children, and society's obligation to its vulnerable immature members, seem to be more well-grounded intuitions than the autonomy to which Thomson appeals. After all, virtuous adults, able to exercise their autonomy in a responsible way, are often the children of parents who did not think of their offspring as products of choice, but rather, as human beings entrusted to their care and whose futures depend on a commitment that cannot be cashed out with the poverty of rights-talk.

But this obligatory relationship is not based strictly on *biology*, for this would make sperm donors morally responsible for children conceived by their seed.[29] Rather, the father's responsibility for his offspring stems from the fact that he engaged in an act, sexual intercourse, which he fully realized could result in the creation of another human being because reproductive organs are ordered to result in reproduction if they are functioning properly, although the father took every precaution to avoid such a result short of abstaining from sex. This is not an unusual way to frame moral obligations, for we do so even in cases when a particular result is merely foreseeable and not naturally ordered. For example, we hold drunk people whose driving results in manslaughter responsible for their actions, even if they did not *intend* to kill someone prior to becoming intoxicated. Such special obligations, although not *directly* undertaken *voluntarily*, are necessary in any civilized culture to preserve the rights of the vulnerable, the weak, and the young, who can offer very little in exchange for the rights bestowed upon them by the strong, the powerful, and the post-uterine in the moral universe of personal autonomy. This is why the burglar illustration I borrowed from Thomson fails (see p. 173, this volume). As Patrick Lee points out: "The woman's action does not cause the burglar to be in the house but only removes an obstacle; the burglar himself is the primary agent responsible for his being in the house. In the voluntary pregnancy case, however, the baby does not cause his or her presence in the mother's womb; rather, the mother and the father do."[30] Consequently, Thomson is wrong when she claims that if a couple has "taken all reasonable precautions against having a child, they do not by virtue of their biological relationship to the child who comes into existence have a special responsibility for it" since "surely we do not have any such 'special responsibility' for a person unless we have assumed it, explicitly or implicitly."[31]

Because Thomson does not adequately address what most of us recognize as the deep moral connection between sexual intercourse, human reproduction, and the pre-political obligations of parents to offspring (as I pointed out in the section on metaphysical objections),[32] her argument languishes in a one-dimensional universe of autonomous adult-choosers who are artificially constructed by Thomson to lack the precise number of natural moral obligations that her science fiction scenario is employed to demonstrate in the first place. Hence, instead of providing reasons for rejecting any special responsibilities for one's offspring, Thomson simply dismisses the concept altogether and presupposes a view of autonomy as obviously true (i.e., "*surely* we do not have any such ... ")[33] that by its nature excludes such special responsibilities. Thus, she begs the question.

Thomson's violinist illustration, of course, makes the correct point that there are times when withholding and/or withdrawing care is morally justified. For instance, I am not morally obligated to donate my kidney to my neighbor Fred, simply because he needs a kidney to live. I am not obligated to risk my life so that Fred may live a few years longer. Fred should not expect that of me. If, however, I donate one of my kidneys to Fred, I will have acted above and beyond the call of duty, since I will have performed a supererogatory moral act. But this case is not analogous to pregnancy and abortion.

In the case of the violinist (as well as my relationship to Fred's welfare), as Michael Levin points out, "the person who withdraws [or withholds] his assistance is not completely responsible for the dependency on him of the person who is about to die, while the mother *is* completely responsible for the dependency of her fetus on her. When one is completely responsible for dependence, refusal to continue to aid is indeed killing." For example, "if a woman brings a newborn home from the hospital, puts it in its crib and refuses to feed it until it has starved to death, it would be absurd to say that she simply refused to assist it and had done nothing for which she should be criminally liable."[34] In other words, just as the withholding of food kills the child after birth, in the case of abortion, it is the *abortion* that kills the child.

Boonin offers a critique of two objections to Thomson's argument – the responsibility objection and the child support objection – portions of which are germane to our discussion in this chapter. I will assess the first here and the second at the end of the next section.

BOONIN'S CRITIQUE OF THE RESPONSIBILITY OBJECTION. Boonin begins the first critique by "noting one reason to be suspicious of analogies that proponents of the responsibility objection generally employ." He then cites my drunk driving illustration (see above) and offers the following analysis:

> But in the case of drunk or negligent driving, we already agree that people have a right not to be run over by cars, and then determine that a person

who risks running over someone with a car can be held culpable if he has an accident that results in a violation of this right. And the same is true in the other sorts of cases that proponents of the objection typically appeal to: It is uncontroversial that you have a right not to be deliberately shot by a hunter's bullet, or to have your food supply intentionally destroyed, and from this we derive a right that people not negligently act in ways that risk unintentionally causing these things to occur. In the case of an unintended pregnancy, on the other hand, the question of whether the fetus has a right to not be deliberately deprived of the needed support the pregnant woman is providing for is precisely the question at issue. So it is difficult to see how an argument from an analogy with such cases can avoid begging the question.[35]

It seems to me that Boonin is offering a response that ultimately undercuts his own case. After all, he, Thomson and McDonagh present uncontroversial examples – such as the violinist story – to extract from them principles that may be applied in the controversial question of justifying abortion if the unborn is a person. It seems odd that Boonin would reject my analogy on the grounds that it is uncontroversial and it is being employed to help justify a particular moral understanding in a controversial case. For that is precisely why people, like Thomson, McDonagh, Boonin, and I use analogies: to illuminate difficult cases by looking at uncontroversial ones and the principles employed in them.

Boonin also seems mistaken about what he calls the "question at issue," which he describes in the following way: "In the case of an unintended pregnancy ... the question ... [is] whether the fetus has a right to not be deliberately deprived of the needed support the pregnant woman is providing for."[36] It seems to me that the question really is: Are persons, who are engaging in an act designed to bring into being dependent persons, justified in depriving a dependent person of life, whose existence results from that act and whose natural, though temporary, home is the womb of one of the persons who brought the dependent person into existence? In the cases of drunk driving or a hunter's bullet, the question is similar (though certainly not identical): Are persons, who are engaging in acts that are inherently dangerous to others, justified in not compensating a harmed person whose injury results from that act and who has a natural right to be compensated for the wrong?

Boonin, however, offers an argument seemingly intended to respond to this sort of clarification. He makes a distinction between (1) one's responsibility for "the needy person's *neediness*" and (2) one's responsibility "for the fact that he is needy, given that he now exists."[37] Concerning (1), if one is responsible for causing someone's neediness – one harmed another as a result of driving drunk, using a hunting rifle, and so on – then one is specially responsible for providing compensation and/or assistance to the victim. However, concerning (2), if one is responsible for bringing a person into existence and that person is in need of assistance, Boonin argues that one has no special responsibility to that person to provide assistance.

Boonin provides a modified version of an example given by Harry S. Silverstein:[38]

> You are the violinist's doctor. Seven years ago, you discovered that the violinist had contracted a rare disease that was on the verge of killing him. The only way to save his life that was available to you was to give him a drug that cures the disease but has one unfortunate side effect: Five to ten years after ingestion, it often causes the kidney ailment described in Thomson's story. Knowing that you alone would have the appropriate blood type to save the violinist were his kidneys to fail, you prescribed the drug and cured the disease. The violinist has now been struck by the kidney ailment. If you do not allow the use of your kidneys for nine months, he will die.[39]

According to Boonin, it is clear that you are responsible for the violinist's existence, for "had you not done it, the violinist would not now exist."[40] However, now that he exists, "you are not...responsible for his neediness."[41] For it was not within your power seven years ago *both* to provide the violinist a drug that would extend his life *and* that he would not require your kidneys in five to ten years to extend his life even further. After all, if you had not given him the drug, he would not exist to be needy. "So," writes Boonin, "you are responsible for the needy violinist's existence, but you are not responsible for his neediness, given that he exists."[42] The application to pregnancy is obvious: "A woman whose pregnancy is the result of voluntary intercourse...is responsible for the existence of the fetus, but is not responsible for the neediness of the fetus, given that it exists."[43] And given that she is not responsible for the neediness of the unborn, she is not required to provide it with assistance.

Because all human beings brought into existence eventually die of something,[44] Boonin's illustration is helpful in showing that just because parents bring a human being into existence does not mean that they are responsible for any or all the harm the child suffers throughout the child's life (assuming that the parents' conduct is *not* the direct cause of the harm the child suffers, e.g., the child shoots himself while playing with a loaded gun left in a conspicuous place by one of the parents). It seems to me, however, that Boonin misses an important distinction between the illustration he offers and the nature of pregnancy. The physician extends the life of a violinist, an already existing person; the physician does not bring a brand-new person into existence. The parents of an unborn child do not extend the life of an already existing person; they bring into being a brand-new person. There are two reasons this distinction is important.[45]

First, *the two cases are not symmetrical relative to increasing or decreasing human neediness.* The physician, by giving the violinist the drug to extend his life for at least another five years, *decreases* his patient's net neediness; after all, the violinist was given the drug at the edge of death. An already existing state of affairs was improved. On the other hand, in the case of pregnancy, net human neediness is increased, for a child-with-neediness, a joint-condition, is actualized by an act that is ordered in such a way that its proper function (though not its only function) is to produce a child-with-neediness. In the case of the violinist, the physician *helps* a violinist to be less needy than he otherwise would have been. In the case of pregnancy, a needy being is brought into existence who otherwise would not exist if not for its progenitors engaging in an act ordered toward producing needy beings.

Second, *the two cases are not symmetrical relative to the actors' responsibility for the neediness of the beings in question.* In the case of the violinist, his future neediness is a foreseeable, though unintended, consequence of extending his life, just as inevitable death is the foreseeable, though unintended, consequence of providing a life-saving measure to any human being. (For example, a person who is given CPR and survives eventually dies of something.) However, in the case of the unborn, his neediness is the *direct result* of his parents' engaging in an act, because the act is ordered to bring *needy persons into existence*. Unlike the physician who is ministering to his violinist patient for the patient's greater good, agents engaged in intercourse are not extending their child's life for his greater good. For there is no child to whom they can minister. Rather, they are engaging in an act, for their own gratification (assuming that they do not intend pregnancy), that is ordered to bring into being a person – an intrinsically valuable being, Boonin grants – who is *needy by nature*, and if brought into existence will be deprived of life *precisely because it is needy* and because those responsible for its needy existence do not want to offer assistance. After all, if sex resulted in the procreation of full-grown responsible adults who were not needy, there would no longer be a justification under the TMB thesis to permit the killing of newly conceived human beings. So, *it is the neediness of the child* that justifies depriving it of life by those responsible for its neediness, one of whom is in a unique position to care and nurture that child. But according to Boonin, when one is responsible for causing someone's neediness, one is specially responsible for providing compensation and/or assistance to the one in need. Consequently, the parents of the unborn *are* responsible for assisting it because they are in fact responsible for bringing into existence a being who is needy by nature and thus are responsible for its neediness.

Consider this illustration. Imagine, as in the story above, you are a physician whose patient is a violinist. However, unlike in the previous tale, your patient is healthy and also happens to be your lover. After arriving at your office for his yearly physical, you suggest a vitamin regimen to him to maintain his health. You offer him what you think is a sample of the vitamin, but it is really a narcotic to which the violinist is highly allergic. You hand him the samples, he swallows one right there in your office, and then moments later he has a severe allergic reaction. He is rushed to the hospital and soon after his arrival the chief of neurology gives you the tragic news: "Your patient, the violinist, will survive, and live quite a long time. However, he has suffered serious brain damage that has resulted in his losing all his memories, abilities, and skills. He will remain in a coma for nine months, but upon awakening he will be able to relearn all his abilities and skills and acquire new memories. It should take about a decade to accomplish this. This means that he is in precisely the same position as the standard fetus." According to Boonin, you are clearly responsible for your patient's neediness and your patient is entitled to your assistance.

However, suppose while the violinist is lying in his hospital bed in a coma, you take some of his DNA to clone him. You rush back to your lab, produce an embryo clone, and then implant the embryo in yourself (you are a woman, after all) because you want to bring into the world *another* human being who is likely to acquire similar characteristics and develop a similar personality as the violinist you dearly love. But suppose you discover a week later that when you implanted the cloned embryo you were pregnant already as a result of sex with the violinist an hour before he had visited your office. You had not intended to become pregnant, but you now are in such a condition. So now there exist three human beings in precisely the same position: identical twin violinists (though decades apart in chronological age) and a child who is the offspring of the senior twin. All three are needy, unconscious, and require time to develop the latent abilities, basic capacities, they have by nature. In all three cases it seems correct to say that you are responsible for their neediness, but in the second and third cases you are also responsible for the being's existence, though in the second case you directly intended a needy being to exist but in the first and third you did not. Yet, according to Boonin, you are only responsible for the neediness of the first, the violinist, but not the second and third because in the latter two cases you are only responsible for the being's existence but not its neediness. But that doesn't seem right. For in the second and third cases neediness is caused simultaneously with existence, because the sort of being brought into existence is needy by nature and the acts performed in each case *are ordered toward* the production of needy human beings. Thus, Boonin's argument fails to show that the distinction he makes between responsibility for neediness and responsibility for existence is applicable to the case of pregnancy.

Thomson's Case Cannot Account for Intuitions That Result in a Pro-Life Understanding of Pregnancy and the Unborn

Most people, pro-life and abortion choice alike, agree that in ordinary circumstances a born child has a natural moral claim upon her parents to care for her, regardless of whether her parents "wanted" her. This is why we prosecute child abusers and parents who abandon their children. Although this understanding of parental obligation is uncontroversial when applied to born children, I argue in this section that it relies on pro-life intuitions, and thus may be applied to the unborn as well.

If the unborn entity is a person (an intrinsically valuable human person [IVHB]), as Thomson and others are willing to grant, why should the unborn's natural prima facie claim to her parents' goods differ before birth? This period of a human being's *natural* development occurs in the womb. This is the journey that *all of us* must take and is a necessary condition for *any* human being's post-uterine existence. Unlike Thomson's violinist who is artificially attached to another person to save his life and is therefore not naturally dependent on any particular human being, the unborn is a human being who is by her very nature *dependent* on her mother, for this is how human beings are at this stage of their development.

Although it should not be ignored that pregnancy and childbirth entail certain emotional, physical, and financial sacrifices on the part of the pregnant woman, these sacrifices are also endemic of *parenthood* in general (which ordinarily lasts much longer than nine months), and do not seem to justify the execution of troublesome infants and younger children whose existence entails a natural claim to certain financial and bodily goods that are under the ownership of their parents.

The moral intuition that parents have a special responsibility for their children and their welfare is reflected in well-established family law. Assuming, as Thomson and others do, that the unborn is a person, this body of law would seem to apply to parents' responsibility for their unborn children. According to legal scholars Dennis J. Horan and Burke J. Balche, "All 50 states, the District of Columbia, American Samoa, Guam, and the U.S. Virgin Islands have child abuse and neglect statutes which provide for the protection of a child who does not receive needed medical care." They further write that "a review of cases makes it clear that these statutes are properly applied to secure emergency medical treatment and sustenance (food or water, whether given orally or through intravenous or nasogastic tube) for children when parents, with or without the acquiescence of physicians, refuse to provide it."[46]

In an example cited by Horan and Balch, a court held in a New York case that the parents of a child with leukemia had acted with neglect when they did not provide the child with medical care: "The parent ... may not deprive a child of lifesaving treatment, however well-intentioned. Even when the parents' decision to decline necessary treatment is based on constitutional grounds, such as religious beliefs, it must yield to the State's interests, as *parens patriae*, in protecting the health and welfare of the child."[47] According to Horan and Balch, "courts have uniformly held that a parent has the legal responsibility of furnishing his dependent child with adequate food and medical care."[48]

It is evident then that child protection laws reflect our deepest moral intuitions about parental responsibility and the utter helplessness of infants and small children. And without these moral scruples the protection of children and the natural bonds and filial obligations that are an integral part of ordinary family life will begin to lose their social force.

But this means that if Thomson's argument (or a version of it) works – that a pregnant woman is not responsible for her unborn child's neediness but only its existence (which is part of Boonin's defense of the argument) – then the moral grounds of our child support laws vanish. For this would mean that deadbeat dads, who consented only to sex but not fatherhood, would not be morally obligated to pay child support because the father, like a pregnant woman, is responsible only for the child's existence but not its neediness. But because we know that deadbeat dads should pay child support regardless of whether they intended for their partners to become pregnant, then the pregnant woman is obligated to remedy her child's neediness regardless of whether she intended to become pregnant when she consented to sex. Thus, Thomson's case fails.[49]

BOONIN'S CRITIQUE OF THE CHILD SUPPORT OBJECTION. Boonin responds to the "deadbeat dad" argument in several ways, two of which are relevant to our analysis here.[50]

(1) He maintains that it is not clear that a man who took every contraceptive precaution to avoid fatherhood, and prior to intercourse plainly conveyed to his female partner that he did not intend to sire a child (as in the example I used above), "is violating the moral rights of the child or the woman."[51] It may very well be legally permissible for the state to require such a father, or one who was not as contraceptively careful but merely did not want paternal responsibilities, to pay child support. Boonin says that a child support law that requires such paternal assistance may be morally "proper" but still "consistent with the claim that there is no independent moral obligation for such men to pay child support."[52] But it's difficult to make sense of this, for at least two reasons.

First, Boonin really understates the force of the intuition that guides our understanding of parental obligation. Clearly, most people would think it bizarre to discard that intuition on the grounds that Boonin is suggesting, that it is inconsistent with an understanding of parental obligation that is grounded exclusively in explicit consent. In fact, most people would think that Boonin's understanding of parental obligation itself *should be* discarded precisely because it morally permits such a counterintuitive state of affairs.

Second, given Boonin's claim that the mother has no moral obligation to assist her unborn child *in any way* because she is only responsible for its existence but not its neediness, it would follow that the father is only responsible for the child's existence but not its neediness and thus has no moral obligation to assist the child *in any way* including the payment of child support. As we have seen, Boonin seems to agree with this analysis. Nevertheless, he also claims that if the state were to require the father to provide assistance in a particular way – namely, the payment of child support – such a requirement is morally proper. But how can a *requirement* be morally proper if it is at the same time *not* a moral obligation? After all, Boonin is saying that there are *no moral grounds* for justifying the obligation to pay child support in our story of the deadbeat dad. But it would seem to follow then that the state has *no moral grounds* for justifying its requirement to pay child support in our story of the deadbeat dad. The state cannot be acting in a morally proper fashion if it is in fact, let's say, garnishing the father's wages and distributing the money to his abandoned children, because that for which one has no moral grounds cannot be morally proper.

Third, if it is morally proper for the state to require the father to pay child support even though he has no moral obligation to pay child support, as Boonin contends, then why can't the state apply the same reasoning to the mother? That is, the state could claim it is morally proper for the law to require that the mother carry the child to term even though she has no moral obligation to do so. Although I believe this makes no sense (for either the mother or the father), it is not clear how Boonin could reject it based on the premises of his case. I suppose he could argue, as he does elsewhere in a different context,[53] that the mother's burdens during pregnancy are so great that requiring her to carry the child to term is morally improper. But what would be the grounds for this judgment? It seems to me that he has to argue that it would be morally improper because the pregnant woman has no moral obligation to bring the child to term. But turn about is fair play, for then the state cannot require the father to pay child support on the grounds that Boonin suggests, namely, that the requirement is morally proper even though the father has no moral obligation to do so.

(2) Boonin offers another argument in reply to the child support objection to Thomson's argument.[54] He asks us to assume that there is a moral obligation for a deadbeat dad to pay child support (even though Boonin does not believe that there really is such a moral obligation). But even if this is the case, argues Boonin, because a woman has unique and greater physical burdens during pregnancy than a man or woman has to his or her child postnatally, the woman lacks during pregnancy the moral obligation to assist her child that she and the child's father have after birth. Moreover, if we would not require a man to undergo a similar physical experience against his will, then we cannot require a woman to remain pregnant against her will. Boonin employs several analogies, comparing the mother's apparent obligation to her unborn child to forced organ donation or temporary use of another's body, which are illegal, and immoral, even if parents are the ones whose bodies are used to help their children:[55]

> Suppose, for example, that in order for the child to survive, the father must go through [an artificial procedure nearly identical to pregnancy]. . . . He must have a pseudo-zygote implanted in him and let it develop into a pseudo-embryo and then pseudo-fetus before giving "birth" to it in a

manner that parallels the nature of childbirth as closely as it is anatomically possible so that a life-saving synthetic drug may then be extracted from it and given to the child. It goes without saying that no court would order him to undergo such a procedure.

Or suppose instead, more mundanely, that in order for the child to survive, the father would have to undergo a painful series of bone marrow transplants, or have one of his kidneys removed. Again, the law would surely not compel him to undergo such procedures.[56]

These analogies seem to turn on two key premises, the first of which Boonin explicitly addresses in the text: (1) there is a distinction between responsibility for existence and responsibility for neediness (which we have already seen fails); and (2) an account of human beings that would show that it is *not rational* to believe that a woman's physical design is ordered toward the caring, sheltering, and nurturing of children (for which Boonin does not offer an account). An involuntary organ donor or lender (even if she is the recipient's parent) is typically *not responsible* for the neediness of the organ recipient, and the donor's body is *not* intrinsically ordered toward the donation of organs for a specific person who by nature needs those organs as the woman's body is intrinsically ordered toward the care of her unborn child. Because I have already dealt with the first premise earlier in this chapter, I will now focus only on the second.

It would require a Herculean effort on Boonin's part to provide a convincing account of human beings suggested by the second premise given what we seem to know about human beings and procreation. For it seems reasonable to believe that it is the mother whose body is designed for pregnancy and child bearing, and whose parts work in concert to make the maternal human organism conducive and receptive to the protection and nurture of an unborn member of the species. This is why there is no market for male surrogate mothers. Thus, during that time of the couple's child's existence it is only the mother who has the physical attributes to provide shelter and sustenance to their unborn child, whose neediness and existence she and the child's father are responsible for.

As Schwarz points out: "So, the very thing that makes it plausible to say that the person in bed with the violinist has no duty to sustain him; namely, that he is a stranger unnaturally hooked up to him, is precisely what is absent in the case of the mother and her child." That is to say, the mother "does have an obligation to take care of her child, to sustain her, to protect her, and especially, to let her live in the only place where she can now be protected, nourished, and allowed to grow, namely the womb."[57]

Although, as I have argued in this chapter, there is good reason to believe that pregnancy is a prima facie good, Boonin is correct that there are burdens that attend the condition of pregnancy that cannot be shared with the male parent, for they are unique to the female of the human species. But it is not clear how the differences in parental burdens between the sexes justifies abortion. It seems to me that the correct comparison is between the burdens to be borne by the child or its mother, not between the father and the mother, if the decision to abort hangs in the balance. For if we were to think of the burden of an ordinary pregnancy as a harm exclusively borne by the woman, as no doubt Boonin does, and compare it to the harm of death borne exclusively by the unborn child if it is aborted, "the harm avoided by the woman seeking the abortion," writes Lee, "is not comparable with the death caused to the child aborted. (Recall that the burden need only involve nine months of pregnancy; the woman can put the child up for adoption.)"[58]

The Rape Exception

Someone may, at this point, respond by agreeing with the criticisms offered here by conceding that Thomson's violinist illustration may not apply in cases of ordinary consensual sexual intercourse, but it does apply in cases in which pregnancy results from rape.[59] After all, the case that I've made against the violinist argument thus far has relied on moral intuitions about one's responsibility for the foreseeable and/or naturally ordered results of one's *consensual* actions. Rape is not a case of consensual sex. Thus, Thomson's violinist argument does seem to apply.

Although Thomson herself does not advance this argument,[60] those who do may choose to argue in the following way. Just as a man whose sperm is extracted and stolen from his body without his consent is not responsible for how it is used or what results from its use (e.g., a woman may inseminate herself with it and give birth to a child), the raped woman, who did not voluntarily engage in intercourse, cannot be held responsible for the unborn human being who is living inside her. And thus, the unborn conceived in rape, like the child resulting from the stolen seed, is not entitled to its parents' goods, bodily, financial, or otherwise.

But there is a problem with this analogy: the man's relinquishing of care for the child *does not result in the death of a human person* while the raped woman's does. The following story should help to illustrate the differences and similarities between these two cases.[61]

Imagine that the sperm was stolen by an unscrupulous physician who then inseminated a woman with the seed. Although the sperm's owner is not morally responsible for the child that results, he is nevertheless forced by an unjust court to pay a large monthly sum for child support, a sum so large that it may drive him into serious debt, maybe even bankruptcy. This would be similar to the woman who became pregnant as a result of rape. She was unjustly violated and is supporting a human being, for whom she is not responsible, at an emotional and financial cost. Is it morally right for the sperm donor to kill the child he is supporting to attempt to right the wrong that has been committed against him? No, for such an act would be unjustified homicide.

Now if we assume, as does Thomson, that the rape victim is carrying a rights-bearing person, the termination of the pregnancy, except if it has a strong possibility of endangering her life, would be as unjust as the sperm donor killing the child he is unjustly forced to support. As the victimized man may rightly refuse to pay the child support, the raped woman may rightly refuse to bring up the child after the pregnancy has come to term. She can choose to put the child up for adoption. But in both cases, the killing of the child is not morally justified. Although neither the sperm donor nor the rape victim may have the same special obligation to their biological offspring as does the couple who voluntarily engaged in intercourse and thus are responsible for its existence and neediness (regardless of whether they directly intended for such a being to exist), it seems that the more general obligation not to directly kill another human person does apply to both the sperm donor and the rape victim.

Consider another case. Suppose a woman, Alice, hears a knock at her door, opens it, and discovers a one-week-old baby at her doorstep, as in the film with Tom Selleck, Ted Danson, and Steve Guttenberg, *Three Men and a Baby*. But unlike that film, Alice lives in northern Alaska as a virtual hermit, residing hundreds of miles from her nearest neighbor and the closest city. She also has no means of communication – no telephone or Internet access. So she cannot call social services for help (assuming her county of residence even has such a government agency). It is the dead of winter, which means that she will not be able to drive to alert someone of what she has found for at least four months, perhaps longer. She has, however, more than enough supplies for a year. So no one but Alice is able to take care of the child, but she has to take care of it for only four months. Because Alice is in her mid-60s, caring for this child will likely result in physical and mental stress that will increase her chance of acquiring other ailments that she has so far avoided by her reclusive and stress-free lifestyle. Suppose, however, that Alice is a devotee of Judith Jarvis Thomson, and reasons this way: "I did not consent to have this child placed on my doorstep. To care for this child will entail physical and mental effort on my part to which I did not consent. Thus, I will return the child to where I found it, thus denying the child shelter, sustenance, care, and attention. This no doubt will result in its death. It may be eaten by wolves or die of exposure to the elements. But since I am not responsible for its neediness and/or its existence, and since I did not consent, either explicitly or implicitly, to care for this child, I have no obligation to this child whatsoever."

It is clear that given the moral principles that guide the examples offered by Thomson, Boonin, and McDonagh, Alice has a right to abandon this child left at her doorstep. Yet something seems deeply wrong with this conclusion. I suspect its wrongness lies in an intuition we have about our moral obligation as a community to those members of the human family who are weak, vulnerable, and defenseless. Because American jurisprudence has generally not recognized a legal duty to rescue,[62] it seems morally obvious to some that a law that would require such would be unjust. But when the parties involved are the reclusive Alice and a baby abandoned on her doorstep, something deep in our souls rises to the surface and we see, with clarity, that if Alice were to apply Thomson's reasoning with complete consistency we would not congratulate her for her analytical skill and/or philosophical insight. We would condemn her and hope that she remain in northern Alaska alone with her books in contemporary moral philosophy.

In a critique of Thomson's argument, U.S. 9th Circuit Judge John T. Noonan raises a point that is particularly relevant to the case of the reclusive Alice. Although not a moral argument, it provides a moral insight into how American tort law views such circumstances. Noonan asserts that "while Thomson focuses on this fantasy [of the violinist story], she ignores a real case from which American tort law has generalized."[63] He briefs the case for us:

On a January night in Minnesota, a cattle buyer, Orlando Depue, asked a family of farmers, the Flateaus, with whom he had dined, if he could remain overnight at their house. The Flateaus refused and, although Depue was sick and had fainted, put him out of the house into the cold night. Imposing liability on the Flateaus for Depue's loss of his frostbitten fingers, the court said: "In the case at bar defendants were under no contract obligation to minister to plaintiff in his distress; but humanity demanded they do so, if they understood and appreciated his condition . . . The law as well as humanity required that he not be exposed in his helpless condition to the merciless elements." Depue was a guest for supper although not a guest after supper. The American Law Institute, generalizing, has said that it makes no difference whether the person is a guest or a trespasser. He has the privilege of staying. His host has the duty not to injure him or put him into an environment where he becomes nonviable. The obligation arises when one "understands and appreciates" the condition of the other.[64]

Noonan concludes that "although the analogy is not exact, the case is much closer to the mother's situation than the case imagined by Thomson; and the emotional response of the Minnesota judges seems to be a truer reflection of what humanity requires."[65]

Let me provide one more illustration. Imagine that there is a mad scientist-physician named Matt and he wants to produce conjoined twins with some new technology that he has manufactured in his laboratory. He abducts one of his patients, Carol, who is about two weeks pregnant with identical (monozygotic) twins. He places her under general anesthesia and removes the tiny embryos from her womb. Matt then, with his new technology, partially re-conjoins them, and re-implants them into Carol, so that they are born as conjoined twins. Clearly, Matt has harmed these twins and has put them in a condition of neediness in which they otherwise would not have been if not for his experiment. Suppose that when the twins are born, the hospital tells their parents that both the twins (two girls) will likely live a long, though difficult, life. Because they share certain organs and glands, both girls, starting at age 15 and ending at age 45, will suffer all the symptoms of pregnancy (except childbirth, of course) for four months straight once every three years. This means that over the course of 30 years each girl will suffer the equivalent of 40 months of pregnancy. Suppose that the girls can be spared this suffering if they are separated. But technology is not advanced enough to separate them.

The girls are now 15 years and six months old, and they have already experienced the suffering that had been predicted at their birth. One of the girls, Hope, is stoic about it and believes that it is simply her cross to bear and is generally optimistic and happy about life. The other girl, Peggy, does not want the burden any more and can't imagine going through it another nine times. Happily, technology now exists that could separate them. But there's a catch. Given the way that they are conjoined, only Peggy will survive the operation. So Peggy plots to kill Hope, the only way that she can convince the hospital to detach Hope from her. She succeeds in her plot, is relieved of her burden, but is eventually arrested for first-degree murder and brought to trial. She hires a clever lawyer who understands that as a matter of law, Peggy has virtually no chance to be acquitted. However, he believes that at sentencing he can offer a persuasive philosophical argument that would induce the jury's sympathy and result in a very short sentence. Well versed in contemporary moral philosophy, he argues thus:

> What my client did may have been against the law, but it is morally justified according to the leading lights of contemporary moral philosophy. Matt, the scientist, wickedly violated the bodily integrity of Peggy and Hope by conjoining them against their will. Peggy and Hope did not consent, either explicitly or implicitly, to this violation, just as a raped woman does not consent to intercourse or to care for the unborn child that results from that wicked union. Like the pregnant woman, my client, Peggy, is not responsible for the neediness of her twin sister, the being which was attached to Peggy and depended on her for life itself. Because of the nature of their relationship, Hope was, tragically, a burden to Peggy, causing her the sort of suffering that is associated with pregnancy, a condition that moral philosophers of incredible wisdom such as Boonin, McDonagh, and Thomson argue is what justifies the termination of pregnancy even if the unborn is a person. Hope needed Peggy to live, but Peggy did not need Hope to live, just as the fetus needs its mother to live and the mother does not need the fetus to live. Carol, their mother, was responsible for their existence but not their neediness; Matt, the scientist, was responsible for producing a new neediness; Peggy was not responsible for Hope's existence or neediness. Consequently, given the bodily burdens lifted, and the absence of any moral responsibility of Peggy for her sister, my client should receive a light penalty. Let me suggest that she be placed on house arrest for a period no longer than two years. This will provide her an opportunity to practice the violin, an instrument with which she is adept. Thank you.

I cannot imagine anyone finding this reasoning persuasive, though it apparently relies on principles derived from the writings of Thomson, Boonin, and McDonagh. Yet there is a glaring difference between, on the one hand, the cases of pregnancy and the conjoined twins, and on the other hand, the case of the violinist: in pregnancy and in the case of the conjoined twins both sets of persons were *simultaneously* victimized by a responsible party (rapist, mad-scientist) in a way that resulted in a relationship of dependency between the two victimized parties; in the case of the violinist, only one party was victimized, the kidney lender, by one responsible party (the kidnapper) who used the relationship he created for the good of another party, the violinist. Thus, it seems right to say that if an individual is one of several co-victims simultaneously placed in a relationship of dependency as the direct result of the same unjust act, she is not required to forfeit her life for the sake of the others merely because her death will relieve them of a burden, less onerous than a permanent loss of life, incurred by the unjust act. For to do so would be to victimize a victim yet again, to use that person merely as a means rather than to treat her as an intrinsically valuable person. Therefore, if one believes it is wrong for Peggy to kill Hope, then one must conclude that Thomson's argument cannot adequately justify abortion of an unborn human being that resulted from rape.

CONCLUSION

In this chapter I critically assessed arguments for abortion choice that either sidestep or concede (for the sake of argument) the personhood of the unborn but nevertheless conclude that abortion is morally permissible. We first evaluated two popular arguments and then moved on to critically assess Judith Jarvis Thomson's famous argument from unplugging the violinist. In the process of that assessment we also critiqued arguments employed by others to support Thomson's case. All these arguments, including Thomson's, fail for a variety of reasons, though they all seem to have one flaw in common: they offer analogies, examples, and illustrations that fail to capture what appears to many of us as the nature of sex, pregnancy, and parental obligation.

PART III

EXTENDING AND CONCLUDING THE ARGUMENT

8

CLONING, BIOETHICS, AND REPRODUCTIVE LIBERTY

Although abortion is the issue that first brought many citizens into the bioethics arena, today bioethics is dominated by other issues that are perceived as more pressing. Nevertheless, the answer to the philosophical question lurking behind abortion – Who and what are we? – turns out to be the key that unlocks the ethical quandaries posed by these other issues. After all, if human persons ought not to be subjects of research or killed without justification, and if the unborn from conception is a full-fledged member of the human community, abortion as well as other procedures, such as certain forms of cloning and embryo manipulation, are prima facie morally wrong.

Some bioethicists seek to sidestep the question of the unborn's full humanity by suggesting a neutral posture toward it. They maintain that bioethical decisions can be made apart from answering this question. Take, for example, the 1994 recommendations of the National Institutes of Health Embryo Research Panel, a body consisting of bioethicists across many disciplines including philosophy, theology, law, and medicine. Formed in 1993, this panel was commissioned to make recommendations about what types of research on the embryo prior to implantation and outside the woman's uterus (ex utero) are appropriate or inappropriate for federal funding. The main ethical concern for the panel was the moral permissibility of creating human embryos for the sole purpose of experimenting on them.

After hearing thousands of hours of testimony by experts on all sides of the debate, the panel concluded in its final report that some research was acceptable for federal support, some warranted further review, and some was unacceptable. But what is remarkable is how the panel attempted to sidestep the issue of personhood, apparently believing that it was possible to make policy without addressing it. In the first 300 words of the report's executive summary, the panel writes that "it conducted its deliberations in terms that were independent of a particular religious or philosophical perspective."[1] Yet, the panel supported federal funding of research on the preimplanted embryo on the basis that "it does not have the same moral status as infants and children" because it lacks "developmental individuation ..., the lack of even the possibility of sentience and most other qualities considered relevant to the moral status of persons, and the very high rate of natural mortality at this stage."[2]

Despite its earlier disclaimer that it would propose recommendations "independent" of any perspective, the panel affirmed (and argued for) a policy that is, by its own admission, dependent on a philosophical perspective, for it was employed by the panel to distinguish between those beings who are and who are not members of the moral community of persons. This is not a neutral perspective. Just like the failed arguments for government neutrality on abortion that we assessed in Chapter 3, the panel's case cannot be sustained.

In this chapter I look at the issue of human cloning. My assessment of this issue relies on much of the work on the nature of human beings found in Chapters 4 and 6. As part of this analysis, I make reference, when appropriate, to the related issue of embryonic stem-cell research. I cover four general topics in this chapter: (1) the science of cloning, and human cloning in particular; (2) the cloning controversy, as well as the political and legal reactions to it; (3) possible uses for cloning, and some objections to the practice, and (4) whether the U.S. Supreme Court's holdings on privacy and reproductive rights establish a right to clone oneself.

WHAT IS CLONING?

In early 1997, Dr. Ian Wilmut, a Scottish scientist, made headlines when he presented Dolly to the world, a sheep that he cloned from a six-year-old ewe. Three and one-half years earlier, Drs. Jerry Hall and Robert Stillman cloned a human embryo by successfully splitting one human embryo into two.[3] This process occurs naturally in the case of identical human twins, but Hall and Stillman were the first to replicate this process artificially. And on October 13, 2001, scientists at Advanced Cell Technology (Worcester, Massachusetts) made biomedical history when they became the first to produce a human embryo by employing the same method used to produce Dolly.[4] These human embryos did not survive for very long, with only one progressing to the six-cell stage.[5]

Although many of us are acquainted with the concept of cloning because of popular films like *The Boys from Brazil*, most people are unaware that cloning has been going on for decades. "Technically, the word 'clone,' in its most simple and strict sense, refers to a precise genetic copy of a molecule, cell, plant, animal, or human being."[6] Cloning has been an important component of the world of horticulture and agriculture for many years. "Genetically identical copies of whole organisms are commonplace in the plant-breeding world and are commonly referred to as 'varieties' rather than clones."[7]

For several decades scientists have been cloning the cells of both humans and animals, for "it provides greater quantities of identical cells or genes for study; each cloned cell or molecule is identical to the others."[8] The clones that result are not copies of whole organisms, but merely fragments of deoxyribonucleic acid (DNA) (as in molecular cloning) or non-germ cells (as in cellular cloning). Both of these types of cloning have important uses in developing new medicines, such as those employed in the treatment of diabetes, heart attack, and kidney disease.[9] The idea of cloning entire organisms can be traced back to a 1938 book by Hans Spemann, an embryologist.[10] In 1952, Thomas King and Robert Briggs were the first to clone frog embryos.[11] In 1962, entire adult frogs were first cloned.[12] Dolly was the first clone resulting from the genetic material of an adult mammal. Researchers at the University of Wisconsin, Madison, employed the technology that produced Dolly to clone members of five different species, including rhesus monkeys.[13] The pregnancies miscarried, but the experiments did show that the technology used to produce Dolly can be employed to generate living embryos of a diversity of animals.[14] Several generations of mice were cloned by scientists at the University of Hawaii who used the Dolly method more efficiently.[15] It is alleged that, in December 1998, South Korean researchers used this more efficient method to create a human embryo cloned from a 30-year-old woman. According to this unconfirmed story, the researchers prevented the embryo from developing past four cells.[16] That same month, scientists in Japan cloned eight calves in 10 attempts by employing a variation on the Dolly method.[17]

When a scientist refers to cloning an entire organism rather than merely a cell or fragment of DNA, she may be speaking of one or both of two procedures – (1) embryo cloning or (2) somatic cell nuclear transfer (SCNT) cloning.

Embryo Cloning

Hall and Stillman employed this type of cloning in their 1993 groundbreaking experiment, in which they cloned a human embryo. Scientists have been successfully using this cloning method with animals for many years. Hall and Stillman began with what is called "in vitro fertilization," or IVF: in a laboratory, they produced human embryos in a petri dish by taking ova and fertilizing them with male sperm. Medical ethicist Scott B. Rae explains the process:

> The embryos they used in their experiments had been fertilized by two sperm instead of one, making them abnormal embryos and destined to die within a week. This cloning process would be no different if the embryo were properly fertilized and had a normal chance at becoming a baby if implanted.[18]

Hart and Stillman produced defective embryos rather than normal ones because they did not intend for either the clones or the defective embryos to develop into babies.[19] They just wanted to see if they could artificially clone a human embryo.

To induce cloning, the scientists followed the subsequent procedure. After they fertilized the ovum, the resulting zygote divided in two, which is what occurs in normal development. The scientists then removed the zona pellucida, "the coating that contains enzymes that promote cell division that is necessary for growth and development."[20] The two cells were then separated. Because development cannot continue unless the zona pellucida is replaced, Hall and Stillman "used an artificial zona pellucida to recoat the two embryonic cells, enabling development to continue. As the cells [grew] they form[ed] genetically identical embryos, a laboratory equivalent to what occurs naturally in the body when identical twins are conceived."[21] However, because the embryos were defective, they perished after six days.[22]

Somatic Cell Nuclear Transfer (SCNT) Cloning

This is the type of cloning that produced Dolly. Because sheep, like human beings, are mammals, scientists were able to clone a human being by this same method in October 2001. The DNA of every cell in the human body, except the sperm and egg, contains the genetic material that, in theory, is capable of producing an identical clone of the body from which the cell is taken. But because nature programs the cells to perform certain functions (i.e., liver cells perform different functions from those of brain cells) and because all other functions are dormant, a scientist must replicate conception to bring into existence a new and genetically identical human being. A scientist may accomplish this by extracting the nucleus of a cell from the human body, fusing that cell with an ovum that has had its nucleus removed, and then electrically stimulating this fused entity. It was by this method that Scottish scientists brought Dolly into existence. But according to molecular biologist Dr. Raymond Bohlin,

> the process was inefficient. Out of 277 cell fusions, 29 began growing in vitro. All 29 were implanted in receptive ewes, 13 became pregnant, and only one lamb was born as a result. This is a success rate of only 3.4%. In nature, somewhere between 33 and 50% of all fertilized eggs develop fully into newborns.[23]

Of course, Dolly is not the same age as her six-year-old twin, whose genetic material was used to clone her. Thus, a human being cloned by SCNT would always be younger than her twin, unlike the adult clones of the character played by actor Michael Keaton in the film *Multiplicity*. As a result, if a 24-year-old woman were to clone herself, her cloned twin would always be 24 years her junior.

Although embryo cloning is an important and controversial topic,[24] this chapter focuses primarily on SCNT, which is what most ethicists, legal scholars, public policy experts, and ordinary citizens mean when they say that they oppose or support human cloning. Nevertheless, some of the moral and legal questions raised by human cloning may apply to embryo cloning as well.

The Cloning Controversy: Legal and Political Reactions

Alarmed by the prospect of human cloning generated by Dolly, Congress and the White House called for legislation in March of 1997 that would ban human cloning. President Bill Clinton, by executive order, prohibited the use of federal funds for cloning.[25] The president also requested that the National Bioethics Advisory Commission (NBAC) evaluate the legal and ethical questions raised by the possibility of human cloning.[26] In arriving at its conclusion and recommendations, the commission conducted hearings over approximately three months in which it heard testimony from scientists, philosophers, bioethicists, legal scholars, theologians, and others.[27] It also commissioned papers by eight scholars from a diversity of fields, and these papers were then published in Volume II of the NBAC's report.[28]

In its June 9, 1997, report, the commission concluded that "it is morally unacceptable for anyone in the public or private sector, whether in research or clinical setting, to attempt to create a child using somatic cell nuclear transfer cloning."[29] The commission gave two sets of reasons for this conclusion: (1) it was concerned with the safety of the procedure for the embryo, fetus, and subsequent child that may result from SCNT; and (2) it "found that concerns relating to the potential harms to children and effects on the moral, religious, and cultural values of society merited further reflection and deliberation."[30] However, the commission also asserted that "whether upon such further deliberation our nation will conclude that the use of cloning techniques to create children should be allowed or permanently banned is, for the moment, an open question."[31]

On November 28, 2001, President George W. Bush, like his predecessor, President Clinton, created his own bioethics commission (Executive Order 13237), The President's Council on Bioethics (PCB).[32] Like the NBAC, it provided to the president its own set of recommendations. PCB offers two recommendations, one by the majority (10 members) and the second by a minority (seven members). The first is summarized in the following way:

> Ten Members of the Council recommend a ban on cloning-to-produce-children combined with a four-year moratorium on cloning-for-bio-medical-research. We also call for a federal review of current and projected practices of human embryo research, pre-implantation genetic diagnosis, genetic modification of human embryos and gametes, and related matters, with a view to recommending and shaping ethically sound policies for the entire field.[33]

The minority recommended **"a ban on cloning-to-produce-children, with regulation of the use of cloned embryos for biomedical research"**[34] (bold typeface in original). This recommendation, though popular among some in the U.S. Congress, would put the government in an unusual position if it were to become law: it would require that researchers *kill embryos* or suffer the penalties of federal law. It is one thing to permit people to kill embryos – as in the case of abortion and certain forms of stem-cell research – it is quite another to *require them* to kill embryos or risk facing hefty fines or imprisonment.

Although it may seem that the PCB majority's recommendation differs little from that of the NBAC, a careful reading of the former, along with the reasons provided for its conclusion, reveals a stronger condemnation of human cloning for reproduction as intrinsically wrong and perhaps, also, for other purposes of cloning (hence, the call for a federal review of current and projected research of preborn human beings). The NBAC also condemns cloning for reproduction, not because it is intrinsically

wrong but rather because it may have bad consequences and society may
not be adequately prepared for it. Hence, its claim that reproductive
cloning is unethical "at this time."[35] In addition, the NBAC report seems
more open to human cloning research outside of reproductive purposes
than does the PCB report.[36]

Since 1997, the U.S. Congress has proposed several bills,[37] in both
the Senate and House of Representatives, that would have resulted in
some ban on human cloning and/or a ban on federal funding of human
cloning research; however, none could command a majority in either
or both houses.[38] This is because disagreements arose over such issues
as whether a federal ban should apply only to government funding or
include private research, whether the law should ban both SCNT and
embryo cloning, and whether the law should ban a gestation of a clone
rather than its creation. These distinctions, apparently subtle but quite
profound, touch on some of the deep issues that divide Americans over
issues such as the nature of human personhood, the importance of the
traditional family for human flourishing, and the weight of competing
values like personal autonomy and the pursuit of scientific knowledge.[39]
The apparent conflict between these values came to the forefront in the
context of another hotly contested issue: the federal funding of stem-cell
research.

Stem cells are found in all animals, including human beings. In adults,
stem cells serve the function of repairing damaged tissue. For example,
"hematopoietic stem cells" are "a type of cell found in the blood."[40]
Their purpose is to repair the tissue of a damaged part of the organ of
which they are a part, for adult stem cells are differentiated. However,
stem cells found in the early embryo (or totipotent cells) – before its cells
differentiate into the cells of particular organs – "retain the special ability
to develop into nearly any cell type."[41] The embryo's germ cells, "which
originate from the primordial reproductive cells of the developing fetus,"
possess similar properties.[42] Although few doubt the potential of human
stem-cell research, the real issue that animates opponents, and raises deep
ethical questions, is how these cells are obtained and from what entity
they are derived. According to the National Bioethics Advisory Commission's (NBAC) 1999 report, these promising "human stem cells can
be derived from" four sources. Embryonic germ cells may be derived
from "human fetal tissue following elective abortion," while totipotent
embryonic stem cells may be extracted from "human embryos that are
created by" IVF "and that are no longer needed by couples being treated
for infertility," "human embryos that are created by IVF with gametes

[i.e., sperm and egg cells] donated for the sole purpose of providing research material," and "potentially, human (or hybrid) embryos generated asexually by somatic cell nuclear transfer cloning techniques [i.e., SCNT cloning]."[43] A fifth source could be embryos brought into being by the cloning technique, or one similar to it, employed by Drs. Hall and Stillman.

With the exception of the first source, extracting the embryo's stem cells can only be accomplished at the cost of killing the embryo itself, which is difficult to justify ethically if the embryo is a full-fledged member of the human community.[44] (With the first source, however, questions have been raised about extracting germ cells of a dead unborn human killed via abortion. Although the moral status of the unborn may be decisive in evaluating this practice, there are some reasons to believe that it may not be in some cases.)[45]

THE USES OF CLONING AND THE REASONS AGAINST IT

There are numerous reasons someone would want to produce a clone (some of which I already alluded to).[46] These reasons can be divided into two general categories: (1) reproductive reasons; and (2) nonreproductive reasons. In the last section, I explore some of the reasons against cloning.

Reproductive Reasons

Human cloning could be used for a number of reproductive reasons, including (1) a method of reproduction for infertile heterosexual couples, (2) a means by which parents may be able to "replace" a dead child or replicate a twin of an already existing child, and (3) a method of reproduction for gay and lesbian couples whose sexual union is biologically incapable of resulting in procreation.

Concerning the first, "human cloning would allow women who have no ova or men who have no sperm to produce offspring biologically related to them."[47] Such potential parents may use the ovum of the female partner with the genetic material of the male, or they may use another's ovum or the genetic material of another individual – including the female partner's or that of a friend, family member, or even a stranger – with a natural talent or an appearance that is thought to be strongly connected to his or her genes (e.g., Michael Jordan, Albert Einstein, Marilyn Monroe). Although it is likely that most couples would choose cloning because of infertility, there are other concerns that may motivate them. For example, one or both partners may have an inheritable disease that they do not want to pass on to their children. Thus, they may choose to use only the genetic material of one of the partners or the genetic material of a third party.

SCNT cloning may also be used by couples as a means to "clone someone who had or has special meaning to them, such as a child who had died."[48] Parents may also elect to use SCNT to clone a living child when the parents, for a variety of reasons (such as medical motives – the living child does not have an inheritable disease), would like another child just like him or her.[49]

It has been suggested by some that gay and lesbian couples may employ SCNT so that they may be able to have children that result from the genetic material of at least one member of the couple.[50] And in the case of lesbians, the ovum of one can be used with the genetic material of the other. Although the resulting child would be the genetic twin of the latter, both partners would have contributed to the child's existence.

Nonreproductive Reasons

Someone may want to clone entire human beings as well as incomplete human beings for purposes other than becoming a parent. Cloning could be a plentiful resource for stem cells, which could "serve as the starter stock for growing replacement nerve, muscle and other tissues that might one day be used to treat patients with a variety of diseases."[51] Nonreproductive cloning also holds out the possibility of increasing the supply of tissues and organs for transplantation by cloning full or intentionally damaged human beings. Although there are other possible nonreproductive uses of cloning (e.g., creating identical embryos to experiment on them in numerous ways), I focus on these two.

Cloning for Organ and Tissue Supplies and as Source of Embryonic Stem Cells

Concerning the latter, cloning – whether embryonic or SCNT – could serve as a nearly unlimited resource for embryonic stem cells. Stem-cell research, according to some scholars, holds out the promise of finding cures for Alzheimer's and Parkinson's disease as well as other ailments.

As far as cloning for organ and tissue supplies, consider the following scenario: a couple's one-year-old child is suffering from two defective kidneys and, if no donor of a healthy kidney can be found within one year, the child will die. If cloning technology were available, the parents could theoretically clone their child so that an identical twin could be produced and that twin could serve as a kidney donor for the dying child. This is not as far-fetched as one may think. Shannon H. Smith tells of a 1990 case in which "the parents of a nineteen-year-old suffering with leukemia chose to have another child in hopes of obtaining a source for a bone marrow transplant."[52] The parents in question, the Ayalas, did conceive and give birth to a child whose bone marrow matched that of their dying 19-year-old. Around the time the Ayalas were going through their travail, an Indiana couple "chose to immediately attempt to have another child to provide fetal stem cells to their newborn, who had been diagnosed with Falconi's Anemia." The mother miscarried. She then "waited a month and got pregnant again. When this child was born, she was an unsuitable donor. Twelve weeks later, the mother was pregnant again, this time with a child who turned out to be compatible."[53] Although these two cases were not cases of SCNT, one can imagine that, if the couples could have had access to such technology, they would have employed it to save their children's lives.

Cloning of incomplete human beings is another possible nonreproductive purpose of cloning. Dan W. Brock cites a proposal by Carol Kahn (which I mention in Chapter 6), in which she argues that "after cell differentiation, some of the brain cells of the embryo or fetus would be removed so that it could then be grown as a brain-dead body for spare parts for its earlier twin."[54] According to Brock, "this body clone would be like an anencephalic newborn or presentient fetus, neither of whom arguably can be harmed, because of their lack of capacity for consciousness."[55]

Objections against Cloning

The following are some, but by no means all of the objections against cloning.[56]

Cloning Will Use and Destroy Prenatal Human Beings

To get to the point where science is capable of cloning human beings with relative ease, literally hundreds of thousands of human embryos will have to be brought into existence and then discarded. Cloning is not a routine procedure. In the case of Dolly, 277 implants were created before Dolly was produced. The numerous human embryos resulting from the work of Hall and Stillman eventually perished. For Dr. Seed's proposed cloning clinic to succeed, thousands of human embryos will have to be purposefully brought into existence and then discarded. And if cloned embryos are brought into being so their stem cells may be extracted for the purpose of research, these beings will be killed as a result. These embryos – in each of these scenarios – will not be treated as intrinsically valuable human subjects but rather as things to be used to further the ends of science or the benefit of others.

Of course, this concern may be countered either metaphysically or legally. Concerning the former, someone may argue that the unborn, at least during most of its gestation, is not a full human person. In reply, I have already made the case in Chapters 4 and 6 that the unborn are full-fledged members of the human community; so there is no need to repeat those arguments here. Legally, however, someone may argue that (in the United States), because the Fourteenth Amendment does not recognize embryos and fetuses as protectable persons,[57] it is permissible to experiment on them for the sake of some greater good for actual persons.[58] It is true that the Supreme Court has ruled that a state's interest in prenatal life may never trump the privacy interests of the pregnant woman, at least prior to fetal viability.[59] But it does not follow from that holding that embryos and fetuses, outside of the context of pregnancy, ought not to be accorded any rights whatsoever.[60] In fact, the rights of embryos and fetuses have been increasingly acknowledged in both tort and criminal law in a growing number of jurisdictions.[61] Given these points, it is possible to argue that a state may prohibit cloning by combining two reasons: (1) cloning involves the destruction of and experimentation on human embryos and fetuses, and (2) the state has an interest in protecting prenatal life outside the context of pregnancy.[62]

Cloning May Undermine the Delicate Balance of Family Life

Imagine if an infertile couple were to produce a clone of the male partner so that they might have a child of their own. This poses some interesting problems. First, the "child" would technically be the father's brother, not the father's son, which would make the "mother" her "son's" sister-in-law. In addition, it would mean that her "son" is also her husband's twin brother. Second, what if this couple were to clone another "child," but this time it is the female partner's clone. This would make the "other," paradoxically, both the biological "father" and "mother" of the clone, her biological twin sister. Technically, this "child" would not be the sister of her "father's" "son." In fact, she would be as much her "brother's" "sister" as her "father" is her "mother's" brother. Thus, the "sister" and "brother" could marry each other and have children the old-fashioned way.

Moreover, if a person were to clone himself, he would literally be giving his parents a new child and his siblings a new heir with whom to compete for inheritance. Also, if this clone in turn were to clone himself, he would be giving to his progenitor another sibling and to his progenitor's parents yet another child. This also poses another peculiar problem: Does the progenitor have a right over his genome to such an extent that his clone may not produce a clone with the progenitor's genome (which is what the progenitor's clone would possess)? If so, then would clones become second-class citizens with less reproductive autonomy than people brought into being the old-fashioned way?

Thus, if cloning is treated as just another exercise in "reproductive rights," the distinctions between parent, child, sister, and brother – the definitions that ground our notion of family life – are at risk of unraveling.

Cloning May Lead Society to View Human Beings as Commodities

Unlike other forms of reproductive assistance, SCNT cloning allows one to choose the particular genome for one's "offspring." Some have argued that this sort of control over and selection of another's genome may result in viewing the child-clone produced as "made" rather than "begotten."[63] That is, some argue that human cloning will have more in common with manufacturing than procreating, and this will lead people to begin to think of these children (and perhaps non-cloned children as well) as commodities selected for their attributes rather than as persons who should be valued for their own sake. Commodities stand in an object-subject relation to their owners and/or their makers; that is, commodities, by virtue of their nature, are inferior to the subjects who make and own them. On the other hand, moral agents stand in a subject-subject relation to other moral agents, including their parents, spouses, children, and siblings. Commodities are replaceable whereas moral agents are not. You can always get a new microwave oven to replace the defective one, but a clone of one's deceased child is not really a replacement.

Nevertheless, defenders of human cloning believe that the "commodities argument" is overstated. After all, as Lawrence Wu points out,

> parents already exercise near absolute control over their children, as evidenced by contraception, the timing of the birth, the choice of where to live, and a host of developmental interventions, ranging from the trivial (e.g., piano lessons) to the considerable (e.g., boarding school or religion). Though selection of the genome certainly does amount to complete control over an aspect of the child's life, such control does not occur within a vacuum, but within a complex network of interactions between

the parent and child, where the parent is almost always exercising some degree of control over the child's life. In this continuum, cloning *per se* does not involve the type of control that will constrain or diminish the child's life (as opposed to bad parenting) because his or her life will still be autonomous and indeterminate. Thus, selecting the genome can be understood as just another aspect of acceptable parental control, albeit at the higher end of the continuum.[64]

It seems, however, that Wu misses the point of the commodities argument. It is not really about a parent's control over her child, for in the cases of accepted control listed by Wu, the child is treated as an end in himself, whom the parent is directing and instructing, so that the child may become a flourishing member of the community. But what troubles opponents of cloning is not that people have the power to become parents and then exercise their parental authority in helping to direct the development of their child. Rather, what troubles them is that cloning will allow parents to have the power to choose their children and their attributes, in much the same way they may choose a toaster, automobile, or computer. For example, J. L. A. Garcia, an opponent of human cloning, argues:

> It strikes me as so transparently demeaning to a human being to make her a product of technological manufacture that it is difficult to understand why some people claim not to see it. This is *not* the way we have ever treated human beings; it *is* the way we have always treated subhuman things we regard as wholly subject to our will. Thus, cloning a human person is treated in a way otherwise reserved only for subhuman beings. It is hard to know a better definition of degrading, depreciating.... Even some advocates of cloning consider it "replication," not reproduction. It is hard to see equal treatment or much acknowledgment of human equality in a situation where one person is planned and designed by another, and then manufactured to the latter's specifications.[65]

Supporters of human cloning, such as Wu, maintain that "the manufacturing aspect of cloning is not limited to this particular [assisted reproductive technology], or even to noncoital reproduction."[66] Some people, for example, direct IVF, artificial insemination, and ordinary sexual procreation for the same purposes to which SCNT will likely be directed. Garcia replies by asserting that this argument "shows not that such perversions are morally unproblematic, but that they should be avoided and condemned everywhere and that forms of reproduction that facilitate or encourage them have a heavy moral presumption against them."[67]

Nonreproductive Uses of Cloning May Lead to Treating Human Beings as Commodities

We may also raise the commodity objection in reply to nonreproductive uses of cloning. Concerning the cloning of entire human beings, we can raise the question, Is it permissible to bring a human being into existence for the primary purpose of using him or her, or his or her parts, as means by which to save or preserve another's life? Although some scholars believe that such a use is morally permissible, and thus ought to be legally permissible in both cloning and non-cloning scenarios,[68] they appeal to a broad interpretation of reproductive liberty[69] that they believe they can find in, and extract from, a string of U.S. Supreme Court decisions tracing back to the middle of the 20th century.[70] The logic of their case goes something like this: the state may not conscript a woman's (or even a man's) body as a means by which to sustain another's life or potential life because people have near absolute bodily autonomy; it follows, then, that there is a fundamental right to reproductive freedom that is broad enough to encompass cloning for both reproductive and nonreproductive reasons.

Ironically, we could employ this same reasoning to critique the justification of the sort of reproduction employed by the Ayalas (and others) that may possibly extend to future uses of cloning human beings. Our reasoning may go something like this: the same woman whose body cannot be conscripted by the state for pregnancy ought not to be conscripted when this body is less developed and the woman's mind less mature. For example, if the parents of a 14-year-old daughter cannot, according to the canons of reproductive freedom, force their daughter to carry her prenatal sister in her womb because her sister's mother is physically incapable of doing so, it is not clear why it would have been permissible to bring that same 14-year-old into existence over 14 years earlier so that her body could be used for the purpose of saving another's life, such as that of her older sibling. Imagine if these parents had combed the adoption rolls to find a suitable organ donor for their dying child. Even if they promised to love that child and nurture her in the same way they had loved and nurtured their dying child, it would not make it less true that the key condition for choosing *that* child, rather than another, was her value as an organ donor for their dying child. Thus, it would seem that the appeal to reproductive liberty to justify cloning a child for organ donation is much more problematic, given the premise – near absolute bodily autonomy – on which reproductive liberty is thought by many to rest.

The cloning of incomplete human beings has its problems as well, as I have already argued in Chapter 6. Even though, as Brock argues, "this body clone" could not arguably be harmed because of its "lack of capacity for consciousness,"[71] "most people would likely find" the practice of purposely creating nonsentient human beings "appalling and immoral, in part because here the cloned later twin's capacity for conscious life is destroyed *solely as a means* to benefit another."[72]

However, given the Supreme Court's claim that the unborn is not protected under the Fourteenth Amendment,[73] as well as Brock's belief (and the belief of many bioethicists; see Chapter 6) that the presentient unborn cannot be harmed, it is not precisely clear what would be wrong with cloning brainless human beings for the purpose of harvesting their organs. (Indeed, it is not clear that it would be morally different from cloning embryos so as to extract their stem cells; for in both cases the unborn is presentient and the fulfillment of their intrinsic purpose is permanently thwarted to benefit others.) That is, if there is no injustice done to another and someone receives a benefit, it is difficult to know where exactly the wrong is to be located in the act. I suspect that some would locate it in the moral intuition that the presentient fetus is deprived of something to which he is entitled. But if that is the case, then current capacity for consciousness is a condition that is sufficient, but not necessary,[74] for a human being to possess both rights and a present capacity to be harmed. Yet what follows is that the intentional creation of brainless children (or embryos) for the purpose of harvesting their organs (or their stem cells) is a serious wrong whose prohibition should be reflected in our laws, for their presentient selves are rights-bearers entitled to some protection by the wider community.[75] But if we were to extract from this insight the principle that seems to ground this wrong – it is prima facie wrong to destroy another's capacity for a yet-to-be-achieved property *solely as a means* to benefit another – then a fundamental aspect of reproductive freedom, the right to abortion, is imperiled by that principle: according to the U.S. Supreme Court, the right to abortion is justified *precisely because* a woman undergoing an abortion is merely destroying the unborn's capacity for, as opposed to its current possession of, actual life.[76]

The Promise of Medical Benefits Begs the Question

As I noted earlier, cloning may result in a plentiful source of embryos from which stem cells may be extracted. In defending cloning for this purpose, proponents are circumspect to ignore or dismiss the moral status of the embryo while stressing the potential benefits that may result from this research. For example, in a position paper called "Human Embryo Research," NARAL Pro-Choice America (formerly the National Abortion and Reproductive Rights Action League) begins its presentation by saying that "the prohibition of federal funding of human embryo research holds the health of millions of Americans hostage to anti-choice politics and severely restricts high-quality scientific research that could lead to a variety of beneficial medical treatments."[77]

This argument – like many of the popular abortion-choice arguments assessed in Chapter 5– begs the question. After all, the law currently forbids conducting fatal experiments on healthy children and the homeless (e.g., injecting them with AIDS), even though such experiments would increase the likelihood that scientists would find cures for diseases such as AIDS, diabetes, and cancer. But merely the promise that many people may (or even will) benefit from these experiments cannot make them just. Consequently, if the unborn are full-fledged members of the human community, intentionally bringing them into existence to conduct experiments on them that will result in their deaths cannot be morally right. However, if the unborn are not fully human, then these experiments may be justified. Thus, the status of the unborn, and not the promise of the research, is what is doing all the moral work.

IS THERE A CONSTITUTIONAL RIGHT TO CLONE?

Is the constitutional right to reproductive liberty broad enough to encompass cloning? It depends.[78] There are aspects of the Supreme Court's decisions on reproductive liberty that seem to point toward personal autonomy on matters of lifestyle, marital choices, and intimacy as being part of the foundation of that liberty. If that is the case, then it seems that there is a constitutional right to clone that states may restrict only if there is a compelling state interest. On the other hand, there are aspects of these same Supreme Court decisions that seem to point toward viewing reproductive liberty as merely allowing individuals the right to reject the burden of pregnancy and subsequent child rearing. That is, there is no jurisprudential basis for affirming a constitutional right either to clone or employ other reproductive technologies that one could reasonably infer from these decisions. Although the Court could go in either direction, it seems to me that a plausible reading of these cases does not entail a constitutional right to clone.

The first hint at a right to reproductive liberty can be found in *Skinner v. Oklahoma*.[79] In that case, the Court ruled in favor of a male plaintiff, an habitual criminal who, after being convicted for his most recent crime, was ordered by the trial court to undergo the "operation of vasectomy"[80] so that his undesirable genetic traits could not be passed on to offspring. Although not dealing with the scientific credibility of such a claim, the Court ruled in the majority opinion (authored by Justice Douglas) that the Oklahoma statute providing the jury its justification to order the punishment violated the Equal Protection Clause of the Fourteenth Amendment because the statute did not allow for the punishment of sterilization for higher classes of thieves (e.g., embezzlers), whose wayward practices could be just as habitual as those of Skinner and other small-time crooks.[81]

Chief Justice Stone pointed out in his concurring opinion that the Equal Protection Clause argument proposed by Justice Douglas does not correctly identify the wrong in the Oklahoma statute. For if the statute had punished all habitual thieves equally – chicken thieves and embezzlers alike – by requiring that the state sterilize them, one would *still* think that there is something wrong with such a statute.[82] Stone believed he had found a solution to this awkward consequence in the Due Process Clause:[83] the State of Oklahoma has the burden to prove, in a fair procedure, that it can justify its intent to surgically and permanently remove the function for which Skinner's reproductive equipment was designed, to sire offspring. Nevertheless, both the holding of the majority, as well as the concurring opinion, seem less like affirmations of reproductive liberty and more like opinions about the morality of equal treatment and the level of judicial scrutiny required to allow state-mandated battery.

However, the aspect of *Skinner*'s majority opinion that seems to have stood the test of time (though it is uncertain whether it was part of the Court's holding) – and seems to have had an influence in the formation of the plurality opinion (authored by Justice Douglas) in *Griswold v. Connecticut* – is the section in which Justice Douglas wrote that "marriage and procreation are fundamental to the very existence and survival of the race. The power to sterilize, if exercised, may have subtle, far reaching and devastating effects."[84] In *Griswold*, the Court ruled as unconstitutional a Connecticut statute that forbade the use of, sale of, and/or the assisting in the use of contraceptive devices.[85] Justice Douglas concluded that the right of privacy grounds this judgment, for the wrongness of this statute lies in its broad scope: it includes the private judgments and activities of couples within the sanctuary of marriage. This right of privacy, according to Douglas, can be gleaned not from a literal reading of the words found in the Bill of Rights but from "penumbras" that stand behind these words, and these penumbras are "formed by emanations

from those guarantees that help give them life and substance."[86] What
was tucked-away in *Skinner* becomes explicit in *Griswold*:

> We deal with a right of privacy older than the Bill of Rights – older than
> our political parties, older than our school system. Marriage is a coming
> together for better or for worse, hopefully enduring, and intimate to the
> degree of being sacred. It is an association that promotes a way of life,
> not causes; a harmony in living, not political faiths; a bilateral loyalty, not
> commercial or social projects. Yet it is an association for as noble purpose
> as any involved in our prior decisions.[87]

It seems that, according to Justice Douglas, the right to marry and
form a family is logically and chronologically prior to the state. What
the Court seems concerned about is that Connecticut, through its anti-
contraception statute, interfered with the sanctity of marriage and the
couple's judgments about intimate matters, including reproduction.[88]
In his concurring opinion, Justice Goldberg understood the plurality's
rejection of the Connecticut statute as firmly grounded in this notion
of marital sanctity.[89] But because of this understanding, Goldberg did
not think that reproductive liberty and the right of privacy were end-
lessly elastic, for he maintained that "the Court's holding today . . . in no
way interferes with a State's proper regulation of sexual promiscuity and
misconduct,"[90] and then approvingly cited Justice Harlan's comments in
Poe v. Ullman: "Adultery, homosexuality and the like are sexual intima-
cies which the State forbids . . . but the intimacy of husband and wife is
necessarily an essential and accepted feature of the institution of marriage which the State not only must allow, but which always and in every
age it has fostered and protected."[91]

In *Eisenstadt v. Baird*, the Court ruled that a Massachusetts statute
violated the Equal Protection Clause because it provided, in its laws
regarding the distribution of contraceptive devices, "dissimilar treatment
for married and unmarried persons who are similarly situated."[92] In the
words of Justice Brennan, author of the majority opinion:

> If under *Griswold* the distribution of contraceptives to married persons
> cannot be prohibited, a ban on distribution to unmarried persons would
> be equally impermissible. It is true that in *Griswold* the right of privacy
> in question inhered in the marital relationship. Yet the marital couple
> is not an independent entity with a mind and heart of its own, but an
> association of two individuals each with a separate intellectual and emo-
> tional makeup. If the right of privacy means anything, it is the right of the
> *individual*, married or single, to be free from unwarranted governmental

intrusion into matters so fundamentally affecting a person as the decision to bear or beget a child.[93]

It seems that, at this point in the historical trajectory of the right of privacy, one could reasonably infer that reproductive liberty was moving in a libertarian direction. That is, the Court was setting into motion certain principles of constitutional liberty that were at such a high level of abstraction that it would become nearly impossible for a community to proscribe in its laws the sorts of research and reproductive technologies that are presently offered, or may soon be offered (e.g., human cloning), in the 21st century.

In *Roe v. Wade*, the Court established a right to abortion based on the right of privacy found in *Griswold* and *Eisenstadt*, as well as other decisions.[94] However, it would be a mistake, the Court explained, to think of this right as absolute,[95] for the Court took into consideration the legitimate state interests of both the health of the pregnant woman and the prenatal life she carries. Concerning the former, the Court allowed States to regulate abortion, as they may regulate other medical facilities and other procedures.[96] In regard to prenatal life, the Court thought the question of metaphysical personhood to be outside the realm of the Court's expertise,[97] even though the Court asserted that the fetus is not a person according to the Constitution.[98] In any event, the state's interest in prenatal life increases as the fetus develops;[99] and when it reaches the point of viability, the state *may* restrict abortion, except in cases in which an abortion is necessary to preserve the health or life of the pregnant woman.[100] Thus, reproductive liberty in the context of *Roe* should be seen as a limited freedom, established within the nexus of three parties: the pregnant woman, the fetus, and the state. The woman's liberty trumps both the value of the fetus and the interests of the state, except when the fetus reaches viability (and an abortion is unnecessary to preserve the life or health of the pregnant woman) and/or when the state has a compelling interest in regulating abortion before and after viability to make sure that the procedure is performed in accordance with accepted medical standards.[101]

As one might guess, this reading of *Roe* is not universally embraced. This is why some courts[102] and some scholars[103] see *Roe* and its predecessors as establishing a near absolute right to reproductive liberty (including the use of reproductive technologies, such as cloning). On the other hand, some courts[104] and scholars[105] embrace a reading similar to the one I am presenting here.

Nevertheless, it seems that the Supreme Court, since the late 1980s, has come to embrace the nonabsolutist interpretation of *Roe*. For this reason, the Court will likely leave the question of human cloning to the state and federal legislatures rather than attempt to settle the issue by judicial fiat. That is, the Court seems to have shifted to a more minimalist perspective when it comes to constitutional interpretation, for there seems to be reluctance to lay down highly abstract principles of moral philosophy that could be extended beyond their intended use in particular cases.[106] There are several reasons to believe this is the case.[107]

In *Casey v. Planned Parenthood* (1992), the Court more carefully defined the right to abortion in terms of a woman's right to avoid the burden of unwanted pregnancy.[108] Although such reasoning was not absent from *Roe*,[109] the *Casey* plurality seems to have crafted its opinion to accentuate the state's interest in prenatal life and that this interest *may only be trumped* by a woman's fundamental right to terminate her pregnancy.[110] Thus, a state's protection of prenatal life, outside of the abortion context, is not impermissible.

Unfortunately for the authors of the plurality opinion, a particular passage from it has been taken by lower courts and some scholars (see below) to establish a near absolute right to personal autonomy:

> Our law affords constitutional protection to personal decisions relating to marriage, procreation, contraception, family relationships, child rearing, and education.... These matters, involving the most intimate and personal choices a person may make in a lifetime, choices central to personal dignity and autonomy, are central to the liberty protected by the Fourteenth Amendment. At the heart of liberty is the right to define one's own concept of existence, of meaning, of the universe, and of the mystery of human life. Beliefs about these matters could not define the attributes of personhood were they formed under compulsion by the State.[111]

In 1994, Federal District Court Judge Barbara Rothstein struck down Washington state's ban on physician-assisted suicide. In her opinion she employed what she thought was the logic of *Casey*: "Like the abortion decision, the decision of a terminally ill person to end his or her life 'involves the most intimate and personal choices a person can make in a lifetime,' and constitutes a 'choice central to personal dignity and autonomy.'"[112] Legal philosopher Ronald Dworkin makes a similar claim:

> Our Constitution takes no sides in these ancient disputes about life's meaning. But it does protect people's right to die as well as live, so far as

possible, in the light of their own intensely personal convictions about "the mystery of human life." It insists that these values are too central to personality, too much at the core of liberty, to allow a majority to decide what everyone must believe.[113]

It is not difficult to imagine, given Rothstein's and Dworkin's interpretation of *Casey*, that one could conclude that there exists a near absolute right to personal autonomy that would include both a right to physician-assisted suicide and a right to clone. However, in *Washington v. Glucksberg*, the Court corrected this interpretation of its "autonomy passage":

> By choosing this language, the Court's opinion in *Casey* described, in a general way and in light of our prior cases, those personal activities and decisions that this Court has identified as so deeply rooted in our history and traditions, or so fundamental to our concept of constitutionally ordered liberty, that they are protected by the Fourteenth Amendment. The opinion moved from the recognition that liberty necessarily includes freedom of conscience and belief about ultimate considerations to the observation that "though the abortion decision may originate within the zone of conscience and belief, it is *more than a philosophic exercise." That many of the rights and liberties protected by the Due Process Clause sound in personal autonomy does not warrant the sweeping conclusion that any and all important, intimate, and personal decisions are so protected, and* Casey *did not suggest otherwise.*[114]

Thus, the *Glucksberg* Court saw its "autonomy passage" in *Casey* as having its application limited to those activities that can be grounded in identifiable and deeply rooted traditions, as well as that which is fundamental to the concept of ordered liberty. Therefore, the Court concluded that there is not a right to physician-assisted suicide as there is a right to abortion.[115]

This provides an important clue as to how the Court may rule concerning the question of whether the right of privacy is broad enough to encompass a right to clone. For, like physician-assisted suicide, cloning, as we have seen, is a matter over which there is a profound debate regarding its morality, legality, and practicality. In addition, cloning, like physician-assisted suicide, is not grounded in our nation's history and traditions.[116] Strong evidence of such is found in the largely negative political, legal, and public reaction to cloning in the United States, as well as the NBAC's and PCB's conclusions and careful analysis of the issue. Therefore, it is likely that the Court will say the same thing about cloning that it has said about physician-assisted suicide:[117] "Throughout the Nation, Americans are engaged in an earnest and profound debate about the morality, legality, and practicality of physician-assisted suicide. Our holding permits this debate to continue, as it should in a democratic society."[118]

Given what we have covered in this chapter, it seems to me that the Supreme Court could reasonably, and is likely to, reject a constitutional right to clone. The Court may employ something like the following argument:

1. The right of privacy establishes the right of contraceptive use. (*Griswold, Eisenstadt*)
2. The right of privacy encompasses the right to abortion, though that right is the result of a balance between three interests: the woman's burden of pregnancy and future child rearing, the state's interest in the unborn, and the state's interest in maternal health.
3. Therefore, it is not unconstitutional for a state to ban or restrict cloning, because such an action would not involve a ban on contraceptive use and/or an absolute prohibition of a woman's right to abortion.
4. Cloning, like physician-assisted suicide, is a controversial matter better left to public discussion, deliberation, and debate. (*Glucksberg*)
5. Given (3) and (4) above, a state may ban cloning on any rational basis, including for the purposes of protecting unborn human life (as has been done in tort and criminal statutes and common law cases), preventing the commodification of children and their parts, or preserving the integrity of the family, an institution whose existence predates the Bill of Rights (*Griswold*).

Therefore, given the Supreme Court's current trajectory on the matter of reproductive liberty, there is no constitutional right to clone.

CONCLUSION

In this chapter we assessed what is perhaps the most intriguing issue in contemporary bioethics: cloning. It is an issue that brings to the forefront of public discussion the question lurking behind the abortion controversy – who and what are we? Although most citizens, and political leaders, have a visceral reaction against cloning, it is not clear that their negative judgment can be sustained if the premises on which many think the abortion right is grounded – for example, the unborn is not a person, reproductive liberty entails near absolute bodily autonomy – cannot logically be prevented from being applied to the practice of cloning. Although the pro-life position on abortion seems to entail that human cloning – as well as embryonic stem-cell research – ought to be prohibited by law, I have argued in this chapter that one need not have to accept the totality of the pro-life position to oppose these practices, either morally or legally. On the other hand, if the medical benefits that may result from research on the unborn become more promising, it will become more difficult to resist these practices unless one has good reasons to believe that the unborn are subjects of rights and must be treated as intrinsically valuable beings deserving of our respect.[119]

9

CONCLUSION: A CASE FOR HUMAN INCLUSIVENESS

The purpose of this final chapter is to offer a summary of the case I make in this book for the argument I offer in the book's introduction:

1. The unborn entity, from the moment of conception, is a full-fledged member of the human community.
2. It is prima facie morally wrong to kill any member of that community.
3. Every successful abortion kills an unborn entity, a full-fledged member of the human community.
4. Therefore, every successful abortion is prima facie morally wrong.

This argument is deductively valid. That is, if the premises are true, the conclusion follows. And if the premises of a valid argument are true, then the argument is sound. And if the above argument is sound, then the pro-life position is morally correct. But are the premises of the above argument true? I believe that the case I made in this book shows that they are true. Let me briefly summarize that case.

First, we saw that the unborn is biologically an individual member of the species, Homo sapiens, from the moment of conception (Chapter 4). Furthermore, we concluded that attempts to exclude the unborn from protection during some or all of its gestation are unsuccessful. Because none of the attempts to isolate the preborn from the community of intrinsically valuable human beings succeeds, and because the substance view of persons provides the best accounting of human beings and their intrinsic value from the moment they come into being (Chapter 6), it follows that *the unborn entity, from the moment of conception, is fully human*, a person entitled to the human community's protection. We saw in Chapter 3 that the government cannot remain neutral on the question of abortion and the unborn's personhood, as the U.S. Supreme Court claimed in its two landmark opinions on abortion, *Roe v. Wade* and *Casey v. Planned Parenthood* (Chapter 2).

Second, it seems intuitively true that it is prima facie wrong to kill an entity that is fully human (Chapter 1). By saying that such killing is prima facie wrong I am only claiming that in ordinary circumstances (that is, "on the face of it") no one is morally justified in killing another human being. This is why none of the popular abortion-choice arguments from pity, tolerance, and ad hominen work, for they try to justify the killing of the unborn on the same grounds for which it would be wrong to kill post-natal human beings (Chapter 5). For the real question – which is begged in virtually all these popular arguments – is whether the unborn is a full-fledged member of the human community.

This does not mean, however, that it is always wrong to kill someone who is fully human, only prima facie wrong. For there could be circumstances in which killing or letting die is *justified*, such as in cases of self-defense or just war. In the case of abortion, the killing of an unborn entity is justified, as I argue in Chapter 6, if her presence in the womb poses a significant threat to the life of her mother. For if the unborn entity is not surgically removed (which will undoubtedly result in her death if performed prior to viability), then both mother and child will die. The *specific* intention of this abortion is not to kill the child but to save the life of the mother. The child's death via abortion is an unfortunate consequence that, although anticipated, cannot be avoided unless one is willing to let *both* mother and child die by permitting the pregnancy to continue. The child is not killed to save the mother. Rather, the pregnancy is terminated to save one life rather than permit two to die.

Some thinkers, such as Judith Jarvis Thomson, although agreeing in principle with premise 2 of my argument, have argued that even if the unborn is fully human with a full right to life, a pregnant woman still has a right to procure an abortion, as no one, not even the unborn, has the right to use another's body against her will. That is to say, the killing of an unborn entity via abortion is not an example of killing that is prima facie wrong. However, there are a number of fundamental problems with both this and other arguments similar to it (see Chapter 7). In sum, it seems that premise 2 is basically correct: it is prima facie wrong to kill an entity that is fully human.

Third, there is no doubt that every successful abortion kills an unborn entity, a full-fledged member of the human community. It seems then that all three premises of this argument are true. And because the conclusion follows logically from the premises, this argument is sound. Therefore, the pro-life position on abortion is morally correct. And because its moral correctness entails the prohibition of the unjust killing of innocent human persons, and because at least one uncontroversial role of government is to protect the powerless from unjust treatment by the powerful, the pro-life position is just the type of moral position that ought to be reflected in our laws. That is, a pro-life law would prohibit exactly the type of activity for which just governments are created to prohibit: an activity in which the powerful unjustly poison, burn, suffocate and/or dismember the powerless. As one ethicist puts it, "Suppose, in the encounter between doctor and child [in an abortion], the child won half of the time, and killed the doctor in self-defense – something he would have every right to do. Very few doctors would perform abortions. They perform them now only because of their absolute power over a small fragile, helpless victim."[1]

We extended the pro-life argument in Chapter 8 in which we dealt with the issue of human cloning. We concluded that it is morally unjustified and ought to be banned. In addition to assessing this issue in light of the view of human beings defended in this book, we concluded that there is no constitutional right to clone even if the Supreme Court's opinions on privacy and reproductive rights are correct.

My good friend Gregory P. Koukl, one of the most gifted minds in the pro-life movement, often tells the fictional story of a father who, while his back is turned, hears his teenage daughter ask the question, "Daddy, can I kill it?" Koukl then asks his audience, "How should the father respond to his daughter's query?" The audience, in every venue at which Greg has told this story, answers: "He should ask her, 'What is it?'" Although largely untutored in the subtle distinctions of moral philosophy, the audience members understand at a visceral level that the permissibility of killing another being depends on what it is and whether the killing is justified. It really matters whether "it" is a cockroach, the girl's infant brother, or an enemy soldier in combat.

This moral truth is the one strand in the tapestry of republican government that, if removed, will put in place premises that will facilitate the unraveling of the understanding of ourselves and our rights that gave rise to the cluster of beliefs on which the rule of law, constitutional democracy, and human equality depend. As my dear friend Hadley Arkes has elegantly argued,[2] if we are, as even the supporters of abortion must assume, bearers of moral rights by nature (including the "right to choose"), then there can be no right to abortion, for the one who has the "right to choose" is identical to her prenatal self. Consequently, the right to abortion can only be purchased at the price of abandoning natural rights and replacing them with the will to power. It is a price not worth paying.

NOTES

Introduction: Who and What Are We and Can We Know It?

1. Of course, an unsuccessful abortion (one in which the fetus survives) is still a wrong, if the unborn is a full-fledged member of the human community, for an act that is intended to kill an innocent person is still wrong even if no harm results or the harm that results is less severe than what was intended.

2. As far as I know, Doris Gordon coined the term "abortion choice." See, for example, her introductory essay in *International Journal of Sociology and Social Policy* 19.3/4 (1999).

3. See Francis J. Beckwith, "Taking Theology Seriously: The Status of the Religious Beliefs of Judicial Nominees for the Federal Bench," *Notre Dame Journal of Law, Ethics & Public Policy* 20.1 (2006): 455–471.

4. Francis J. Beckwith, "A Critical Appraisal of the Theological Arguments for Abortion Rights," *Bibliotheca Sacra* 148 (July–September 1991): 337–355.

5. Francis J. Beckwith, "The Court of Disbelief: The Constitution's Article VI Religious Test Prohibition and the Judiciary's Religious Motive Analysis," *Hastings Constitutional Law Quarterly* 33.2 & 3 (Winter and Spring 2006): 337–360.

1. Abortion and Moral Argument

1. For an overview of the abortion debate from different sides, see Louis P. Pojman and Francis J. Beckwith, eds., *The Abortion Controversy 25 Years after* Roe v. Wade: *A Reader*, 2nd ed. (Belmont, CA: Wadsworth, 1998). Ironically, this book was the result of a debate I had with my co-editor and dear friend, the late Lou Pojman (d. 2005), at Taylor University (Upland, Indiana) in 1993. A defender of abortion rights, Pojman was no relativist, and thus much of what I say in this chapter does not apply to sophisticated abortion-choice supporters such as Pojman.

2. The ideas and argument of this section have been significantly shaped by a portion of the book by Hadley Arkes, *First Things: An Inquiry into the First Principles of Morals and Justice* (Princeton, NJ: Princeton University Press, 1986), 20–22.

3. Arkes's work (ibid.) was instrumental in helping me to better understand the differences between the two statements.

4. See, for example, Louis P. Pojman, *Ethics: Discovering Right and Wrong*, 3rd ed. (Belmont, CA: Wadsworth, 1998). As I noted in note 1, Pojman, a supporter of abortion rights, was a critic of moral relativism as well as a defender of moral objectivism. For his defense of the abortion-choice position, see Pojman, "Abortion: A Defense of the Personhood Argument," in *The Abortion Controversy*. Another well-known defender of abortion-choice, David Boonin, seems to be no friend of moral relativism. See David Boonin, *In Defense of Abortion* (New York: Cambridge University Press, 2002), 13–14.

5. For an assessment of the apparent incoherence of this position, see Hadley Arkes, *Natural Rights and the Right to Choose* (New York: Cambridge University Press, 2002)

6. Arkes, *First Things*, 149.

7. Ibid., 132

8. See Tim Sutter, "Salem Witchcraft: The Events and Causes of the Salem Witch Trials" (2003), *The Salem Witch Trials* (website) at http://www.salemwitchtrials.com/salemwitchcraft.html (12 July 2006).

9. Ibid.

10. I say the latter because it seems to me that if certain religious traditions may have rational warrant, it would not be irrational for believers in those traditions to legitimately judge certain practices (e.g., witchcraft) as evil without criminalizing the practice. For some interesting arguments on the rationality of certain religious traditions, see Alvin Plantinga, *Warranted Christian Belief* (New York: Oxford University Press, 2003); and Francis J. Beckwith, William Lane Craig, and J. P. Moreland, eds., *To Everyone an Answer: A Case for the Christian Worldview* (Downers Grove, IL: InterVarsity Press, 2004).

11. Judith Jarvis Thomson, "A Defense of Abortion," in *Philosophy and Public Affairs* 1 (1971): 57–66; Eileen McDonagh, *Breaking the Abortion Deadlock: From Choice to Consent* (New York: Oxford University Press, 1996); Boonin, *A Defense of Abortion*, 133–281.

12. J. P. Moreland, *Scaling the Secular City* (Grand Rapids, MI: Baker Book House, 1987), 92.

13. Moreland offers a similar illustration in ibid.

14. Ibid., 243.

15. Tom L. Beauchamp, *Philosophical Ethics: An Introduction to Moral Philosophy* (New York: McGraw-Hill, 1982), 42.

16. This dialogue is presented in slightly different form in Francis J. Beckwith and Gregory P. Koukl, *Relativism: Feet Firmly Planted in Mid-Air* (Grand Rapids, MI: Baker, 1998), 74.

17. Xiaorang Li, "Postmodernism and Universal Human Rights: Why Theory and Reality Don't Mix," *Free Inquiry* 18.4 (Fall 1998): 28.

18. Arkes, *First Things*, 24.

19. *The Collected Works of Abraham Lincoln*, ed. Roy P. Basler (New Brunswick, NJ: Rutgers University Press, 1953), 3: 256–257, as quoted in Arkes, *First Things*, 24.

20. Arkes, *First Things*, 24–25.

21. Ibid., 25.

22. *The Collected Works of Abraham Lincoln*, 2: 222, as quoted in Arkes, *First Things*, 43–44 (emphasis in original).

23. Arkes, *First Things*, 43.

2. The Supreme Court, *Roe v. Wade,* and Abortion Law

1. *Roe v. Wade,* 410 U.S. 113 (1973).
2. Abortion-choice advocate, and Harvard law professor, Laurence Tribe writes: "A decade and a half after the Court handed down its decision in *Roe* v. Wade McCorvey explained, with embarrassment, that she had not been raped after all; she made up the story to hide the fact she had gotten 'in trouble' in the more usual way" (Laurence Tribe, *Abortion: The Clash of Absolutes* [New York: W. W. Norton, 1990], 10).
3. For example, in Missouri and Pennsylvania modest restrictions were allowed due to the Court's rulings in *Webster v. Reproductive Health Services,* 492 U.S. 490 (1989) and *Casey v. Planned Parenthood,* 505 U.S. 833 (1992).
4. *Roe,* 410 U.S. 164–165.
5. "Appellant and some *amici* argue that the woman's right is absolute and that she is entitled to terminate her pregnancy at whatever time she alone chooses. With this we do not agree" (ibid). The Court writes elsewhere in *Roe:* "The privacy right involved, therefore, cannot be said to be absolute. In fact, it is not clear to us that the claim asserted by some *amici* that one has an unlimited right to do with one's body as one pleases bears a close relationship to the right of privacy previously articulated in the Court's decisions. The Court has refused to recognize an unlimited right of this kind in the past. *Jacobson v. Massachusetts,* 197 U.S. 11 (1905) (vaccination); *Buck v. Bell,* 274 U.S. 200 (1927) (sterilization)" (ibid., 154).
6. *Akron v. Akron Center for Reproductive Health, Inc.,* 462 U.S. 416, 459 (1983) (O'Connor, J., dissenting).
7. Nevada Revised Statute, 442.250, subsection 3.
8. *Doe v. Bolton,* 410 U.S. 179, 192 (1973).
9. Report, Committee on the Judiciary, U.S. Senate, on Senate Resolution 3, 98th Congress, 98–149, June 7, 1983, 6. In another report, the Judiciary Committee concludes: "The apparently restrictive standard for the third trimester has in fact proved no different from the standard of abortion on demand expressly allowed during the first six months of the unborn child's life. The exception for maternal health has been so broad in practice as to swallow the rule. The Supreme Court has defined 'health' in this context to include 'all factors – physical, emotional, familial, and the woman's age – relevant to the well-being of the patient.' *Doe v. Bolton,* 410 U.S. 179, 192 (1973). Since there is nothing to stop an abortionist from certifying that a third-trimester abortion is beneficial to the health of the mother – in this broad sense – the Supreme Court's decision has in fact made abortion available on demand throughout the pre-natal life of the child, from conception to birth" (Report on the Human Life Bill – S. 158; Committee on the Judiciary, United States Senate, December 1981, p. 5).
10. *Thornburgh v. American College of Obstetricians and Gynecologists,* 476 U.S. 747 (1986).
11. See, for example, Victor G. Rosenblum and Thomas J. Marzen, "Strategies for Reversing *Roe* v. Wade through the Courts," in *Abortion and the Constitution,* ed. Dennis Horan, Edward R. Grant, and Paige C. Cunningham (Washington, DC: Georgetown University Press, 1987), 199–200; Thomas O'Meara, "Abortion: The Court Decides a Non-Case," *The Supreme Court Review* (1974): 344; Stanley M. Harrison, "The Supreme Court and Abortional Reform: Means

to an End," *New York Law Forum* 19 (1974): 690; Robert A. Destro, "Abortion and the Constitution: The Need for a Life-Protective Amendment," *California Law Review* 63 (1975): 1250; Jacqueline Nolan Haley, "Haunting Shadows from the Rubble of *Roe's* Right to Privacy," *Suffolk University Law Review* 9 (1974): 152–153; John Hart Ely, "The Wages of Crying Wolf: A Comment on *Roe v. Wade*," *Yale Law Journal* 82 (1973): 921; John T. Noonan Jr., "Raw Judicial Power," in *The Zero People*, ed. Jeff Lane Hensley (Ann Arbor, MI: Servant Books, 1983), 18; Charles E. Rice, "Overruling *Roe v. Wade*: An Analysis of the Proposed Constitutional Amendments," *Boston College Industrial and Commercial Law Review* 15 (December 1973): 309; Lynn D. Wardle and Mary Anne Q. Wood, *A Lawyer Looks at Abortion* (Provo, UT: Brigham Young University Press, 1982), 12; William R. Hopkin Jr., "*Roe v. Wade* and the Traditional Legal Standards Concerning Pregnancy," *Temple Law Quarterly* 47 (1974): 729–730; John Warwick Montgomery, "The Rights of Unborn Children," *Simon Greenleaf Law Review* 5 (1985–1986): 40; Stephen M. Krason, *Abortion: Politics, Morality, and the Constitution* (Lanham, MD: University Press of America, 1984), 103–104; and Roger Wertheimer, "Understanding Blackmun's Argument: The Reasoning of *Roe v. Wade*," in *Abortion: Moral and Legal Perspectives* (Amherst: University of Massachusetts Press, 1984), 120–121.

12. *Roe*, 410 U.S. 163.

13. *Colautti vs. Franklin*, 439 U.S. 379, 387 (1979), quoting from ibid. However, given the Court's analysis in *Casey* (see following) and that opinion's understanding of *Roe*, it may reject *Colautti's* definition of "meaningful life," though one may never really know for sure.

14. *Griswold v. Connecticut*, 381 U.S. 479 (1965).

15. *Eisenstadt* v. Baird, 405 U.S. 438 (1972). In the words of Justice Brennan, author of the majority opinion: "If under *Griswold* the distribution of contraceptives to married persons cannot be prohibited, a ban on distribution to unmarried persons would be equally impermissible. It is true that in *Griswold* the right of privacy in question inhered in the marital relationship. Yet the marital couple is not an independent entity with a mind and heart of its own, but an association of two individuals each with a separate intellectual and emotional makeup. If the right of privacy means anything, it is the right of the *individual*, married or single, to be free from unwarranted governmental intrusion into matters so fundamentally affecting a person as the decision to bear and beget a child."

16. This is not to say that one may raise objections to the "right of privacy." For its proponents admit that this right has no connection to the actual language of the Constitution's text. According to Justice William O. Douglas, who penned the plurality opinion in *Griswold*, this right of privacy can be gleaned, not from a literal reading of the words found in the Bill of Rights, but from "penumbras" that stand behind these words, and these penumbras are "formed by emanations from those guarantees that help give them life and substance" (*Griswold*, 381 U.S. at 484 [Douglas, J.]). Douglas goes on to say: "We deal with a right of privacy older than the Bill of Rights – older than our political parties, older than our school system. Marriage is a coming together for better or for worse, hopefully enduring, and intimate to the degree of being sacred. It is an association that promotes a way of life, not causes; a harmony in living, not political faiths; a bilateral loyalty, not commercial or social projects. Yet it is an

association for a noble purpose as any involved in our prior decisions" (ibid., 486).

17. Ibid.

18. As Justice Blackmun writes in *Roe*: "The pregnant woman cannot be isolated in her privacy. She carries an embryo and, later, a fetus, if one accepts the medical definitions of the developing young in the uterus....The situation therefore is inherently different from marital intimacy, or bedroom possession of obscene material, or marriage, or procreation, or education....As we have intimated above, it is reasonable and appropriate for a State to decide that at some point in time another interest, that of health of the mother or that of potential human life, become significantly involved. The woman's privacy is no longer sole and any right of privacy she possesses must be measured accordingly" (*Roe*, 410 U.S. 159) (citations omitted).

19. Justice Blackmun writes: "It has been argued that a State's real concern in enacting a criminal abortion law was to protect the pregnant woman, that is, to restrain her from submitting to a procedure that placed her life in serious jeopardy" (ibid., 149).

20. Ibid., 132–136. Justice Blackmun writes: "It is thus apparent that at common law, at the time of the adoption of the Constitution, and throughout the major portion of the 19th century, abortion was viewed with less disfavor than under most American statutes currently in effect. Phrasing it another way, a woman enjoyed a substantially broader right to terminate a pregnancy than she does in most States today. At least with respect to the early stage of pregnancy, and very possibly without such a limitation, the opportunity to make this choice was present in this country well into the 19th century" (ibid., 140–141).

21. Ibid., 132 (footnote omitted).

22. "Mortality rates for women undergoing early abortions, where the procedure is legal, appear to be as low or as lower than the rates of normal childbirth. Consequently, any interest of the State in protecting the woman from an inherently dangerous procedure, except when it would be equally dangerous for her to forgo it, has largely disappeared" (*Roe*, 410 U.S. 149).

23. *Roe*, 410 U.S. 129–151.

24. Ibid., 139 (emphasis added).

25. Dellapenna, "The History of Abortion." 389.

26. Among these many works are the following: see, for example, James S. Witherspoon, "Reexamining *Roe*: Nineteenth-Century Abortion Statutes and the Fourteenth Amendment," *St. Mary's Law Journal* 17 (1985); Krason, *Abortion*, 134–157; Dennis J. Horan and Thomas J. Balch, "*Roe* v. Wade: No Justification in History, Law, or Logic," *The Abortion Controversy 25 Years after* Roe v. Wade: *A Reader*, 2nd ed., ed. Louis P. Pojman and Francis J. Beckwith (Belmont, CA: Wadsworth); Joseph W. Dellapenna, "Abortion and the Law: Blackmun's Distortion of the Historical Record," in *Abortion and the Constitution*; and Joseph W. Dellapenna, "The History of Abortion: Technology, Morality and Law," *University of Pittsburgh Law Review* 40 (1979); Martin Arbagi, "*Roe* and the Hippocratic Oath," in *Abortion and the Constitution*; Harold O. J. Brown, "What the Supreme Court Didn't Know: Ancient and Early Christian Views on Abortion," *Human Life Review* 1.2 (Spring 1975); Robert M. Byrn, "An American Tragedy: The Supreme Court on Abortion," *Fordham Law Review* 41 (1973); John R. Connery, S.J., "The Ancients and the Medievals on

Abortion: The Consensus the Court Ignored," in *Abortion and the Constitution*; John Gorby, "The 'Right' to an Abortion, the Scope of Fourteenth Amendment 'Personhood' and the Supreme Court's Birth Requirement," *Southern Illinois Law Review* (1979); John Keown, *Abortion, Doctors, and the Law: Some Aspects of the Legal Regulation of Abortion in England from 1803 to 1982* (Cambridge, UK: Cambridge University Press, 2002), 3–25; Stephen Krason and W. Hollberg, *The Law and History of Abortion: The Supreme Court Refuted* (1984); Janet LaRue, "Abortion: Justice Harry A. Blackmun and the *Roe v. Wade* Decision," *Simon Greenleaf Law Review: A Scholarly Forum of Opinion Interrelating Law, Theology and Human Rights* 2 (1982–1983); Marvin Olasky, *Abortion Rites: A Social History of Abortion in America* (Wheaton, IL: Crossway, 1992); and Robert Sauer, "Attitudes to Abortion in America, 1800–1973," *Population Studies* 28 (1974).

27. See, generally, Witherspoon, "Reexamining *Roe*."

28. Ibid.

29. Ibid., 70.

30. Cyril Means, "The Phoenix of Abortional Freedom: Is a Penumbral or Ninth Amendment Right about to Rise from the Nineteenth-Century Legislative Ashes of a Fourteenth-Amendment Common Law Liberty," *New York Law Forum* 17 (1971); and Cyril Means, "The Law of New York Concerning Abortion and the Status of the Foetus: 1664–1968," *New York Law Forum* 14 (1968).

31. In addition to Witherspoon's article, see Byrn, "An American Tragedy"; Krason, *Abortion*, 134–157; Horan and Balch, "*Roe v. Wade*: No Justification in History, Law, or Logic"; Dellapenna, "Abortion and the Law"; and Dellapenna, "The History of Abortion."

32. See, for example, Tribe, *Abortion: The Clash of Absolutes*, 27–41, 119–120; Ronald M. Dworkin, *Life's Dominion: An Argument about Abortion, Euthanasia, and Individual Freedom* (New York: Random House, 1993), 112; and Susan Estrich, "Abortion Politics: Writing for an Audience of One," *University of Pennsylvania Law Review* 138 (1989): 152–154.

33. *Roe*, 410 U.S. 132.

34. Ibid., 133.

35. Obviously, false beliefs may be widely held. The point here is that an ancient belief may be abandoned because it is *false*. That is, a belief's age has no bearing on its truthfulness.

36. Krason, *Abortion*, 148.

37. The Human Life Bill: Hearings on S. 158 before the Subcommittee on Separation of Powers of the Senate Committee on the Judiciary, 97th Congress, 1st Session (statement of Victor Rosenblum, Professor of Law, Northwestern University), 474.

38. John Warwick Montgomery, *Slaughter of the Innocents* (Westchester, IL: Crossway, 1981), 37.

39. Witherspoon, "Reexamining *Roe*," 32.

40. "The right of privacy, whether it be founded in the Fourteenth Amendment's concept of personal liberty and restrictions upon State action, as we feel it is, or, as the District Court determined, in the Ninth Amendment's reservation of rights to the people, is broad enough to encompass a woman's decision whether or not to terminate her pregnancy" (*Roe*, 410 U.S. 153).

41. "The appellee and certain amici argue that the fetus is a 'person' within the language and meaning of the Fourteenth Amendment. In support of this, they

outline at length and in detail the well-known facts of fetal development. If this suggestion of personhood is established, the appellant's case, of course, collapses, for the fetus' right to life would then be guaranteed specifically by the Amendment. The appellant conceded as much on reargument. On the other hand, the appellee conceded on reargument that no case could be cited that holds that a fetus is a person within the meaning of the Fourteenth Amendment" (*Roe*, 410 U.S. 157–158).

42. Ibid., 157.

43. Ibid. In a note that followed this quote, the Court writes: "When Texas urges that a fetus is entitled to Fourteenth Amendment protection as a person, it faces a dilemma. Neither in Texas nor in any other State are all abortions prohibited. Despite broad proscription, an exception always exists. The exception contained in Art. 1196, for an abortion procured or attempted by medical advice for the purpose of saving the life of the mother, is typical. But if the fetus is a person who is not to be deprived of life without due process of law, and if the mother's condition is the sole determinant, does not Texas' exception appear to be out of line with the Amendment's command?" (ibid., 157–158 n. 54). Given the sui generis nature of pregnancy, the life of the mother exception is perfectly consistent with, and incorporates the principle that grounds, the common law notion of justified homicide for self-defense. Because a continued pregnancy that imperils a woman's life will likely result in the death of both mother and child, the law, by permitting this exception, allowed physicians and patients the freedom to make a medical judgment that would result in at least one life being saved.

44. Following the comments made in the above note, the Court presents another argument: "There are other inconsistencies between Fourteenth Amendment status and the typical abortion statute. It has already been pointed out...that in Texas the woman is not a principal or an accomplice with respect to an abortion upon her. If the fetus is a person, why is the woman not a principal or an accomplice? Further, the penalty for criminal abortion specified by Art. 1195 is significantly less than the maximum penalty for murder prescribed by Art. 1257 of the Texas Penal Code. If the fetus is a person, may the penalties be different?" (ibid., 158 n. 54). Although I address this and a similar argument in greater detail in the text of Chapter 5, I will make a few brief comments here in this note. First, if Blackmun is correct that Texas's laws are inconsistent with its claim that the unborn is a Fourteenth Amendment person, it does not prove that the unborn are not human persons or that abortion is not a great moral evil. It simply proves that Texas was unwilling to "bite the bullet" and consistently apply its position. The unborn may still be a Fourteenth Amendment person, even if the laws of Texas do not adequately reflect that. Texas's inconsistency, if there really is one, proves nothing, for if the unborn is a Fourteenth Amendment person, then Texas's laws violate the unborn's equal protection; but if the unborn is not a Fourteenth Amendment person, then Texas's laws violate the pregnant woman's fundamental liberty. How a statute treats the unborn's assailants has no bearing on what the unborn in fact is. Second, as I state in Chapter 5, the *Roe* Court did not take into consideration the possible *reasons* that Texas's statutes and those of other states granted women immunity or light sentences and specified penalties for abortionists not as severe in comparison to penalties for nonabortion homicides. These reasons, I argue, were thought by legislators to justify penalties they believed had the best chance of limiting the most abortion-homicides possible.

Thus, Texas's penalties as well as those of other states were not inconsistent with affirming the unborn as a Fourteenth Amendment person.

45. Ibid., 157.

46. Ibid.

47. Krason, *Abortion*, 168.

48. *Steinberg v. Brown*, 321 F. Supp. 741 (ND Ohio 1970).

49. *Roe*, 410 U.S., 155 (citing *Steinberg*, 321 F. Supp., as well as other cases in which courts have sustained anti-abortion statutes).

50. *Steinberg*, 321 F. Supp. 746–747.

51. See Francis J. Beckwith, "Baha'ism," in *Dictionary of Contemporary Religion in the Western World*, ed. Christopher Partridge et al. (Downers Grove, IL: InterVarsity Press, 2002), 168–171.

52. This is why some conservative legal scholars, such as Robert Bork, are mistaken when they say that the Fourteenth Amendment cannot in principle be applied to the unborn. See Nathan Schlueter and Robert H. Bork, "Constitutional Persons: An Exchange on Abortion," *First Things* 129 (January 2003). Thank you to Jim Stoner for bringing this essay to my attention.

53. See Krason's historical analysis and citations of the relevant literature in Krason, *Abortion*, 164–173.

54. One of our Ph.D. candidates at Baylor University, T. Hunter Baker (who served as my graduate assistant from 2003 to 2005), made the observation to me that this is tricky because children and noncitizens do not have the full panoply of constitutional rights as adult citizens. There is no doubt that Hunter is correct: there are rights and privileges that are specific to one's age or citizenship. The question, then, is whether the right to life should depend on those contingencies. After all, those rights that are contingent on maturity or nationality presuppose that the being in question is the sort of being who can in principle have the full panoply of legal rights. For example, a 17-year-old citizen will acquire the right to vote when she turns 18, but a baboon, at whatever age, will never have the right to vote. A certain level of maturity on the part of a citizen is required for the state to grant her the right to vote. However, all that is necessary for a right to life is to be alive. This is why we cannot murder illegal aliens or five-year-olds, even though neither group can vote or be elected to Congress.

55. *Roe*, 410 U.S. 160.

56. Ibid., 163.

57. Ibid., 157–158.

58. See, for example, *Danforth*, 428 U.S. 52 (held as unconstitutional parental and spousal consent requirements as well as state ban on saline [or salt poisoning] abortions, a procedure that literally burns the skin of the unborn); *Colautti*, 439 U.S. 379 (state may not define viability or enjoin physicians to prove the fetus is viable to require that they have a duty to preserve the life of the fetus if a pregnancy termination is performed; "viability" is whatever the physician judges it is in a particular pregnancy); *Akron*, 462 U.S. 416 (held as unconstitutional: informed consent requirement, 24-hour waiting period, parental consent requirement, compulsory hospitalization for second trimester abortions, and humane and sanitary disposal of fetal remains); *Thornburgh*, 476 U.S. 747 (struck down as unconstitutional Pennsylvania statute that required informed consent of

abortion's possible risks to woman, that required that the pregnant woman be informed of agencies that would help her if she brought child to term, that the abortion provider report certain statistics about their patients to the state, and that a second physician be present at abortion when fetal viability is possible).

59. See *Harris v. McRae*, 448 U.S. 297 (1980).

60. *Webster v. Reproductive Health Services*, 492 U.S. 490 (1989).

61. Ibid., 504, quoting from Mo. Rev. Stat. §§ 1.205.1(1), (2) (1986) (parenthetical insertions are the Court's).

62. Ibid., 504, quoting from Mo. Rev. Stat. §§ 1.205.2 (1986) (footnote omitted).

63. Ibid., 513, quoting from Mo. Rev. Stat. § 188.029 (1986).

64. Mo. Rev. Stat. § 188.029 (1986), as found in ibid.

65. *Webster*, 492 U.S. 520. "No abortion of a viable unborn child shall be performed unless necessary to preserve the life or health of the woman." (Mo. Rev. Stat. § 188.030 [1986]).

66. *Webster*, 492 U.S. 519.

67. Ibid.

68. *Casey*, 505 U.S. 844.

69. Ibid., 877.

70. "Yet it must be remembered that *Roe v. Wade* speaks with clarity in establishing not only the woman's liberty but also the State's 'important and legitimate interest in potential life.'.... That portion of the decision in *Roe* has been given too little acknowledgment and implementation by the Court in its subsequent cases. Those cases decided that any regulation touching upon the abortion decision must survive strict scrutiny, to be sustained only if drawn in narrow terms to further a compelling state interest.... Not all of the cases decided under that formulation can be reconciled with the holding in *Roe* itself that the State has legitimate interests in the health of the woman and in protecting the potential life within her. In resolving this tension, we choose to rely upon *Roe*, as against the later cases" (ibid., 871).

71. The Court in fact explicitly overrules *Akron*, 462 U.S. and *Thornburgh*, 476 U.S.: "To the extent *Akron I* and *Thornburgh* find a constitutional violation when the government requires, as it does here, the giving of truthful, nonmisleading information about the nature of the procedure, the attendant health risks and those of childbirth, and the 'probable gestational age' of the fetus, those cases go too far, are inconsistent with *Roe*'s acknowledgment of an important interest in potential life, and are overruled" (*Casey*, 505 U.S. 882).

72. Ibid., 872.

73. Ibid., 870.

74. *Roe*, 410 U.S. 163.

75. Justice Blackmun's dissenting opinion in *Webster* (492 U.S. 553) seems to bear this out:

> For my part, I remain convinced, as six other Members of this court 16 years ago were convinced, that the *Roe* framework, and the viability standard in particular, fairly, sensibly, and effectively functions to safeguard the constitutional liberties of pregnant women while recognizing and accommodating the State's interest in potential human life. The viability line reflects the biological facts and truths of fetal development; it marks the threshold moment prior to which a fetus cannot survive separate from the woman and

cannot reasonably and objectively be regarded as a subject of rights or interests distinct from, or paramount to, those of the pregnant woman. At the same time, the viability standard takes account of the undeniable fact that as the fetus evolves into its postnatal form, and as it loses its dependence on the uterine environment, the State's interest in the fetus' potential human life, and in fostering a regard for human life in general, becomes compelling.

76. Stuart Rosenbaum, "Abortion, the Constitution, and Metaphysics," *Journal of Church and State* 43 (2001): 715.

77. "Beckwith's charge of circularity is a 'strawman' reading of Blackmun" (ibid., 716).

78. *Roe*, 410 U.S. 163.

79. In response to this sort of analogy, David Boonin writes: "One common objection to the viability criterion is that it excludes from the class of individuals with a right to life people who clearly have such a right, such as, according to one such critic people with pacemakers or on heart-lung machines" (David Boonin, *A Defense of Abortion* [New York: Oxford University Press, 2003], 130, citing Richard Werner, "Hare on Abortion," *Analysis* 36.4 [June 1976]: 204). This is a puzzling response, for it seems to make the very point the objection is making: if physical dependence is morally relevant in determining the ontological status of any being, then why should it matter if the being is dependent on another being (e.g., its mother or its conjoined twin) or a machine (e.g., an incubator or a heart-lung machine)? But, as the objection points out, if it is morally irrelevant in the latter case, then it is morally irrelevant in the former as well. Consequently, physical dependence on another (whether a person or a machine) is not a morally relevant property in assessing one's ontological status. Boonin, nevertheless, replies that because "viability means merely the ability to survive outside the womb of the woman in whom the fetus is conceived," and because "we can distinguish between being dependent on a particular person and being dependent on some person or other," and because "the viability criterion maintains that the former property is morally relevant, while the purported counterexamples [e.g., heart-lung machine] establish only that the latter is morally irrelevant," and because "the moral relevance of the former is not entailed by the latter," these counterexamples "are ultimately ineffective" (Boonin, 130). This reply begs the question, for all that Boonin is doing is restating the viability criterion and that its proponents maintain that an unborn human being's unique physical dependence on its mother is morally relevant while a postnatal human being's dependence on some person or other is not. But that is *precisely* the distinction the proponent of the viability criterion has to demonstrate, and Boonin fails to do so. The power of the counterexamples is that they extract from the viability criterion the property that is doing all the moral work, dependence. The key for Boonin is to show that the inability to survive outside the womb in which one was conceived is a type of dependence that when ended results in one's ontological status changing from a being that does not have a right to life to one that does.

Although Boonin evaluates the viability criterion as a criterion of personhood (see Chapter 6 of this volume for more on the question of personhood) rather than the point at which the state has a compelling interest in the unborn (as the Court does), his assessment of the viability criterion is applicable to the latter as well.

80. Boonin replies to this type of argument by offering a counterexample: "Consider...an adult human being with a particular form of brain injury that has caused him to lapse into an irreversible coma. Most people would agree that he does not have the same right to life as you and I. But it is of course possible that technological advances might some day make it possible to bring people with precisely the same form of brain injury out of their comas. Were that to happen, we would surely say that the individual did have the same right to life as you or I, since this is what we say of people who are only temporarily unconscious. This would be to make his moral standing relative to the existing state of technology, and in a way that seems perfectly appropriate" (Boonin, 131). Setting aside the question of whether the irreversibly comatose have the same right to life as you or I, Boonin seems to miss the point of this objection by finding in it a principle its more sophisticated advocates are not employing: moral standing is *never* relative to technological advances. After all, a pro-lifer would argue that an abortion morally permissible in times past to save the life of the mother may not be permissible today due to advances in medical technology. Rather, the objection is making the point that there is no moral difference between two human beings that are identical in every way *except* that one is dependent on technology and the other on its mother. So, to conscript Boonin's counterexample: if the comatose person could be brought back by either new technology or a newly discovered herb, his moral standing would not hinge on whether his recovery depended on artificial or natural means.

81. Blackmun reveals this confusion in his dissent in *Webster* (492 U.S. 553): "The viability standard takes account of the undeniable fact that as the fetus evolves into its postnatal form, and as it loses its dependence on the uterine environment, the State's interest in the fetus' potential human life, and in fostering a regard for human life in general, becomes compelling."

82. Hadley Arkes, *First Things: An Inquiry into the Principles of Morals and Justice* (Princeton, NJ: Princeton University Press, 1986), 378–379.

83. For a revealing response to my arguments against Blackmun's use of the viability criterion, see Rosenbaum, 716–719 (responding to arguments that appeared in Francis J. Beckwith, "Law, Religion, and Metaphysics: A Reply to Simmons," *Journal of Church and State* 43.1 [Winter 2001]: 19–33). Rosenbaum does not actually engage my arguments but rather dismisses them as not relevant because, according to Rosenbaum, Blackmun was discussing the constitutional permissibility of abortion and did not intend for the viability criteron to be an answer to any philosophical question on the nature of human beings and/or persons (ibid., 716). But this response is a red herring, for, as we have seen, the viability criterion was advanced by Blackmun as a standard by which the law marks off one set of human beings (prenatal ones) as objects that may be killed without justification and marks off another set of human beings as subjects that may do the killing with the law's permission. To employ an illustration: imagine that the law were to allow whites to own blacks, as it did prior to the passage of the Thirteenth Amendment. Suppose that the Supreme Court upheld this law and based its opinion on the "pigment standard," a criterion that asserts that when one's flesh reaches a certain dark hue then one could be a slave to the first white man to come along. It would seem perfectly sensible, and entirely legitimate, on the part of the Court's critics to say that this criterion is arbitrary, flimsy, and without warrant because skin color carries no moral weight to

justify such a judicial opinion. And the critics could offer arguments to support the conclusion on which this criticism is based: there is no *ontological* difference between whites and blacks that warrants treating blacks as property. A Rosenbaum-like comeback to such arguments – "issues of ontology are issues for metaphysicians, philosophers, and theologians" or "Supreme Court justices, and ontologically modest others, pursue issues in the historical world of human society and human practice" (ibid., 717) – is no response to these arguments. It is a red herring, a rhetorical distraction, that does not engage the arguments for the case for which they have been offered. However, what is more troubling is that Rosenbaum labels me as exhibiting a lack of wisdom (Rosenbaum, 717), "metaphysical imperialism" (ibid.), and "paternalism" (ibid.) as well as claiming that I lack modesty (ibid.), do not live "in the real world" (ibid.), and that I raise "arcane issues" (ibid.). (He also calls me a "philosophical fundamentalist" [ibid., 723].) Although Rosenbaum claims that "genuinely reasonable people will surely detect the inadequacy of the alleged reasons Beckwith suggests might deter them from accepting the viability standard of Blackmun and Simmons" (ibid., 718), he does not present the actual grounds by which these reasonable people would reject my *reasons* qua reasons. He merely points out that they are irrelevant to an opinion of the Supreme Court on a question of constitutional law. At some point Rosenbaum has to actually get his hands dirty and engage the arguments rather than resort to name calling.

84. Ibid., 870.

85. The "reliance interest" is a term of art from contract law that refers to "the interest a nonbreaching party has in recovering costs stemming from that party's reliance on the performance of the contract" (*Black's Law Dictionary*, ed. Bryan A. Garner, 7th ed. [St. Paul, MN: West Group, 1999], 816). The Court took this term from contract law and applied it to the public's apparent reliance on the right to abortion and the personal and economic benefits that right supposedly entails. Consequently, according to the Court, if it had overturned *Roe*, it would have "breached" its social contract with the public, which would have suffered personal and economic costs as a result.

86. "For two decades of economic and social developments, people have organized intimate relationships and made choices that define their views of themselves and their places in society, in reliance on the availability of abortion in the event that contraception should fail" (*Casey*, 505 U.S. 869).

87. "A decision to overrule *Roe*'s essential holding under the existing circumstances would address error, if there was error, at the cost of both profound and unnecessary damage to the Court's legitimacy, and to the Nation's commitment to the rule of law" (*Casey*, 505 U.S. 869).

88. *Casey*, 505 U.S. 844–853.

89. Oddly enough, the Court does claim it will not reexamine *Roe* "because neither the factual underpinnings of *Roe*'s central holding nor our understanding of it has changed (and because no other indication of weakened precedent has been shown)" (ibid., 864). This is a curious argument, for it is unlikely that the Court and its clerks did not know that there exists a massive volume of scholarly literature that shows that the *Roe* opinion is significantly flawed in its history and its logic. Unless the Court means something else by the term "factual underpinnings," nothing but willful ignorance can account for the Court's not taking this scholarship into serious consideration when assessing the merits of this case and crafting an opinion for it.

90. Ibid., 966 (Rehnquist, J., dissenting).

91. See "Partial Birth Abortion," Center for Reproductive Rights Home Page, available at http://www.crlp.org/hill pba.html (January 22, 2003).

92. *Stenberg* v. Carhart, 120 S. Ct. 2597 (2000).

93. Ibid., citing *Casey* 505 U.S. 879.

94. Ibid., 2610.

95. Ibid., 2628 (Kennedy, J., dissenting).

96. As Justice Kennedy points out in his dissent, there is impressive medical opinion that D & X abortion is not any less risky and may in some cases increase the risk to a woman's health. See ibid., 2626–2631 (Kennedy, J., dissenting).

97. *Webster*, 492 U.S. 519.

98. *Casey*, 505 U.S. 871. The Court writes: "Even in the earliest stages of pregnancy, the State may enact rules and regulations designed to encourage [a woman] to know that there are philosophic and social arguments of great weight that can be brought to bear in favor of continuing the pregnancy to full term and there are procedures and institutions to allow adoption of unwanted children as well as a certain degree of state assistance if the mother chooses to raise the child herself" (ibid., 872) (insertion mine).

99. *Stenberg*, 120 S. Ct. 2628 (Kennedy, J., dissenting).

100. Ibid., 2606.

101. "Were there any doubt remaining the statute could apply to a D & E procedure, that doubt is no ground for invalidating the statute. Rather, we are bound to first consider whether a construction of that statute is fairly possible that would avoid the constitutional question" (ibid., 2644, citing *Erznoznick* v. Jacksonville, 422 U.S. 205, 216 [1975] and *Frisby* v. Schultz, 487 U.S. 474, 482 [1988] [Thomas, J., dissenting]). See also ibid., 2631 (Kennedy, J., dissenting).

102. Ibid., 2640–2643 (Thomas, J., dissenting).

103. Ibid., 2640.

104. 18 USCS § 1531 (2003).

105. This is what the 2003 federal law asserts: "This subsection does not apply to a partial-birth abortion that is necessary to save the life of a mother whose life is endangered by a physical disorder, physical illness, or physical injury, including a life-endangering physical condition caused by or arising from the pregnancy itself." (18 USCS § 1531 [2003][a])

106. Robert B. Bluey, "Lawsuits Challenge Partial-Birth Abortion Ban," CNSNews.com (31 Oct. 2003), available at http://www.cnsnews.com/Culture/archive/200310/CUL20031031c.html (27 Jan. 2004).

107. *Gonzales v. Carhart*, 550 U.S. ___ (2007).

108. Although published before the act became law, one should read Arkes's elegant account of the act's history as well as his public encounters with certain members of Congress: Hadley Arkes, *Natural Rights and the Right to Choose* (New York: Cambridge University Press, 2002), 234–294.

109. Ibid., 89.

3. Abortion, Liberalism, and State Neutrality

1. John Rawls seems to argue that even though the pro-life position on abortion is consistent with Roman Catholic moral theology (as it is, I might add, consistent with traditional Protestant and Orthodox moral theology as well), it still may be legitimately reflected in our laws if it is supported by public reason and is

able to win a majority. See John Rawls, *The Laws of Peoples* (with "The Idea of Public Reason Revisited") (Cambridge, MA: Harvard University Press, 1999), 155–156. Admittedly, not everyone will agree with my reading of Rawls on this matter.

2. John Rawls, *Political Liberalism*, 2nd ed. (New York: Columbia University Press, 1996), lvi n. 31, citing Judith Jarvis Thomson, "Abortion: Whose Right?" *Boston Review* 20.3 (Summer 1995). Rawls, however, adds that he "would want to add several addenda" to the piece. Thomson's essay is available at http://bostonreview.mit.edu/BR20.3/thomson.html. All references to Thomson's piece in this chapter are from the online version.

3. Although Rawls recommends Thomson's essay in *Political Liberalism*, he seems more open than Thomson to the possibility that the pro-life position may be reflected in our laws (lvi–lvii including notes), a position he may finally embrace in *The Laws of Peoples* (155–156). See my comments in footnote 1.

4. Paul D. Simmons, "Religious Liberty and Abortion Policy: *Casey* as 'Catch-22,'" *Journal of Church and State* (Winter 2000): 69–88.

5. *Roe v. Wade* 410 U.S. 113 (1973).

6. *Planned Parenthood v. Casey* 505 U.S. 833 (1992).

7. See ibid.

8. See *Bray v. Alexandria Women's Health Clinic* 113 S. Ct. 753 (1993). In *Hill v. Colorado* (2000), in a 6–3 decision, the U.S. Supreme Court upheld a Colorado Revised Statute, §18–9–122(3), "that makes it unlawful for any person within 100 feet of a health care facility's entrance to 'knowingly approach' within 8 feet of another person, without that person's consent, in order to pass 'a leaflet or handbill to, displa[y] a sign to, or engag[e] in oral protest, education, or counseling with [that] person'" (from the syllabus of *Hill v. Colorado* [98–1856] 973 P.2d 1246).

9. Simmons, "Religious Liberty and Abortion Policy," 70.

10. Ibid., 88.

11. Although the original purpose of the Establishment Clause of the First Amendment was to restrain Congress ("*Congress* shall make no law respecting an establishment of religion"), the Supreme Court has incorporated the First Amendment through the Fourteenth Amendment and now applies the former to the states as well. The Court first incorporated the freedom of speech and press clauses, eventually incorporating the entire First Amendment. See *Gitlow v. New York*, 268 U.S. 652, 666 (1925) (freedom of speech and press "are among the fundamental personal rights and 'liberties' protected by the Due Process Clause of the Fourteenth Amendment from impairment by the states"); *Near v. Minnesota*, 283 U.S. 697, 707 (1931) ("It is no longer open to doubt that the liberty of the press and of speech is within the liberty safeguarded by the due process clause of the Fourteenth Amendment from invasion by state action"); *De Jorge v. Oregon*, 299 U.S. 353, 364 (1937) ("The right of peaceable assembly is a right cognate to those of free speech and free press as fundamental"); *Cantwell v. Connecticut* 310 U.S. 296, 303–304 (1940) ("The First Amendment declares that Congress shall make no law respecting an establishment of religion or prohibiting the free exercise thereof. The Fourteenth Amendment has rendered legislatures of the States as incompetent as Congress to enact such laws"); and *Everson v. Board of Education* 330 U.S. 1 (1947) (justices unanimously agreed that the Establishment Clause applies to the states through the Fourteenth Amendment).

12. Simmons, "Religious Liberty and Abortion Policy," 88.

13. See, for example, Francis J. Beckwith and John Peppin, "Physician-Value Neutrality: A Critique," *Journal of Law, Medicine, and Ethics* 28.1 (Spring 2000); and Francis J. Beckwith, "Is Statecraft Soulcraft? Faith, Politics, and Legal Neutrality," in *Bioethics and the End of Consensus*, ed. Nigel Cameron, Scott Daniels, and Barbara White (Grand Rapids, MI: Eerdmans, 2000).

14. There are some, though not many, who argue that the moral question of abortion is *not* contingent upon the status of the fetus. They include Judith Jarvis Thomson ("A Defense of Abortion," *Philosophy and Public Affairs* 1 [1971]); Frances M. Kamm (*Creation and Abortion: A Study in Moral and Legal Philosophy* [New York: Oxford, 1992]); Eileen McDonagh (*Breaking the Abortion Deadlock: From Choice to Consent* [New York: Oxford, 1996]); Laurence Tribe (*Abortion: The Clash of Absolutes* [New York: Norton, 1990], chapter 6); and David Boonin, *A Defense of Abortion* (New York: Oxford, 2002), chapter 4. For replies to this perspective, see Chapter 7 of this book as well as Francis J. Beckwith, "Personal Bodily Rights, Abortion, and Unplugging the Violinist," *International Philosophical Quarterly* 32 (1992); Patrick Lee, *Abortion and Unborn Human Life* (Washington, DC: Catholic University of America Press, 1996), chapter 4; Keith Pavlischek, "Abortion Logic and Paternal Responsibilities: One More Look at Judith Thomson's Argument and a Critique of David Boonin-Vail's Defense of It," in *The Abortion Controversy 25 Years after* Roe v. Wade: *A Reader*, 2nd ed., ed. Louis P. Pojman and Francis J. Beckwith (Belmont, CA: Wadsworth, 1998); and John T. Wilcox, "Nature as Demonic in Thomson's Defense of Abortion," *The New Scholasticism* 63 (Autumn 1989). Because Simmons's essay seems to be affirming *Roe* as normative, I am assuming that he accepts Justice Harry Blackmun's conditional challenge: "The appellee and certain amici argue that the fetus is a 'person' within the language and meaning of the Fourteenth Amendment. In support of this, they outline at length and in detail the well-known facts of fetal development. If this suggestion of personhood is established, the appellant's case, of course, collapses, for the fetus' right to life would then be guaranteed specifically by the Amendment. The appellant conceded as much on reargument. On the other hand, the appellee conceded on reargument that no case could be cited that holds that a fetus is a person within the meaning of the Fourteenth Amendment" (*Roe v. Wade*, 157–158). In an earlier article ("Religious Liberty and the Abortion Debate," *Journal of Church and State* 32 [Summer 1990]: 569), Simmons seems to agree with Blackmun: "Whether and/or in what sense gestating life should be defined as a person for purposes of constitutional protections is the foundation question of the debate. Whether it is truly the *central* issue or not may be debatable since other motives and wider agendas are certainly involved. But it is arguably the key issue in fashioning public policy." Consequently, the political and legal reality is that the status of the unborn is doing all the moral work, even though some moral philosophers and legal and political theorists argue that it does not and/or should not.

15. Simmons, "Religious Liberty and Abortion Policy," 71.

16. Ibid.

17. Ibid.

18. *Roe v. Wade*, at 158.

19. Simmons, "Religious Liberty and Abortion Policy," 71.

20. Ibid.

21. Ibid.

22. Simmons, "Religious Liberty and Abortion Policy," 71. Critiques of the viability standard are plentiful in the literature on abortion, though Simmons does not cite any of them. See, for example, Chapter 2 of this volume as well as Lee, *Abortion and Unborn Human Life*, 72–74; Stephen Schwarz, *The Moral Question of Abortion* (Chicago: Loyola University Press, 1990), 44–47; and Andrew Varga, *The Main Issues in Bioethics*, 2nd ed. (New York: Paulist Press, 1984), 62–63.

23. Simmons, "Religious Liberty and Abortion Policy," 71.

24. However, as I note in my original essay, Simmons uses the viability criterion as a standard by which to distinguish persons from non-persons whereas Blackmun uses it to determine when the state has a compelling interest in prenatal life. See Beckwith, "Law, Religion, and the Metaphysics of Abortion," 23–24.

25. Stuart Rosenbaum, "Abortion, the Constitution, and Metaphysics," *Journal of Church and State* 43.4 (Autumn 2001): 714–716.

26. Simmons, "Religious Liberty and Abortion Policy," 71.

27. Ibid., 71.

28. See Chapter 2 of this volume.

29. J. P. Moreland in *Body and Soul: Human Nature and the Crisis in Ethics* by J. P. Moreland and Scott B. Rae (Downers Grove, IL: InterVarsity, 2000), 52.

30. Simmons, "Religious Liberty and Abortion Policy," 71.

31. See Baruch Brody, *Abortion and the Sanctity of Human Life: A Philosophical View* (Cambridge, MA: MIT Press, 1975).

32. See Mary Anne Warren, "On the Moral and Legal Status of Abortion," in *The Problem of Abortion*, 2nd ed., ed. Joel Feinberg (Belmont, CA: Wadsworth, 1984).

33. See Michael Tooley, "In Defense of Abortion and Infanticide," in *The Abortion Controversy 25 Years after Roe v. Wade*, 2nd ed., ed. Louis Pojman and Francis J. Beckwith (Belmont, CA: Wadsworth, 1998); and Michael Tooley, *Abortion and Infanticide* (New York: Oxford, 1983).

34. See Peter Singer, "Sanctity of Life or Quality of Life?" *Pediatrics* 73 (July 1973); Helga Kuhse and Peter Singer, *Should the Baby Live? The Problem of Handicapped Infants* (New York: Oxford, 1985); and Peter Singer, *Rethinking Life and Death: The Collapse of Traditional Ethics* (New York: St. Martin's Press, 1994).

35. David Boonin, *A Defense of Abortion* (New York: Cambridge University Press, 2002), 115–128.

36. See L. W. Sumner, *Abortion and Moral Theory* (Princeton, NJ: Princeton University Press, 1981).

37. Simmons, "Religious Liberty and Abortion Policy," 72 n. 6. The book cited is Beverly Harrison, *Our Right to Choose* (Boston: Beacon, 1983).

38. Cited in *Policy Review* (32 [Spring 1985]: 14–15) in answer to the question posed to a number of partisans (including Harrison) on the issue of abortion, "Is there a moral difference between feticide and infanticide?"

39. See, for example, Fletcher's comments in Joseph Fletcher and John Warwick Montgomery, *Situation Ethics: Is It Sometimes Right to Do Wrong?* (Minneapolis: Bethany House, 1972).

40. See Joseph Fletcher, "Indicators of Humanhood: A Tentative Profile of Man," *Hastings Center Report* 2 (1972); and Joseph Fletcher, "Four Indicators of Humanhood: The Enquiry Matures," *Hastings Center Report* 4 (1974).

41. Paul D. Simmons, "Religious Liberty: A Heritage at Stake" at www.rcrc.org/religion/es/liberty.html (14 May 2000).
42. "Words of Choice: Countering Anti-Choice Rhetoric" at www.rcrc.org/pubs/words.html (14 May 2000).
43. John Swomley, "When Does Life Begin?" section 2 of the essay "Abortion: A Christian Ethical Perspective" at www.rcrc.org/religion/es8/section2.html (14 May 2000). This argument has been critiqued by a number of different authors. See, for example, Chapter 9 of this volume; Harold O. J. Brown, *Death before Birth* (Nashville: Thomas Nelson, 1977), 123–124; and John Jefferson Davis, *Abortion and the Christian* (Phillipsburg, NJ: Presbyterian and Reformed, 1984), 101–102.
44. Simmons, "Religious Liberty and Abortion Policy," 71.
45. See, for example, Chapter 6 of this volume as well as Robert P. George, "Public Reason and Political Conflict: Abortion and Homosexuality," *Yale Law Journal* 106 (1997); Robert E. Joyce, "Personhood and the Conception Event," *New Scholasticism* 52 (1978); Gregory P. Koukl, *Precious Unborn Human Persons* (San Pedro, CA: Stand to Reason, 1999); Lee, *Abortion and Unborn Human Life*; Moreland and Rae, *Body and Soul*; Dianne Nutwell Irving, "Scientific and Philosophical Expertise," *Linacre Quarterly* (February 1993); Patrick Lee and Robert P. George, "The Wrong of Abortion," in *Contemporary Debates in Applied Ethics*, ed. Andrew I. Cohen and Christopher Wellman (New York: Blackwell Publishers, 2005); Patrick Lee, "The Pro-Life Argument from Substantial Identity," *Bioethics* 18.3 (2004); A. A. Howsepian, "Who or What Are We?" *Review of Metaphysics* 45 (March 1992); and Schwarz, *The Moral Question of Abortion*.
46. J. P. Moreland, "Humanness, Personhood, and the Right to Die," *Faith and Philosophy* 12.1 (January 1995); 101.
47. Moreland in *Body and Soul* by Moreland and Rae, 206.
48. Ibid., 178.
49. Ibid.
50. Lee, *Abortion and Unborn Human Life*, 55.
51. See, for example, Peter McInerny, "Does a Fetus Already Have a Future-Like-Ours?" *The Journal of Philosophy* 87 (1990); and Derek Parfit, *Reasons and Persons* (Oxford: Oxford University Press, 1984).
52. This is a name coined by Lee in *Abortion and Unborn Human Life*, 37.
53. Simmons, "Religious Liberty and the Abortion Debate," 572.
54. See, for example, Moreland and Rae, *Body and Soul*; and Lee, *Abortion and Unborn Human Life*, chs. 1 and 2.
55. Paul Churchland, *Matter and Consciousness* (Cambridge, MA: M.I.T. Press, 1984), 12.
56. See, for example, Boonin, *A Defense of Abortion*, ch. 2, and Dean Stretton, "The Argument from Intrinsic Value: A Critique," *Bioethics* 45 (2000): 228–239.
57. Simmons writes that prior to viability "the fetus simply is not sufficiently developed to speak meaningfully of it as an independent being deserving and requiring the full protection of the law, i.e. a person. The notion of viability correlates biological maturation with personal identity in a way that can be recognized and accepted by reasonable people" (Simmons, "Religious Liberty and Abortion Policy," 71). He writes in an earlier article, "Viability, by definition,

deals with that stage of gestation at which the fetus has a developed neo-cortex and physiological maturation sufficient to survive outside the womb. Biological maturation is correlated with personal identity that can be recognized and accepted by reasonable people" (Simmons, "Religious Liberty and the Abortion Debate," 573).

58. Rosenbaum claims there is conceptual difficulty in understanding what I mean in saying that an organism is "ontologically prior to its parts" (Rosenbaum, 720). The notion has been ably, and clearly, articulated and defended by others in the literature, such as by J. P. Moreland in his book with Scott B. Rae, *Body and Soul*, 157–228. I offer a brief definition earlier in this chapter. Granted, this view may be wrong, but it does have an understandable meaning. However, what is particularly strange about Rosenbaum's comments is that he claims that I attribute to Simmons the view that an organism is ontologically prior to its parts, when in fact I say that it is a view that Simmons *does not* hold (as I do in this chapter, a large portion of which appeared as the article to which Rosenbaum responded). Rosenbaum writes: "As an aside, one might take note of the conceptual difficulty in understanding the content of Beckwith's charge against Simmons that he 'would seem to be accepting the view that the human person is a substance ontologically prior to its parts.'" (Rosenbaum, 720). Rosenbaum misquotes me. Here's what I actually said (which I say in this chapter as well): "Or if one ties the achievement of personhood to the acquisition and development of certain physical properties – as Simmons apparently does – one would seem to be accepting the view that the human person is merely a physical system, denying that a human person is ontologically prior to its parts" (Francis J. Beckwith, "Law, Religion, and Metaphysics: A Reply to Simmons," *Journal of Church and State* 43.1 [Winter 2001]: 31).

59. Simmons, "Religious Liberty and Abortion Policy," 75.

60. Ibid., 72.

61. Ibid., 71.

62. Ibid.

63. Ibid., 73.

64. Ibid., 69–70.

65. Ibid., 73.

66. Simmons is more explicit in his 1990 essay: "Anti-choice groups adopt what Daniel Callahan calls a *genetic* definition of personhood; a person is their genetic code.... Pro-choice groups operate with a more complex and sophisticated definition of person.... The fatal fallacy of the *genetic* definition of personhood is its radical reductionism – a terribly complex entity (person) is reduced to a genetic code" ("Religious Liberty and the Abortion Debate," 570). As we have seen, this depiction of the pro-life position is simply inaccurate.

67. Beckwith, "Law, Religion, and Metaphysics."

68. Rosenbaum, 719.

69. Simmons, "Religious Liberty and Abortion Policy," 71.

70. Simmons, "Religious Liberty and the Abortion Debate," 573.

71. Ibid., 572.

72. Rosenbaum, nevertheless, writes that "Simmons ... clearly suggests to any attentive reader ... that viability offers a standard that, *in the absence of knowledge about when the fetus becomes a person*, is useful to reasonable people in correlating the biological facts of fetal development with customary understandings of personal identity. These customary understandings of personal identity, I should

add, are just those understandings of personal identity that do not depend on particular and contested metaphysical, theological, or philosophical views about personhood or personal identity" (Rosenbaum, 714–715). This is not a response to the argument I make. It is a synonymous repetition of the original claim made by Simmons, a claim, as we have seen, for which he provides reasons that do depend on "particular and contested metaphysical, theological, or philosophical views about personhood or personal identity." The fact that an understanding of personal identity is customary does not mean that it is not contested or that it is reasonable to hold. After all, there was a time in the United States when it was customary to permit slavery and treat women as second-class citizens. I cannot imagine Rosenbaum saying that these practices were justified because they were customary and that any resistance to them was unwarranted because there was a diversity of opinion on the matter.

73. Beckwith, "Law, Religion, and the Metaphysics of Abortion," 23, 30, 31 n. 48.

74. Rosenbaum, 720.

75. Here's a typical example of what I mean: "Beckwith quotes Simmons repeatedly in order to justify his own claim that Simmons holds and defends a particular metaphysical view about persons, the view he calls 'the *no-subject* view.' Nonetheless, reading the quotes he cites, as well as reading more widely in Simmons's work, is enough to persuade serious readers that Simmons in fact believes that he is avoiding metaphysical views about persons and that he intends to avoid such views. Simmons intends, and palpably intends, to attentive readers, that his perspective about abortion is an attempt to bracket, skirt, side-step, elude, or set aside all metaphysical views about 'the nature of the human person'" (Rosenbaum, 720).

76. Rosenbaum labels my arguments as exhibiting a lack of wisdom (Rosenbaum, 717), "metaphysical imperialism" (ibid.), and "paternalism" (ibid.) as well as claiming that I lack modesty (ibid.), do not live "in the real world" (ibid.), and that I raise "arcane issues" (ibid.). In at least a half-dozen places in his essay he employs the term "fundamentalist" to describe me and my views, including in one place where he calls me an "imperialistic fundamentalist" (ibid., 721). In another place he writes: "Beckwith believes that if one is not a natural law metaphysician and ethicist, or some variety of absolutist 'fellow-traveller,' then one must be a metaphysical materialist and a 'might makes right' thinker about moral issues, or some variety of nihilist, relativist, materialist 'fellow-traveller.' Beckwith is mistaken about these issues" (ibid., 714). This latter comment by Rosenbaum is particularly bizarre, since I never even address these issues in my essay. A reader who reads only Rosenbaum's piece will get the impression that Rosenbaum is actually referring to something in my article, but he is not.

77. Ibid., 721.

78. Ibid.

79. Writes Rosenbaum, "Genuinely reasonable people will surely detect the *inadequacies of the alleged reasons* Beckwith suggests might deter them from accepting the viability standard of Blackmun and Simmons" (ibid., 718; emphasis added).

80. Writes Rosenbaum, "Beckwith, and these other 'philosophical fundamentalists,' are *wrong* to see intellectual, moral, religious, or cultural disaster in yielding to the American and continental traditions' efforts to undermine the cultural authority of reason" (ibid., 723; emphasis added).

81. Those he corrects are not merely mistaken but "philosophical fundamentalists" who are so morally challenged that they "inevitably resort to 'strawman' strategies to distort their opponents' views in order to make those opponents appear silly, unsophisticated, unskilled in argument, or simply mistaken" (ibid., 722). Perhaps I can take solace in Alvin Plantinga's humorous retort that the term "fundamentalist" has no actual cognitive content in these sorts of discussions, but is merely a visceral reaction on the part of some people to label the "'stupid sumbitch [son of a bitch] whose theological opinions are considerably to the right of mine'" (Alvin Plantinga, *Warranted Christian Belief* [New York: Oxford, 2000], 245).

82. Ibid., 723.

83. Ibid.

84. Writes Rosenbaum, "Blackmun *wisely* and deliberately avoided metaphysics. Paul Simmons, too, *wisely* and deliberately avoided metaphysics" (ibid., 723; emphasis added). In another place, Rosenbaum writes, "The ways of thinking about persons, infants, and fetus's [sic] characteristic of those cultures [e.g., Chinese, Indian] are radically different from ways allowed by Beckwith's rigidly schematic presentation of metaphysical alternatives. No *understanding*, no progress toward *understanding*, the diverse practices of these diverse cultures comes from following Beckwith's rigidly narrow conception of allowable perspectives on the issue of abortion and personhood" (ibid., 721; emphasis added). This last comment is inexplicable, for I clearly say in my essay (and this chapter) that there is a wide diversity of philosophical and religious views on the question (see Beckwith, "Law, Religion, and the Metaphysics of Abortion," 28), and briefly present at least six of them. Of course, I don't deal with every view, but that wasn't the purpose of my essay. Its purpose was to make a particular philosophical point and to offer arguments for it. Just because I do not mention a view does not mean that I do not think the view is allowable or unallowable. Of course, I believe some views are better than others, but so does Rosenbaum, for he no doubt maintains that his view is better than mine or he would not have written his rebuttal to that effect.

85. "In such a real world, *tolerance* of diversity and plurality is a mark of wisdom. The *Roe v. Wade* decision embodies that wisdom in its accommodation of the diversities and pluralities of American, and Western, practices and opinions about fetal life" (Rosenbaum, 717; emphasis added).

86. Concerning my interpretation of a portion of *Roe*, Rosenbaum writes: "This argument by Beckwith is palpably, even naively, mistaken" (ibid., 715). Concerning my interpretation of Simmons: "In informal logic, Beckwith's strategy here falls into the 'strawman' category. Beckwith is reading Simmons in accord with his own predispositions about what Simmons *must* mean or intend" (ibid., 719).

87. "Thinkers like Beckwith inevitably resort to 'strawman' strategies to distort their opponents' views" (ibid., 722).

88. For example, Rosenbaum commends Justice Blackmun for resisting to interpret "the Constitution in accord with any particular philosophical, theological, or moral perspective," for "he wrote the majority opinion in *Roe* deliberately seeking accord only with the content of the Constitution and its interpretation by previous courts" (ibid., 712). Of course, the command to interpret the Constitution "correctly" is itself not found in the Constitution, but is a

principle logically prior to reading it. It is, some would say, a principle of natural law.

89. Ibid., 723; emphasis added.

90. Ibid., 722.

91. Ibid.

92. See note 87.

93. Although not everyone who affirms the unborn's full humanity embraces natural law theory (e.g., some Reformed thinkers and others skeptical of natural theology of any sort), Rosenbaum correctly links natural law theory as the moral application of reason that I believe is the correct one. See ibid., 713–714, 722. For my works on this question, see Francis J. Beckwith and Gregory P. Koukl, *Relativism: Feet Firmly Planted in Mid-Air* (Grand Rapids, MI: Baker, 1998); Francis J. Beckwith, "Why I Am Not a Relativist," in *Why I Am a Christian*, ed. Norman L. Geisler and Paul Hoffman (Grand Rapids, MI: Baker, 2001); and Francis J. Beckwith, "The Metaphysics and Theology of Political and Legal Disagreement: A Review Article," *Philosophia Christi* 4.2 (2002).

94. Thomson, "A Defense of Abortion."

95. Thomson, "Abortion: Whose Right?"

96. Thomson writes: "But if abortion were murder, all that [i.e., the harms that may follow from constraining a woman's liberty to abort] would amount to little. Suppose a fetus is a product of rape, or that allowing it to develop would constitute a threat to the woman's health or make it impossible for her to supply a decent life to other already existing children, or that it is deformed, or that allowing it to develop would interfere with plans that are central to her life. If killing the fetus were murder, the woman would have to carry it to term, despite the burden on her of doing so. Morality, after all, does not permit us to commit murder in the name of avoiding such burdens. You certainly may not murder your five-year-old child just because it is a product of rape, or because its demands on your attention get in the way of your career" (Thomson, "Abortion," 2).

97. I would like to thank several of my Baylor University colleagues who took the time to read this section when it was the large part of a paper that was the topic of discussion at an April 16, 2004, philosophy department colloquium at Baylor: Mark T. Nelson (visiting from the University of Leeds), C. Stephen Evans, Robert C. Roberts, J. Daryl Charles (visiting from Taylor University), Todd Buras, and Margaret Tate. They offered me important suggestions and critical questions. Todd and Mark were particularly helpful in providing me with detailed notes of their analyses. Because of the input I received at the colloquium, this section of the book is better than it otherwise would have been, though all of its flaws remain mine.

98. Thomson, "Abortion," 8.

99. Of course, an unsuccessful abortion (one in which the fetus survives) is still a wrong, if the unborn is a full-fledged member of the human community, for an act that is intended to kill an innocent person is still wrong even if no harm results or the harm that results is less severe than what was intended.

100. Ibid.

101. See, for example, the work by Boonin, *A Defense of Abortion*.

102. Ibid.

103. Ibid., 8.

104. See Robert Marshall and Charles Donovan, *Blessed Are the Barren: The Social Policy of Planned Parenthood* (San Francisco: Ignatius Press, 1991), 239–266.
105. Ibid., 7.
106. Thomson, "Abortion: Whose Right?" 6.
107. Simmons, "Religious Liberty and Abortion Policy," 71.
108. Thank you to my Baylor colleague, C. Stephen Evans, for encouraging me to use this illustration in print after I had used it in my oral presentation of this argument at the colloquium I mention above.

4. Science, the Unborn, and Abortion Methods

1. Take, for example, the work of Michael Tooley, one of the foremost defenders of abortion choice (and the moral permissibility of infanticide): *Abortion and Infanticide* (New York: Oxford University Press, 1983), 50–86. In another publication, Tooley (with Laura Purdy) writes: "The first part of the claim [made by pro-lifers] is uncontroversial. A fetus developing inside a human mother is certainly an organism belonging to *homo sapiens*" (Laura Purdy and Michael Tooley, "Is Abortion Murder?" in *Abortion: Pro and Con*, ed. Robert Perkins [Cambridge, MA: Schlenkman, 1974], 140).
2. I would like to thank the following individuals for comments on earlier versions of, or portions of, this chapter: Dianne Nutwell Irving, Patrick Lee, Joseph Francis, Michael Buratovich, Scott Klusendorf, and Jonathan Wells.
3. The facts in this section are taken from the following works which deal with the unborn's development: Lewis Wolpert, *The Triumph of the Embryo* (New York: Oxford University Press, 1991); Ronan O'Rahilly and Fabiola Muller, *Developmental Stages in Human Embryos* (Washington, DC: Carnegie Institution of Washington, 1987); Ronan O'Rahilly and Fabiola Muller, *Human Embryology and Tetratology*, 2nd ed. (New York: Wiley-Liss, 1996); Ulrich Drews, *Color Atlas of Embryology* (New York: Georg Thieme Verlag Stuttgart, 1995); Stephen M. Krason, *Abortion: Politics, Morality, and the Constitution* (Lanham, MD: University Press of America, 1984), 337–349; F. Beck, D. B. Moffat, and D. P. Davies, *Human Embryology*, 2nd ed. (Oxford: Blackwell, 1985); Keith L. Moore, *The Developing Human: Clinically Oriented Embryology*, 2nd ed. (Philadelphia: W. B. Saunders, 1977); Bart T. Hefferman, "The Early Biography of Everyman," in *Abortion and Social Justice*, ed. Thomas W. Hilgers and Dennis J. Horan (New York: Sheed & Ward, 1972), 3–25; Edwin C. Hui, *At the Beginning of Life: Dilemmas in Theological Ethics* (Downers Grove, IL: InterVarsity Press, 2002), 58–83; and *Motion and Brief Amicus Curiae of Certain Physicians, Professor and Fellows of the American College of Obstetrics and Gynecology in Support of Appellees*, submitted to the Supreme Court of the United States, October Term, 1971, No. 70–18, *Roe v. Wade*, and No. 70–40, *Doe v. Bolton*, prepared by Dennis J. Horan, et al. (the List of Amici contains the names of over 200 physicians), as quoted extensively in Stephen D. Schwarz, *The Moral Question of Abortion* (Chicago: Loyola University Press, 1990), 2–6. I do, however, rely on Krason's presentation as a template by which to present the data derived from these works including Krason and the works on which he relies.
4. Michael Buratovich, a developmental biologist (Ph.D., U.C., Irvine), points out, in private e-mail correspondence, that because of chromosomal abnormalities,

an ovum may undergo complete fertilization but fail conception. Buratovich refers to a work by S. Munne, "Preimplantation genetic diagnosis of numerical and structural chromosone abnormalities," *Reprod Biomed Online* 4.2 (March–April 2002): 183–196. Hence, that is the reason I define conception as the result of a fertilization process that is *successful*.

5. Robert E. Joyce, "Personhood and the Conception Event," *The New Scholasticism* 52 (1978): 101.

6. For an overview of the different points of view, see Dianne Nutwell Irving, *Philosophical and Scientific Analysis of the Nature of the Early Embryo* (Ph.D. dissertation, Georgetown University, 1991). Although much has been published on this subject since the appearance of Dr. Irving's work, her presentation of the debate, its cast of characters, and the types of arguments are most helpful.

7. David Boonin, *A Defense of Abortion* (New York: Cambridge University Press, 2002), 37–40.

8. Although the normal number of chromosomes is 46, some people are born with fewer (people with Turner's syndrome have 45) and some people are born with more (people with Down syndrome have 47). But one's humanity does not rest necessarily on the number of chromosomes one may have, but on the fact that one is a *human organism*. That is, the human organism may have a human genetic structure that subsists in an abnormal number of chromosomes (genes are contained in the chromosomes within the nuclei of a person's cells), but such a human being is no less human than one with an abnormal number of more obvious parts. For example, a human being born with six fingers, one arm, or one leg is a human being.

9. Technically, identical twins have the same DNA (i.e., genomic sequence), and if a human being is cloned, the clone would have the same DNA as its progenitor. However, what is important to understand is that at conception a *new human individual* with its a human genetic code and its own genomic sequence comes into being, even if its DNA happens to be the same as that of another individual being, such as its twin or clone-parent. That is, the new human being, which begins as a zygote, is not a part of either its mother, father, clone-parent, or identical twin, but is a *whole organism* with its own intrinsically directed nature and basic capacities that make certain properties and powers possible for it to exercise.

10. The Human Life Bill: Hearings on S. 158 Before the Subcommittee on Separation of Powers of the Senate Judiciary Committee, 97th Congress, 1st Session (1981), as quoted in Norman L. Geisler, *Christian Ethics: Options and Issues* (Grand Rapids, MI: Baker, 1989), 149.

11. The Human Life Bill – S. 158, Report together with Additional and Minority Views to the Committee on the Judiciary, United States Senate, made by its Subcommittee on Separation of Powers, 97th Congress, 1st Session (1981): 9.

12. Ibid., 7–8.

13. Ibid., 8.

14. Ibid.

15. O'Rahilly and Muller, *Human Embryology and Teratology*, 2nd ed., 8.

16. Ibid., 11.

17. Hefferman, "The Early Biography of Everyman," 4.

18. From Hymie Gordon, M.D., "Genetical, Social, and Medical Aspects of Abortion," *South African Medical Journal* (20 July 1968), as quoted in ibid., 5.

19. James J. Diamond, M.D., "Abortion, Animation and Biological Hominization," *Theological Studies* (June 1975): 305–342. Although rare, twinning may occur after fourteen days, sometimes resulting in conjoined twins. See O'Rahilly and Muller, *Human Embryology and Teratology*, 50.

20. Krason, *Abortion*, 341.

21. Ibid., citing the work of Geraldine Lux Flanagan, *The First Nine Months of Life* (New York: Simon & Schuster, 1962, 1965), 47, 51

22. Krason, *Abortion*, 341.

23. Amicus curiae, as quoted in Schwarz, *The Moral Question of Abortion*, 2

24. Ibid., 3

25. Ibid.

26. Ibid., 3–4.

27. Ibid., 5.

28. See Mortimer Rosen, "The Secret Brain: Learning before Birth," *Harper's* (April 1978): 46–47.

29. Bernard Nathanson (with Richard Ostling), *Aborting America* (New York: Doubleday, 1979), 216.

30. Ibid., 217.

31. Dr. Buratovich pointed out to me in personal correspondence that a "scientific problem" with Nathanson's argument "is that the embryo makes low levels of hCG before implantation occurs. Human chorionic gonadotropin maintains the corpus luteum and keeps it producing estrogen and progesterone. Thus, if chemical communication is the criterion, then it occurs well before implantation." He cites B. M. Carlson, *Patten's Foundations of Embryology* (New York: McGraw-Hill, 1996), 287–288

32. Ibid., 214.

33. Ibid.

34. Although somewhat dated, Andrew Varga offers a wise and insightful summary of the philosophical and scientific problems surrounding human cloning in his book *The Main Issues in Bioethics*, 2nd ed. (New York: Paulist Press, 1984), 119–126.

35. As cited in John Jefferson Davis, *Abortion and the Christian* (Phillipsburg, NJ: Presbyterian and Reformed, 1984), 60. Davis, however, is skeptical of these statistics and offers a critical analysis of them (see ibid., 60–61). For a more detailed critical evaluation of these statistics, see Thomas W. Hilgers, M.D., "Human Reproduction," *Theological Studies* 38 (1977): 136–152.

36. Thomas Shannon and Allan Wolter, "Reflections on the Moral Status of the Pre-Embryo," *Theological Studies* 51 (1990): 619, as cited in Patrick Lee, *Abortion and Unborn Human Life* (Washington, DC: Catholic University of America Press, 1996), 103.

37. "Such vast embryonic loss intuitively argues against the creation of a principle of immaterial individuality at conception. What meaning is there in the creation of such a principle when there is such a high probability that this entity will not develop to the embryo stage, much less come to term?" (Shannon and Wolter, "Reflections," 619, as quoted in Lee, *Abortion*, 103–104.)

38. Lee points out that "for centuries . . . the infant mortality rate has been higher than" the 55% miscarry rate suggested by Shannon and Wolter (Lee, *Abortion*, 104).

39. Lee, *Abortion*, 104, citing Benedict Ashley and Albert Moraczewksi, "Is the Biological Subject of Human Rights Present from Conception?" in *The Fetal Tissue*

Issue: Medical and Ethical Aspects, ed. Peter Cataldo and Albert Moraczewksi (Braintree, MA: Pope John Center, 1994), 47.

40. Norman L. Geisler, *Christian Ethics: Options and Issues* (Grand Rapids, MI: Baker Book House, 1989), 153.

41. Shannon and Wolter write: "Maximally, one could argue that full individuality is not achieved until the restriction process is completed and cells have lost their totipotency" (Shannon and Wolter, "The Moral Status of the Pre-Embryo," 620, as quoted in Lee, *Abortion*, 94).

42. Shannon and Wolter, "The Moral Status of the Pre-Embryo," 612, as quoted in Lee, *Abortion*, 91.

43. Norman Ford, *When Did I Begin?* (Cambridge: Cambridge University Press, 1988), 139.

44. Hui, *At the Beginning of Life*, 238.

45. Lee, *Abortion*, 93.

46. Varga, *Issues in Bioethics*, 65.

47. Lee, *Abortion*, 95.

48. Hui, *At the Beginning of Life*, 69.

49. Ibid., 70.

50. Ibid., citing Teresa Iglesias, "What Kind of Being Is the Human Embryo?" in *Embryos and Ethics: The Warnock Report in Debate*, ed. Nigel M. de S. Cameron (Edinburgh: Rutherford House, 1987), 69.

51. Ashley and Moraczewksi, "Is the Biological Subject of Human Rights Present from Conception?" 49, as quoted in Lee, *Abortion*, 98.

52. Antony Fisher, "'When Did I Begin?' Revisited," *Linacre Quarterly* 58 (1991): 60, as quoted in Lee, *Abortion*, 96.

53. Lee, *Abortion*, 96.

54. Ibid.

55. Ibid.

56. Ann McLaren, "The Embryo," in *Reproduction in Mammals*, bk. 2, *Embryonic and Fetal Development*, ed. C. R. Austin and R. V. Short, 2nd ed. (Cambridge: Cambridge University Press, 1982), 682–683, as quoted in Lee, *Abortion*, 96.

57. Lee, *Abortion*, 96.

58. Ibid., 97. Lee quotes an embryology textbook's description of compaction: "Starting at the eight-cell stage of development, the originally round and loosely adherent blastomeres begin to flatten, developing an inside-outside polarity that maximizes cell-to-cell conact among the blastomeres at the center of the mass. As differential adhesion develops, the outer surfaces of the cells become convex and their inner surfaces becomes concave. This reorganization, called *compaction*, involves the activity of cytoskeletal elements in the blastomeres" (William J. Larsen, *Human Embryology* [New York: Churchill Livingstone, Press, 1993], 19, as quoted in ibid., 97).

59. Ibid., citing Benedict Ashley, "Delayed Hominization: Catholic Theological Perspective," in *The Interaction of Catholic Bioethics and Secular Society*, Proceedings of the Eleventh Bishops' Workshop in Dallas, TX, ed. Russell E. Smith (Braintree, MA: Pope John Center, 1992), 167–168.

60. Personal e-mail correspondence from Michael Buratovich to Francis J. Beckwith (12 June 2003) (on file with author).

61. C. A. Bedate and R. C. Cefalo, "The Zygote: To Be or Not to Be," *Journal of Medicine and Philosophy* 14 (1989): 641–645.

62. Shannon and Wolter, "The Moral Status of the Pre-Embryo," 608 (relying on ibid).
63. Bedate and Cefalo, "The Zygote," 644.
64. Shannon and Wolter, "The Moral Status of the Pre-Embryo," 608.
65. See Antoine Suarez, "Hydatidiform Moles and Teratomas Confirm the Human Identity of the Preimplantation Embryo," *Journal of Medicine and Philosophy* 15 (1990): 627–635. It should be noted, as Patrick Lee indicated to me in private correspondence (e-mail from P. Lee to F. Beckwith, 28 January 2004), that there is a difference between complete hyditidiform moles and partial ones. The latter, unlike the former, in some cases do contain an embryo but cannot be implanted because of a developmental problem.
66. Lee, *Abortion*, 101.
67. Ibid. (citations omitted).
68. I owe this illustration to Michael Buratovich.
69. Centers for Disease Control and Prevention, "Abortion Surveillance – United States, 2002," *Morbidity and Mortality Weekly Report* 54, ss-7 (November 25, 2005): 1 (CDC, "2002 Abortion" hereafter). According to the CDC, this statistic does not include Alaska, California, and New Hampshire, which did not report their legal abortions in 2002 (ibid., 13).
70. Ibid., 16.
71. Ibid., 15.
72. See Carmine E. Williams, M.D., et al., "Dilation and Curettage," in *EMedicine* (April 21, 2001), available at http://www.emedicine.com/aaem/topic156.htm (June 5, 2003).
73. CDC, "2002 Abortion," 3, 4.
74. According to the Planned Parenthood Federation of America (PPFA), "the usual method of *early* abortion is suction curettage. It is performed from *about six to 14 weeks after the last period*" (Planned Parenthood Federation of America, "How Abortion Is Provided," available at http://www.plannedparenthood.org/library/ABORTION/howabort˙fact.html [June 5, 2003] [hereafter PPFA, "How Abortion is Provided"]).
75. See CDC, "2002 Abortion," 13–15. In 1972, for example, 23.4% of all abortions were performed by employing a "sharp curettage" method (Centers for Disease Control and Prevention, "Abortion Surveillance – United States, 1999," *Morbidity and Mortality Weekly Report* 51, ss-9 [November 29, 2002]: 12) (CDC, "1999 Abortion" hereafter). In 2002, only 2.4 % of all the abortions were performed by a sharp curettage method (CDC, "2002 Abortion," 15).
76. See PPFA, "How Abortion Is Provided."
77. Michigan Department of Community Health, "Suction Curettage," available at http://www.michigan.gov/mdch/0,1607,7–132–2940_4909_6437_19077–46301–,00.html (June 5, 2003) (hereafter MDCH, "Suction Curettage"). See also, PPFA, "How Abortion Is Provided."
78. PPFA, "How Abortion Is Provided."
79. Warren Hern, *Abortion Practice*, 1st ed. (Philadelphia: J. B. Lippincott, 1984), 114.
80. Francis A. Schaeffer and C. Everett Koop, M.D., *Whatever Happened to the Human Race?* (Old Tappan, NJ: Fleming H. Revell, 1979), 41.
81. CDC, "2002 Abortion," 15.
82. Ibid., 31.

83. K. Kaufmann, *The Abortion Resource Handbook* (New York: Simon & Schuster, 1997), 152.

84. PPFA, "How Abortion Is Provided."

85. Warren Hern, "WHAT ABOUT US? Staff Reactions to the D&E Procedure," a lecture given at the Association of Planned Parenthood Physicians convention in San Diego (October 26, 1978), as quoted in Rachel M. McNair, "The Nightmares of Choice: The Psychological Effects of Performing Abortions," *Touchstone Magazine* 16.7 (September 2003), available at http://touchstonemag.com/archives/article.php?id = 16-07-022-f (no pagination found in online version) (15 July 2006).

86. Warren Hern, *Abortion Practice*, 2nd ed. (Philadelphia: J. B. Lippincott, 1990), 154.

87. PPFA, "How Abortion Is Provided."

88. Ibid. (citation omitted).

89. Ibid. (citation omitted).

90. Ibid. (citation omitted).

91. CDC, "2002 Abortion," 5.

92. PPFA, "How Abortion Is Provided."

93. CDC, "2002 Abortion," 5.

94. Schaeffer and Koop, *Whatever Happened to the Human Race?* 41.

95. Creator of the technique, Martin Haskell, M.D., writes that it "can be used successfully in patients 20–26 weeks" and that he "routinely performs this procedure on all patients 20 through 24 weeks LMP [last menstrual period] with certain exceptions . . . [and] on selected patients 25 through 26 weeks LMP" (Martin Haskell, M.D., "Dilatation and Extraction for Late Second Trimester Abortion," paper delivered at the National Abortion Federation conference proceedings [September 13–14, 1992]: 27, 28) (paper on file with author).

96. Haskell, "Dilatation and Extraction for Late Second Trimester Abortion," 27, 30–31.

97. Ibid., 28.

98. William Powers, "Partial Truths," *The New Republic* (March 24, 1997): 19.

99. Ibid.

100. Ibid.

101. David Stout, "An Abortion Rights Advocate Says He Lied about Procedure," *New York Times* (February 26, 1997): A11.

102. Schaeffer and Koop, *Whatever Happened to the Human Race?* 42.

103. CDC, "1999 Abortion," 28.

104. Centers for Disease Control and Prevention, "Abortion Surveillance – United States, 1996," in *Morbidity and Mortality Weekly Report* 48, ss-4 (July 20, 1999), Table 18, available at http://www.cdc.gov/mmwr/preview/mmwrhtml/ss4804a1.htm (June 6, 2003).

105. Schwarz, *The Moral Question of Abortion*, 23–25. In addition to the data I supplied for this figure from the CDC 2002 report on abortion surveillance and from other sources cited in this section concerning the times during pregnancy in which certain abortion methods are performed, Schwarz writes that the other "data for this table are taken from *Amicus Curiae*, 8–21. Data for weeks 9 and 10 are also from Flanagan [*The First Nine Months*, 80–81]. . . . Data for week 4.5 is from a brochure, *Life? When Did Your Life Begin?* (Value of Life Committee, Inc.: Brighton, MA). Data assembled by physician members of this

committee, using a number of standard scientific texts, including [Robert Rugh, Laundrum B. Shettles, and Richard N. Einhorn, *From Conception to Birth: The Drama of Life's Beginnings* (New York: Harper & Row, 1971)].... Some items appear in more than one place" (Schwarz, *The Moral Question of Abortion*, 251 n. 10).

5. Popular Arguments: Pity, Tolerance, and Ad Hominem

1. James B. Freeman, *Thinking Logically: Basic Concepts for Reasoning* (Englewood Cliffs, NJ: Prentice-Hall, 1988), 74.
2. From the *Informal Logic Newsletter*, vol. II, Supplement, June 1980, as quoted in ibid.
3. Mary Anne Warren, "On the Moral and Legal Status of Abortion," in *The Problem of Abortion*, 2nd ed., ed. Joel Feinberg (Belmont, CA: Wadsworth, 1984), 103.
4. Philosopher Craig Walton alludes to this argument in his Socratic dialogue, "Socrates Comes to His Senses during Meeting with Bush," *Las Vegas Review-Journal* (November 3, 1988): 11B.
5. Baruch Brody, *Abortion and the Sanctity of Human Life: A Philosophical View* (Cambridge, MA: M.I.T. Press, 1975), 36–37.
6. See the arguments in the Planned Parenthood Federation of America brief (for *Roe v. Wade*), as cited in Stephen M. Krason, *Abortion: Politics, Morality, and the Constitution* (Lanham, MD: University Press of America, 1984), 315–319.
7. Sidney Callahan, "Talk of 'Wanted Child' Makes for Doll Objects," *National Catholic Reporter* (3 December 1971): 7, as quoted in James T. Brutchaell, *Rachel Weeping: The Case against Abortion* (San Francisco: Harper & Row, 1982), 80.
8. For an excellent overview of the major birth defects, their causes, and the chances of their occurring (for every 100,000 babies born alive), see "Birth Defects," in *The American Medical Association Encyclopedia of Medicine*, ed. Charles B. Clayman, M.D. (New York: Random House, 1989), 172–173.
9. Peter Singer and Helen Kuhse, "On Letting Handicapped Infants Die," in *The Right Thing to Do: Basic Readings in Moral Philosophy*, ed. James Rachels (New York: Random House, 1989), 146.
10. As quoted in Bernard Nathanson (with Richard Ostling), *Aborting America* (New York: Doubleday, 1979), 235.
11. Ibid., 235–236.
12. Peter Kreeft, *The Unaborted Socrates* (Downers Grove, IL: InterVarsity, 1982), 40.
13. For a jurisprudential analysis of the case and the political and legal disputes that followed, see Hadley Arkes, *Beyond the Constitution* (Princeton, NJ: Princeton University Press, 1990), 232–244.
14. George Will, "The Killing Will Not Stop," in *The Zero People*, ed. Jeff Lane Hensley (Ann Arbor, MI: Servant 1983), 206–207. This article originally appeared as a syndicated column in the *Washington Post* (April 22, 1982).
15. *AMA Encyclopedia of Medicine*, 104.
16. Krason, *Abortion*, 387. See Germain Grisez, *Abortion: The Myths, the Realities, and the Arguments* (New York: Corpus Books, 1970), 28–30. It should be noted, however, that Grisez, according to Krason, believes that there may

be some cases of anencephaly in which the preborn's humanness is uncertain. Krason argues that "there are two ways we may view the 'anencephalic monster,' depending on when the abnormality originates." One way, "when the abnormality or the genetic certainty of it is present from conception, is to view the organism as human in its conception, but incapable of developing beyond a few hours, a few days, or a few weeks." He argues "that in such cases, especially if the specifically human genetic pattern is greatly transformed, we may not consider the conceptus a human individual" (Krason, *Abortion*, 386–387; see Grisez, 30). In my earlier monograph on abortion (*Politically Correct Death: Answering the Arguments for Abortion Rights* [Grand Rapids, MI: Baker, 1993], 68), I affirmed Grisez's view. Since that time, however, I have embraced the view of Edwin C. Hui (*At the Beginning of Life: Dilemmas in Theological Bioethics* [Downers Grove, IL: InterVarsity Press, 2002], 363–366]) who, in his wonderfully insightful way, makes the point: "In the event that such an unfortunate one is born alive, she is born a human person, and her short life as a person must be respected and treated with dignity as we would treat any irreversibly dying person. No heroic or futile treatments need to be provided, but neither should her organs be harvested for transplant [which has been suggested by scholars who deny the anencephalic's personhood]. She dies and rests in peace as a person" (ibid., 366).

17. Virginia Ramey Mollenkott, "Reproductive Choice: Basic to Justice for Women," *Christian Scholar's Review* 17 (March 1988): 286–293.

18. Ibid., 289.

19. Concerning this, Krason writes: "A number of studies have shown that pregnancy resulting from rape is very uncommon. One, looking at 2190 victims, reported pregnancy in only 0.6 percent [Charles R. Hayman, M.D., 'Pregnancy and Sexual Assault,' *American Journal of Obstetrics and Gynecology* 109 (1971): 480–486]. Barbara M. Sims, who once served as an assistant district attorney in Erie County, New York (Buffalo and vicinity), wrote in 1969 that the district attorney's office in her county 'contain[ed] no reported complaints of pregnancy from forcible rape or incest for the past thirty years' [Barbara M. Sims, 'A District Attorney Looks at Abortion,' *Child and Family* 8 (1969): 176, 178]. In one study of 117 rape victims in Oklahoma City over a one-year period, there were no pregnancies reported [Royice B. Everett, M.D., and Gordon K. Jimmerson, 'The Rape Victim: A Review of 117 cases,' *Obstetrics and Gynecology* 50 (1977): 88, 89]. The Cook County, Illinois (which includes Chicago), States Attorney's Office could not recall a single instance of pregnancy in about nine years of prosecuting rape [Eugene F. Diamond, M.D., 'ISMS Symposium on: Medical Implications of the Current Abortion in Illinois,' *Illinois Medicine* 131 (May 1967): 678]. St. Paul, Minnesota, did not report a single pregnancy from rape in over ten years [Fred E. Mecklenburg, M.D., 'The Indications for Induced Abortion: A Physician's Perspective,' in *Abortion and Social Justice*, ed. Thomas W. Hilgers and Dennis J. Horan (New York: Sheed and Ward, 1972), p. 38]" (Krason, *Abortion*, 281).

20. See Andrew Varga, *The Main Issues in Bioethics*, rev. ed. (New York: Paulist Press, 1984), 67–68. Varga himself, however, does not believe that abortion is morally justified in the cases of rape and incest.

21. Stephen Schwarz, *The Moral Question of Abortion* (Chicago: Loyola University Press 1990), 146, 151.

22. Ibid., 148.

23. Michael Bauman, *Pilgrim Theology: Taking the Path of Theological Discovery* (Grand Rapids, MI: Zondervan, 1992), 197.
24. Ibid.
25. Ibid., 198.
26. Michael Davis, "Foetuses, Famous Violinists, and the Right to Continued Aid," *Philosophical Quarterly* 33 (1983): 268, as quoted in Patrick Lee, *Abortion and Unborn Human Life* (Washington, DC: Catholic University of America Press, 1996), 122.
27. See James Witherspoon, "Reexamining *Roe*: Nineteenth Abortion Statutes and the Fourteenth Amendment," *St. Mary's Law Journal* 17:1 (1985): 31–50, 61–71. See also Dennis J. Horan and Thomas J. Balch, *Roe v. Wade*, "No Justification in History, Law, or Logic," in *Abortion and the Constitution: Reversing* Roe v. Wade *through the Courts*, ed. Dennis J. Horan, Edward R. Grant, and Paige C. Cunningham (Washington, DC: Georgetown University Press, 1987), 57–88; Joseph W. Dellapenna, "Abortion and the Law: Blackmun's Distortion of the Historical Record," in *Abortion and the Constitution*, 137–158; and Krason, *Abortion*, 119–179.
28. *Roe v. Wade*, 410 U.S. 113, 157–158 n. 54 (1973).
29. Witherspoon, "Reexamining *Roe*," 58–59. For a different point of view, see Jean Rosenbluth, "Abortion as Murder: Why Should Women Get Off? Using Scare Tactics to Preserve Choice," *Southern California Law Review* 66 (March 1993).
30. Although the state penalties for an abortionist unjustly killing an unborn person were less severe than for somebody unjustly killing a born person, the reduced severity of the penalties does not mean that the unborn were seen as less than fully human under the law. Rather, like the immunity granted to pregnant women in most states, the punishments for abortionists may have taken into consideration several variables, none of which affirms that the unborn is less than a full person. For a brief survey of the legal punishments for those who attempted to procure abortions, and why these punishments are not inconsistent with the state's affirmation of the unborn's full humanity, see ibid., 51–56.
31. See, for example, David C. Reardon, *Aborted Women: Silent No More* (Westchester, IL: Crossway Books, 1987).
32. This is one of the points brought out by Witherspoon as to why in the pre-*Roe* era the penalties for physicians who performed abortions were less severe than the penalties for other forms of homicide. See Witherspoon, "Reexamining *Roe*," 51–56.
33. *Webster v. Reproductive Health Services*, 492 U.S. 490, 557 (Blackmun, J., dissenting).
34. Laurence Tribe, *Abortion: The Clash of Absolutes* (New York: W. W. Norton, 1990), 105.
35. As quoted in the *New York Times* (May 10, 1988).
36. Nancy S. Erickson, "Women and the Supreme Court: Anatomy Is Destiny," *Brooklyn Law Review* 41 (1974): 242.
37. n.a., Sound Advice for All Prolife Activists and Candidates Who Wish to Include a Concern for Women's Rights in Their Prolife Advocacy: Feminists for Life Debate Handbook (Kansas City, MO: Feminists for Life of America, n.d.), 17.
38. Eileen E. Padberg, "Gender Gap, Republicans and Abortion," *Los Angeles Times* (Orange County Edition) (10 July 2000): B13.
39. Ibid.

40. *Webster*, 492 U.S., 557–558. Blackmun's assertion that hundreds of thousands of women will resort to illegal abortions is highly questionable. See Krason's (*Abortion*, 301–310), Daniel Callahan's (*Abortion: Law, Choice and Morality* [New York: Macmillan, 1970], 132–136), and Robert Marshall and Charles Donovan's (*Blessed Are the Barren: The Social Policy of Planned Parenthood* [San Francisco: Ignatius Press, 1991], chapters 6, 7, and 9) critiques of the statistics used to verify the number of illegal abortions prior to *Roe* v. Wade. In addition, it is conceded by sophisticated abortion-choice advocates that 90% of the "backalley abortions" of which Blackmun writes were, according to former Planned Parenthood president Mary Calderone, performed by licensed physicians in good standing (Mary Calderone, "Illegal Abortion as a Public Health Problem," *American Journal of Public Health* 50 [July 1960]: 948–954). Moreover, as I pointed out earlier in this chapter, arguments from the dangers of illegal abortions, such as Blackmun's, beg the question as to the full personhood of the unborn.

41. Mollenkott, 291.

42. See especially the nontheological defense of the pro-life position by former abortion-choice activist Bernard Nathanson (*Aborting America*) and *The Abortion Papers: Inside the Abortion Mentality* (New York: Frederick Fell, 1983). For other examples of nontheological defenses of the pro-life position, see J. P. Moreland and Scott B. Rae, *Body and Soul: Human Nature and the Crisis in Ethics* (Downers Grove, IL: InterVarsity Press, 2000); Brody, *Abortion and the Sanctity of Human Life;* David Clark, "The Quality of Life Argument for Infanticide," in *Simon Greenleaf Law Review* 5 (1985–1986): 91–112; Peter Kreeft, *The Unaborted Socrates* (Downers Grove, IL: InterVarsity Press, 1984); Don Marquis, "Why Abortion Is Immoral," *Journal of Philosophy* 86 (April 1989): 183–202; A. Chadwick Ray, "Humanity, Personhood, and Abortion," in *International Philosophical Quarterly* 25 (1985): 233–245; Stephen D. Schwarz, *The Moral Question of Abortion* (Chicago: Loyola University Press, 1990); Andrew Varga, *The Main Issues in Bioethics*, rev. ed. (New York: Paulist Press, 1984), 59–65; Hui, *At the Beginning of Life;* and Lee, *Abortion and Unborn Human Life.*

43. See, for example, the official statements of denominations and religious groups that are "pro-choice": *We Affirm: National Religious Organizations' Statements on Abortion Rights* (Washington, DC: Religious Coalition for Abortion Rights, n.d.).

44. Tribe, *Abortion*, 116.

45. George Mavrodes, "Abortion and Imagination: Reflections on Mollenkott's 'Reproductive Choice,'" in *Christian Scholar's Review* 18 (December 1988): 168–169.

46. For a philosophical defense of this position, see Robert P. George, *Making Men Moral: Civil Liberties and Public Morality* (Oxford: Clarendon, 1992).

47. Barbara J. Syska, Thomas W. Hilgers, M.D., and Dennis O'Hare, "An Objective Model for Estimating Criminal Abortions and Its Implications for Public Policy," in *New Perspectives on Human Abortion*, ed. Thomas Hilgers, M.D., Dennis J. Horan, and David Mall (Frederick, MD: University Publications of America, 1981), 178. For a summary of the scholarly dispute over the prelegalization statistics, see Callahan, *Abortion*, 132–136; Krason, *Abortion*, 301–310; and Marshall and Donovan, *Blessed Are the Barren*, chapters 6, 7, and 9.

48. As cited in Hadley Arkes, *First Things: An Inquiry into the First Principles of Morals and Justice* (Princeton, NJ: Princeton University Press, 1986), 383.
49. Ibid., citing the *New York Times*, February 3, 1975.
50. Ibid., citing the *Boston Globe*, July 4, 1979; and the *New York Times*, July 12, 1984.
51. Nathanson, *Aborting America*, 193.
52. Laurence Lader, *Abortion* (Indianapolis: Bobbs-Merrill, 1966), 3.
53. Burtchaell, *Rachel Weeping*, v. 93.
54. *New York Times*, September 7, 1967, 38.
55. Callahan, *Abortion*, 134.
56. From the U.S. Bureau of Vital Statistics, Centers for Disease Control, as cited in Dr. and Mrs. J. C. Willke, *Abortion: Questions and Answers*, rev. ed. (Cincinnati: Hayes Publishing, 1988), 101–102. It turns out that the Willkes statistics are correct. According to a publication of the Centers for Disease Control and Prevention (CDC), the number of women who died from illegal abortions in 1972 was 39: CDC, "Abortion Surveillance – United States, 1999," *Morbidity and Mortality Weekly Report* 51, ss-9 (November 29, 2002): 28.
57. From Dr. Helleger's testimony before the U.S. Senate Judiciary Committee on Constitutional Amendments, April 25, 1974, as cited in John Jefferson Davis, *Abortion and the Christian* (Phillipsburg, NJ: Presbyterian and Reformed, 1984), 75.
58. Reardon, *Aborted Women*, 319.
59. Ibid., 319–320. For studies showing the plausibility of this view, see the works cited by Reardon.
60. Nathanson, *Aborting America*, 267.
61. Frank R. Zindler, "Human Life Does Not Begin at Conception," in *Abortion: Opposing Viewpoints*, ed. Bonnie Szumski (St. Paul, MN: Greenhaven Press, 1986), 24.
62. Schwarz, *The Moral Question of Abortion*, 197.
63. Ibid.
64. Ibid., 197–198
65. Nicholas Capaldi, *The Art of Deception: An Introduction to Critical Thinking*, rev. ed. (Buffalo, NY: Prometheus Books, 1987), 92.
66. "Abortion Foes Challenged to Help," in Dear Abby column, in *Las Vegas Review-Journal* (October 4, 1989): 4f.
67. See Pregnancy Centers Online, available at http://www.pregnancycenters.org (21 April 2003).
68. Special thanks to my good friend, Dan Green, for sharing with me this important observation.
69. See, for example, Ron Sider, *Completely Pro-Life: Building a Consistent Stance* (Downers Grove, IL: InterVarsity, 1987).
70. I am afraid that I cannot take full credit for "arguments don't have penises." The credit goes to Mark Wiegand, my ex-brother-in-law who helped prep me for that December 1989, debate.
71. Example taken from Nathanson, *Aborting America*, 189.
72. See, for example, Michael Tooley, *Abortion and Infanticide* (New York: Oxford University Press, 1983); Michael Tooley, "In Defense of Abortion and Infanticide," in *The Abortion Controversy 25 Years after Roe v. Wade: A Reader*, 2nd ed., ed. Louis P. Pojman and Francis J. Beckwith (Belmont, CA: Wadsworth,

1998); Mary Anne Warren, "On the Moral and Legal Status of Abortion," *Monist* 57.1 (1973); Paul D. Simmons, "Religious Liberty and Abortion Policy: Casey as "Catch-22," *Journal of Church and State* 42.1 (Winter 2000); and David Boonin, *A Defense of Abortion* (New York: Oxford University Press, 2003), 19–90.

73. See, for example, Judith Jarvis Thomson, "A Defense of Abortion," *Philosophy and Public Affairs* 1 (1971); Boonin, *A Defense of Abortion*, 133–281; and Eileen McDonagh, *Breaking the Abortion Deadlock: From Choice to Consent* (New York: Oxford University Press, 1996).

74. *Roe*, 410 U.S. 157–158.

75. Gregory P. Koukl, *Precious Unborn Human Persons* (San Pedro, CA: Stand to Reason, 1996), 4.

6. The Nature of Humanness and Whether the Unborn Is a Moral Subject

1. David Boonin, *A Defense of Abortion* (New York: Cambridge University Press, 2002), xiii–xiv; and Dean Stretton, "The Fallacy of Essential Moral Personhood" (May 2003), available at http://www.pcug.org.au/~dean/femp.html (17 February 2004) (no pagination).

2. Boonin, *A Defense of Abortion*, xiii, xiv.

3. W. Norris Clarke, *Explorations in Metaphysics* (Notre Dame, IN: University of Notre Dame Press, 1994), 105.

4. J. P. Moreland, "Humanness, Personhood, and the Right to Die," *Faith and Philosophy* 12.1 (January 1995): 101.

5. J. P. Moreland in *Body and Soul: Human Nature and the Crisis in Ethics* by J. P. Moreland and Scott B. Rae (Downers Grove, IL: InterVarsity, 2000), 206

6. Ibid., 178.

7. Ibid.

8. Robert E. Joyce, "Personhood and the Conception Event," *The New Scholasticism* 52 (Winter 1978): 106, 113. Although Joyce is writing about what he calls "the gradualist thesis," Joyce's critique may be applied to the case we are assessing here.

9. See Stretton, "Fallacy."

10. See Don Marquis, "Why Abortion Is Immoral" and "A Future Like Ours and the Concept of a Person: A Reply to McInerny and Paske," in *The Abortion Controversy 25 Years after Roe v. Wade: A Reader*, 2nd ed., ed. Louis P. Pojman and Francis J. Beckwith (Belmont, CA: Wadsworth, 1998); and Don Marquis, "Fetuses, Futures, and Values: A Reply to Shirley," *Southwest Philosophy Review* 6.2 (1995): 263–265.

11. Boonin, *A Defense of Abortion*, 78.

12. Lee, "A Christian Philosopher's View," 8–9.

13. For a fuller explanation of the distinction between first-order and second-order capacities, see Moreland in *Body and Soul*, 202–204.

14. Carol Kahn offers this proposal in her essay, "Can We Achieve Immortality?: The Ethics of Cloning and Other Life Extension Technologies," *Free Inquiry* (Spring 1989): 14–18.

15. Dan W. Brock, "Cloning Human Beings: An Assessment of the Ethical Issues Pro and Con," in National Bioethics Advisory Commission, *Cloning Human*

Beings, vol. 2 (Rockville, MD: The Commission, 1997), E8 (hereinafter, NBAC 2)

16. Ibid., E9.
17. See, for example, Ronald Dworkin, *Life's Dominion: An Argument about Abortion, Euthanasia, and Individual Freedom* (New York: Random House, 1993), 11–15. Boonin offers a similar argument in which he grounds his case in the unborn's acquisition of organized cortical brain activity, which occurs between 25 and 32 weeks' gestation. See Boonin, *A Defense of Abortion*, 115–129. I critique this argument below.
18. Dean Stretton, "The Argument from Intrinsic Value: A Critique," *Bioethics* 45 (2000): 228–239.
19. The example of a dog is mine, not Stretton's.
20. Lee writes: "Though not all arguments starting from thought-experiments are useless, this one is circular. According to it, human A's cerebrum is transplanted into nonhuman animal B's body. I don't think our intuitions are clear about what to say here.... One could say [that] B continues to exist but now becomes rational. This is Stretton's interpretation, because (I think) he already believes that being rational/free is in every sense an accidental characteristic" (Patrick Lee, "The Pro-Life Argument from Substantial Identity," *Bioethics* 18 [2004]: 255).
21. Ibid.
22. Ibid., 255–256.
23. Joyce, "Personhood and the Conception Event," 101.
24. Lee, "The Prolife Argument," 4–5.
25. Dean Stretton, "Essential Properties and the Right to Life" (December 2002) available at http://www.pcug.org.au/dean/epatrtl.html/ (17 February 2004) (no pagination).
26. See Alvin Plantinga, *Warrant and Proper Function* (New York: Oxford University Press, 1993).
27. Thomson, "Abortion: Whose Right?" 3, quoting Dworkin, *Life's Dominion*, 15.
28. Thomson, "Abortion: Whose Right?" 5.
29. Ibid., 6.
30. Ibid.
31. Ibid.
32. Robert Wennberg, *Life in the Balance: Exploring the Abortion Controversy* (Grand Rapids, MI: Eerdmans, 1985), 98.
33. Lee, *Abortion and Unborn Human Life*, 7–31.
34. Ibid., 30.
35. Ibid., 30, 31.
36. Boonin, *A Defense of Abortion*, 115–129.
37. Ibid., 64–69.
38. Ibid., 122.
39. Ibid., 123–124.
40. Boonin correctly points out that Marquis does not commit himself to conception as the time at which an individual human being (and thus one with a future-like-ours) comes into existence (ibid., 61 n. 26), though, according to Boonin, "Marquis clearly maintains that *if* a new individual human being comes to exist

at conception, then the future-like-ours argument provides grounds for accepting the conception criterion" (ibid., 61 n. 26). But it is clear that Marquis believes that such a being comes into existence long before it acquires organized cortical brain activity.

41. Ibid., 126 (footnote omitted).

42. Lee, *Abortion and Unborn Human Life*, 7–31.

43. See, for example, L. W. Sumner, *Abortion and Moral Theory* (Princeton, NJ: Princeton University Press, 1981).

44. Wennberg, *Life in the Balance*, 59.

45. Boonin responds to what he calls "The Uncertainty Argument": If one is uncertain about the unborn's moral status, one should err on the side of life and not countenance most abortions (Boonin, *A Defense of Abortion*, 312–324). Although the argument Boonin critiques has similarities to the argument I offer in response to the agnostic argument, both in this chapter and Chapter 2 (Justice Blackmun's version in *Roe v. Wade*) and Chapter 3 (J. J. Thomson's argument), there is a significant difference: the argument Boonin critiques calls for a prohibition on most abortions based on the lack of certainty of the unborn's status; the argument I am offering calls for a prohibition on most abortions based on the apparent equal plausibility of the differing views of the unborn's moral status.

46. Ernest Van Den Haag, "Is There a Middle Ground?" *National Review* (December 12, 1989): 29–31

47. Ibid., 30.

48. John Jefferson Davis, *Abortion and the Christian* (Phillipsburg, NJ: Presbyterian and Reformed, 1984), 58.

49. Ibid., 59.

50. John T. Noonan, "An Almost Absolute Value in History," in *The Morality of Abortion*, ed. and intro. John T. Noonan (Cambridge, MA: Harvard University Press, 1970), 53.

51. Ibid.

52. Wennberg, *Life in the Balance*, 77.

53. Peter Singer and Helen Kuhse, "On Letting Handicapped Infants Die," in *The Right Thing to Do: Basic Readings in Moral Philosophy*, ed. James Rachels (New York: Random House, 1989), 146.

54. Wennberg, *Life in the Balance*, 77–78.

55. Baruch Brody, *Abortion and the Sanctity of Human Life: A Philosophical View* (Cambridge, MA: M.I.T. Press, 1975), 108–109.

56. Ibid., 102. As one would guess, Boonin disagrees with Brody's account of brain activity (see Boonin, *A Defense of Abortion*, 108, 110–111). Boonin writes that "Brody . . . seem[s] to have conflated simple brain activity in general with the specific sort of organized cortical brain activity that produces the familiar patterns found in EEG waves" (ibid., 111). However, one could more charitably interpret Brody to be saying that the brain's presence, however primitive, signals the beginning of the existence of a being with a *capacity* for consciousness, not the beginning of a being with an immediate capacity for consciousness, one with organized cortical brain activity. Of course, whether the brain's presence at 40–42 days after conception is sufficient or necessary to declare abortion prima facie homicide from that point forward is another question. In

any event, I will assume the more charitable interpretation in assessing Brody's argument.

57. Brody, *Abortion and the Sanctity of Human Life*, 83.
58. "Cartesian" in this context, is shorthand for the philosophical anthropology of French philosopher, Rene Descartes (1591–1650), who held that the real person is the immaterial conscious mind and that the physical body is a machine to which the immaterial mind is accidentally, but not essentially, attached. "Man is thus not the rational animal of Aristotelian tradition, but an incorporeal mind lodged mysteriously in a mechanistic extended body" (*A Dictionary of Philosophy*, ed. Antony Flew [New York: St. Martin's Press, 1982], 85).
59. Lee, *Abortion and Unborn Human Life*, 82.
60. Ibid., 83.
61. For a defense of this view of the soul, see Moreland and Rae, *Body and Soul*.
62. See, for example, Lee, *Abortion and Unborn Human Life*, 74–79; Stephen D. Schwarz, *The Moral Question of Abortion* (Chicago: Loyola University Press, 1990), 50–53; Edwin C. Hui, *At the Beginning of Life: Dilemmas in Theological Bioethics* (Downers Grove, IL: InterVarsity Press, 2002), 311–315; and Andrew Varga, *The Main Issues in Bioethics*, 2nd ed. (New York: Paulist Press, 1984), 61–62.
63. Varga, *The Main Issues in Bioethics*, 61–62.
64. Ibid., 62.
65. Schwarz, *The Moral Question of Abortion*, 52.
66. Brody, *Abortion*, 113–114.
67. An essay that was very helpful in my developing this response is by A. Chadwick Ray, "Humanity, Personhood, and Abortion," *International Philosophical Quarterly* 25 (1985): 233–245.
68. Brock, "Cloning Human Beings," E8, citing the work of Carol Kahn, "Can We Achieve Immortality?" 14–18.
69. Brock, "Cloning Human Beings," E8.
70. Ibid., E9.
71. This means that if one can identify actual persons by determining whether they have a current capacity for consciousness (C), it only follows that C is a sufficient condition for being an actual person. That is, if a person (X) were to lack C, it would not follow that X is *not* an actual person, for if a condition is sufficient it does not follow that it is necessary. For example, being a sister is a sufficient condition for being female, though not a necessary condition, for one may be a female and an only child. However, being female is a necessary condition for being a sister, though not a sufficient one, for one may have no siblings. Thus, we could reject C as a necessary condition for being an actual person on the grounds that we have good independent reasons to believe that there are actual persons that lack C, for example, pre-sentient fetuses or the comatose.
72. Schwarz, *The Moral Question of Abortion*, 15–19.
73. Ibid., 15.
74. Ibid., 16.
75. Ibid., 17.
76. Peter K. McInerny, "Does a Fetus Have a Future-Like-Ours?" *Journal of Philosophy* 87 (May 1990): 266. Professor Frank R. Zindler offers a similar argument

in "Human Life Does Not Begin at Conception," in *Abortion: Opposing View-points*, ed. Bonnie Szumski (St. Paul, MN: Greenhaven, 1986), 27. This article originally appeared under the title, "An Acorn Is Not an Oak Tree," in *American Atheist* (August 1985).

77. As I point out in the text of Chapter 4, there is a dispute among human embry-ologists concerning the point in the fertilization process at which a new human being comes to be. Many maintain that this occurs *before* syngamy, the time at which the maternal and paternal chromosomes cross over and form a diploid set. Some, for example, argue that a human being comes to be when the sperm penetrates the ovum; others argue that this occurs when the pronuclei of the maternal and paternal chromosomes blend in the oocyte. It seems to me that the penetration criterion is flawed because the sperm and ovum still seem to be two distinct entities and thus no new individual human substance – human being – exists. The pre-syngamy pronuclei standard is less problematic as sperm and ovum have ceased to exist as distinct entities and the oocyte, though not possessing the diploid set of chromosomes of the zygote and embryo, seems to behave like an individual living organism with an intrinsically directed nature. Nevertheless, even though a new human being *may have* come to be prior to syngamy (and there is good reason to hold this view), it seems indisputable that at syngamy a new human being, an individual human substance, exists and is in the process of development and is not identical to either the sperm or the ovum from whose uniting it arose. (For an overview of the different points of view, see Dianne Nutwell Irving, *Philosophical and Scientific Analysis of the Nature of the Early Embryo* [Ph.D. dissertation, Georgetown University, 1991]). As I wrote in the text in Chapter 4, David Boonin argues that the dispute about the precise moment at which a new human organism comes into existence counts against the conception criterion (Boonin, *A Defense of Abortion*, 37–40). Although he brings up many of the same points I have briefly outlined in this footnote (as well as in Chapter 4), it seems to me that Boonin's raising of this important epistemological question (when do we know X is an individual organism and its germ cell progenitors cease to be?) does not detract from the strongly supported ontological claim offered by pro-life advocates: a complete and living zygote is a whole organism, with certain capacities, powers, and properties, whose parts work in concert to bring the whole to maturity. It may be that one cannot, with confidence, pick out the precise point at which a new being comes into existence between the time at which the sperm initially penetrates the ovum and a complete and living zygote is present. But how does it follow from that acknowledgment of agnosticism that one cannot say that zygote X is a human being? It seems to me that Boonin commits the fallacy of the beard: just because I cannot tell you when stubble ends and a beard begins does not mean that I cannot distinguish bearded faces from clean-shaven ones. After all, abortion-choice advocates typically pick out what they consider value-making properties – such as rationality, having a self-concept, sentience – that they maintain jus-tify one in concluding that a being lacking one or all of them does not have a right to life. But these value-making properties are typically not all-or-nothing affairs, for they are degreed properties that run along a continuum through-out one's life. So, for example, it may be nearly impossible to pick out at what precise point a being becomes rational enough to warrant a right to life. But it's

doubtful whether the abortion-choice advocate would abandon her position on those grounds.

78. For example, see Peter Singer, *Animal Liberation* (New York: Avon, 1977).

79. Marquis presents a similar argument in his "Why Abortion Is Immoral," 346.

80. I use the Vulcan illustration to show that the Fourteenth Amendment would apply to such a creature if it were to reside in the United States. See Francis J. Beckwith, "Taking Theology Seriously: The Status of the Religious Beliefs of Judicial Nominee for the Federal Bench," *Notre Dame Journal of Law, Ethics, and Public Policy* 20.1 (2006): 468–470.

81. My reply to this question follows some of the reasoning offered by Schwarz in *The Moral Question of Abortion*, 214–215.

82. My reply to this question follows some of the reasoning offered by Schwarz in *The Moral Question of Abortion*, 214–215.

83. I credit Schwarz for bringing this question to my attention (ibid., 214), though I answer it a little differently from the way he does.

84. Ibid.

85. Zindler, "Human Life Does Not Begin at Conception," 27.

86. Robert P. George and Patrick Lee, "Acorns and Embryos," *The New Atlantis: A Journal of Technology and Society* (Fall 2004/Winter 2005): 93.

87. *Words of Choice* (Washington, DC: Religious Coalition for Abortion Rights, 1991), 11.

88. Daniel Callahan, "Abortion: Some Ethical Issues," in *Abortion, Medicine, and the Law*, 3rd ed., ed. J. Douglas Butler and David F. Walbert (New York: Facts on File Publications, 1986), 345.

89. C. Everett Koop, "Deception on Demand," *Moody Monthly* 80 (May 1980): 26.

90. Zindler, "Human Life Does Not Begin at Conception," 27.

91. Schwarz, The Moral Question of Abortion, 85.

92. Ibid.

93. I credit Schwarz's work for bringing this question to my attention (see Schwarz, *The Moral Question of Abortion*, 211–212). My reply to this question follows some of the reasoning offered by Schwarz in ibid.

94. Ibid., 211.

95. Ibid., 212.

96. See James Witherspoon, "Reexaming *Roe*: Nineteenth-Century Abortion Statutes and the Fourteenth Amendment," *St. Mary's Law Journal* 17 (1985): 29–77; Joseph W. Dellapenna, "Abortion and the Law: Blackmun's Distortion of the Historical Record," in *Abortion and the Constitution: Reversing* Roe v. Wade *through the Courts*, ed. Dennis J. Horan, Edward R. Grant, and Paige C. Cunningham (Washington, DC: Georgetown University Press, 1987), 137–158; and Dennis J. Horan and Thomas J. Balch, "*Roe v. Wade:* No Justification in History, Law, or Logic," in *Abortion and the Constitution*, 57–88.

97. Scott B. Rae in *Body and Soul*, 275.

98. I credit Schwarz for bringing this question to my attention (see Schwarz, *Moral Question of Abortion*, 213).

99. Ibid., 212.

100. Ibid., 213.

101. Ibid.

102. Ibid.

103. I credit Schwarz for bringing this question to my attention (see ibid.). My reply to this question follows much of the reasoning offered by Schwarz in ibid.

104. Ibid.

105. Ibid.

7. Does It Really Matter Whether the Unborn Is a Moral Subject? The Case from Bodily Rights

1. Judith Jarvis Thomson, "A Defense of Abortion," in *The Problem of Abortion*, 2nd ed., ed. Joel Feinberg (Belmont, CA: Wadsworth, 1984), 173–187. This article was originally published in *Philosophy and Public Affairs* 1 (1971): 47–66. References to Thomson's article in this chapter are to the former piece.

2. David Boonin, *A Defense of Abortion* (New York: Cambridge University Press, 2002), 133–281.

3. Eileen McDonagh, *Breaking the Abortion Deadlock: From Choice to Consent* (New York: Oxford University Press, 1996).

4. Thomson, "A Defense of Abortion," 174.

5. Ibid., 174–175.

6. Ibid., 180.

7. Boonin comments on a sentence of mine that is similar: "[Thomson] rejects the idea that the fetus has a right to life that overrides the mother's right to her own body" (Louis P. Pojman and Francis J. Beckwith in *The Abortion Controversy: A Reader*, ed. Louis P. Pojman and Francis J. Beckwith [Boston: Jones & Bartlett, 1994], 131, as quoted in Boonin, *A Defense of Abortion*, 136). Boonin then comments:

> But this is a mistake. Thomson's example is not meant to deny that the violinist's right to life outweighs your right to control your body. If there were a genuine conflict between your right to control your body and the violinist's right to life, Thomson would surely agree that his right to life would trump your right to control your body. If you met the violinist at one of his concerts and wanted to exercise your right to control your body by swinging your fists in a manner that would cause him to be pummeled to death, for example, she would plainly acknowledge that his right to life would outweigh your right to control your body. But Thomson's claim is precisely that there is no such conflict between these two rights in the case she has presented, that unplugging yourself from the violinist does not violate his right to life in the first place. Even though he has a right to life, that is, he has no right to the use of your kidneys. So, unplugging yourself from him, you do nothing that conflicts with his right to life, even though you do something that brings about his death. The lesson of the story, therefore, is not that it is sometimes permissible for you to violate the violinist's right to life, but rather that the violinist's right to life does not include or entail the right to be provided with the use or the continued use of whatever is needed in order for him to go on living. And if, as Thomson suggests, the rights-based argument against abortion proceeds in a relevantly similar manner, then this will be the objection to that argument as well: not that the fetus's right to life does not outweigh a woman's right to control her body. Surely if the fetus has the same right to life as you and I, then the right does outweigh a woman's right to control her body, and if the two come into conflict, then it is the fetus's right to life that must prevail. Rather, the objection will turn on the claim that the fetus's right to life does not include or entail the right to be provided with the use or the continued use of whatever is needed in order to go on living. (Boonin, *A Defense of Abortion*, 136–137)

I still stand by my sentence, and here's why. When we reflect on the nature of young human beings – infants, toddlers – it is apparent that they cannot fend for themselves without the assistance of adults, and we correctly believe that prima facie the burden of that assistance falls squarely on the shoulders of their parents. But we don't think that the obligation on the parents is the result of mere consent on their part, that the child's presence in this world is absolutely contingent on the nonobligatory charity of his parents. That is, we would be rightly horrified if we found out that our neighbors let their newborn child starve to death because sustaining the child requires extra money, time, and bodily and mental effort to purchase and prepare the appropriate foods for the child and to monitor his well-being. It seems correct to say that the child's "right to life" entails providing these basic necessities to him even if it means more physical and mental effort and personal attention for the child's benefit and less income and time by which the parents may enjoy other activities. But when the child is a fetus there are similar basic necessities it requires to survive. These necessities also demand physical and mental effort and personal attention for the child's benefit and less income and time by which his mother may enjoy other activities. Consequently, if the child's right to life entails certain parental obligations after birth, and these parental obligations provide the same goods that a child needs for survival before birth (i.e., food, shelter), but one maintains that the child may be killed before birth even though its death is justified on the grounds that it is not entitled to those goods before birth that it is entitled to after birth, then it is fair to say that "[Thomson] rejects the idea that the fetus has a right to life that overrides the mother's right to her own body."

8. For example, in clarifying her own view, Thomson criticizes the absolutist position that it is morally impermissible to have an abortion even if the life of the mother is in significant danger. Needless to say, I agree with Thomson that this view is seriously flawed and have spelled out my reasons for this in Chapter 6.

9. Thomson writes: "If the room is stuffy, and I therefore open a window to air it, and a burglar climbs in, it would be absurd to say, 'Ah, now he can stay, she's given him a right to use her house – for she is partially responsible for his presence there, having voluntarily done what enabled him to get in, in full knowledge that there are such things as burglars, and that burglars burgle" (ibid., 182).

10. Stephen D. Schwarz and R. K. Tacelli, "Abortion and Some Philosophers: A Critical Examination," *Public Affairs Quarterly* 3 (April 1989): 85.

11. *Hope Clinic v. Ryan*, 195 F.3d 857, 876–90 (1999).

12. Richard A. Posner, *The Problematics of Moral and Legal Theory* (Cambridge, MA: Harvard University Press, 1999), 54–55 (footnotes omitted), quoting from Michael S. Burnhill, "Reducing the Risks of Pregnancy Termination," in *Prevention and Treatment of Contraceptive Failure: In Honor of Christopher Tietze*, ed. Uta Landy and S. S. Ratman (New York: Plenum Press, 1986), 145.

13. Some portions of this section are co-authored with Steven D. Thomas, a Biola University graduate student. These sections originally appeared as parts of our article, "Consent, Sex, and the Pre-Natal Rapist: A Brief Critique of McDonagh's Suggested Revision of *Roe v. Wade*," *Journal of Libertarian Studies* 17.2 (Spring 2003): 1–16. The portions of the article employed in this chapter have been edited and reworked by me for inclusion here.

14. For example, Boonin writes: "Indeed, it is the central thesis of this book [*In Defense of Abortion*] that the moral case against abortion can be shown to be

unsuccessful *on terms critics of abortion can, and already do, accept.*" He writes
elsewhere that he defends a version of Thomson's argument by showing that the
pro-life case against it "should . . . be rejected on the abortion critic's own terms"
(133).

15. Michael Sandel, *Democracy's Discontent: America in Search of a Public Philosophy* (Cambridge, MA: Harvard University Press, 1996), 12. Although Sandel
is not explicitly writing about Thomson or Boonin, it is fair to say that he is
addressing a view of the person or self that their arguments assume.

16. For Thomson, pregnancy is, after all, like being hooked up to a violinist and
can only be justified if the pregnant person, like the temporary organ loaner,
explicitly consents to it. This hardly sounds like a prima facie good.

17. In arguing that consent to sex does not entail tacit consent to pregnancy, Boonin
writes: "A person's act cannot reasonably be taken as evidence of tacitly consenting to something unless it takes place in a context in which it is generally
understood as constituting such consent" (Boonin, 164; footnote omitted).

18. Eileen L. McDonagh, "My Body, My Consent: Securing the Constitutional Right
to Abortion Funding," *Albany Law Review* 62 (1999): 1059–1060.

19. Boonin writes: "My claim has simply been that the fact that [the woman's] engaging in intercourse was voluntary provides no good reason to suppose that she
has in fact [tacitly agreed to give up the right to the exclusive control of her
body]. . . . But the assumption that the right to control one's body is inalienable
is open to doubt. Suppose, after all, that a woman made the following explicit
agreement: Give me some money today, and tomorrow you can use my body in
any way that you want even if by that time I have changed my mind and no longer
want you to. Most of us would think this sort of contract to be simply invalid.
As at least one writer sympathetic to the good samaritan argument [i.e., Thomson's argument] has urged, 'one cannot legitimately enslave oneself by waiving
in advance one's right to control one's body.' . . . And if this is so, then even if
we thought that by her actions the woman could legitimately be understood as
attempting to consent to waive this right, we would still have to conclude that she
had not in fact done so" (Boonin, 166–167, quoting Roderick T. Long, "Abortion, Abandonment, and Positive Rights: The Limits of Compulsory Altruism,"
Social Philosophy and Policy 10.1 [1993]: 189).

20. McDonagh, *From Choice to Consent*, 11–12. For McDonagh, coercive pregnancy is the result of the implantation of the zygote, not the result of rape or
incompetent sterilization. It is wholly the "fault" of the fetus.

21. Boonin, 166–167, quoting Long, "Abortion, Abandonment, and Positive
Rights," 189.

22. McDonagh writes:

> The distinction between being responsible for a benefit and the obligation to continue
> the benefit is clarified by reference to the common law tort of "conversion." Under tort
> law, one's negligence in conferring a benefit to another does not entitle that other person
> to the benefit. For example, if a woman places her personal property at risk of being
> stolen, she nevertheless is entitled to the property's return, even though she is responsible
> for having placed the property at risk in the first place. Thus, even if a woman consents
> to sexual intercourse without minimizing the probabilities that pregnancy will ensue, no
> matter how stupid or negligent this action might be, the fact that an ensuing pregnancy
> benefits a fetus does not constitute grounds for conversion of pregnancy into a fetal
> benefit (McDonagh, "My Body, My Consent," 1102–1103) (footnotes omitted).

Of course, there is another tort that may apply here as well – *attractive nuisance* – that does not fare as well for McDonagh's case. According to §339 of the Restatement (Second) of Torts, ARTIFICIAL CONDITIONS HIGHLY DANGEROUS TO TRESPASSING CHILDREN:

> A possessor of land is subject to liability for physical harm to children trespassing thereon caused by an artificial condition upon the land if
> (a) the place where the condition exists is one upon which the possessor knows or has reason to know that children are likely to trespass, and
> (b) the condition is one of which the possessor knows or has reason to know and which he realizes or should realize will involve an unreasonable risk of death or serious bodily harm to such children, and
> (c) the children because of their youth do not discover the condition or realize the risk involved in intermeddling with it or in coming with the area made dangerous by it, and
> (d) the utility to the possessor of maintaining the condition and the burden involved of eliminating the danger are slight as compared with the risk to children involved, and
> (e) the possessor fails to exercise reasonable care to eliminate the danger or otherwise to protect the children. (As quoted in James A. Henderson, Jr., Richard N. Pearson, and John A. Siliciano, *The Torts Process*, 5th ed. [New York: Aspen Law & Business, 1999], 255–256.)

The woman in McDonagh's story engages in an act, sexual intercourse, whose instrinsic purpose is to bring into existence a child (an artificial condition, since the couple, and not nature, is the proximate cause of the child coming to be) who the couple does not want to have and who will thus be killed by abortion. So the woman knows that the condition "will involve an unreasonable risk of death or serious bodily harm to such" a child, whose youth makes it impossible for it to realize or escape its circumstances.

23. McDonagh, "My Body, My Consent," 1087, 1092, 1095.
24. Boonin, 157.
25. J. P. Moreland, "James Rachels and the Active Euthanasia Debate," *Journal of the Evangelical Theological Society* 31 (March 1988): 86.
26. See, for example, Boonin, *A Defense of Abortion*, 148–167.
27. One may raise, as one anonymous referee has, several objections to our suggested alternative to what we think is TMB's teleology (or dysteleology) of human sexuality. We do not dispute that there are difficult questions that proponents of our suggested alternative must address. But that misses the point of our analysis. All we are trying to do is to show that TMB do not a have a prima facie case, which means that our burden is minimal. To meet this burden we just have to show that it is reasonable (*not* rationally required) to believe a view that maintains that procreation is part of the purpose of sexual intercourse. We believe we have done that.
28. See "State and Local IV-D Agencies on the Web" (15 June 2006), Office of Child Support Enforcement, Administration for Children and Families, U.S. Department of Health and Human Services, available at http://acf.hhs.gov/programs/cse/extinf.htm (18 July 2006). Boonin mistakes my citation of child support laws, which I have also employed in other publications, as a *moral reason* for the case I am making. He writes: "It is clear from Beckwith's comment about the sperm donor case that when he says the father has an obligation in his example, he means a moral obligation and not merely a legal one. And since the good

Samaritan argument [that is, Thomson's argument] is an argument about whether abortion is morally impermissible, and not about whether it would be morally permissible to make abortion illegal even if it is not morally impermissible, this is what [Beckwith] must mean if his objection is to have any chance of succeeding. But the only support Beckwith provides for this claim is the observation that there are many laws that would require the man to pay child support. And it simply does not follow from this fact that the man stands under a moral obligation to pay such support" (Boonin, *Defense of Abortion*, 247). I do not believe this is a correct reading of my case. I do not cite the child support laws as a *moral reason* for the father's obligations. Rather, I mention those laws as best accounted for by the father's moral responsibility that arises from the act of intercourse in which he voluntarily engaged. This is why I place the phrase "*precisely because*" directly after my citation of child support laws. Their presence in our legal system is the *result of* our pre-political moral understanding of paternal responsibility.

29. An anonymous referee asks: "Why should sperm donors be so different from a man having sexual intercourse? The act of the donor more surely leads to conception than the contracepted sex of the man having intercourse." I'm not sure sperm donors are so different. After all, such donors typically sign contracts that relieve them from responsibility for, and surrender parental rights over, the children that result from their donated seed. These children are often brought up by two parents, one of whom is the adoptive father. It is to this individual that the sperm donor transfers his paternal responsibilities and obligations. Consequently, if these sperm donors had no responsibilities or obligations to the children they sire, as the referee suggests, no contracts that transfer their responsibilities and obligations would be necessary. Moreover, if the donated sperm is being used by unmarried women to bring children into single-parent homes, I think one can question the ethics of men who provide genetic material that brings fatherless children into the world.

30. Lee, *Abortion and Unborn Human Life*, 119.

31. Thomson, "A Defense of Abortion," 186.

32. The lengths to which Thomson will go to deny the *natural* relationship between sex, reproduction, and filial obligations is evident in her use of the following analogy: "If the room is stuffy, and I therefore open a window to air it, and a burglar climbs in, it would be absurd to say, 'Ah, now he can stay, she's given him a right to use her house – or she is partially responsible for his presence there, having voluntarily done what enabled him to get in, in full knowledge that there are such things as burglars, and that burglars burgle" (ibid., 182). Because there is no *natural* dependency between burglar and homeowner, as there is between child and parent, Thomson's analogy is way off the mark. Burglers *don't belong* in other people's homes, whereas preborn children belong in *no other place except* their mother's womb. Patrick Lee adds that "the woman's action does not cause the burglar to be in the house but only removes an obstacle; the burglar himself is the primary agent responsible for his being in the house. In the voluntary pregnancy case, however, the baby does not cause his or her presence in the mother's womb; rather, the mother and the father do" (Patrick Lee, *Abortion and Unborn Human Life* [Washington, DC: The Catholic University of America Press, 1996], 119).

33. Thomson, "A Defense of Abortion," 186 (emphasis added).
34. Michael Levin, *Feminism and Freedom* (New Brunswick, NJ: Transaction Books, 1987), 288–289.
35. Boonin, 168. Boonin is referring to my use of the drunk driving analogy in Francis J. Beckwith, "Personal Bodily Rights, Abortion, and Unplugging the Violinist," *International Philosophical Quarterly* 32.1 (March 1992): 111–112.
36. Ibid.
37. Ibid., 170.
38. Harry S. Silverstein, "On a Woman's 'Responsibility' for the Fetus," *Social Theory and Practice* 19.3 (Fall 1997): 106–107, cited in Boonin, 172 n. 27.
39. Ibid., 172–173.
40. Ibid., 173.
41. Ibid.
42. Ibid.
43. Ibid., 175.
44. As a former professor of mine used to say, "The death rate is still the same: one per person."
45. Steve Thomas graciously offered me several helpful suggestions on how to better, and more clearly, present these reasons.
46. Dennis J. Horan and Burke J. Balch, *Infant Doe and Baby Jane Doe: Medical Treatment of the Handicapped Newborn*, Studies in Law and Medicine Series (Chicago: Americans United for Life, 1985), 2. Although this study is 20 years old, the law on parental obligation has not weakened. If anything, it has become stronger.
47. *In re Storar*, 53 N.Y. 2d 363, 380–381, 420 N.E. 2d 64, 73, 438 N.Y.S. 2d 266, 275 (1981), as quoted in ibid., 2–3.
48. Horan and Balch, *Infant Doe*, 3–4.
49. See Keith Pavlischek, "Abortion Logic and Paternal Responsibility: One More Look at Judith Thomson's 'Defense of Abortion,'" *Public Affairs Quarterly* 7.4 (October 1993); and Keith Pavlischek, "Abortion Logic and Paternal Responsibility: One More Look at Judith Thomson's 'Defense of Abortion' and a Critique of David Boonin-Vail's Defense of It," in *The Abortion Controversy 25 Years after* Roe v. Wade: *A Reader*, 2nd ed., ed. Louis P. Pojman and Francis J. Beckwith (Belmont, CA: Wadsworth, 1998). The latter is a revised version of the former.
50. I deal with one of his other responses in footnote 27.
51. Boonin, 248.
52. Boonin, 248–249.
53. Boonin, 249–254.
54. Ibid.
55. See, for example, Boonin, 249–252.
56. Ibid., 249–250.
57. Stephen D. Schwarz, *The Moral Question of Abortion* (Chicago: Loyola University Press, 1990), 118.
58. Lee, *Abortion and Unborn Human Life*, 118.
59. Mary Anne Warren brings up this point when she writes: "The plausibility of such an argument is enough to show that the Thomson analogy can provide a clear and persuasive defense of a woman's right to obtain an abortion only with respect to those cases in which the woman is in no way responsible for her

pregnancy, e.g., where it is due to rape" (Mary Anne Warren, "On the Moral and Legal Status of Abortion," in *The Problem of Abortion*, 108).

60. "Surely the question of whether you have a right life at all, or how much of it you have, shouldn't turn on the question of whether or not you are the product of rape" (Thomson, "A Defense of Abortion," 175).

61. For other responses to the general argument from rape, see Chapter 5.

62. Judge Posner, however, writes that "it is by no means obvious that the law should *not* impose a general duty to rescue strangers when the rescue can be effected without moral peril to the rescuer. The laws of many European countries and now of several U.S. states do impose such duties; the objections to them are of a practical character unrelated to the morality of refusing to be a Good Samaritan" (Posner, *The Problematics of Moral and Legal Theory*, 54, citing John P. Dawson, "*Negotiorum Gestio*: The Altruistic Intermeddler," *Harvard Law Review* 74 [1961]; and Alberto Cadoppi, "Failure to Rescue and the Continental Criminal Law," in *The Duty to Rescue: The Jurisprudence of Aid*, ed. Michael A. Menlowe and Alexander McCall Smith [Brookfield, VT: Dartmouth, 1993)]).

63. John T. Noonan, "How to Argue about Abortion," in *Morality in Practice*, 2nd ed., ed. James P. Sterba (Belmont, CA: Wadsworth, 1988), 150. This article is from Noonan's "Responding to Persons: Methods of Moral Argument in Debate over Abortion," *Theology Digest* (1973): 291–307.

64. Ibid.

65. Ibid.

8. Cloning, Bioethics, and Reproductive Liberty

1. National Institutes of Health, "Executive Summary," in Final Report of the Human Embryo Research Panel (27 September 1994), as reprinted in *Do the Right Thing: A Philosophical Dialogue on the Moral and Social Issues of Our Time*, ed. Francis J. Beckwith (Belmont, CA: Wadsworth, 1996) 285.

2. Ibid. I respond to these and similar criteria in greater detail in Chapters 4 and 6 of this volume See also Patrick Lee, *Abortion and Unborn Human Life* (Washington, DC: The Catholic University of America Press, 1996), chapters 1–3; and Edwin C. Hui, *At the Beginning of Life: Dilemmas in Theological Ethics* (Downers Grove, IL: InterVarsity, 2002), chapters 1–6.

3. Gina Kolata, "Scientist Clones Human Embryos, and Creates an Ethical Challenge," *New York Times* (October 24, 1993): A1; Rebecca Kolberg, "Human Cloning Reported," *Science* 262 (1993): 652; Kathy Sawyer, "Researchers Clone Human Embryo Cells; Work Is 'Small Step' in Aiding Infertile," *Washington Post* (October 25, 1993): A4; Philip Elmer-DeWitt, "Cloning: Where Do We Draw the Line?" *Time* (November 8, 1993): 65; Jerry Adler et al., "Clone Hype," *Newsweek* (November 8, 1993): 60.

4. Jose B. Cibelli, Robert P. Lanza, and Michael D. West (with Carol Ezzell), "The First Human Cloned Embryo," *Scientific American* (November 24, 2001), available at http://www.sciam.com/explorations/2001/112401ezzell/ (last visited October 11, 2002).

5. Ibid.

6. National Bioethics Advisory Commission, *Cloning Human Beings*, vol. 1 (Rockville, MD: The Commission, 1997), 13 (hereinafter, NBAC 1).

7. Ibid., 14.

8. Ibid.

9. Ibid.

10. Gina Kolata, *Clone: The Road to Dolly, and the Path Ahead* (New York: W. Morrow, 1998), 47–51, 61. *See also* Hans Spemann, *Embryonic Development and Induction* (New Haven, CT: Yale University Press, 1938).

11. Kolata, *Clone*, 61–65; Robert Briggs and Thomas King, "Transplantation of Living Nuclei from Blastula Cells into Enucleated Frogs' Eggs," *Proceedings of the National Academy of Sciences* 38 (1952): 455.

12. Kolata, *Clone*, 67.

13. "5 Species Cloned Using Cow's Eggs," *San Francisco Chronicle* (January 19, 1998): A1. I first read of this story and the subsequent ones listed in this paragraph in Stephanie J. Hong, "And Cloning Makes Three: A Constitutional Comparison between Cloning and Other Assisted Reproductive Technologies," *Hastings Constitutional Law Quarterly* 28 (Spring 1999): 747–748.

14. "5 Species," ibid.

15. Ellen Ruppel Shell, "Cloning of Humans Will Be Inevitable; What Have We Done, Done, Done?" *Cincinnati Enquirer* (January 5, 1999): A6.

16. "Human Embryo Clone, S. Korean Team Claims," *Sacramento Bee* (December 17, 1998): A1.

17. David Derbyshire, "Made in Japan, a Herd of Cloned Calves," *Daily Mail* (December 8, 1998): 9; and "Japanese Clone 8 Genetically Identical Calves from a Cell of Single Adult Cow," *Transplant News* (December 17, 1998).

18. Scott B. Rae, *Brave New Families* (Grand Rapids, MI: Baker Book House, 1996), 172–173.

19. Connie Cass, "Spotlight Thrust on Scientists Who Cloned Human Embryos," *Las Vegas Review-Journal* (October 23, 1993): 1A, 2A.

20. Rae, *Brave New Families*, 173.

21. Ibid.

22. Rae's description of the technical procedure is taken from Elmer-Dewitt, "Cloning," 67.

23. Raymond G. Bohlin, "The Little Lamb that Made a Monkey of Us All" (March 7, 1997), available at http://www.probe.org/docs/lambclon.html (last visited Oct. 11, 2002). Dr. Bohlin's analysis is confirmed by the findings of the NBAC 1, 22. However, a variation of the Dolly technique used by University of Hawaii researchers proved more efficient, with an 80% success rate when employed by Japanese scientists who cloned four calves in five attempts. See Derbyshire, "Made in Japan."

24. See, for example, Rae, *Brave New Families*, 169–188; and NBAC 1, 13–34.

25. "Restrictions have been in place in January 1996 which prohibit the Department of Health and Human Services (DHHS) from using Federal funds to support cloning research involving human embryos. President Clinton's March 4 directive to all Executive departments and agencies extends this ban to all federally supported research, but does not apply to research done in the private sector" ("Cloning Technology: Scientific Developments and Current Guidelines," *Congressional Digest* Cong. Dig. 77 [February 1998]: 38).

26. "The Clone Age," *ABA Journal* (July 1997): 68.

27. "To aid in these tasks NBAC invited testimony from an array of scientists, scientific societies, ethicists, theologians, and legal experts, and heard from a variety

of interested parties during the public comment session at each meeting" (NBAC 1, 9).

28. National Bioethics Advisory Commission, *Cloning Human Beings*, vol. 2 (Rockville, MD: The Commission, 1997) (hereinafter NBAC 2). The scholars who contributed papers are Stuart H. Orkin, Janet Rossant, Elisa Eiseman, Courtney S. Campbell, Dan W. Brock, Lori B. Anderson, Bartha Maria Knoppers, and Robert Mullan Cook-Deegan.

29. NBAC 1, iii.

30. Ibid.

31. Ibid.

32. President's Council on Bioethics, *Human Cloning and Human Dignity: An Ethical Inquiry* (July 2002), available at http://www.bioethics.gov/cloningreport/ (last visited October 11, 2002).

33. Ibid.

34. Ibid.

35. According to the NBAC, scientific and professional "societies should make clear that any attempt to create a child by somatic cell nuclear transfer and implantation into a woman's body at this time" is "an irresponsible, unethical, and unprofessional act" (NBAC 1, iii).

36. An overview of the commission's recommendations can be found in ibid., iii–v, 107–110.

37. See, for example, Human Cloning Prohibition Act, H.R. 923, 105th Cong. § 2 (1997) (asserting that "it shall be unlawful for any person to use a human somatic cell for the process of producing a human clone"); see also Human Cloning Prohibition Act, S. 1601, 105th Cong. § 3 (1997) (asserting that "it shall be unlawful for any person or entity, public or private, in or affecting interstate commerce, to use human somatic cell nuclear transfer technology"); H.R. 922, 105th Cong. (1997); S. 368, 105th Cong. (1997) (a bill, proposed by Senators Ashcroft and Bond, seeking to codify President Clinton's executive order to ban federal funding of cloning research); H.R. 2264, 105th Cong. (1997) (a bill banning federal funding for "the creation of a human embryo or embryos for research purposes"); S. 1061, 105th Cong. (1997); S. 1602, 105th Cong. (1998) (proposed by Senators Kennedy and Feinstein, this bill would not forbid embryo cloning but would make it illegal to "perform or use somatic cell nuclear transfer with the intent of introducing the product of that transfer into a woman's womb or in any other way creating a human being"); Cloning Research Prohibition Act, H.R. 3133, 105th Cong. (1998); Cloning Prohibition Act of 1998, S. 1599, 105th Cong. (1998); Prohibition on Cloning Human Beings Act of 1998, S. 1611, 105th Cong. (1998); Cloning Prevention Act of 1999, H.R. 571, 106th Cong. (1999); Cloning Research Prohibition Act, H.R. 2326, 106th Cong. (1999); S. 2439, 107th Cong. (2001) ("To prohibit human cloning while preserving important areas of medical research, including stem cell research"); S. 1899, 107th Cong. (2001) ("to amend title 18, United States Code, to prohibit human cloning"); H.R. 1644, 107th Cong. (2001) ("to amend title 18, United States Code, to prohibit human cloning"); Human Cloning Prohibition Act of 2003, H.R. 534, 108th Cong. (2003) ("to amend title 18, United States Code, to prohibit human cloning").

38. Many states, however, now have statutes that forbid some form of human cloning and/or state funding of the practice. See, for example, Cal. Health & Safety Code § 24185 (West 1997); La. Rev. Stat. Ann. § 40:1299.36.2 (West 1999); Mich. Stat. Ann. § 333.16274 (Michie 1999); Mo. Rev. Stat. § 1.217 (1998); R.I. Gen. Laws § 23–16.4 (1998).

39. For differing views on these questions, see John A. Robertson, "Liberty, Identity, and Human Cloning," *Texas Law Review* 76 (1998); and Leon R. Kass, "The Wisdom of Repugnance: Why We Should Ban the Cloning of Humans," *Valparaiso University Law Review* 32 (1998).

40. National Bioethics Advisory Commission, *Ethical Issues in Human Stem Cell Research*, vol. I (Rockville, MD: NBAC, 1999), i (hereinafter NBAC I, *Stem Cell*).

41. Ibid.

42. Ibid.

43. Ibid., i, ii.

44. On August 9, 2001, President Bush called for (1) no federal funding for the production of human embryos for the purpose of extracting their stem cells, and (2) federal funding for research on "more than sixty genetically-diverse stem cell lines [that] already exist" (President George Bush, "Remarks by the President on Stem Cell Research" [August 9, 2001], available at http://www.whitehouse.gov/news/releases/2001/08/20010809-2.html [last visited October 12, 2002]. According to the president,

   > [These stem-cell lines] were created from embryos that have already been destroyed, and they have the ability to regenerate themselves indefinitely, creating ongoing opportunities for research. I have concluded that we should allow federal funds to be used for research on these existing stem cell lines, where the life and death decision has already been made.

45. See, for example, Scott B. Rae, "Spare Parts from the Unborn?: The Ethics of Fetal Tissue Transplantation," in *Do the Right Thing: Readings in Applied Ethics and Social Philosophy*, 2nd ed., ed. Francis J. Beckwith (Belmont, CA: Wadsworth, 2002); and NBAC I, *Stem Cell*, 45–49.

46. For an extensive list and evaluation of reasons for and against cloning, including possible individual and social harms and benefits, see Dan W. Brock, "Cloning Human Beings: An Assessment of the Ethical Issues Pro and Con," in NBAC 2.

47. Ibid., E7.

48. Ibid., E9.

49. This is suggested by Robertson, "Liberty," 1392–1394.

50. See, for example, Anita Manning, "Pressing a 'Right' to Clone Humans: Some Gays Foresee Reproduction Option," *USA Today* (March 6, 1997): D1; Timothy F. Murphy, "Our Children, Our Selves: The Meaning of Cloning for Gay People," in *Flesh of My Flesh: The Ethics of Human Cloning*, ed. Gregory E. Pence (Lanham, MD: Rowman & Littlefield, 1998), 141.

51. Cibelli et al., "The First Human Cloned Embryo."

52. Smith, "Ignorance Is Not Bliss," 325. According to Smith, "The father underwent surgery to reverse a vasectomy (a procedure with a 40% success rate), and the mother became pregnant at the age of 43, knowing that the odds were one in four that the baby's bone marrow would match" (ibid., n. 61). See Lance Morrow, "When One Body Can Save Another: A Family's Act of Lifesaving Conception

Was on the Side of Angels, but Hovering in the Wings Is the Devilish Ghost of Dr. Mengele," *Time* (June 17, 1991): 54.

53. Smith, "Ignorance Is Not Bliss," 325. See Morrow, "When One Body Can Save Another," 58.

54. Brock, "Cloning Human Beings," E8, citing the work of Carol Kahn, "Can We Achieve Immortality? The Ethics of Cloning and Other Life Extension Technologies," *Free Inquiry* (Spring 1989): 14–18.

55. Brock, "Cloning Human Beings," E8.

56. For more extensive criticisms of cloning, see Forsythe, "Human Cloning," 527–542; Kass, "Wisdom of Repugnance"; and J. L. A. Garcia, "Human Cloning: Never and Why Not," in *Life and Learning IX: Proceeding of the Ninth University Faculty for Life Conference*, ed. Joseph Koterski (Washington, DC: University Faculty for Life, 1998).

57. *Roe v. Wade*, 410 U.S. 113, 157 (1973): "The Constitution does not define 'person' in so many words. Section 1 of the Fourteenth Amendment contains three references to 'person.' . . . But in nearly all these instances, the use of the word is such that it has application only postnatally. None indicates, with any assurance, that it has any possible pre-natal application."

58. See, for example, Gregory P. Pence, *Who's Afraid of Human Cloning?* (Lanham, MD: Rowman & Littlefield, 1998), 85–98. Pence writes: "What is true about human embryogenesis . . . will never be known precisely until we do experiments with such human embryos. To say we cannot do such experiments because such embryos are 'tiny persons' or because it violates the 'sanctity of life' is to say that humans are never meant to know truths about how embryos develop, how genes regulate such development or fail to do so in deleterious ways, and how it all goes together with the uterine environment to create a baby's genotype" (ibid., 96–97).

59. *Roe*, 410 U.S. at 163–165; *Planned Parenthood v. Casey*, 505 U.S. 833, 846 (1992).

60. The Supreme Court, in *Casey*, seems to say as much when it writes: "Before viability, the State's interests are not strong enough to support a prohibition of abortion or the imposition of a substantial obstacle to the woman's effective right to elect the procedure . . . the State has legitimate interests from the outset of the pregnancy in protecting the health of the woman *and* the life of the fetus that may become a child" (*Casey*, 505 U.S. at 846 [emphasis added]).

61. See Forsythe, "Human Cloning," 494–501. Forsythe writes:

> Although the Supreme Court in 1973 virtually abolished abortion law, *Roe* did not touch assaults on the unborn child outside the context of abortion. *Roe* stifled an ongoing process of increasing state protection for unborn human life through state criminal and tort law. But, despite *Roe*, that progressive process has continued outside the immediate context of abortion. The upshot of this progressive protection in both tort and criminal law has been an increasing abolition of the obsolete born alive rule and a growth in protection of the unborn child, even if stillborn, without regard to the stage of gestation. In tort law [as of 1997], virtually all states allow suits for prenatal injuries for children later born alive. (Obviously, if the child is not born alive, the suit would be for wrongful death.) A majority of state courts have expressly or implicitly rejected viability as a limitation on liability for nonfatal prenatal injuries. . . . Some states, by statute, have eliminated gestational time limits for recovery for injury or death to the unborn child. (ibid., 497)

Forsythe continues that, as of 1997:

> more than half of all states treat the killing of an unborn human being, at some stage
> of gestation, as a form of homicide, even though the child is not born alive (stillborn).
> Eleven states, including Illinois and Minnesota, define by statute the killing of an unborn
> child as a form of homicide, regardless of the stage of pregnancy. One state defines by
> statute the killing of an unborn human being after eight to ten weeks gestation as a form
> of homicide. Eight states define by statute the killing of an unborn child after quickening
> as a form of homicide. Five states define by statute or by caselaw the killing of an unborn
> human being after viability as a form of homicide. In several cases, courts have rejected
> constitutional challenges to statutes of this type, including statutes applying throughout
> gestation. State and federal courts have recognized that *Roe* only limits state protection
> for the unborn human being when the woman's privacy interest is asserted. (ibid., 499–
> 500) (footnotes omitted)

62. For a defense of this reading of the Supreme Court's view of reproductive liberty,
    see Chapter 2 and the part of this chapter titled "Is There a Constitutional Right
    to Clone?"

63. See, for example, Kass "Wisdom of Repugnance," 693–698. Kass writes:
    "Human cloning would also represent a giant step toward turning begetting
    into making, procreation into manufacture . . . a process already begun with
    IVF and genetic testing of embryos. With cloning, not only is the process in
    hand, but the total genetic blueprint of the cloned individual is selected and
    determined by the human artisans . . . we here would be taking a major step
    into making man himself simply another one of the man-made things" (ibid.,
    696).

64. Wu, "Family Planning," 1504–1505.

65. Garcia, "Human Cloning," 13.

66. Wu, "Family Planning," 1474–1485. Wu writes, "the Constitution protects an
    affirmative right to procreate through the use of cloning technology. Such tech-
    nology compromises no measure of individuality or humanity, and its use is con-
    sonant with the principle that procreation is protected as a fundamental right
    because of the value of having children, and not because of the mode used to
    create the children" (ibid., 1515). Wu also writes:

    > Whenever a couple decides they want to "try" for a child and acts on that desire, the
    > resulting child will always, to some degree, be a product of their will, and will thus have
    > been "made." Parents, after all, seek to procreate for all sorts of reasons that sound
    > in the objectification of children – for instance, to replace a recently deceased child, to
    > give their first child a playmate, to save their marriage, to stem boredom, or because the
    > family already has two daughters and the father wants to try for a son. The particular
    > mode of reproduction used does not alter that manufactured aspect. Society, however,
    > does not police such motivations for having children, because it is generally assumed
    > that parents will care for their children regardless of the motivations for having them.
    > (ibid., 1505)

67. Garcia, "Human Cloning," 13.

68. Smith, "Ignorance Is Not Bliss," 326 ("If cloning is held protected under procre-
    ative liberty, cloning for purposes of having a child that is an acceptable organ
    donor would fall under that protection as well"). See Robertson, "Liberty,"
    1393–1421 ("The idea of cloning an existing child is plausibly foreseeable in
    several circumstances. . . . [One circumstance] is one in which an existing child

might need an organ or tissue transplant" [ibid., 1394]). Citing the example of the case of the Ayalas, Robertson writes:

> If the Ayalas acted ethically because they were prepared to love the child whose conception was motivated by another child's potential need for bone marrow, then using an existing child's DNA in order to have another child as a source of organs or tissue should also be acceptable.... The fact that the child was also desired to serve as a source of tissue or organ does not negate the love that parents will have for that child.
>
> The question of objectification is somewhat different if cell biology advances to the point that tissue or organs for transplant can be obtained from embryonic stem cells or early abortions. In that case cloning another to obtain tissue or organs for transplant need only produce cloned embryos or fetuses, and not live-born children, thus avoiding the problem of instrumentalizing a child created in part to serve as an organ source. (ibid., 1421)

Moffat writes:

> In the case of the child conceived to produce a bone marrow match, some critics object, in a naive form of Kantianism, that the younger child is being treated solely as a means to an end. When the child grows up and learns the story of her place in the family, will she feel that she was created only to be used as an instrumentality? Actual experience with such situations indicates that the child is loved not only as a member of the family, but is valued even more as the one who saved the life of the older sibling. (Moffat, "Cloning Freedom," 587–588)

69. Wu, "Family Planning," 1474–1485. Wu writes:

> The Constitution protects an affirmative right to procreate through the use of cloning technology. Such technology compromises no measure of individuality or humanity, and its use is consonant with the principle that procreation is protected as a fundamental right because of the value of having children, and not because of the mode used to create the child... Furthermore, granting constitutional protection is also more consistent with the longstanding recognition that decisions regarding matters of fundamental concern, like procreation, are best left to the decisionmaker, and not to the majority. Viewed properly, therefore, the cloning of humans presents no threat to society or to the nature of reproduction or to the family; rather, human cloning is a promising, new technology that can help would-be parents have children and create new families (ibid., 1515).

See also Smith, "Ignorance Is Not Bliss," 320–323; and Hong, "And Cloning Makes Three," 752–755. Hong writes, "The Court has found this right [to privacy] to be nearly inviolate in the context of the right to procreate" (ibid., 753).

70. These cases usually include the following: *Skinner v. Oklahoma*, 316 U.S. 535 (1942); *Griswold v. Connecticut*, 381 U.S. 479 (1965); *Eisenstadt v. Baird*, 405 U.S. 438 (1972); *Roe v. Wade*, 410 U.S 113; *Doe v. Bolton*, 410 U.S. 179 (1973); *Thornburgh v. American College of Obstetricians and Gynecologists*, 476 U.S. 747 (1986); and *Planned Parenthood v. Casey*, 505 U.S. 833 (1992).

71. Brock, "Cloning Human Beings," at E8.

72. Ibid., E9.

73. *Roe*, 410 U.S. 157.

74. This means that if one can identify actual human beings by determining whether they have a current capacity for consciousness (C), it only follows that C is a sufficient condition for being an actual human being. That is, if a human being (X) were to lack C, it would not follow that X is *not* an actual human being,

for if a condition is sufficient it does not follow that it is necessary. For example, being a sister is a sufficient condition for being female, though not a necessary condition, for one may be a female and an only child. However, being female is a necessary condition for being a sister, though not a sufficient one, for one may have no siblings. Thus, we could reject C as a necessary condition for being an actual human being on the grounds that we have good independent reasons to believe that there are actual human beings that lack C, for example, pre-sentient fetuses, the comatose, and others.

75. According to this view (which I defend in Chapter 6), each kind of living organism or *substance*, including the human being, maintains identity through change and possesses a nature or essence that makes certain activities and functions possible. "A substance's **inner nature** is its ordered structural unity of ultimate capacities. A substance cannot change in its ultimate capacities; that is, it cannot lose its ultimate nature and continue to exist" (J. P. Moreland, "Humanness, Personhood, and the Right to Die," *Faith and Philosophy* 12.1 [January 1995]: 101).

76. In the majority and plurality opinions of the leading cases that affirm a woman's right to abortion – *Roe, Doe, Thornburgh*, and *Casey* – the Court refers to the unborn as *potential*, rather than actual, life. This is important because if the unborn were considered actual life by the Court, then there would be no right to abortion. For, in *Roe*, Justice Blackmun concedes that the most important premise in establishing the right to abortion is the non-personhood of the unborn: "If the suggestion of personhood [of the unborn] is established, the appellant's case, of course, collapses, for the fetus' right to life is then guaranteed specifically by the [Fourteenth Amendment]" (*Roe*, 410 U.S. 157–158). But Blackmun writes elsewhere in *Roe*, "We need not resolve the difficult question of when life begins. When those trained in the respective disciplines of medicine, philosophy, and theology are unable to arrive at any consensus, the judiciary, at this point in the development of man's knowledge, is not in a position to speculate" (ibid., 160). But, as I argued in Chapter 2, this poses a curious problem for the justification of abortion rights. For if, as Blackmun admits, the right to abortion is contingent upon the status of the fetus, then the allegedly disputed fact about life's beginning means that the right to abortion is disputed as well. For a conclusion's support – in this case, "abortion is a fundamental right" – is only as good as the truth of its most important premise – in this case, "the fetus is not a human person." As a result, the Court's admission that abortion-choice is based on a widely disputed fact, far from establishing a right to abortion, entails that the Court not only does not know when life begins, but it does not know when, if ever, the right to abortion begins.

77. NARAL Pro-Choice America, "Human Embryo Research" (2003), 1, available at http://www.naral.org/mediaresources/fact/embryo.pdf (May 8, 2003).

78. Cass Sunstein has authored an article that includes two imaginary Supreme Court decisions, one in which the Court rules that reproductive liberty encompasses cloning and a second in which the Court rules that reproductive liberty is not broad enough to include cloning. See Cass Sunstein, "The Constitution and the Clone," in *Clones and Clones*, 207–220.

79. 316 U.S. 535 (1942). The analysis that follows is similar to one offered by Hadley Arkes, *First Things: An Inquiry into the First Principles of Morals and Justice* (Princeton, NJ: Princeton University Press, 1986), 347–350.

80. Ibid., 537 (Douglas, J.).
81. Ibid., 538–541.
82. Ibid., 543–544 (Stone, J., concurring).
83. Ibid., 544–545.
84. Ibid., 541 (Douglas, J.).
85. *Griswold v. Connecticut*, 381 U.S. 479 (1965).
86. Ibid., 484.
87. Ibid., 486.
88. "We do not sit as a super-legislature to determine the wisdom, need, and propriety of laws that touch on economic problems, business affairs, and social conditions. This law, however, operates directly on an intimate relation of husband and wife and their physician's role in one aspect of that relation" (ibid., 48).
89. In his concurrence, Justice Goldberg stated:

    The entire fabric of the Constitution and the purposes that clearly underlie its specific guarantees demonstrate that the rights to marital privacy and to marry and raise a family are of similar order and magnitude as the fundamental rights specifically protected.... The fact that no particular of the Constitution explicitly forbids the State from disrupting the traditional relation of the family – a relation as old and as fundamental as our entire civilization – surely does not show that Government was meant to have the power to do so. (ibid., 495–496 [Goldberg, J., concurring])

90. Ibid., 498–499.
91. Ibid., 499 (citing *Poe v. Ullman*, 367 U.S. 497, 553 [1961]).
92. *Eisenstadt*, 405 U.S. 454.
93. Ibid., 453.
94. "This right of privacy, whether it be founded in the Fourteenth Amendment's concept of personal liberty and restrictions upon state action, as we feel it is, or, as the District Court determined, in the Ninth Amendment's reservation of rights to the people, is broad enough to encompass a woman's decision whether or not to terminate her pregnancy" (*Roe*, 410 U.S. 153).
95. "Appellant and some *amici* argue that the woman's right is absolute and that she is entitled to terminate her pregnancy at whatever time she alone chooses. With this we do not agree" (ibid.). The Court writes elsewhere in *Roe* (ibid., 154):

    The privacy right involved, therefore, cannot be said to be absolute. In fact, it is not clear to us that the claim asserted by some amici that one has an unlimited right to do with one's body as one pleases bears a close relationship to the right of privacy previously articulated in the Court's decisions. The Court has refused to recognize an unlimited right of this kind in the past. *Jacobson v. Massachusetts*, 197 U.S. 11 (1905) (vaccination); *Buck v. Bell*, 274 U.S. 200 (1927) (sterilization).

96. "The State has a legitimate interest in seeing to it that abortion, like any other medical procedure, is performed under circumstances that ensure maximum safety for the patient" (ibid., 150).
97. "We need not resolve the difficult question of when life begins. When those trained in the respective disciplines of medicine, philosophy, and theology are unable to arrive at any consensus, the judiciary, at this point in the development of man's knowledge, is not in a position to speculate" (ibid., 160).
98. "The Constitution does not define 'person' in so many words. Section 1 of the Fourteenth Amendment contains three references to 'person.' . . . But in nearly all

these instances, the word is such that it has application only postnatally. None indicates, with any assurance, that it has any possible pre-natal application" (ibid., 157).

99. The Court went on to declare (ibid., 162–163):

> The State does have an important and legitimate interest in preserving and protecting the health of the pregnant woman, whether she be a resident of the State or a nonresident who seeks medical consultation and treatment there, and that it has still *another* important and legitimate interest in protecting the potentiality of human life. These interests are separate and distinct. Each grows substantially as the woman approaches term and, at a point during pregnancy, each becomes 'compelling.' ... With respect to the State's important and legitimate interest in potential life, the 'compelling point' is at viability. This is so because the fetus then presumably has the capability of meaningful life outside the mother's womb.

100. "If the State is interested in protecting fetal life after viability, it may go so far as to proscribe abortion during that period, except when it is necessary to preserve the life or health of the mother" (ibid., 163–164).

101. As I noted in Chapter 2, because the Court accepts the view that the primary reason for states prohibiting abortion by criminal statute in the nineteenth century and in the early twentieth century was to "protect the pregnant woman ... from submitting to a procedure that placed her life in serious jeopardy," and since "modern medical techniques have altered this situation" for the better, there is no compelling reason to criminalize abortion prior to viability (ibid., 149). For a reply to this argument, see Chapter 2 and James Witherspoon, "Reexamining *Roe:* Nineteenth-Century Abortion Statutes and the Fourteenth Amendment," *St. Mary's Law Journal* 17 (1985).

102. See, for example, *Lifchez v. Hartigan*, 735 F. Supp. 1361, 1376 (N.D. Ill. 1990), *aff'd without opinion*, 914 F.2d 260 (7th Cir. 1990), *cert. denied sub nom.*, *Scholberg v. Lifschez*, 498 U.S. 1069 (1991) (striking down the state statute that prohibited fetal experimentation because it was unconstitutionally vague and violated "a woman's right of privacy, in particular, her right to make reproductive choices free of governmental interference with those choices"); see also *Margaret S. v. Treen*, 597 F. Supp. 636 (E.D. La. 1984), *aff'd on other grounds*, *Margaret S. v. Edwards*, 794 F.2d 994, 999 (5th Cir. 1986) ("the use of the terms 'experiment' and 'experimentation' makes the statute impermissibly vague").

103. See, for example, Wu, "Family Planning," 1474–1485; and John A. Robertson, "Decisional Authority over Embryos and Control of IVF Technology," *Jurimetrics Journal* 28 (1988): 292.

104. See, for example, *Jane L. v. Bangerter*, 794 F. Supp. 1537 (D. Utah 1992) (upholding a state statute that forbids using prenatal children in experimentation).

105. See, for example, Forsythe, "Human Cloning," 517–527; and Paul L. Linton, "*Planned Parenthood v. Casey*: The Flight from Reason in the Supreme Court," *St. Louis University Public Law Review* 13 (1993): 15–137.

106. For a provocative defense in favor of this type of judicial minimalism, see Cass R. Sunstein, "*Dred Scott v. Stanford* and Its Legacy," *Great Cases in Constitutional Law*, ed. Robert P. George (Princeton, NJ: Princeton University Press, 2000).

107. One may cite as an exception to this *Lawrence v. Texas*, 123 S.Ct. 2472 (2003), in which the Court overturned *Bowers v. Hardwick*, 478 U.S. 186 (1986), and argued that private sexual acts between consenting adults cannot be prohibited by the state on exclusively moral grounds. But in *Lawrence*, the Court,

according to the majority opinion's account, was dealing with the narrow question of self-regarding private sexual acts between consenting adults. It did not establish a principle from which one could argue support for a fundamental right to any reproductive technologies, such as cloning, that may have far-reaching implications on the human beings cloned and society's view of its own humanity as well as our responsibilities to others. Granted, one could argue that the Court is making an incoherent claim when it holds that a law may not be based exclusively on morality, as the claim that "law may not be based exclusively on morality" is a moral claim on how judges and legislatures should make law and thus is itself not a claim of law but of morality. One could also argue that the Court has underestimated the corrosive influence of placing its imprimatur on homosexual sodomy, that the Court has no idea how its opinion may undermine our important and indispensable institutions, such as the family and marriage, whose preservation depends on a cluster of social stigmas and incentives, once reinforced by law and government and now cavalierly discarded, that have served us well to tame an otherwise depraved human nature for the sake of advancing the public good. However, for our present purposes, it is enough to say that *Lawrence*, though a flawed opinion, is consistent with judicial minimalism.

108. See *Casey*, 505 U.S. 852:

> Though abortion is conduct, it does not follow that the State is entitled to proscribe in all instances. That is because the liberty of the woman is at stake in a sense unique to the human condition and so unique to the law. The mother who carries a child to full term is subject to anxieties, to physical constraints, to pain that only she can bear.... Her suffering is too intimate and personal for the State to insist, without more, upon its own vision of the woman's role, however dominant that vision has been in the course of our history and our culture. The destiny of the woman must be shaped to a large extent on her own conception of her spiritual imperatives and her place in society.

109. See *Roe*, 410 U.S. 153:

> The detriment that the State would impose on the pregnant woman by denying this choice altogether is apparent. Specific and direct harm medically diagnosable even in early pregnancy may be involved. Maternity, or additional offspring, may force upon the woman a distressful life and future. Psychological harm may be imminent. Mental and physical health may be taxed by child care. There is also the distress, for all concerned, associated with the unwanted child, and there is the problem of bringing a child into a family already unable, psychologically and otherwise, to care for it. In other cases, as in this one, the additional difficulties and continuing stigma of unwed motherhood may be involved. All these are factors the woman and her responsible physician necessarily will consider in consultation.

110. See *Casey*, 505 U.S. at 869:

> From what we have said so far it follows that it is a constitutional liberty of the woman to have some freedom to terminate her pregnancy. We conclude that the basic decision in *Roe* was based on a constitutional analysis which we cannot now repudiate. The woman's liberty is not unlimited, however, that from the outset the State cannot show its concern for the life of the unborn, and at a later point in fetal development the State's interest in life has sufficient force so that the right of the woman to terminate the pregnancy can be restricted ... the urgent claims of the woman to retain the ultimate control over her destiny and her body, claims implicit in the meaning of liberty, require us to perform that function.

111. Ibid., 851 (citations omitted).
112. *Compassion in Dying v. Washington*, 850 F. Supp. 1454, 1459 1460 (W.D. Wash. 1994).
113. Ronald Dworkin, "When Is It Right to Die?" *New York Times* (May 17, 1994): A19.
114. *Washington v. Glucksberg*, 521 U.S. 702, 727–728 (1997) (citations omitted) (first emphasis in original; second emphasis, in final sentence, added).
115. Susan F. Appleton, however, argues that "a closer look at the majority's analysis [in Glucksberg] ... raises questions about whether a constitutional right to abortion truly escapes unscathed" (Susan F. Appleton, "Assisted Suicide and Reproductive Freedom: Exploring Some Connections," *Washington University Law Quarterly* 76 [1998]: 19). She draws this conclusion from the Court's two tests in its analysis of the claim that physician-assisted suicide is a constitutional right: (1) is the claimed right deeply rooted in our Nation's tradition and history? and (2) can one provide a careful description of precisely what fundamental liberty interest is claimed, as substantive due process cases require? Appleton argues that subjecting the abortion right to these two tests may make the right less stable because (1) if the Court were to argue that the relevant tradition and history for assessing the abortion right is the time in which the Fourteenth Amendment was adopted, this test becomes problematic for sustaining a right to abortion, even though the Court's historical case in *Roe* is more persuasive, according to Appleton, when one includes its presentation of ancient and common law attitudes toward abortion, and (2) if abortion is viewed as situated "in more expansive protection that includes bodily integrity, family autonomy, and freedom of conscience ... that formulation would then fail the 'precision' test," even though it "offers considerable support from this country's history and tradition" (ibid., 19, 20) (citations omitted).
116. *Glucksberg*, 521 U.S. 708–719 (presenting a history of the prohibition of suicide and assisting suicide from common law until the mid-1990s).
117. Appleton comes to a similar conclusion: "No doubt, the two-part test announced in *Glucksberg* would create significant obstacles for an expansive constitutional right to reproductive choice that includes protection for access to assisted conception and other 'high-tech' procedures" (Appleton, "Assisted Suicide," 20). Presumably, one such procedure could be cloning.
118. *Glucksberg*, 521 U.S. 735.
119. Special thanks to Professor Susan F. Appleton (Washington University School of Law, St. Louis) for her feedback on an earlier draft of this chapter, which was published in 2002 in *Nevada Law Journal*. Because of her insights, it is a much better chapter, though I take full responsibility for all of its flaws.

9. Conclusion: A Case for Human Inclusiveness

1. Stephen D. Schwarz, *The Moral Question of Abortion* (Chicago: Loyola University Press, 1990), 143.
2. See Hadley Arkes, *Natural Rights and the Right to Choose* (New York: Cambridge University Press, 2002).

SELECTED BIBLIOGRAPHY

Arkes, Hadley. *First Things: An Inquiry into the First Principles of Morals and Justice.* Princeton, NJ: Princeton University Press, 1986.

———. *Natural Rights and the Right to Choose.* New York: Cambridge University Press, 2002.

Bauman, Michael. *Pilgrim Theology: Taking the Path of Theological Discovery.* Grand Rapids, MI: Zondervan, 1992.

Beauchamp, Tom L. *Philosophical Ethics: An Introduction to Moral Philosophy.* New York: McGraw-Hill, 1982.

Beckwith, Francis J. "A Reply to Keenan: Thomson's Argument and Academic Feminism." *International Philosophical Quarterly* 32 (September 1992).

———. "Cloning and Reproductive Liberty." *Nevada Law Journal* 3.1 (Fall 2002).

———. "Defending Abortion Philosophically: A Review-Essay of David Boonin's *A Defense of Abortion.*" *Journal of Medicine and Philosophy* 31 (April 2006).

———. "Law, Religion, and the Metaphysics of Abortion: A Reply to Simmons." *Journal of Church and State* 43.1 (Winter 2001).

———. "Of Souls, Selves, and Cerebrums: A Reply to Himma." *Journal of Medical Ethics* 31.1 (January 2005)

———. "Personal Bodily Rights, Abortion, and Unplugging the Violinist." *International Philosophical Quarterly* 32 (March 1992).

———. *Politically Correct Death: Answering the Arguments for Abortion Rights.* Grand Rapids, MI: Baker Book House, 1993.

———. "The Supreme Court, *Roe v. Wade,* and Abortion Law." *Liberty University Law Review* 1.1 (2006)

———. "Taking Abortion Seriously: A Philosophical Analysis of the New Prolife Rhetorical Shift." *Ethics and Medicine: An International Journal of Bioethics* 17:3 (Fall 2001).

———. "The Explanatory Power of the Substance View of Persons." *Christian Bioethics* 10.1 (April, 2004).

_____. "Thomson's 'Equal Reasonableness' Argument for Abortion Rights: A Critique." *American Journal of Jurisprudence* 49 (2004).

_____. "When You Come to a Fork in the Road, Take It? Abortion, Personhood, and the Jurisprudence of Neutrality." *Journal of Church and State* 44.3 (Summer 2003).

Beckwith, Francis J., and Gregory P. Koukl. *Relativism: Feet Firmly Planted in Mid-Air.* Grand Rapids, MI: Baker, 1998.

Beckwith, Francis, and Steven D. Thomas. "Consent, Abortion, and the Pre-Natal Rapist: A Brief Critique of McDonagh's Suggested Revision of *Roe v. Wade.*" *Journal of Libertarian Studies* 17.2 (Spring 2003).

Boonin, David. *A Defense of Abortion.* New York: Cambridge University Press, 2002.

Burtchaell, James T. *Rachel Weeping: The Case against Abortion.* San Francisco: Harper & Row, 1982.

Clarke, W. Norris. *Explorations in Metaphysics.* Notre Dame, IN: University of Notre Dame Press, 1994.

Davis, John Jefferson. *Abortion and the Christian.* Phillipsburg, NJ: Presbyterian and Reformed, 1984.

Dellapenna, Joseph W. "Abortion and the Law: Blackmun's Distortion of the Historical Record." In *Abortion and the Constitution: Reversing* Roe v. Wade *Through the Courts.* Washington, DC: Georgetown University Press, 1987.

Destro, Robert A. "Abortion and the Constitution: The Need for a Life-Protective Amendment." *California Law Review* 63 (1975).

Dworkin, Ronald. *Life's Dominion: An Argument about Abortion, Euthanasia, and Individual Freedom.* New York: Vintage Books, 1993.

Ely, John Hart. "The Wages of Crying Wolf: A Comment on *Roe v. Wade.*" *Yale Law Journal* 82 (1973).

George, Robert P. *The Clash of Orthodoxies: Law, Religion, and Morality in Crisis.* Wilmington, DE: ISI Press, 2001.

_____. "Public Reason and Political Conflict: Abortion and Homosexuality." *Yale Law Journal* 106 (1997).

Gordon, Doris. "Introduction." *International Journal of Sociology and Social Policy* 19.3/4 (1999).

Hefferman, Bart T. "The Early Biography of Everyman." In *Abortion and Social Justice.* New York: Sheed & Ward, 1972.

Hern, Warren. *Abortion Practice.* 1st ed. Philadelphia: J. B. Lippincott, 1984.

Horan, Dennis, Edward R. Grant, and Paige C. Cunningham, eds. *Abortion and the Constitution.* Washington, DC: Georgetown University Press, 1987.

Hui, Edwin C. *At the Beginning of Life: Dilemmas in Theological Ethics.* Downers Grove, IL: InterVarsity Press, 2002.

Joyce, Robert E. "Personhood and the Conception Event." *New Scholasticism* 52 (1978).

Kass, Leon. "The Wisdom of Repugnance: Why We Should Ban the Cloning of Humans." *Valparaiso University Law Review* 32 (1998).

Kolata, Gina. *The Road to Dolly, and the Path Ahead*. New York: W. Morrow, 1998.

Koukl, Gregory P. *Precious Unborn Human Persons*. San Pedro, CA: Stand to Reason, 1999.

Krason, Stephen M. *Abortion: Politics, Morality, and the Constitution*. Lanham, MD: University Press of America, 1984.

Kreeft, Peter. *The Unaborted Socrates*. Downers Grove, IL: InterVarsity Press, 1982.

Lee, Patrick. *Abortion and the Unborn Human Life*. Washington, DC: The Catholic University of America Press, 1996.

_____. "The Pro-Life Argument from Substantial Identity." *Bioethics* 18.3 (2004).

Li, Xiaorang. "Postmodernism and Universal Human Rights: Why Theory and Reality Don't Mix." *Free Inquiry* 18.4 (Fall 1998).

Marquis, Don. "Why Abortion Is Immoral." In *The Abortion Controversy 25 Years after* Roe v. Wade: *A Reader*. 2nd ed. Edited by Louis P. Pojman and Francis J. Beckwith. Belmont, CA: Wadsworth, 1998.

Marshall, Robert, and Charles Donovan. *Blessed Are the Barren: The Social Policy of Planned Parenthood*. San Francisco: Ignatius Press, 1992.

McDonagh, Eileen L. *Breaking the Abortion Deadlock: From Choice to Consent*. New York: Oxford University Press, 1996.

Mollenkott, Virginia Ramey. "Reproductive Choice: Basic to Justice for Women." *Christian Scholar's Review* (March 1988).

Moreland, J. P. *Scaling the Secular City*. Grand Rapids, MI: Baker Book House, 1987.

Moreland, J. P., and Scott B. Rae. *Body and Soul: Human Nature and the Crisis in Ethics*. Downers Grove, IL: InterVarsity Press, 2000.

O'Meara, Thomas. "Abortion: The Court Decides a Non-Case." *The Supreme Court Review* (1974).

Pavlischek, Keith. "Abortion Logic and Paternal Responsibility: One More Look at Judith Thomson's 'Defense of Abortion.'" *Public Affairs Quarterly* 7.4 (October 1993).

Pojman, Louis, and Francis J. Beckwith, eds. *The Abortion Controversy 25 Years after* Roe v. Wade: *A Reader*. 2nd ed. Belmont, CA: Wadsworth, 1998.

Posner, Richard A. *The Problematics of Moral and Legal Theory*. Cambridge, MA: Harvard University Press, 1999.

Powers, William. "Partial Truths." *The New Republic* (March 24, 1997).

Rachels, James. "A Critique of Ethical Relativism." In *Philosophy: The Quest for Truth*. Edited by Louis P. Pojman. Belmont, CA: Wadsworth, 1989.

Rae, Scott B. *Brave New Families*. Grand Rapids, MI: Baker Book House, 1996.

Rawls, John. *Political Liberalism*. New York: Columbia University Press, 1993.

————. *Political Liberalism*. 2nd ed. New York: Columbia University Press, 1996.

Rosenbaum, Stuart. "Abortion, the Constitution, and Metaphysics." *Journal of Church and State* (Autumn 2001).

Schaeffer, Francis A., and C. Everett Koop. *Whatever Happened to the Human Race?* Old Tappan, NJ: Fleming H. Revell, 1979.

Schwarz, Stephen D. *The Moral Question of Abortion*. Chicago: Loyola University Press, 1990.

Schwarz, Stephen D., and Ronald K. Tacelli. "Abortion and Some Philosophers: A Critical Examination." *Public Affairs Quarterly* 3 (April 1989).

Simmons, Paul D. "Religious Liberty and Abortion Policy: Casey as 'Catch-22.'" *Journal of Church and State* (Winter 2000).

————. "Religious Liberty and the Abortion Debate." *Journal of Church and State* 32 (Summer 1990).

Singer, Peter, and Helen Kuhse. "On Letting Handicapped Infants Die." In *The Right Thing to Do: Basic Readings in Moral Philosophy*. Edited by James Rachels. New York: Random House, 1989.

Stetson, Brad, ed. *The Silent Subject: Reflections on the Unborn in American Culture*. Westport, CT: Praeger Books, 1996.

Stretton, Dean. "The Fallacy of Essential Moral Personhood" (May 2003), available at http://www.tip.net.au/~dean/femp.html (5 January 2004).

Thomson, Judith Jarvis. "A Defense of Abortion." *Philosophy and Public Affairs* 1.1 (1971).

————. "Abortion: Whose Right?" *Boston Review* 20.3 (Summer 1995).

Tooley, Michael. *Abortion and Infanticide*. New York: Oxford University Press, 1983.

Tribe, Laurence. *Abortion: The Clash of Absolutes*. New York: W. W. Norton, 1990.

Wennberg, Robert. *Life in the Balance: Exploring the Abortion Controversy*. Grand Rapids, MI: Eerdmans, 1985.

Willke, Jack, and Barbara Willke. *Abortion: Questions and Answers*. Rev. ed. Cincinnati: Hayes Publishing, 1988.

Witherspoon, James. "Reexamining *Roe*: Nineteenth Century Abortion Statutes and the Fourteenth Amendment." *St. Mary's Law Journal* 17, no. 1 (1985).

INDEX